The New York Times

PUZZLE IT OUT

Published in the United States by St. Martin's Griffin,
an imprint of St. Martin's Publishing Group

THE NEW YORK TIMES PUZZLE IT OUT.
Copyright © 2023 by The New York Times Company. All rights reserved.
Printed in the United States of America. For information, address
St. Martin's Publishing Group, 120 Broadway, New York, NY 10271.

www.stmartins.com

ISBN 978-1-250-87578-5

Our books may be purchased in bulk for promotional, educational,
or business use. Please contact your local bookseller or the Macmillan Corporate and
Premium Sales Department at 1-800-221-7945, extension 5442, or by email
at MacmillanSpecialMarkets@macmillan.com.

First Edition: 2023

10 9 8 7 6 5 4 3 2 1

The New York Times

PUZZLE IT OUT
200 Easy to Hard Crossword Puzzles

Edited by Will Shortz

ST. MARTIN'S GRIFFIN
NEW YORK

Looking for more Easy Crosswords?

The New York Times

The #1 Name in Crosswords

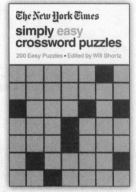

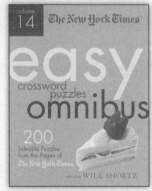

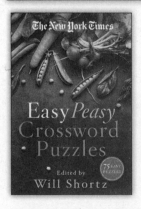

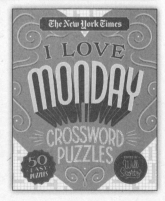

ACROSS

1 Honorific given to 17-, 27-, 43- and 58-Across
6 Agreements between nations
11 CBS series with spinoffs set in Miami and New York
14 Rocker Vedder or Van Halen
15 Menotti's "___ and the Night Visitors"
16 ". . . yadda, yadda, yadda"
17 Disco
19 Bread for a Reuben sandwich
20 Montero Lamar Hill a.k.a. Lil ___ X
21 Socially distant
22 "u up?," e.g.
23 "___ the season to be jolly"
25 "Mona ___," painting with an enigmatic smile
27 Soul
34 Keep away from
35 What a bride gets fitted for
36 Dude
37 "Aye-aye" guy
38 Most common surname in the U.S. (ahead of Johnson and Williams)
39 Trickster of Norse myth
40 Get a move on, quaintly
41 Japanese dog breed
42 Like emails at the top of an inbox
43 Jazz
46 Stops procrastinating
47 Purchase at a pump
48 Sank, as a putt
50 Cowboy's cow catcher
54 "For ___ a jolly good fellow . . ."
57 ___ Man Winter
58 Country
61 Coffee, slangily
62 "Carmen" or "Elektra"
63 Nintendo villain with an upside-down "M" on his cap
64 Opposite of 'neath
65 Like maples but not pines
66 Won the World Series in four games, say

DOWN

1 Proof-ending letters
2 Thick Japanese noodle
3 Woman's name hidden in "United Nations"
4 He postulated $E = mc^2$
5 Grant-issuing cultural org.
6 Bandmate of John, George and Ringo
7 Hunter's supply, for short
8 Hunter's garb, for short
9 Justice League member who's super-speedy
10 35mm camera type
11 Good name for a postseason football game sponsored by General Mills?
12 Mythological river around the underworld
13 Rapper/actor on "Law & Order: SVU"
18 Pageant wear
22 "For shame!"
24 "___ be my pleasure"
26 Shoo-___ (sure winners)
27 Be of use
28 Access to a treehouse, maybe
29 "You gotta ___ . . ."
30 On the ___ (broken)
31 Mark down for a sale, say
32 Cheesed off
33 Dark film genre
34 Feel sore
38 Black diamond trail, e.g.
39 Ordinance for dog-walkers
41 Toward the stern
42 Org. supporting the Second Amendment
44 Blackjack card with two values
45 Acronym for a multiaward accomplishment
48 Magical power, informally
49 ___ vera
51 Vicinity
52 Feudal worker
53 Dog command often issued with an outstretched palm
55 Brontë's Jane
56 Scissor sound
58 "u r so funny!"
59 Reactions to cute puppies
60 "Just kidding!"

by Carl Larson

ACROSS

1 Analyze grammatically
6 Extreme devotee, informally
11 Org. for Pistons and Rockets
14 Overact
15 Egypt's Sadat
16 Common street name in the Northeast
17 "God in his wisdom made the fly / And then forgot . . ."
19 ___ Sports (video game)
20 Card in Uno
21 Word after square or plus
22 Brings home
24 "Tell me, O Octopus, I begs, / Is those things arms . . . ?"
28 Festival that awards the Palme d'Or
31 Best possible
32 Eschew
33 Voiced, as grievances
35 Something often lent, but never returned
38 Eye of ___ (part of a witch's brew)
39 Poet Nash, who wrote the lines in 17-, 24-, 47- and 58-Across
40 Long part of a horse, short part of a giraffe
41 Places with frontline workers, for short
42 Vibes
43 Parts of a Facebook feed
44 Bring out
46 "Let's be real"
47 "The cow is of the bovine ilk; / One end is moo, . . ."
51 Alternative to Google or AOL
52 One-named singer born Gabriella Sarmiento Wilson
53 Straw, basically
57 Thanksgiving dinner ending
58 "The trouble with a kitten is that / Eventually it . . ."
62 Flub
63 They protect the QB
64 Beth Harmon's weakness in "The Queen's Gambit"
65 "Yes, captain"
66 Ocean's motions
67 Like a good biscuit

DOWN

1 Adoptees from the A.S.P.C.A.
2 One way to run
3 Indian flatbread
4 "Go, go, go!"
5 Fish that may have only vestigial fins
6 Mr. Tumnus in the "Narnia" books and others
7 Zoomed-in map
8 "Blech!"
9 "I'll pass"
10 Impassive
11 Netflix debut, perhaps
12 Ice you can wear
13 Not quite right
18 Lowry who wrote "The Giver"
23 ___ mode
25 Like a low battery icon
26 Puts on the payroll
27 Genesis garden
28 Walking aid
29 Profess
30 "Listen, bub!"
33 What the nouns and verb in this clue doesn't do
34 Civil rights activist ___ B. Wells
36 Prefix with inflammatory
37 Doctor's generic recommendation
39 "That's gotta hurt!"
40 Shirley Temple, e.g.
42 Decepticon's enemy in the "Transformers" films
43 Chum
45 Scooby-___
46 Something said to be in the eyes or belly
47 Like an overachieving personality
48 Dangerous, as a situation
49 French wine valley
50 Much internet humor
54 Home of the Bruins
55 Refuse to continue
56 E-commerce site for homemade goods
59 One of the Manning brothers
60 El ___ (Spanish hero)
61 UV blocking measure

by Jennifer Lee and Victor Galson

ACROSS

1 Alternative to subway or taxi
4 Privately includes on an email
8 Farm towers
13 "Hold on ___!"
15 Most populous Hawaiian island
16 Scoring 100% on
17 Last runner in a relay
19 French writer Jean
20 1986 #1 hit by Falco
22 Capable
24 Prefix with -ceps
25 Dance with clicking sounds
26 In ___ (as found)
27 Place that's an appropriate rhyme for "aah"
29 Ones foretelling the future
31 Title lyric heard 41 times in a 1965 Beach Boys hit
34 Big name in ice cream
35 Persian Gulf land: Abbr.
36 Designer item from Hermès or Kate Spade
37 "Cogito ergo ___"
40 Red-haired toy craze of 1996
43 They say this "ain't over until the fat lady sings"
45 "Yes, cap'n"
46 "99 Luftballons" singer, 1984
47 "No ___ do!"
48 Large wine container
50 Bonus item
51 Request from the voracious plant in "Little Shop of Horrors"
55 "Color me impressed!"
56 Comment after getting off a dizzying amusement park ride
59 Christopher who directed "Dunkirk"
60 V.I.P.s at board meetings
61 Falco of "The Sopranos"
62 Symbols in movie ratings
63 Stitches
64 Which came first . . . this or the chicken?

DOWN

1 Call to Little Bo-Peep
2 Mil. branch for sailors
3 On the down-low
4 When tripled, catchphrase of the Muppets' Swedish Chef
5 Completely zen
6 World's fastest land animal (up to 70 m.p.h.)
7 Icing, essentially
8 It's a long story
9 Lemonade + ___ = Arnold Palmer
10 Like the equation $y = 2x + 3$
11 Outdoes in a back-and-forth
12 Superiors to cpls.
14 Slice and dice
18 Mo. for trick-or-treaters
21 Call wrongly
22 Arthur ___ Stadium, U.S. Open locale
23 Ran out of battery
27 Italy's Blue Grotto is a famous one
28 School for 3- and 4-year-olds, informally
30 Sharp part of a knife
32 Conservationist John who co-founded the Sierra Club
33 Heed
37 Activity for a snow day
38 "Er, I think I'll pass"
39 Gripe
40 Make the rounds?
41 Penalty for missing the payment deadline
42 Ultimate purpose
43 Large feline kept as a pet by Salvador Dalí
44 Classic Spanish rice dish
49 Adidas competitor
50 Big inits. in 1990s internet
51 Signs of nearby sharks
52 Clothing store department
53 "#@&%! My toe!"
54 Military cafeteria
57 "Butt"
58 Large beer container

by Ian Rathkey

4 EASY

ACROSS

1 Key above Caps Lock
4 Depletes, as of energy
8 Goes on the offensive
15 Suffix with expert
16 "___ the case!"
17 Many an evergreen
18 With 63-Across, "The end" . . . or what can be said about the novels in the clues for 25-, 38- and 52-Across
20 Sometimes it's "not an option"
21 Stella ___ (beer)
22 Sculler's tool
23 ___ score (400 to 1600)
24 Prefix with bot
25 Author of "The Bell Jar" (1963)
30 Sending a Slack message, say
32 Secure, as a boat
33 NPR host Cornish
34 "___ away!" ("Hit me!")
35 Paths of lobs
37 Actress Mirren
38 Author of "Black Beauty" (1877)
41 Sealy competitor
43 Bit of fishing equipment
44 Many a college prof
47 Difficult tooth for a dentist to fill
48 Help (out)
50 Mystical energy fields
52 Author of "Wuthering Heights" (1847)
55 Slugger Sammy in the 1998 home run chase
56 Bit of fishing equipment
57 Prey for a barracuda
58 "You don't even want to know"
60 Question of apathy
63 See 18-Across
65 Guaranteed
66 Met highlight
67 Earn the most votes, say
68 Abhors
69 Some August births
70 Inc., abroad

DOWN

1 Fairy queen in "A Midsummer Night's Dream"
2 Hindu retreats
3 Many a character in Kerouac's "On the Road"
4 Enthusiastic Spanish approval
5 Collect in volume
6 One shaking hands and kissing babies, stereotypically
7 Weekly show famously filmed in Studio 8H, in brief
8 Secret relationship
9 Small crown
10 El ___ (nickname for the Mexican national soccer team)
11 Falcons, on a scoreboard
12 Vigorous campaign
13 Protein in horns and hair
14 Keep one's anger at a low boil
19 Yogi Bear or Fred Flintstone
22 Egg: Prefix
26 It often has a gym and pool
27 The "1" in a 15–1 record
28 Dish associated with the Valencia region of Spain
29 Slow period
31 Overhead support for interstate signs
36 Tiny messenger
37 ___-haw
38 Asia's ___ Sea
39 Popular name for an Irish girl
40 Swollen mark
41 "Can't say who"
42 Snooty
44 N.F.L. all-star game
45 Makes an enthusiastic attempt
46 Wrong turn in a maze
47 Repaired
48 American Kennel Club list
49 Former Time Warner partner
51 Leningrad's land, for short
53 Visorless cap
54 Letters heard after "cow," "pig" and "horse"
59 "___ the night before Christmas . . ."
61 Chalk one up?
62 Horace's "___ Poetica"
63 Narrator of "On the Road"
64 Charlemagne's domain: Abbr.

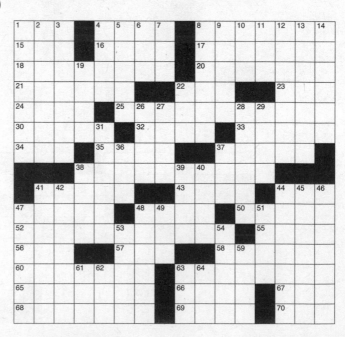

by Drew Schmenner

ACROSS

1 Bottom of a shoe
5 Had on
9 Insurance worker
14 Work by a composer
15 Skating leap
16 Outdoor party locale
17 Pastime for armchair sports enthusiasts
20 Corrosive substance
21 ExxonMobil's business
22 Toy that goes up slow and comes down fast
23 Close, as a jacket
26 What a grocery scanner scans, for short
29 Unidentifiable protein
34 They're paid to play
36 Grp. that extends from Canada to Chile
37 Lustful, informally
38 Sightseeing on wheels
40 Finally starts talking
42 Like draft beers
43 "Baby Cobra" comic Wong
44 Christmas season
45 Holy site in Jerusalem
49 When a plane is due in, in brief
50 Hair stylist, fancily
52 Old Glory, for one
56 Sch. in Fort Worth
57 "The very idea!"
61 Spanish or French, but not German
64 "Tosca" or "Turandot"
65 Opening for a coin
66 Speak to a deaf person, in a way
67 What the start of 17-, 29-, 45- or 61-Across is, in a bookstore
68 Tickle Me Elmo maker, once
69 Otherwise

DOWN

1 Living room seat
2 Iridescent gem
3 Meathead
4 Abbr. before a date on a business shingle
5 Question to a suspected culprit
6 Popular acne medication
7 Starts up again, as a computer
8 Pal of Jerry on "Seinfeld"
9 Primate with no tail
10 Talks on and on
11 And others: Abbr.
12 River on which Cleopatra cruised
13 Couldn't keep a secret
18 Grad
19 Shpeak indishtinctly
24 Ruler in pre-Communist Russia
25 Heap for burning
26 Instruction for a violinist
27 Dehydrated plum
28 Things weighed against benefits
30 Not just a few
31 Come next
32 One who's 18 or older
33 Like an impatient and competitive personality
35 "Now!" in the operating room
39 Intl. group that has no members in Europe or North America
40 Minnesota's St. ___ College
41 Enter en masse, as a car
43 In a terrible way
46 Coll. military program
47 Most pleasant
48 Where inhaled air goes
51 Find a second function for
52 Creature that goes "ribbit!"
53 Run easily
54 "You said it, brother!"
55 Actress Teri
58 Colorado skiing mecca
59 Objects in an Easter hunt
60 Surrealist Magritte
62 Scottish negative
63 Member of a D.C. "Squad"

by Stella Zawistowski

ACROSS

1 "Money, Money, Money" group
5 Toughs . . . or an anagram of TOUGHS minus a letter
10 Slightly open
14 Thick slice
15 Old but back in fashion
16 Agricultural giant founded in Hawaii in 1851
17 Atmosphere
18 Font akin to Helvetica
19 "What time?"
20 Sort of investment suggested by the ends of 3-, 11- and 29-Down
23 First half of a Senate vote
24 "Oh, bleah!"
25 Indent key
27 Exclamation upon reaching a customer service representative, maybe
31 Measurement for passes and rushes: Abbr.
34 It's 99.9% "empty space"
36 "___ you are you! That is truer than true!": Dr. Seuss
37 Rapper fronting the heavy metal band Body Count
38 Late-night host O'Brien
40 Profs' helpers
41 Silly
42 Where chess is believed to have originated
43 Qty.
44 Curving billiards shot
45 Car company that shares its name with an inventor
46 Longtime CBS police drama
47 Flicked, as a cigarette

48 In a risky situation
51 Nicholas I or II
54 They have ears, it's said
55 Intimidates
59 Had in one's hands
60 Blacksmith's block
61 Place to cook a turkey
62 Behind, in England
63 Part of an act
64 Reviled Roman emperor
65 Deserving a D
66 "Able was I ___ . . ."
67 Picked a card

DOWN

1 "Get on it!"
2 Sad
3 M.L.B. record-holder for most career home runs

4 Humiliate
5 Kind of visa for just passing through an airport
6 Greek goddess of marriage
7 Gas or elec.
8 Tennis's Steffi
9 How best to hit a ball for a home run
10 Coke vs. Pepsi, e.g.
11 Singer profiled in the biopic "Walk the Line"
12 Smart ___
13 Philosopher Descartes
21 Big doofus
22 "I disagree"
25 Understood
26 Make reparations
28 "Impossible!"
29 N.B.A. commissioner starting in 2014
30 Trailing all others

32 Tightly packed
33 Horse for a knight
35 Alternative to in-store
37 "I'll be right with you"
39 Tandoor bread
41 Apple desktop
49 Contraction starting a Christmas poem
50 Archipelago part
51 Bloke
52 It doesn't mean a thing
53 In addition
56 Lead-in to "the hill" or "the top"
57 "What ___ you thinking?"
58 Reason for a school day off

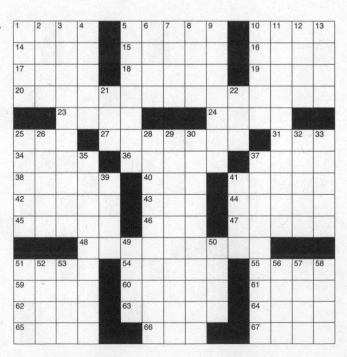

by Eric Bornstein

ACROSS

1 Soldier who deserted
5 Daughters' counterparts
9 Archcompetitor
14 Sitarist Shankar who tutored the Beatles
15 "Shall I compare ___ to a summer's day?"
16 Upper crust
17 Something on a list
18 Taj Mahal locale
19 Closes with a bang
20 Hoped-for experience at a casino
23 Residences that may have groundskeepers
24 Oaty cereal
28 Sprinkle often paired with salt
31 ___ Diamond, author of popular science books
34 Modern love?
35 Pledge drive giveaway
36 "What ___ the chances?"
37 Digital birthday greeting
39 Classic doll with "Shaving Fun" and "Mod Hair" versions
40 Degs. for entrepreneurs
42 On the ___ (fleeing)
43 Ominous note from a boss
45 Fashion designer's purchase
49 Designer Giorgio
50 Eavesdropping range
54 Early advantage . . . or what 20-, 28- and 45-Across each have?
57 Apple tablets
60 Tweak, as text
61 "On top of that . . ."
62 Lakeside rental
63 Nintendo competitor
64 Bad cafeteria food, say
65 College boards, e.g.
66 Powdered drink once used by NASA
67 Desires

DOWN

1 Get out of bed
2 Actress Naomi
3 For all to see
4 Mouth-puckering green drink
5 Belmont ___
6 "Goodness gracious!"
7 Kind of ball it's hard to hurt anyone with
8 ___ of approval
9 Sort of dog that's ready for a new home
10 Poorly hidden, as a secret
11 By way of
12 Prez dispenser?
13 Broadway's "___ Misérables"
21 Just slightly
22 Called strikes and balls at a game
25 Broke the silence, in a way
26 "See if I care what they do!," informally
27 Cara who sang "Flashdance . . . What a Feeling"
29 Michelle with the best-selling memoir "Becoming"
30 Distant
31 Big name in smoothies
32 Ann ___, Mich.
33 Sphere of influence
37 Spritelike
38 Half-___ (latte option)
41 Fame in the field of sports or entertainment
43 Lancelot and Gawain of legend
44 Blissful state
46 Burdens of proof
47 Harmless
48 Motley, as a crew
51 Actress and spokesmodel Berry
52 Cinema legend Welles
53 Sporty car roofs
55 Tweets often come from here
56 "What's the big ___?"
57 Swelling soother
58 Roman peace
59 Actress de Armas of "No Time to Die"

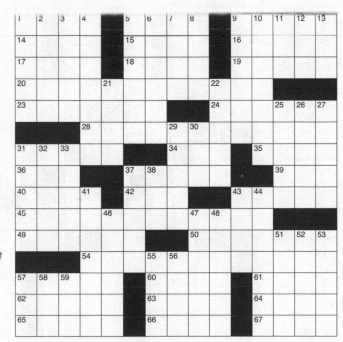

by Enrique Henestroza Anguiano

ACROSS

1 Exam for some coll. seniors
5 Actress Kurylenko
9 Stow away
14 The singer Lorde's given name
15 Home of many of the world's alpacas
16 Philadelphia N.F.L.er
17 Cadillac rims?
18 Work at a news desk, maybe
19 Bygone Italian coins
20 Sign outside a Stratego tournament?
23 Greek goddess of wisdom
24 2011 Jay-Z/Kanye West hit that pays tribute to singer Redding
25 Sign outside a Scrabble tournament?
31 Web portal once owned by Verizon
34 Contract period
35 Dazzles
36 Facebook Messenger activity
38 "You rang?"
40 Astronomical event
41 Among, as friends
44 Up for anything
47 Happenin', modernly
48 Sign outside a Taboo tournament?
51 Mystique
52 Many a plaza has one
56 Sign outside a dominoes tournament?
60 Finland's largest company by revenue
61 Circular earring
62 Certain sausage, informally
63 Play, as a guitar
64 Doughnuts, topologically
65 Workplace org. created in 1970
66 "Same with me"
67 Schedule opening
68 Mafia V.I.P.s

DOWN

1 Destination for many pilgrims
2 Shoe spike
3 The beginning of the Hebrew world?
4 Takes a first bite of
5 Do surgery
6 Start of an article, in journalist lingo
7 Moxie
8 Wilde or Wilder
9 Not willing to share
10 Dizzying decline
11 Noted mausoleum site
12 Smelting byproduct
13 "___ a real nowhere man" (Beatles lyric)
21 Mile or mole
22 Data for airport limo drivers, for short
26 Destroy, as a motherboard
27 The end of the Greek world?
28 Carbon compound
29 First name in denim
30 Exam for some coll. seniors
31 Very harsh, as comments
32 Cry of horror
33 Spot for a campaign sign
37 Element named after a group in Greek myth
39 Noticed
42 Overwhelming amount
43 Notoriously fast starter
45 Where you might bump into a metal fan
46 Art Deco icon
49 Sails in style, in a way
50 Flabby male physique (that's not exclusive to fathers)
53 Work of art that goes to waist?
54 Beehive State resident
55 These, in Madrid
56 Camp beds
57 Vegetable that's often fried
58 Level or lever
59 One seeing red?
60 Home to many cybersafety experts, in brief

by Billy Ouska

ACROSS

1 Thick rugs
6 Like some exams and medicines
10 Pack (down)
14 No-no
15 Actress Moore of "Ghost"
16 ___ 51 (U.F.O. landing site? . . . hmm)
17 Toward the back
18 Rule by a small group
20 Early addendum to the Constitution
22 Radio host Glass
23 Doves' home
24 Stag's mate
27 Crying . . . or laughing hysterically
31 "I've got it!"
33 Train unit
34 Gutenberg invention
37 Coup d'___
39 "Woo-hoo!"
40 NSFW stuff
41 Sauna plus massage at a spa, perhaps
46 ". . . ___ he drove out of sight . . ."
47 Traveling, as a band
48 Slowly burn
50 N, E, W and S, on a compass: Abbr.
51 Follower of open or pigeon
54 Spartans' sch.
55 1998 Hanks/Ryan rom-com . . . or a hint to the starts of 20-, 34- and 41-Across
60 Welcoming environment for everyone
63 Dwelling
64 Someone sought by mil. police

65 Semihard Dutch cheese
66 What some couples do with their wedding vows
67 Outside of an orange
68 Almanacs and atlases, for short
69 Tire pattern

DOWN

1 Wild guess
2 Mata ___ (W.W. I spy)
3 Brother betrayed in the Bible
4 Heavily padded hockey player
5 Sisterly
6 Febreze target
7 Ancient artifact
8 "Adios, ___!"
9 Something waved at concerts prior to the age of cellphones
10 Covers with black goo
11 Section of a circumference
12 "I'm not impressed"
13 Equal ___ for equal work
19 Avidly enjoyed
21 Taxi charge
24 Adjudged
25 "Fine, works for me"
26 Occasion for an egg roll
27 Frozen summer treat
28 Floating on water
29 Land parcels
30 Ocular affliction
32 $200 Monopoly properties: Abbr.
35 Little bit

36 Snake ___ (dice roll)
38 Boxing ruling, for short
42 Dealership inventory
43 Large-mouthed food fish
44 Peas, to some classroom pranksters
45 Writing in script, nowadays
49 Wood for building
52 Give the slip
53 Java without the jolt
55 Holler
56 Pearls and peridots
57 First-class
58 Notion
59 Raunchy
60 What tapping a maple yields
61 Dazzle
62 Dr. No, to James Bond

by Emily Rourke

ACROSS

1 Truck weigh station unit
4 Enter one's password
9 Contents of an hourglass
13 Boston's Mass. ___
14 Birth announcement units
16 Charlie's Angels, e.g.
17 'Tis the season: Abbr.
18 One remedy for a hangover, supposedly
20 Place to attach a surfboard leash
22 Big ___ (cheapo's opposite)
23 Place to pick up a pepperoni pie, perhaps
27 Card in Uno or action on Spotify
29 Actress Glazer of "Broad City"
30 U.F.C. sport
33 Popeye's Olive ___
34 Thorny part of a rose
35 Listens to
37 Close follower of the "horse race"
41 Poker-faced
42 "Oh, OK"
43 Sinister fish in "The Little Mermaid"
44 Reactions to stepping on Legos, say
45 Late-night coffee order
47 What's stronger than "might"
48 Aircraft that's 1% full?
51 Farm measure
54 Astronomer Hubble
57 Some Xmas card attire . . . or a hint to 18-, 23-, 37- and 48-Across
61 Keats's "To Autumn," e.g.
62 Worry
63 Distribute cash at the end of a shift, in restaurant lingo
64 "Oedipus ___"
65 Snafu
66 Snapple cap fodder
67 Kit ___ bar

DOWN

1 Self-congratulatory cry
2 Have a bun in the ___
3 Aid for sleeping on a plane
4 Singer/actress Jennifer
5 "Yes, madame!"
6 Big inits. in protein powder
7 "Gross!"
8 Half ___ (wrestling hold)
9 Fall guys?
10 Like Death Valley
11 Pleasant French city?
12 Go-getter
15 Filter that gives photos a vintage look
19 Former Biden White House press secretary Psaki
21 Sass
24 Pasta popular on "The Sopranos"
25 Smart ___
26 Birthplace of Rastafarianism
27 Absorbs, as with bread
28 Capital of Japan for more than a thousand years
31 Iconic encouragement from Tim Gunn on "Project Runway"
32 The Little Mermaid
34 Teen's bedroom, stereotypically
35 Peach or periwinkle
36 Vend
38 Checks out
39 Challenge for a future atty.
40 Spanish boss, with "el"
45 8 or 9, but not 10
46 Were it possible that
47 Get hitched
49 When doubled, enthusiastic
50 Jokes around
51 Radio switch
52 Safekeeping
53 Google Maps might provide several of them: Abbr.
55 Starting place for an inventor
56 In the on-deck circle, say
58 4.0 is an excellent one
59 African American or Asian American, e.g., for short
60 Stick (out)

by Margaret Seikel

ACROSS

1 Flows out, as the tide
5 One who's always complaining, complaining, complaining
9 Prevent through intimidation
14 Prefix with -naut
15 ___ gras (goose or duck delicacy)
16 Contents of a .jpeg file
17 Grand Central, for one
20 Host Harvey of "Family Feud"
21 Music genre often labeled "heavy"
22 Psychedelic substance
23 ___ year (2020 or 2024)
25 Actor/musician whose name sounds like a drink
27 Santa ___ winds
29 Event of October 1929
35 A long way away
36 Bird symbolizing grace
37 Figure skater Harding
38 Spoiler of a perfect record
40 Skiing or skating
43 Legal wrong
44 Love on the Loire
46 Listening device for an undercover officer
48 Inconclusive score
49 Pastry with a swirl
52 "I've ___ enough out of you!"
53 Bridge
54 Narrowly defeat, with "out"
56 La ___ (Bolivian capital)
59 "If only!"
62 Continental currency units
65 Fire safety technique . . . or 17-, 29- and 49-Across together
68 Where to sit for the bar?

69 Where baby Moses was found
70 Go back, when editing
71 "Yum!"
72 Mother Nature's blanket
73 Ooze

DOWN

1 Elves have big ones, stereotypically
2 Musical rhythm
3 Star of "Room" and "Captain Marvel"
4 Do a crossword, say
5 Money manager, in brief
6 Wander about
7 Right-hand person
8 Closest pal
9 Cockney vis-à-vis English
10 An essential worker, for short
11 A sea horse has a prehensile one
12 Big heads
13 Tear up
18 Printing paper units
19 What you may use when turning down an invitation
24 Canine "handshake" offerings
26 Gait for a horse with a buggy
27 Fortune 500 company whose name rhymes, appropriately, with "quack"
28 Tennis champ Osaka
30 Grammy genre since 1988
31 In the public consciousness
32 Terse request to a bartender
33 Damascus is its capital
34 Word repeated in Roger Ebert's "I ___, ___, ___ This Movie"

39 Phoenix N.B.A. team
41 Poke fun at
42 "You're right"
45 With haste
47 Came to a close
50 Bryn ___ (women's college)
51 Liver and ___ (dish)
55 Spiritual guides
56 [Hey! Over here!]
57 Lead in to boy or girl
58 They have everything from aardvarks to zebras
60 Whirl
61 Sign of saintliness
63 Ye ___ Shoppe
64 Pigs' supper
66 What calls the kettle black, in an expression
67 Fresh

by Tomas Spiers

ACROSS

1 Policy nerd
5 P.F. ___ (restaurant chain)
11 Query
14 Gaelic language
15 Actor Pattinson
16 Actress Farrow
17 Northern European region
19 Cozy lodging
20 Kind of beef from Japan
21 Like the richest soufflé
23 County of Newark, N.J.
26 Oil-drilling structure
27 Feeling of dejection
30 Its flag has a blue 61-Across
34 Lyrical dedication
35 Scare off
37 Play dirty
38 "Star Wars" racing vehicles
40 Flier with a tail
42 Fiona or Shrek
43 Swords with blunted ends
45 Radium discoverer
47 Mr. ___ (Tootsie Pop's avian mascot)
48 Its flag has a white 61-Across
50 Beguile, to Brits
52 "___ been meaning to mention . . ."
53 Military helicopters, colloquially
54 2021 Elizabeth Warren book
58 Two kings or two queens, e.g.
60 Chopper
61 Flag symbol seen twice in this puzzle's grid
66 Rapper ___ Wayne
67 Novelist Graham
68 Opera highlight
69 It's a mess!
70 Was in a state of suppressed agitation
71 Actor Jon of "Good Omens"

DOWN

1 Director Anderson
2 Tolkien monster
3 Secretive org.
4 Logic puzzle invented by a math teacher as a teaching tool
5 Baby's bed
6 Refine, as a skill
7 Lawyers' group, for short
8 Actress Campbell
9 Climber's belaying device
10 Job for a play director
11 Female friend in France
12 Gluttony and lust, for two
13 Philosopher Immanuel
18 Outed maliciously online
22 Home with a northern exposure
23 Got married in Vegas, perhaps
24 "That's awesome!"
25 Its flag has a yellow 61-Across
28 Little bit of time
29 Soup starter
30 "___ Jacques, dormez-vous?"
31 Popular vote winner of 2000
32 Its flag has a blue-and-white 61-Across
33 Lingers (on)
36 Second-tallest bird on earth
39 Penultimate matches
41 10th anniversary gift
44 Nest egg
46 Set of moral principles
49 Vacation destination
51 "Yay!"
54 Friends
55 Sign at a highway cloverleaf
56 Depend (on)
57 See 58-Down
58 With 57-Down, car air freshener shape
59 Got an A on
62 Drops on the grass?
63 Hour, in Italy
64 Virtual citizen in a popular video game franchise
65 Symbolic U.S. "uncle"

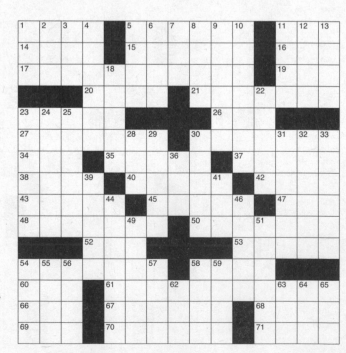

by Tao Platt

ACROSS

1 Actress Raquel
6 Slightly wet
10 ___-retentive
14 Nebraska city nicknamed the "Gateway to the West"
15 Female French friend
16 It's good for what ails you
17 Prince or princess
18 Held in high esteem
20 Prompt action when things are unraveling
22 Number of provinces in Canada
23 Nay's opposite
24 Rear end, in slang
28 Ground-breaking tool
29 Watery expanse
31 In the mail
32 Beat around the bush
36 "Well, ___-di-dah!"
37 Cry of pity
38 Shoe bottoms
40 "The ___ Duckling" (fairy tale)
41 Relieved (of)
42 "Oh, blast!"
44 One of three in Orion's belt
46 Bundle of money
47 Poetic praise
48 Prefix meaning "different"
50 "A work of ___ that did not begin in emotion is not ___": Cézanne
51 Letter before chi
54 What ties everything together, including 20-, 32- and 42-Across?
58 Pulsating
61 Like coincidences that make you go "hmm"
62 The "h" in m.p.h.
63 Brewed beverages in bottles
64 Fauna's partner
65 Piece with a view
66 Exam
67 Annual theater awards

DOWN

1 Lowest of the low
2 Act poorly?
3 Stockpile
4 Chew the fat
5 Like the good old days
6 Title girl in a bygone MTV cartoon
7 "You said it!"
8 Fine spray
9 Pumpkin seed
10 Means of entry
11 Hexagonal bit of hardware
12 "___ we cool?"
13 Was in first place
19 Outback bird
21 Obeys
25 Andrew Wyeth portrait subject
26 Counting everything together
27 Antiknock fluid
28 Contains
29 One getting dressed for lunch?
30 Wide-mouthed jug
32 Caustic
33 Of the highest standard
34 Angry with
35 Host Kotb of morning TV
39 Sound from a pug
40 Salt Lake City athlete
43 Goal of phishing schemes, informally
45 "Let the ___ show . . ."
46 Outback animal
49 Burgle
50 Frequent teenage sensation
51 The Evita of "Evita"
52 Opposite of clean-shaven
53 They're symbolized by light bulbs in cartoons
55 One of about 93 million between Earth and the sun
56 Change for a five
57 Move, in real estate lingo
58 Howe'er
59 You might do it after stubbing a toe
60 Feel sorry about

by Anne Rowley

ACROSS

1 Bygone Russian ruler
5 Rock band whose name also forms the call letters for a rock radio station in San Antonio
9 Like some sprays
14 "The Simpsons" character with a palindromic name
15 Part of a foot
16 "The best is ___ come"
17 Capture the attention of
18 Not quite shut
19 Sing smoothly
20 Hawk's home
22 Russia's ___ Mountains
24 Dating ___
25 Skiing and snowboarding
28 Fulfill completely
29 With special importance
32 Sewing shop supply
35 Puts money (on)
36 Lens holder
37 Work hard for
38 B or C of the Spice Girls
39 Building with a loft
40 Prominent feature of a fennec fox
41 Pesky plant
43 Card suit that symbolizes a medieval weapon
45 Hare ___
47 Sight near an exit sign
48 Display of mentalism . . . or a hint to this puzzle's shaded squares
52 www.nytimes.com, for one
53 Attempt, metaphorically
54 Reserve
56 Give away, as a story's ending
58 Smooth (out)
60 Walkie-talkie word
61 Pinky and the Brain, for two
62 It may be printed on a place mat
63 ___-do-well
64 Put into the pot
65 First place?
66 Wapitis

DOWN

1 Caesar dressing?
2 Scatter
3 Developer of the game Breakout
4 M.L.B.'s first Rookie of the Year (1947)
5 Sorento automaker
6 Cause harm to
7 Lasting marks
8 Explosion fragments
9 Home of the Met, the Whitney and the Frick, in brief
10 Make fizzy
11 Halts abruptly
12 Crowning
13 Actor Chaney nicknamed "The Man of a Thousand Faces"
21 List shortener: Abbr.
23 Plundered goods
26 U.F.O. pilots
27 Some N.F.L. blockers
30 Orpheus' instrument
31 Urges
32 Ask for
33 Talk show host Jack
34 Ingredient in perfume and potpourri
35 Furniture depicted in Frida Kahlo's "The Dream" (1940)
38 Interim period
39 Singing voice meaning "heavy-sounding"
41 Question of identity
42 First and only chimpanzee to orbit Earth
43 Cronus, to Uranus
44 Whale groups
46 Long, thin strip used in building construction
47 Prepare, in a way, as chicken
49 Exposed for all to see
50 Work of fiction
51 One of Cyprus's two official languages
52 "___ the housetop, click, click, click . . ."
55 Goofs
56 Subway stop: Abbr.
57 It may give you visuals
59 Sister

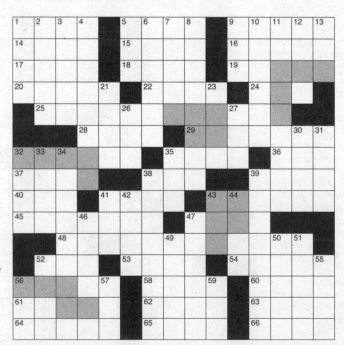

by Guilherme Gilioli

ACROSS

1 "Ain't that the truth!"
7 Use a swizzle stick
11 "You don't need to be ___, Roy" (rhyming Paul Simon lyric)
14 Human beings
15 Keister, in Leicester
16 Filmmaker DuVernay
17 *TV remote inserts, often
19 Implement with ink
20 Technical detail, for short
21 *Sobriety support group session, informally
23 Give off, as vibes
26 Little criticism
27 Pub barrel
30 *Animal whose name means "earth pig" in Afrikaans
35 Line on a sales receipt
36 Skirmish
38 Lena of "Chocolat"
39 Floor cover
40 *"Winnie-the-Pooh" writer
42 Lacto-___ vegetarianism
43 Element that also names a household appliance
45 Acknowledges with a head tilt
46 Snag
47 *4.0 on a transcript
49 Shapes made in the snow
51 Swing ___ (when big bands were big)
52 Disney snow queen
53 *Three-time Emmy winner for "Breaking Bad"
58 Word with butter or Stadium
62 What's central in heliocentrism
63 Tennessee Smokies or Portland Sea Dogs . . . or what the answers to the starred clues comprise?

66 Words from an altar ego?
67 Fairy tale menace
68 Section of a sentence
69 What's inside an inner tube
70 Fly high
71 Summer wear with a T-shirt

DOWN

1 Many hoppy brews, in brief
2 ___ of faith
3 One of four in the human brain
4 Actress Sissy
5 Ctrl-___-Del
6 Nonetheless
7 Singer Bareilles
8 Minor haircut
9 "Ah, gotcha"
10 Forward, as mail
11 Banking giant that makes the Venture card
12 Bakery hot spot
13 Yin's opposite
18 "Don't starve yourself!"
22 Big name in DVRs
24 Prefix with physics
25 Tropical lizard
27 Indoor spaces with lots of natural light
28 First lady Bush
29 Arnold Schwarzenegger or Ronald Reagan, for California
30 Parenthetical comment
31 "___ Well That Ends Well"
32 Car for a vacationer
33 Archcompetitor
34 Some volume controls
37 Pollution in city skies
41 Like, forever!
44 Emperor during the Great Fire of Rome

48 Total strangers, in modern slang
50 Prefix with enterologist
52 Right-angle shape
53 Home of seven -stans
54 A4 automaker
55 Jumping stick
56 Vibe
57 Lyft competitor
59 Consider, as a judicial case
60 Down ___ (Maine)
61 Iowa campus town
64 Mini-albums, in brief
65 "Say ___" (doctor's request)

by Adam Aaronson

ACROSS
1 Piquancy
5 British fellow
9 Treasure holder
14 Pretentious in a painterly way
15 March ___ (Lewis Carroll character)
16 Recluse
17 Racket handle
18 Letter-shaped bridge support
19 Extremely
20 Food topping used at Abe Lincoln's birthplace?
23 Stein filler
25 Wash for gold
26 Drunkard
27 Ambulance letters
28 Dairy product used at the Seven Dwarfs' dwelling?
32 Lug around
33 Tulsa sch.
34 Sellout indicator
35 Rant and rage
37 "Good Morning America" network
39 Took notice
43 Old TV's "The Adventures of ___ Tin Tin"
45 Always, in poems
47 Vegetable whose name is also slang for "money"
48 Turkey stuffing used at the Ewings' Southfork?
51 Michael of "S.N.L."
53 Calendar block
54 Zoom or TikTok
55 ___ Palmas, city in the Canary Islands
56 Spreads using 20-, 28- and 48-Across?
60 Jumper cable connection
61 "Make it ___"
62 Big lugs

65 Candidate for a Booker Prize
66 Helper: Abbr.
67 Capital of Latvia
68 Lead-in to line or setter
69 Does as the sun does in the evening
70 Kentucky's Fort ___

DOWN
1 Evasive maneuver
2 Slip up
3 Shoe named after a dagger
4 Slip-up in writing
5 Where Michelle Obama was born
6 Dance named after Cuba's capital
7 Prized mount
8 Come to an end
9 Groups of grapes, e.g.

10 Word in many cathedral names
11 Main course
12 Injection at a hospital
13 Pitfalls
21 4.0 for a valedictorian, maybe
22 Rejections
23 ___ of the Apostles
24 Heist haul
29 Earth, in science fiction
30 Raised to the third power
31 Enjoys a long, hot bath, say
36 Vulcan's telepathic link
38 Pottery maker
40 Bad situation for an airplane
41 Wrist/elbow connector

42 Clothes holders on a clothesline
44 March Madness org.
46 Expresses sorrow for one's wrongdoing
48 Jettison
49 Mythical Greek monsters
50 Destination for a rest cure
51 "U.S.A.! U.S.A.!," e.g.
52 Being named valedictorian, for one
57 Heaven on earth
58 Simplicity
59 Frolic
63 Narcissist's flaw
64 Instrument in most jazz combos

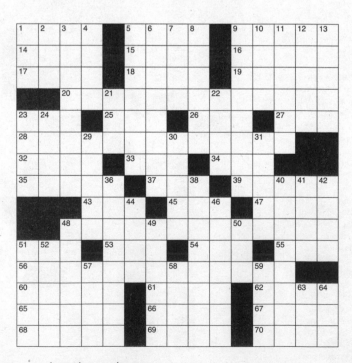

by Kathy Wienberg

ACROSS

1 "First, do no ___" (physician's maxim)
5 Claim on some food packaging
10 Simplicity
14 Cookie often dipped in milk
15 Barclays Center in Brooklyn, for one
16 Ending with Insta-
17 Telepathic sort
19 Halliwell of the Spice Girls
20 Makeup mogul Lauder
21 Determines the money needed to get out of jail
23 Affirmative response to "Shall we dance?"
26 Greek letter that one might expect to come last
27 Embedded spy awaiting a mission
32 Minor-league level
35 With 59-Across, "Madam Secretary" star
36 Curbside coin collector
37 Scattered here, there and everywhere
42 Animal that dances ballet in "Fantasia"
43 Apple mobile devices run on it
44 Locale for clouds
45 "Quit arguing, kids!"
50 Cuatro + cuatro
51 1988 Best Picture winner starring Dustin Hoffman
55 People who "sow" evil
59 See 35-Across
60 Antioxidant-rich berry
61 Intuition without logical explanation, or a hint to this puzzle's circled letters

64 Dryer fuzz
65 "Ciao" in Chihuahua
66 Singer India.___
67 Border
68 H. Ross ___, candidate of 1992 and 1996
69 Banana skin

DOWN

1 Invitingly warm and cozy
2 Come up, as issues
3 Amounts on Monopoly cards
4 X and Y, for Tesla
5 Scottish refusal
6 Pop star Rita
7 Doc's prescriptions
8 "Gesundheit!" elicitor
9 Hose holder, or a kind of snake
10 Breakfast roll with another breakfast staple added in
11 Locale
12 Dress in India
13 Jannings who won the first Best Actor Oscar
18 Highlight ___ (sports compilation)
22 "Forever" purchase
24 Head: Fr.
25 Clairvoyant sort
28 Outdoor furniture setting
29 Sched. listings at JFK or LAX
30 Long part of a giraffe
31 Card above deuce
32 Oohs and ___
33 Landed, as on a wire
34 Fido fare, maybe
38 Night, to day
39 Soprano or alto
40 60 minutes
41 This: Sp.

46 Something to "mind" at a British train station
47 "What's up, my man?!"
48 ___ E. Coyote
49 Up and back, in a pool
52 Wavy-patterned fabric
53 Photographer Leibovitz
54 ___ Barker, fashion photographer and reality TV judge
55 Bundle of hay
56 You'll trip on it if you drop it
57 "Shoot!"
58 Commotion
62 Rock's ___ Fighters
63 Ballpark guess: Abbr.

by Beth Rubin and Trent H. Evans

ACROSS

1 Upper-left keyboard button
4 Hinders, as one's style
10 Federal loan agcy.
13 Aloe vera product
14 Entertain lavishly
15 #1
16 Kitchen gadget brand
17 Spotted wild cat
18 Screenplay abbr. indicating "outside"
19 Start of an optimistic quote by 57-Across
22 Kind of diagram that the Mastercard logo resembles
23 School grps. without students
24 "He'd be a broader guy if he had dropped ___ once": Steve Jobs on Bill Gates
26 Snow day toys
28 Strike from the Bible?
29 Part 2 of the quote
34 "Smooches!"
35 Part 3 of the quote
41 Knockoff
42 Virtual holiday greeting
44 Cranberry farms
45 N.B.A. team with a gorilla mascot, strangely enough
49 Kuwaiti ruler
50 Shoot the breeze
51 "Spiffy!"
53 Big name in the freezer aisle
54 End of the quote
57 First puzzle editor of The New York Times
61 Like a thumbs-down vote
62 Anklebones
63 With 66-Across, fizzy drink
64 Lasers read them from the inside out
65 Proofreader's "Actually, don't delete this"
66 See 63-Across

DOWN

1 Lead-in to mania
2 Risqué costume for a holiday party
3 George of "Hail, Caesar!"
4 Foam clog
5 Make a long story short?
6 Bond is a special one
7 Island nation south of Sicily
8 Schemes
9 Rogen of "Superbad" and "This Is the End"
10 Artist's shortcut
11 Airborne toy with no tail
12 Like Usain Bolt's last name
20 Edit menu option
21 Poetic foot with a short and long syllable
22 Letters on a bottle of brandy
25 ___ Moines, Iowa
27 Blacken, as a reputation
28 Almost too smooth
30 Caviar
31 Sports bar array
32 ___ Speedwagon
33 Popeye's Olive
35 "Mind. Blown."
36 School where students learn to spell?
37 Ones with access
38 It makes a "clink" in a drink
39 Make it well known that you know someone well-known well
40 Many a city street layout
41 Popular sammie
43 Like some humor and martinis
45 Word after booty or Bermuda
46 Remove from office
47 Parent company of Lean Cuisine
48 Considered it right (to)
51 60 minuti
52 Ode title starter
55 Movie f/x
56 B&O and Short Line: Abbr.
57 & 58 Words before cheese
59 Kerfuffle
60 Bust a rhyme

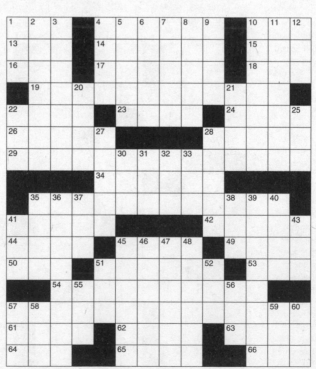

by David Bukszpan

ACROSS

1 Police officers
5 Activity with a lotus position
9 Word before Actor and Actress at the Oscars
13 Tie score
14 Emerged, as an issue
16 Story about Zeus or Hera, say
17 Where to get one's Kix?
19 Have on
20 Birds in a gaggle
21 Dig in at dinner
23 ___ Lanka
24 Jeans or jodhpurs
25 Singer/songwriter nicknamed "Piano Man"
28 "___-Man" (Paul Rudd superhero film)
29 Gloomy atmosphere
30 In the countryside
31 Forlorn, directionless type
34 Some hotel and restaurant staffers
35 Place for a ship's captain
36 Top-of-the-line
37 Places among the troops, as a journalist
40 Survey of Election Day voters
44 Somewhat, informally
45 Street ___ (acceptance among peers)
46 One of 435 in D.C.
47 Greener energy source
49 Skedaddles
51 Org. promoting oral health
52 Source for maple syrup
53 Derisive cries from the audience
54 Jab
56 Categorize simplistically
60 Diabolical
61 Marine animals with flippers
62 "___ go bragh!" ("Ireland forever!")
63 Cold and damp, as a basement
64 Barbecue skewer
65 1-Across in Manhattan, for short

DOWN

1 U.S. public health agcy.
2 Common herb in pizza
3 Perennial embarrassments for teens
4 Like most desserts
5 New Haven alma mater of five presidents
6 Sphere
7 Melted chocolate, e.g.
8 To boot
9 Luxury German carmaker
10 Blight on the landscape
11 Fix one's gaze on
12 Sensations at amusement parks
15 Carrier based at Ben Gurion Airport
18 Nincompoop
22 Ruthless ruler
24 Chum
25 "The Wonderful Wizard of Oz" writer
26 Under the weather
27 Minty drink at Churchill Downs
29 Capitol insiders, informally
32 Letter before iota
33 Many family cars
34 Emptiness
36 Figure skating jump
37 Got away
38 Neighbor of Ukraine once part of the U.S.S.R.
39 Burglary, e.g.
40 Noted stretch of time
41 Grand speechmaking
42 Reveal inadvertently
43 Discs on hi-fis
45 Xeroxes, e.g.
48 Mushroom parts
49 George or Louis, to William and Kate
50 Leonard who wrote the song "Hallelujah"
53 The late Alex Trebek, for one
55 Antlered animal
57 Distinct disparity
58 Pharmacist/philanthropist Lilly
59 Finale

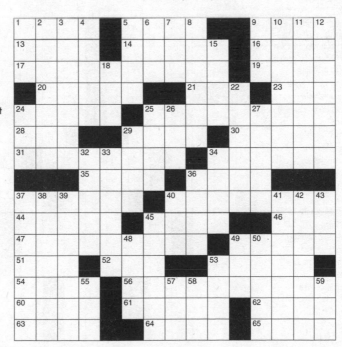

by Lynn Lempel

ACROSS

1 Positive particles
8 Fending (off)
15 Brand X
16 Precipice of exposed bedrock
17 & 18 Emmy-winning "Ugly Betty" actress
19 Festive French season
20 Goddess often depicted holding a staff of papyrus
21 Lunch with Skippy, briefly?
24 Tricky thing to get caught in
25 Nabokov's longest novel
26 QB Newton who popularized dabbing
29 Ate away
31 Author of "An Inconvenient Truth"
33 Spelling of "BH90210"
34 Enlighten
38 Deeply regrets
39 65-Across justifiers, in a saying
40 Year, in ancient Rome
41 "The Queen's Gambit" actress Taylor-Joy
42 Newswoman Paula
44 Remark further
45 Sondheim's "___ the Woods"
46 Fellows
47 When viewed
50 ___-runner (bootlegger)
52 One calling you out, perhaps
53 Bunch of numbers for crunching
54 N.B.A.'s ___ Ming
55 Charge
56 Come over the top, in poker
57 Certain camera, for short
58 Journalist ___ Rogers St. Johns
60 Path of a pop-up
61 Threepio's "Star Wars" companion

63 Site of a Massachusetts tourist shop named "Witch Way Gifts"
64 Nothing
65 See 39-Across
66 Amazon voice assistant
67 Actor Billy ___ Williams
68 Shopping ___

DOWN

1 ___ Tour
2 Sleep stage, in brief
3 Unified
4 Bird on a beach
5 Baltimore bird
6 "Great thinking!"
7 Common bathroom device
8 Bulgaria's capital
9 They always come 48 hours before Thanksgiving
10 Relating to a heart chamber
11 Some old tape players, briefly
12 Wrath
13 Here/there go-between
14 Transcript fig.
21 Court great Sampras
22 Prize for third place
23 Oscar-winning director of "Get Out"
26 Grand Ole Opry performer . . . or a hint to 17-/18-Across and 23- and 36-Down
27 "Can we talk privately?"
28 Bit of Southwest topography
30 Share juicy gossip

32 2008 Clint Eastwood film "___ Torino"
35 Half of a double helix
36 Grammy-winning singer of "Little Things"
37 Chocolate treat on a stick
43 Rhyming descriptor for Obama
45 Groups fixing computer crashes, for short
46 Scar's brother in "The Lion King"
48 Scot's refusal
49 "Mama ___ Crazy," 1984 hit by the Judds
51 Gloomy
59 "Superman" antagonist ___ Luthor
62 Dem.'s opposite

by Ross Trudeau

ACROSS

1 ___ and downs
4 John or John Quincy
9 Off-the-wall
14 Org. for the Flyers and Red Wings
15 First toy to be called an "action figure"
16 Congresswoman ___ Omar
17 Teenage military leader canonized in 1920
19 Country singer Patsy
20 ___ Domini
21 Not inclined to reveal one's feelings
23 "Goodness gracious!"
26 Sign of an old wound
27 Word before trap or prize
30 Marx's collaborator on "The Communist Manifesto"
34 Clown accessory that's often bright red
37 Skin soothers
39 Furniture megastore
40 Insignificant amount . . . or hint to this puzzle's shaded squares
44 Genuine
45 Actress Rigg of "The Avengers"
46 "___ sells seashells . . ."
47 Rachel of MSNBC
50 Sign of fire
52 Places where the cucumbers aren't for eating
54 Dragonlike creature of fantasy
58 Big-dollar election-influencing grp.
62 Smoothie berry
63 Deadly nerve gas
64 "Tell someone who gives a hoot"
67 Use a stencil on
68 Instrument in Hindustani music
69 TV remote button
70 Turned white
71 Major pipes
72 Rap's Dr. ___

DOWN

1 Dislodge, as printer paper
2 Bogus
3 "Tea" for "gossip," e.g.
4 In the past
5 "What's the ___?"
6 Cracked, as a door
7 Glutton's demand
8 Religious offshoots
9 One who worships the Triple Goddess and Horned God
10 Itchy, say
11 Keep this up when you're down
12 Philosopher Immanuel
13 Number on a foam finger
18 Beginner, in modern lingo
22 Rocks, in a drink
24 Dove or Dial
25 Hindu festival of colors
28 "___, James ___"
29 Himalayan cryptids
31 Scrapes (out)
32 Jacob's first wife
33 Reasonable
34 In the 70s or 80s, say
35 Bit of inspiration
36 Mortarboard tosser
38 Bogus
41 Male grooming brand
42 Sufficient, to Shakespeare
43 Describing chardonnay, e.g.
48 Uncorked
49 Mindless two-player card game
51 Emergency relocation of people, for short
53 Twitch
55 Digital holiday greeting
56 Like uranium vis-à-vis carbon
57 Girl at a family reunion
58 ___ Lee (dessert brand)
59 Russian river
60 Home to the Hang Seng and Nikkei 225 indexes
61 Commercial prefix with bank
63 Indy 500 sponsor
65 Aid on a hot summer day
66 1040 org.

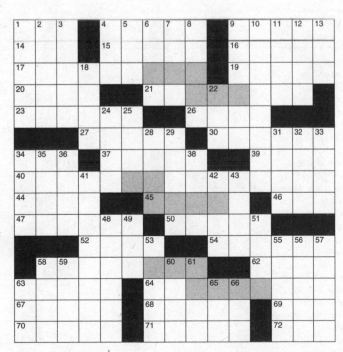

by Evan Mahnken

ACROSS

1 "I feel pretty, ___ pretty" ("West Side Story" lyric)
5 Spray lightly
9 Sore from exercise, say
13 Chicken or duck
14 Artificial feature in New York's Central Park
15 Oak or beech
16 Possible requirements for joining a tattoo club?
19 Zero
20 It's "the word"
21 Not great, as chances
23 Material easily mistaken for aluminum
24 A healthy person regularly calling in sick, e.g.?
28 Drifting sheet
30 Italian author Umberto
31 Lil ___ X
32 Give up
33 Point
35 Italian author Ferrante
37 What a nervous public speaker sounds like?
41 As an ___ (parenthetically)
44 Outdoor "carpet"
45 Intro to girl
49 Word in a "Batman" balloon
50 Org. that creates the G.R.E.
53 "Carrying the Banner" musical
55 Preceded in commenting on an adorable kitten photo, say?
58 Megan Thee Stallion genre
59 Annual festival in Austin, Tex.
60 Sigma/upsilon go-between
61 Tabloid twosome
63 Lucy's empty-booth sign in "Peanuts" . . . or a hint to 16-, 24-, 37- and 55-Across
68 Uncommon

69 Single-serve coffee holder
70 Cannabis strain named for its regional origin
71 Yemeni port
72 Prop for a tilting bookcase, say
73 Dog command

DOWN

1 Frequently, in poetry
2 "Isn't that special!"
3 Reacted to a dreamboat, maybe
4 Lena or Ken of film and TV
5 Reform leader memorialized in the Stone of Hope, for short
6 Billie Eilish's "Therefore ___"
7 Economize
8 Academic job security
9 Cash-out spot?
10 It may be found above the mantle
11 The difference between a mini and a midi
12 Confident shout from an optimist
17 Singer Young or Diamond
18 Apple offering
22 High, flat land feature
23 Idiosyncrasy
25 Good dirt
26 "Star Wars" princess-turned-general
27 Ethan or Joel of filmmaking
29 "Family ___"
34 Hosts, informally
36 Grassy expanses
38 Come face to face
39 Sharpen
40 "What's the big ___?"
41 Transmissions triggering manhunts, for short

42 Really overdoing it, in slang
43 "They conned me!"
46 Exhaust
47 Olympic group with a red, white and blue insignia
48 Cleopatra's snake
51 Pet transported in a bike basket amid a whirlwind
52 Library area
54 Event with V-E Day and V-J Day
56 Quaint contraction
57 Rabbit holder
62 Wordless admonishments
64 Family room
65 Paris accord?
66 Dashboard reading, for short
67 "Hallowed be ___ name"

by Kate Schutzengel

ACROSS

1 Drains of strength
5 Top celebs
10 Witch
13 Jazzy Fitzgerald
14 Tongue sense
15 Contented cat's sound
16 It doesn't need time to rise before baking
18 Monster often seen wielding a club
19 Actress Thurman
20 Rarin' to go
21 Commence
22 Bed and breakfast, e.g.
23 Bill known as the "Science Guy"
24 "___ word is a lamp unto my feet . . .": Psalms
26 Director DuVernay
27 The "N" in TNT
29 One of two "royal" sleeping options
31 U.K. award
33 Web address
34 "What ___ have you got?"
35 Social crafting event
38 Created yarn or tales
40 Industrial tub
41 Help
42 ATV with four tires
44 ___ nodes
48 Coffee dispenser
49 "___ your head!"
50 "Chairman" of Chinese Communism
52 U.N. agcy. awarded the 1969 Nobel Peace Prize
53 Fall bloom that resembles a daisy
55 Big name in shapewear clothing
57 Apt rhyme for "grab"
58 Actor Guzmán of "Traffic"

59 Key member of a football team, in brief . . . or a feature of 16-, 29-, 35- and 42-Across?
61 Elevate
62 Spooky
63 Chimney duct
64 Pig's wallowing spot
65 Rises and shines
66 Sediment in a wine barrel

DOWN

1 Sparkly bit on a gala gown
2 College reunion attendees
3 Flexible
4 Cul-de-___
5 Kept in check
6 Size above medium
7 "Now it's clear"

8 Breakout movie role, say
9 CNN founder Turner
10 Cuddle-worthy
11 Shows up
12 Hand-held explosive
15 Author of "The Gold-Bug"
17 Obi-Wan ___ (Jedi master)
21 "See ya!"
25 Mate for Hägar the Horrible
28 Spherical
29 Extremely
30 Like a partner who can't spend a second apart from you
32 Grammy winner Costello
35 Put a number on

36 Enjoys a late-afternoon snack, as a Brit might
37 Mississippi city on the Gulf of Mexico
38 Sudden storms with whipping winds
39 Hobby
43 Prickly seedcase
45 Socialize at a party
46 Commemorative tablet
47 Calvin's tiger companion, in the comics
50 Curie who coined the term "radioactivity"
51 Pays for a hand
54 Superlative suffix
56 Playground place
59 Stitch
60 Super Bowl org.

by John Guzzetta

ACROSS

1. Smug expression
6. Gentle attention-getter
9. "Fidelio" is Beethoven's only one
14. Be honest (with)
15. Tide competitor
16. Tongue, but not cheek
17. Make amends
18. Hi or lo follower
19. _____ boson (the so-called "God particle")
20. General's responsibility?
23. Foxy
24. "_____ Te Ching"
25. In which head shots can be taken
29. Apology from Iago?
32. Take stock of
35. Peculiar light in the sky, in brief
36. Millennium, at the beginning and end?
37. Lure (in)
38. University entrance exam, for short
39. It turns red litmus paper blue
40. 60 minuti
41. Click of disapproval
42. Wears
44. Antitrust concern?
48. Requests from
49. Big name in ice cream
50. Formerly named
53. Editors of crossword puzzles, e.g.?
57. Dagger's partner
60. "Come as you _____"
61. They may be locked or blown
62. Hooded snake
63. Singer Cooke
64. Country with the highest percentage of vegetarians
65. Reuben ingredient
66. "The Last O.G." channel
67. One of the Affleck brothers

DOWN

1. Cabbage dishes
2. Rock genre
3. Highbrow tower material?
4. Home to the Atlantis casino
5. Thieving condors of Mario games
6. Holy _____
7. πr^2, for a circle
8. Bygone
9. "Pick me! Pick me!"
10. One-named singer who pioneered the Minneapolis sound
11. The hundred folds on a chef's toque are said to represent the number of ways to prepare this
12. Scott Joplin tune
13. T or F, say: Abbr.
21. Corn units
22. :, in an analogy
26. Pellucid
27. Part of a horror film address, for short
28. National floral emblems of the U.S.
29. Date regularly
30. Gross
31. Not seldom, poetically
32. Pleasant whiff
33. Billionaire philanthropist George
34. Defeat soundly, so to speak
38. It has colloquial gestures like "kiss-fist" and "shaking L": Abbr.
39. _____ choy
41. Miso soup cubes
42. Affirmative or negative, in a debate
43. Medium
45. Trio for Daniel Day-Lewis
46. Bohemian folk dances
47. Takes up or lets down, say
50. Passionate learners, to some
51. Bert's buddy on "Sesame Street"
52. College application part
54. One wicked witch's home in "The Wizard of Oz"
55. Baltimore seafood specialty
56. Hawaii's _____ Coast
57. IV amounts
58. Make oneself heard in a herd
59. Kimono sash

by Ray Brunsberg and Ellen Brunsberg

ACROSS

1 Fertile soil
5 Send too many emails
9 Infuriate
14 Pay to get in a card game
15 "Night" author Wiesel
16 Totally pointless
17 Inverted pose seen in break dancing and yoga
19 Sports network that airs "Courtside Cinema"
20 & 21 Broadcast unit that may operate with 50,000 watts
23 Chowder morsel
25 Misled deliberately
27 & 30 Numbers displayed in rows and columns
32 Locale for a home garden
34 Open room with natural light
36 Others
38 The present
39 Renders null
40 Jar cover
41 2010s White House family name
43 Little hellion
44 Ink stain
46 "Mad Money" host Jim
47 Fine sediment
49 & 51 Long-lasting cover for a house
52 Life or Lucky Charms
54 Smart guy?
56 & 58 What this puzzle's circled letters are . . . or what they're doing
62 Biden's debate opponent in 2008
64 Fell asleep quickly
66 Iridescent gems
67 Great burden
68 Online marketplace for crafts
69 Secret meeting between lovers
70 "Is the ___ Catholic?"
71 Location

DOWN

1 Bert who played the Cowardly Lion
2 Fit for military service
3 Not much
4 Federal program for health care coverage
5 Mathematical grouping
6 Blood bank donation
7 "___ No Sunshine" (Bill Withers classic)
8 Won gold, silver or bronze
9 Little redhead in a long-running Broadway show
10 Fake name given by Odysseus to the Cyclops
11 Cuba's ___ Bay
12 Winter setting in N.Y.C.
13 Fire (up)
18 Fifth note in an octave scale
22 Traditional Father's Day gifts
24 Cash withdrawal spot, in brief
26 Start of Juliet's "What's in a name?" speech
27 Actress Viola of "Fences"
28 Invisibly small
29 Impressive feat in baseball
31 Water filter brand
33 Dopey or Sneezy
35 Kind of computer port, for short
37 Home of the Raptors, on scoreboards
40 Something to lick on a stick
42 Checkout lines?
45 Exam for an aspiring atty.
46 Collectible toon image
48 Hiking paths
50 Touches base before running home, say
53 Iowa senator Joni
55 Lamb's mother
57 One-billionth: Prefix
59 Unleavened flatbread in Indian cuisine
60 Makeup of some "bunnies"
61 Affliction that aptly rhymes with "eye"
62 Cauldron
63 Figure that a bank charges for a loan, for short
65 180° from NNW

by Eric Bornstein

ACROSS

1 Smurf with red pants
5 Performed in a choir
9 Overly proper
13 Homecoming guest, informally
14 Algeria has the largest one among African countries
15 Capital where natives say "Arrivederci!"
16 Chinese New Year, celebrated on Feb. 1, 2022
19 Trunk in a studio
20 Star's negotiator
21 Lines at a theater?
26 Jewish New Year, celebrated on Sept. 25, 2022
32 Nevada's third-largest city
33 A long way off
34 Follow, as orders
36 List-ending abbr.
37 "The Good Place" actress Rudolph
38 Became threadbare
39 Impudence
40 Pigs' hangouts
41 Barbecue spice mixes
42 Big seller of flat-pack furniture
43 Blackthorn fruit
44 Pac-12 team
45 Haggard of country music
47 Clear sky's color
48 Approximate fig.
49 Came to a halt
54 Ave. crossers
55 Thai New Year, celebrated on April 13, 2022
57 Big toucan feature
60 Stadium level
61 Squared up
65 Prepare for takeoff
66 Fashion designer Tahari
67 Tick off
68 Bit of a dance
69 Tear to pieces
70 Highly skilled

DOWN

1 Days gone by
2 Pedigree competitor
3 Sound from a contented cat
4 "Time's Arrow" novelist Martin
5 Old couch's problem
6 Sheepdog's greeting
7 Formerly called
8 Methane, e.g.
9 Uptight type
10 Wander around
11 Mogadishu-born model and cosmetics mogul
12 Brewing ingredient
17 Quick bite
18 "Bye now!"
22 Tourney winners
23 Tennis's Nadal
24 "Thumbs down!"
25 Sentence segment
26 Movie do-overs
27 Standing guard
28 Korean New Year, celebrated on Feb. 1, 2022
29 Iranian New Year, celebrated on March 21, 2022
30 Explanatory page on a company's website
31 President between Calvin and Franklin
32 Government in power
35 Affirmatives
46 ___-warrior (environmental activist)
47 Org. on a mouthwash bottle
50 Go in
51 Like ballet dancers
52 Unit of yarn
53 Messed up
55 Not attend
56 Peter Parker in "Spider-Man," for one
57 "Dynamite" K-pop band
58 Dine
59 Tool on a fire truck
62 Fight (for)
63 Pointy-eared toymaker
64 Acrobat's safeguard

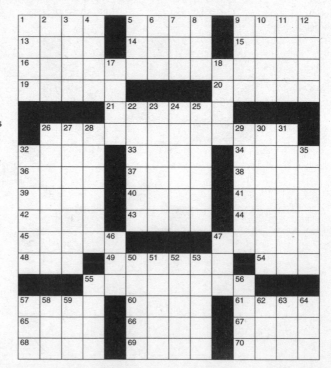

by Zhouqin Burnikel

ACROSS

1 Director Almodóvar
6 "Excuse me"
10 Dallas basketball squad, informally
14 French farewell
15 Word sung twice after "Que"
16 Somewhat
17 Good accessory for the owner of a shedding dog
19 "Raw" facts
20 Blend, as batter
21 Big beer order
22 Popular pie nut
23 Nothing to write home about
27 "r u serious?!"
29 Short snooze
30 What a horseshoe is attached to
31 One who might smoke ganja as a sacrament, informally
33 Director Anderson
34 Ibiza, e.g., to a Spaniard
38 Emulated Dr. Frankenstein . . . or what you did after you filled in the shaded parts of 17-, 23-, 50- and 61-Across?
42 Sparkling Italian wine
43 Bagel and ___
44 Starting squad
45 Exam with a logical reasoning section: Abbr.
47 Motor oil brand
49 Ask intimate questions, say
50 Move reluctantly
55 Race with a baton
56 Consume
57 Needing directions, say
60 Leave out
61 June celebration honoring the Stonewall uprising
64 Sneaker giant headquartered in Beaverton, Ore.

65 Doofus
66 Comment from a stage actor directly to the audience
67 Some co-parents
68 Dish from a slow cooker
69 Easy mark

DOWN

1 Buds
2 Move some text around, say
3 Matching table and chairs in a kitchen
4 Vintage-inspired
5 "___ Father, who art in heaven . . ."
6 Snoozing
7 Hägar the Horrible's wife
8 Poet's "before"
9 Damage
10 Prepared to play rock paper scissors
11 One way to be taken
12 Curriculum ___
13 Obsessive fans, in slang
18 Vegetable that becomes gooey when cooked
22 Vietnamese noodle soup
24 Swarming pest
25 Nonbinary pronoun
26 Middling
27 Killer whale
28 Locale of the Perseverance rover
32 Pregame activities in the parking lot
33 Hair removal option
35 Hits the accelerator
36 Shakespearean king
37 Large group of ants
39 Exuberance
40 Lavish affection (on)
41 Back of the neck

46 Plant milk option
47 It's shortest when the sun is directly overhead
48 Head: Fr.
50 Aid in filming aerial shots
51 Club version of a song, often
52 How great minds think, it's said
53 Grab
54 Novelist Mario Vargas ___
58 Norms: Abbr.
59 "What were ___ thinking?"
61 Network supported by "Viewers Like You"
62 Poppycock
63 Treasure hunter's aid

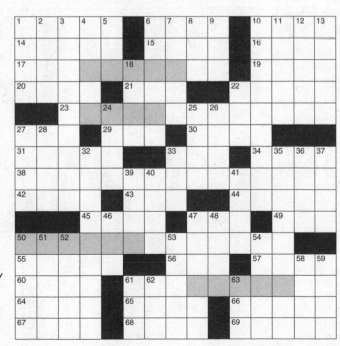

by Rebecca Goldstein

ACROSS

1 River-crossing platforms in Frogger
5 World soccer org.
9 Follow, with "by"
14 Egg-shaped
15 Lines at a wedding
16 He sold his namesake company to Disney for over $4 billion
17 Tart snacks [pressure]
19 Professional negotiator
20 Thin pancakes
21 Manipulates, as an election
23 "Like, obviously!"
24 Cruising, say
25 Kiss for a señor or señorita
26 Jeer
27 ___ for tat
28 Movie scale with a "Certified Fresh" tier [length]
31 Atmospheric condition that can be caused by wildfires
33 Bird in Duolingo's logo
34 One of three in Fiji?
35 Long stretches
37 Freaks out
40 Super-duper
41 ___-Town (Windy City)
42 Window customization at an auto shop
44 Scrabble relative played without a board [mass]
49 Vientiane local
50 Love for a señor or señorita
51 Spoiled kid
52 Not appropriate
54 The Pentagon houses it: Abbr.
55 Reynolds of "Deadpool"
56 Playful response to "You're a funny one!"
57 Actress Witherspoon
59 Longtime Nabisco cookie [force]
61 People have counted on them for centuries
62 Sticky strip
63 The constructors of this puzzle, e.g.
64 Michael of Monty Python
65 Side dish whose name comes from the Dutch for "salad"
66 Heavy drinkers

DOWN

1 Memes with captions like "I can has cheezburger?"
2 Extra sports period
3 Big retailer of Nintendo and Xbox products
4 It may be slippery
5 White lies
6 Memphis's ___ B. Wells Plaza
7 "Seriously?"
8 Basketball datum
9 [sigh]
10 Issue for a programmer
11 Treated a sprained ankle, say
12 Longest non-Russian river in Europe
13 Purim heroine
18 Nifty
22 What a three-point shooter needs
25 German luxury cars
26 Question after a poorly delivered joke
29 "This is gonna be good!"
30 Sun. follower
32 Achieve great things
36 Certain recyclable
37 Cool, in the '90s
38 Herb that tastes soapy to some
39 "Get going!"
41 Skull-related
43 Brand of pizza rolls
44 Undeserved criticism, informally
45 Tiny shape-shifter
46 "I refuse your offer"
47 Transplants
48 Title for a king
53 Some members of the family Salamandridae
55 Hand-holding at equestrian school?
56 Once again
58 Comp ___
60 College app stat

by Adam Aaronson, Jack Joshi and Jackson Janes

ACROSS

1 Genre for the boy band BTS
5 Palm that yields deep purple fruit
9 Rotating barbecue rod
13 Befuddled state
14 Nut from an oak
15 Answer to Gollum's riddle in "The Hobbit" "This thing all things devours: Birds, beasts, trees, flowers . . ."
16 Morning waker-upper
18 "Terrible" czar
19 ___ the Frog
20 Vigor
21 The one for Starbucks shows a two-tailed mermaid
22 Peeved
23 Step counter
25 Baghdad currency
27 Skin art, in brief
28 "Friend or ___?"
31 Furthermore
33 Upstate New York city
37 Orienteering aid
40 Trove of business contacts
42 Singing group often in robes
43 Wise one in "Star Wars"
45 "Didn't I call it?"
46 Helper for Santa
48 Upbeat and cheerful
51 What many a home movie was once shot on
55 Cocktail favored by Carrie Bradshaw on "Sex and the City"
59 Home of the N.B.A.'s Jazz
60 Goof up
61 Repeated verbatim
62 ___ fides (credentials)
63 Device that can replace 16-, 23-, 37-, 40- and 51-Across

65 Profession for many an M.I.T. grad: Abbr.
66 Do, re, mi, etc.
67 Guesstimate words
68 Aisle, window or middle, on a plane
69 Harbinger
70 Muscat's land

DOWN

1 Army uniform material
2 Like pastels compared to primary colors
3 Missouri's ___ Mountains
4 Set in waves, as hair
5 ___ tear (athlete's injury)
6 Cask makers
7 Rainbow-shaped
8 Receptacle into which a quill is dipped
9 Shoe sometimes called a "spike heel"
10 Turn on an axis
11 Publicist's concern
12 Pavarotti's vocal range
14 Part of a play
17 Skirt length that ends midcalf
23 ___-walsy (chummy)
24 Handle roughly
26 Music's Lil ___ X
28 5G-regulating org.
29 Reaction to fireworks
30 Moody music genre
32 Command accompanying a pounding gavel
34 Drivers' licenses and such
35 So-so grade
36 Body spray brand
38 Apt infographic for showing a bakery's sales
39 Woody's folk-singer son
41 Rowing implement

44 Perform surgery
47 Largest inland city in California
49 Single-serving coffee pod
50 "Hello-o-o-o!"
51 Shapes of most sugar lumps
52 Do penance
53 Japanese comics style
54 She may take your temp before tucking you in
56 Hurricane or typhoon
57 High-I.Q. group
58 Classical theater
61 Four of these make a gal.
64 Kylo ___ of "Star Wars"

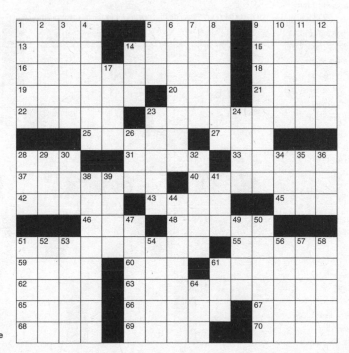

by Alan Siegel

ACROSS

1 Rise to the challenge
7 Anthony Hopkins's role in the "Thor" film franchise
11 Foldable bed
14 Element essential to thyroid function
15 Director/screenwriter Ephron
16 "___ you good?"
17 Might have, informally
18 Parched, as land
19 Upstate N.Y. campus
20 Catastrophe at a tennis match?
23 Overjoy
25 "%&$@," in comics
26 Author Morrison
27 Leased
28 Prefix with futurism
29 Ransacks like a pirate
30 Uncertainties at a football game?
34 Promise to pay
35 !!!!, in a text
36 Security alerts at a boxing match?
44 Country singer LeAnn
45 Stars might have big ones
46 "A mouse!"
47 Two times quadri-
48 Signify
49 Pal, in Pamplona
51 Supplies at a swim meet?
54 Traveler's approx.
55 Honolulu's island
56 Season for pumpkin-spiced everything
59 "Oh, ___ on!"
60 Common songbird
61 Rude looks
62 Revolutionary Turner
63 Campus anti-D.U.I. group
64 Montana's capital

DOWN

1 Editor's bracketed disclaimer
2 "___ cute!"
3 Teach
4 Spirit guide?
5 Excessive
6 Prickly ___ (cactus variety)
7 How some risks are taken
8 Chips brand whose "Cool Ranch" flavor is called "Cool American" in Europe
9 "Fighting" Notre Dame team
10 Diddly-squat
11 "SpongeBob SquarePants," for one
12 Points in the right direction
13 Falling block game
21 Stir-fry protein option
22 Moe, Larry or Curly
23 Figure in a Grimm story
24 Neckwear in Honolulu
28 Ocean shade
29 Arm or branch
31 Of direct descent
32 Some four-footed friends
33 Casual shoe brand
36 Lasagna filling
37 "Things don't look good for me!"
38 Restrained
39 Beached, as a boat in sand
40 TV streaming device
41 Off-duty time
42 Part of a relay race
43 Reggae relative
44 Ensnare using deceptive strategies
48 Comedian Anne
49 Less than 90°
50 Valuable part of ore
52 Exercises on an ergometer
53 Not well thought through
57 "___ Explain Things to Me" (Rebecca Solnit essay collection)
58 Covert org.

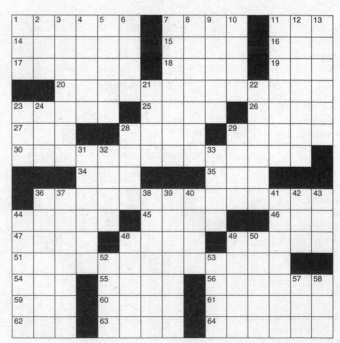

by Claire Rimkus

ACROSS

1 Title character in a Tyler Perry film franchise
6 Actress Foster of "The Silence of the Lambs"
11 Actor Efron
14 Select group of celebs
15 Relatively safe investment security
16 "That tastes terrible!"
17 On a whim [#35]
19 West with the classic movie line "I'm no 45-Across . . ."
20 Largest movie theater chain in the U.S.
21 Facts and figures, in brief
22 Baseball slugger's stat
23 Denim pants with a red tab label [#36]
29 Complete one round of reps
31 It may fill up during a vacation
32 Inter ____ (among others)
33 "Love your work!"
35 Longtime electronics company
38 Where domestic meals are enjoyed [#32]
42 Den fixtures
43 Give an earful
44 Padlock fastener
45 Heavenly sort
46 Nuclear experiments, for short
48 "On the other hand . . ." [#33]
53 "That's a joke"
54 Schlep
55 Chart-topper
58 Magic spell
59 In the distant past [#43]
64 Fútbol cheer
65 One of a pair for a podcast listener
66 Juliet's love
67 Photographer Goldin
68 Dick ____, comic strip detective
69 Calms

DOWN

1 "The Naked ____" (Goya painting)
2 School reunion attendee, informally
3 Denies any association with
4 "To the max" suffix
5 When happy hour often begins
6 ____ Dylan, lead singer of the Wallflowers
7 Kimono sash
8 Only dwarf with a three-letter name
9 Pen fluid
10 Mag. staffers
11 Dance-based fitness program
12 Once more
13 "The Queen's Gambit" game
15 Pound sounds
18 "Don't bet ____"
22 Tyrannosaurus ____

24 Actor Morales
25 Jungle vine
26 Not suitable, as for a job
27 Israeli statesman Abba
28 "Fear of Flying" author Erica
29 Absurd or foolish
30 Patron saint of Norway
33 Keeps the engine running, without moving
34 Actress Jovovich of "The Fifth Element"
35 Christmas entrees
36 Tag line?
37 Electrical units
39 Country singer Loretta
40 Safecracker
41 Relative of an ostrich or emu
45 Assistance
46 Lead-in to girl

47 "And ____ off!" (start of a race)
48 Spousal greeting
49 "The Jungle Book" wolf
50 One of Santa's reindeer
51 He troubleshoots Macs and PCs
52 Pulitzer-winning columnist Maureen
56 Frozen drink brand
57 Some boxing decisions, in brief
59 Understand
60 Rowboat propeller
61 Savings for old age, for short
62 "S.N.L." network
63 ____ constrictor.

by Natalie Murphy

ACROSS

1 Waiting room fare, in brief
5 TV's "The Good ___"
9 Michelle ___ West of the L.P.G.A.
12 Yankees manager whose teams never missed the postseason
13 Near the North or South Pole, say
16 Gather, as information
17 Championing
18 "Uncool, man"
20 Like Thor or Loki
21 Well-trodden, as a path
22 Communicated through channels
25 Horse's bit
26 ___ Ghiberti, sculptor of Florence's Gates of Paradise
29 ___ pro quo
32 Bake, as eggs
34 German article
35 Son of, in Arabic names
36 Calendar column . . . or a punny hint to the circled squares
38 Pen that's full of oink?
39 After tax
40 Like much Three Stooges humor
41 Shortcut to highlighting the address bar on most internet browsers
42 Beowulf's first combatant
44 In the past
46 ___ Pieces
48 Enters unannounced, with "in"
52 "I'm speechless!"
54 Bad, but better than the alternatives
56 Patron of the Met, say
59 Birthplace of Zeus, in myth
60 Where ships are outfitted

61 First-stringers
62 Bad result for a QB
63 "___ in Show"
64 Third degrees, for short

DOWN

1 Very, on a music score
2 "You ___ Beautiful"
3 "American Gothic" artist
4 Title for Eva Perón
5 D.C. media giant, for short
6 Sign on a vintage appliance at a flea market, maybe
7 To's counterpart
8 "Nightmare" street
9 Oddity
10 B&Bs
11 Brink
12 "The weekend's almost here, yay!"

14 Lead-in to "Be happy"
15 Squirrel away
19 Explosion maker
23 Skip over
24 "Sleepless in Seattle" director Ephron
27 Pasta that's often baked
28 Shade of black
29 Last Chinese dynasty (1644–1912)
30 Lyft competitor
31 What parallel lines never do
32 Bobby of the Black Panthers
33 Buying channel on TV
36 Water channel that rises and falls
37 Quelques-___ (a few: Fr.)
41 Home of the Texas Motor Speedway, with

seating for more than 150,000 spectators
43 Foster professional connections
44 Lawyers' org.
45 Screw-off car part
47 Cafeteria trays on snowy days, perhaps
49 Vice encouraged by capitalism
50 These: Sp.
51 Part of a flower or watch
52 Writer Picoult with the 2021 novel "Wish You Were Here"
53 Well informed about
55 Lead-in to while
57 Chatterbox's "gift"
58 Earth deposit

by Jacob McDermott

ACROSS

1 Bunch of wolves or cards
5 Busy with other things
11 The Beatles' "Till There ___ You"
14 Jai ___ (sport)
15 Francis of old TV's "What's My Line?"
16 It clinks in a drink
17 Nurses, as a drink
18 Swamp in "Pogo"
20 In few words
22 Museum-funding org.
23 Like auto shop rags
24 1990s cartoon series featuring Yakko, Wakko and Dot
27 Org. featured in the documentary "This Film Is Not Yet Rated"
28 Abbr. meaning "and others"
29 Arizona college town
31 Some Best Buy buys, for short
34 Doggie doc
36 Bones next to ulnae
39 Baby-boomer series that starred Ken Olin
44 Indian stringed instrument
45 Around 50.25% of the world's adult population
46 Letters before an alias
47 Meters and liters
50 Eve's man
53 Pinnacle
55 Poet William who wrote "The Prelude"
60 Play opener
61 Flamenco cheer
62 Reproductive cell for a fern
63 South American rodent with soft, dense fur
67 One may be half-baked or brilliant
68 "___ soon?"
69 "Slouching Towards Bethlehem" author Joan
70 Must-have

71 ID in the form xxx-xx-xxxx
72 X-ray follow-up, perhaps
73 Deities

DOWN

1 Linguine or fettuccine
2 Not from Earth
3 ___ pants (cropped style popularized in the 1960s)
4 Instruction to Kate in a Cole Porter title
5 "___ Te Ching"
6 Rub the wrong way
7 Justice Kagan
8 Reason for a markdown
9 Disquieted state
10 Writing implement filled with 37-Down
11 Popular online reference

12 Amtrak express train
13 "So long!"
19 Tuba sound
21 Enjoy a meal
25 Dark shade of blue
26 Parts of a French archipelago
30 Actor with the famous line "I pity the fool!"
31 Six for a TD, e.g.
32 Ho ___ Minh City
33 Word before room or comedy
35 Male cat
37 10-Down filler
38 "Hometown proud" supermarket
40 Jeannette ___, first woman elected to Congress
41 Prefix between bi-and quad-
42 Cultural anthropologist Margaret
43 Make ___ meet

48 Like some well-pitched games
49 One side in eight-ball pool
51 "How cute!" sounds
52 In a sulk
53 Agreements
54 Amazon speakers introduced in 2014
56 Archaeologist's find
57 Contest with roping and riding
58 Cornered, in a way
59 Two are better than one, they say
64 Public health agcy.
65 Mauna ___ (Hawaiian volcano)
66 Journalist Curry

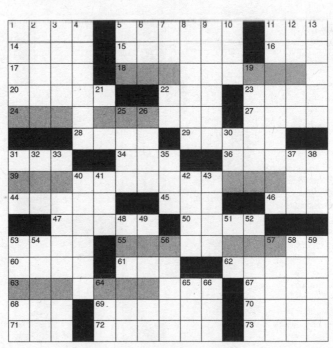

by Zach Sherwin and Andrea Carla Michaels

ACROSS

1 Yaks
5 *Gulf Coast waterway
10 Simpson family member who says "Get bent!"
14 Eye layer containing the iris
15 Reunion attendees, informally
16 "Never Have I ___" (Mindy Kaling Netflix series)
17 Aspiring doc's exam
18 Imam's holy book
19 Campbell of "Scream"
20 Sandwich known by its initials
21 Not taking sides
23 ___ de plume
24 One-up
26 "Yay, me!"
28 *Main drag of the French Quarter
34 *Celebration with king cakes
35 Chick's chirp
38 Eccentric
39 Varieties
43 No power?
44 "Absolutely!"
45 Singer Celine
46 What nephology is the study of
49 Foe of Austin Powers
51 Wombs
53 Bird in a gaggle
54 Rapper Mos ___
56 Nickname for New Orleans, celebrated by the answers to the starred clues and suggested by the shaded squares
58 N.Y.C. airport
61 Psyched about
63 Once around the track
64 Harlem Renaissance writer Locke
66 "Later!"
67 Mine find
68 "I put the sing in single" singer
69 Ship's backbone
70 *___ Square (translation of "Vieux Carré")
71 [Wrong answer!]

DOWN

1 *Cajun stew
2 Pop culture site created as a supplement to The Onion
3 Arrive at ahead of
4 Parked oneself
5 Prepare, as a king cake
6 Baseball family name
7 Steppes dwelling
8 Actor Epps
9 Annapolis inst.
10 Actor Platt of "Dear Evan Hansen"
11 *St. Charles or Esplanade
12 Uprising
13 *2010–13 HBO series set shortly after Hurricane Katrina
21 Screenwriter Ephron
22 Former Italian money
25 Empty, as a purse
27 Lives (in)
29 "Hang on a sec," in texts
30 Singer Anita of the swing era
31 Evening, in ads
32 Some NCOs
33 Attempt
35 Plastic pipe material, in brief
36 ___ sauce (sushi roll topper)
37 *Cajun shellfish-over-rice dish
40 *Music heard at Preservation Hall
41 Colorful pond fish
42 NBC hit since '75
47 Actress Messing
48 ___ Lanka
49 Uno + uno
50 Queenly
52 Ice house
53 Stared in wonder
54 Twilight time
55 Fencing event
57 ___ Grey tea
59 Soda's pop?
60 Shoelace or muscle problem
62 Popeye's Olive
65 Women's ___

by Lisa Senzel and Jeff Chen

ACROSS

1 Sea: Fr.
4 Capital of North Macedonia
10 26 things learned in kindergarten
14 Gibbon or gorilla
15 Arctic mammal with tusks
16 Be introduced to
17 Actress Tyler
18 The "i" of Roy G. Biv
19 Farming-focused govt. org.
20 *Dessert for which "I scream"
22 When doubled, popular 1990s sitcom featuring Tia and Tamera Mowry
24 Sports org. for Rangers and Red Wings
25 Group of whales
27 ___ Moines, Iowa
28 Pop singer Lady ___
30 *Traditional English pub order of fish in a set stock
34 Meeting handout
36 Undergarment with cups
37 Bread for a Reuben
38 ___ Lanka
39 Slugger's stat, for short
41 A dozen minus one
43 *Picnic bowlful
47 Event that may be proctored
48 Where the biceps and triceps are found
49 Election mo.
50 Benchmark: Abbr.
51 "That's curtains for me"
54 *Tomato-based summer soup
58 Sci-fi princess
59 Part of an unruly mob
61 "___ the fields we go . . ."

62 The "I" of M.I.T.: Abbr.
63 Pretend shot, in basketball lingo
64 Slow Wi-Fi annoyance
65 Like a used firepit
66 Be released from prison
67 Like wine labeled "sec"

DOWN

1 Timbuktu's country
2 "The ___ of Gilgamesh"
3 With 11-Down, proverb about delayed retribution, with a hint to the answers to this puzzle's starred clues
4 Pattern that might induce hypnosis

5 "Citizen" played by Orson Welles
6 "Ripe" time of one's life
7 Fundamental, as an urge
8 Moonshine container
9 Those: Sp.
10 Finding it funny
11 See 3-Down
12 Give up, as land
13 Constellation part
21 Jackie known for doing his own stunts
23 As good as it gets
26 Sports org. for Rangers and Red Sox
28 Shocked reaction
29 Taj Mahal city
30 Boxers' punches
31 Steaming mad
32 The ":" of :-)
33 Pre-Easter period
35 What gossipy people love to stir up

40 McKellen who played Gandalf
42 "At Last" singer James
44 Agreement between nations
45 Conclude use of a computer, e.g.
46 Sci-fi blockbuster of 2009
50 Shop-till-you-drop adventure
51 Pelvic bones
52 Suit-and-tie section in a department store
53 Pharmaceutical product
55 ___ Elliott, three-time N.F.L. Pro Bowler, to fans
56 Listen to
57 Bacchanalian party
60 Wall St. debut

by Sam Acker

ACROSS

1 Bacall's partner in a classic Hollywood romance, informally
6 Apple pick?
10 Races, as an engine
14 "Easy on Me" singer, 2021
15 Wine valley in California
16 Fathom or foot
17 1966 Swedish Literature Nobelist who wrote about the struggles of the Jewish people
19 Was a passenger
20 Feathery neckwear
21 Successful singer or producer of popular music
23 1988 American Nobelist in Physiology or Medicine who helped develop the first drug used to fight rejection in organ transplants
25 Knight's title
27 Hurricane's center
28 Old atlas inits.
29 Tehran's country
31 Bio class subject
33 Bit role
38 2018 Canadian Physics Nobelist who helped implement chirped pulse amplification
42 Computer command
43 Rank below capt.
44 In the thick of
45 Grp. that welcomed girl Cubs in 2018
48 Casual affirmative
50 Commercials
51 1976 Peace Nobelist from Northern Ireland who co-founded Community of Peace People
57 Diplomatic envoy
58 Spanish Mrs.
59 Nothin'
60 1911 Polish/French Chemistry Nobelist who pioneered research in radioactivity
65 Level
66 Strait-laced
67 Get around
68 Bygone G.M. car
69 Locale spelled out in a Village People song
70 Allowed by law

DOWN

1 Forbid
2 Poet Amanda Gorman's "___ to Our Ocean"
3 Toothpaste type
4 "Imagine that!"
5 Pooh's down-in-the-dumps friend
6 One ___ million
7 ___ Picchu, Peru
8 Sap-sucking bugs
9 Levels of social status in India
10 Like farm country
11 Mushroom in miso soup
12 YouTube upload
13 Back of a ship
18 Mythical goat-men
22 Big pharma company
23 Research money
24 Lease (out)
25 One of nine on a nonagon
26 A hot one makes a good impression
30 Opposite of SSW
32 Rainbow shape
34 ___ carte
35 Some fiercely protective "bears"
36 Oklahoma city named for a Camelot woman
37 Bettor's chances
39 Fast-food chain with a cowboy hat logo
40 Pastoral poem
41 Royal Caribbean trip
46 Like marshes
47 Military aviation wing
49 Package
51 Japanese box lunch
52 Message sent with a click
53 Satisfied for now, with "over"
54 Bygone Russian rulers
55 Line of a song
56 Pale purple
61 The Monkees' "___ Believer"
62 Cleaning cloth
63 Journalist ___ B. Wells
64 Sushi fish

by Mary Lou Guizzo

ACROSS

1 Little hopper
5 Tied, as sneakers
10 It springs eternal
14 Replacement for the franc and lira
15 Remains
16 Narrow
17 Neighbor on "Family Matters"
19 Brain
20 Summer suit material
21 Plural suffix with good, hood and food
22 Online personal journals
23 Santa ___ winds
24 Letter after sigma
26 Wedding vow
28 Neighbor on "Full House"
34 Ones with negative views on humanity
37 Unit of resistance
38 Four-star review
39 ___ 66 (classic highway)
40 Winter hrs. in St. Louis
41 Strongly disliked
42 Gawk at
43 Exclamation from Homer Simpson
44 Lets down
45 Neighbor on "Home Improvement"
48 Old cloth
49 Peculiar
50 Olympic women's gymnastics powerhouse
53 What a tree provides on a hot, sunny day
57 Boise's home: Abbr.
59 Writer Joyce Carol ___
61 Secret recording device
62 Bygone TV host with a famous "neighborhood"
64 Notion

65 Narrow street
66 Shallowest of the Great Lakes
67 A good one is square
68 Lesser-played half of a 45
69 Sort (through)

DOWN

1 Car company with a "T" logo
2 ___ the cold (left stranded)
3 Big sports venue
4 Hawk's opposite
5 Baton Rouge sch.
6 Central room of a Roman house
7 "Well, that takes the ___!"
8 20/20, for example
9 Aging broadband inits.
10 Web designer's code
11 Youngstown's home
12 ___-Pong
13 Concludes
18 Lure
22 Hairstyle akin to a pageboy
25 Mornings, for short
27 Bright's opposite
28 Toys with tails
29 Dinosaur in Super Mario games
30 Brain's counterpart
31 How fashionable people arrive, it's said
32 At any point
33 Crimson and scarlet
34 Bird that caws
35 Cartoon character who's "smarter than the av-er-age bear"
36 ___ and void

40 Some rodeo riders
41 Something that brings bad luck
43 Genetic stuff
44 Psychedelic inits.
46 Refinery rocks
47 Rich, rich, rich
50 Gestation locations
51 Typographical flourish
52 Positive quality
53 Do the breaststroke, e.g.
54 Conceal oneself
55 Neighborhood
56 Successful conclusion to negotiations
58 Place to get a sandwich
60 Improves, as wine
62 Super-duper
63 Seeded loaf, often

by Stephen Hiltner

ACROSS

1 90° from norte
5 Bit in Bartlett's
10 Dogs' "dogs"
14 Start of a description of a nursery rhyme spider
15 Remove from a UPS package, maybe
16 Periods in history
17 Classic martini garnish
19 Laura of 2017's "Twin Peaks"
20 Reason to get gussied up
21 Rapper with the line "I'm not a businessman, I'm a business, man"
22 "Conan" channel
23 Locale for baccarat or roulette
28 "Gimme a break!"
30 Nosh
31 Game with Skip cards
32 Mauna ___
34 Barbecue residue
35 Unlike Eton College
36 Daytona International Speedway, for one
39 Company originally called AuctionWeb
41 1989 play about Capote
42 Bird in Liberty Mutual ads
43 Huge amount
44 Big entree from the oven
46 English town known for its salt
50 Philharmonic's home
53 Outrage
54 Reminder to arrive with good spirits?
55 Gymnast Aly with three Olympic gold medals
57 PC alternatives

58 "Awful!" . . . or a hint to the common element of 17-, 23-, 36- and 50-Across
61 Worship leader
62 Capital near Casablanca
63 Guinness of film
64 Some G.I. attire
65 Crystal Castles console
66 Work well together

DOWN

1 Fourscore
2 Flashing light
3 Tropical African fly
4 Sized up
5 Target percentage
6 "Wait, what if . . ."
7 Kimono sash
8 "Mazel ___!"
9 PC file name extension
10 Brake or accelerator
11 Words of concern
12 Combat area
13 Govt.-issued ID
18 Cheesy restaurant order
21 D.D.E. follower
24 Hurriedly
25 Cartoonist who created the G.O.P. elephant
26 Earthy pigment
27 Word after hot or lightning
29 Vanquish, as a dragon
33 Person in a cast
35 Certain bra spec
36 Home-monitoring device
37 "I smell ___" (words of suspicion)
38 Title heroine of a 2001 French film

39 List-shortening abbr.
40 Four-footed resident of the White House from 2009–17
44 Yank's opponent
45 Calculus, in dentistry
47 "Snug as a bug in a rug," e.g.
48 Speaks grandly
49 Person of integrity
51 First name of Kramer on "Seinfeld"
52 Christine of "The Blacklist"
56 Target of a filter
57 Source of unwanted feedback?
58 Savings plan inits.
59 Bit of ink
60 Lender to a mom-and-pop shop: Abbr.

by Michael Lieberman

ACROSS

1 Actress Christina of "The Addams Family"
6 Amusement park attraction
10 Ink "oops"
14 French romance
15 Taiwanese tech giant
16 Assistant
17 Classic Sylvester Stallone part
18 Alfresco spot for a "spot"
20 Greater responsibility, often as part of a promotion
22 Furious
23 "College GameDay" broadcaster
26 Pointing out minuscule annoyances
33 Lo-o-ong time
35 "Let me clarify . . ."
36 Flying saucer fliers, in brief
37 Org. for pet rescue
38 Reality star sister of Kim and Kourtney
42 Congers and morays
43 Academic's degree
44 Jordanian landmark described as "a rose-red city half as old as time"
45 Sign of a packed performance
46 Goal of some core workouts
49 This, in Spanish
51 Anatomical pouch
52 One helping in a band . . . or what can be found in each set of circled letters?
60 Rigorous email management strategy
63 Vital artery
64 "Dagnabbit!"
65 Novelist Kingsley
66 Exams for aspiring attorneys, in brief
67 Reedy wind instrument
68 Civil rights icon Parks
69 Really energize

DOWN

1 Uncommon
2 Extra-large movie format
3 Workers' ___ (on-the-job insurance)
4 Havana is its capital
5 Excavation site for a steelmaker
6 Suitable for all ages, as a movie
7 Like many a summertime beverage
8 Cherished
9 Latin "therefore"
10 Exposes, as one's teeth or soul
11 Part of the eye that blinks
12 Poem of praise
13 "Count to ___" (calming advice)
19 Certain tavern pours
21 QB Marino
24 Pumpkin seed, by another name
25 Like diets that cut out bread and pasta
26 Spearlike weapons of medieval times
27 Text from a waiting car pool driver
28 String quartet instruments
29 Evil organization on "Get Smart"
30 Dorky sorts
31 "___ be my pleasure!"
32 Airport screening grp.
34 Grandmas
37 Backyard building
39 Speed measure on European hwys.
40 Some sushi tuna
41 Kellogg's breakfast cereal
46 Cajole
47 Spanish wife
48 ___ Vegas, Nev.
50 Steakhouse option
53 Industry bigwig
54 ___ Sabe (the Lone Ranger, to Tonto)
55 Leon ___, "Exodus" author
56 What glasses rest on
57 Color of an overcast sky
58 "___, Brute?"
59 Carpenter's file
60 Altar promise
61 Catch in the act
62 Dude

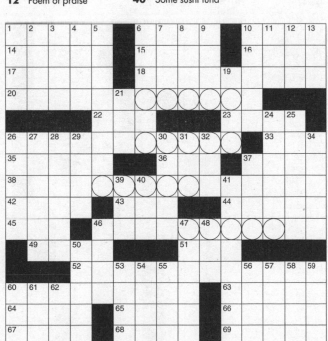

by John Ewbank and Jeff Chen

ACROSS

1 Prepared, with "up"
7 Snake in ancient Egyptian art
10 Crowdsourced map app
14 Final syllable of a word, in linguistics
15 Singer Rawls
16 Wide-eyed with wonder
17 Oxymoronic stage name for the D.J. Norman Cook
19 Puddle-jumper?
20 "Phooey!," to Shakespeare
21 Frontiersman Wyatt
22 Admit, with "up"
23 Rashida Jones's role on "Parks and Recreation"
25 Unquestioning followers, in slang
27 First three words famously said by Kamala Harris to Joe Biden upon winning the 2020 election
30 Gradually increased
33 Hard-to-find game cards, in collector's lingo
35 "Am I the problem here?"
36 Reverberate
39 In ___ words
41 Sound likely not made by a Tyrannosaurus rex, despite what "Jurassic Park" would have you believe
42 Welcomed at the door
44 Streaming service rebranded with the suffix Max in 2020
46 Fragrance
48 Singularity
52 Gentleman: Sp.
54 "The Simpsons" storekeeper
55 Vodka brand that sounds like a toast
57 Reassuring words after a fall
58 ___ Jose, Calif.
59 "Ple-e-e-ease?"
60 Ones with minority views
64 Oodles
65 Before, poetically
66 Act as a go-between
67 Icy hazard at sea
68 When doubled, a 2010s dance fad
69 Object represented visually twice in this puzzle

DOWN

1 Belly laugh
2 Julia Louis-Dreyfus role on "Seinfeld"
3 Go to
4 ___-eye steak
5 Punk offshoot
6 Word with latter or red-letter
7 Deity of Islam
8 Fancy evening party
9 Lifted weights, informally
10 Breakfast appliance
11 Shook on
12 Places where you might find okapis and gnus (besides crossword puzzles!)
13 ___ Benedict
18 Six-line stanza
24 Vaccine approver, in brief
26 Newspaper parts: Abbr.
28 Debris from welding or power drilling
29 Heavy metal band whose name includes an actual heavy metal
31 Actress Thurman
32 According to
34 Movie theater reproof
36 Mentalist's power
37 Third letter in an alphabet song
38 Judge Judy title
40 Kindle purchases
43 Birth control option, for short
45 "I hadn't thought of it that way"
47 New York city where Mark Twain is buried
49 Enter gingerly, as a hot tub
50 Few and far between
51 Slowly phase out, in lingo
53 "Look for yourself"
55 It may cover a cut
56 Feminist Millett who popularized the concept of the patriarchy
61 Stately tree
62 Actress Long
63 @, as a verb

by Adam Wagner

ACROSS

1 Officially accepted works
6 Follow orders
10 Section of grass-covered dirt
13 Be melodramatic on stage
14 Actor Carell of "The Office"
15 Wonderment
16 Q.U.E.U.E.S.
18 The "N" of N.Y.C.
19 Opera highlight
20 Direction of the morning light
21 Site to buy and sell handicrafts
22 Share, as a Twitter post
24 Barack, Michelle, Sasha or Malia
27 E+X+T+R+A+S
31 Seventh planet from the sun
34 Money for a mortgage
35 Salt Lake City collegian
36 Longer-lasting nail polish options
37 Highest number on a die
38 Give credit in a footnote
39 "Wonder Woman" star Gadot
40 Places to relax while getting all steamed up?
42 Himalayan country that's home to the world's highest unclimbed mountain
44 W/H/E/E/L/S
47 Lamb's cry
48 Continuously
52 Floating marker on a swim course
54 Prussia's ___ von Bismarck
56 Get smaller, as the moon
57 ___-compliant (wheelchair-accessible, say)
58 D-R-E-A-M-S
61 Neither's partner
62 Prove helpful
63 School vacation
64 Finale
65 Calendar boxes
66 In a strange way

DOWN

1 Fragrant wood
2 Love, to Michelangelo
3 Cry heard at the start of a game of tag
4 Residents of Canada's capital
5 Once named
6 Redding who sang "(Sittin' On) The Dock of the Bay"
7 Compartmented Japanese lunch
8 Allhallows ___
9 "I'd love to!"
10 Costume for St. Nick
11 Is behind financially
12 Like grass on a misty morning
14 Bluish gray hue
17 Owners' papers
21 Bird that can sprint up to 30 m.p.h.
23 Alternative to .com and .org
25 Feathery neckwear
26 Raggedy ___ (doll)
28 Classification for the barely famous
29 "At Last" singer James
30 Sighted
31 Popular brand of sheepskin boots
32 Authentic
33 Train conductor's cry
37 "Lamentably . . ."
38 Bit of foul language
40 "That's all ___ wrote"
41 Split ___ soup
42 Hatchlings for a 43-Down
43 Coop mother
45 Sneaky
46 Spy's gathering
49 Recorded on cassette
50 15-time N.B.A. All-Star Shaquille
51 Nettlesome
52 ___ of one's existence
53 Thick Japanese noodle
55 The one right here
58 Father
59 Director DuVernay
60 "Game of Thrones" airer

by Leslie Rogers

ACROSS

1 Carne ___ taco
6 Ski mountain transport
10 Hairdo
14 Substance used by gymnasts and cellists
15 Major or Minor in astronomy?
16 Cry just before the guest of honor arrives at a surprise party
17 Staged, as a disappearance
18 The country music industry
20 The lobbying industry
22 So far
23 Blog message
24 Like facts, but not fiction
26 The high-tech industry
31 Valuable violin, informally
32 Leave out
33 Japanese honorific
35 Ja's opposite
36 Banksy's "Girl With Balloon," e.g.
38 Low-ranking NCOs
39 Office linkup letters
40 Vegan protein source
41 Think "OMG! OMG!"
42 The advertising industry
46 Makes a choice
47 Ancient Roman statesman known as "the Censor"
48 Rocky outcrops
51 The automotive industry
54 The film industry
57 More bizarre
59 Actress Fanning
60 Carmaker with a four-ring logo
61 Conceal
62 National symbol

63 Put on display, with "out"
64 Friend of Forman and Fez on "That '70s Show"

DOWN

1 Sound from a little dog
2 Marinate, e.g.
3 Shows curiosity
4 Nutritionist's offering
5 Smartphone operating system with the biggest market share
6 Find on the radio dial
7 Sitter's handful
8 Ninny
9 Encouraging word
10 Sculptor's tool
11 Like canned sardines and olives, typically
12 Just twiddling one's thumbs
13 Three in a yard
19 Strongroom
21 "Emergency" keyboard key
24 Rating for non-kid shows
25 Train travel
26 Use a rice cooker, e.g.
27 Olympic figure skater Slutskaya
28 Like some tights and baseball games
29 College sports channel
30 New Haven Ivy Leaguer
31 NBC weekend skit show, for short
34 Situation Room grp.
36 Not quite all
37 Alien transports

38 Make out
40 A bit lit
41 Gag gift in a ventilated box
43 Fairway challenge
44 Scored 100 on an exam
45 Brewery fixture
48 Sous-___
49 Get moving, casually
50 Spaghetti ___ carbonara
51 Chowderhead
52 "White Wedding" singer Billy
53 Oolong and Darjeeling
55 Angkor ___ (Cambodian temple)
56 Fox drama "___ Kind of People"
58 Onetime movie studio rival of MGM

by Jamey Smith

ACROSS

1 Part of the leg between the knee and ankle
5 Certain athletic honorees, for short
9 Lodging near a highway interchange
14 Crazy, in Cancún
15 Strap attached to a horse's bit
16 Proverbial saying
17 Enthusiastic
18 Crumbly salad cheese
19 Karate studios
20 Dinosaur whose name means "swift seizer"
23 Sneaky devil
24 Cause for a confession
25 To the ___ degree
28 Impose (upon)
31 Bonus performance
33 Total pro
36 Dinosaur whose name means "winged finger"
38 Designer Chanel
40 Fooled
41 Indefinite quantity
42 Dinosaur whose name means "three-horned face"
47 Barbie's beau
48 Easter decorating need
49 Rip into bits
51 Insult, informally
52 Prefix with genetics or Pen
54 Go by, as time
58 Dinosaur whose name means "thunder lizard"
61 Sci. class for many future pre-meds
64 Jason's ship, in Greek myth
65 ___ a move (start dancing)
66 Gem from an oyster
67 Fully cooked, as steak

68 Falco of "Nurse Jackie"
69 Letters on a gearshift
70 Crossed (out)
71 A buck or two?

DOWN

1 Many Balkan inhabitants
2 Squalid dwelling
3 In a standoffish manner
4 Fall asleep on the couch, perhaps
5 Handy Andy, by another name
6 Go off course suddenly
7 Gyro bread
8 Loses it
9 One-named singer called the "Queen of Pop"
10 Bad smell
11 ___ Mahal
12 Narcissist's problem
13 "___ Miz"
21 Henhouse
22 Like the score 4–4
25 Unacceptable
26 "I might, if you're willing to ask"
27 ___ of Troy
29 Genesis console maker
30 Steady equestrian gaits
32 Loops into an online convo
33 Played a role
34 Buckingham Palace dog breed
35 Modern smokes
37 Alternatively, in a text
39 Condition that may involve repetitive urges, for short
43 Reaction of silent but obvious disapproval

44 Car at an auction, maybe
45 Reserved for a select customer
46 Actress Ward
50 Applied, as foundation or powder
53 Filled with wonder
55 One who's easily shocked or scandalized
56 "Wake Up Little ___" (1957 hit for the Everly Brothers)
57 Perfuming compound
58 Loon or dodo
59 "King" of this puzzle?
60 Rudely stare
61 Zoom, for one
62 The "p" of m.p.h.
63 Prohibit

by Derek J. Angell

ACROSS

1 Doesn't include
6 Very top
10 Vegetable in borscht
14 ___ cat
15 Drifting ice
16 Stow, as cargo
17 Fragile art form crafted with air and heat
19 Chair parts that tend to wear out quickly
20 Source of bills, for short
21 Paint application
22 Piece of material used to strengthen a garment
23 Props for "It's the Hard-Knock Life" in "Annie"
25 Starter on the mound, often
28 Censoring sounds
30 ___ Gatos, Calif.
31 Sch. in Columbus
32 Supplement
33 Longtime home appliance brand
35 What "X" might mean
36 Type who's out of touch with reality
39 Veer sharply
42 Church donation
43 Some frozen drinks
47 Wrath
48 Something about nothing, perhaps
49 Candy piece with white sprinkles
50 Metaphorical source of some government funds
54 Snack (on)
55 Running on ___
56 Burden
58 Situation that might lead to extra time
59 "By Jove!"
60 Comment before a stupid stunt . . . or a hint to the ends of 17-, 25-, 36- and 50-Across
63 Jay with a "Garage"
64 It's a thought
65 Desktop accessory
66 Home of the tree of knowledge
67 Nuisance
68 Gets ready to wash, say

DOWN

1 Classic rock standard with Spanish lyrics
2 Considering everything
3 Walked heavily
4 London's ___ Gardens
5 Align, as multiple devices
6 Company with a "spokesduck"
7 Division of the earth's crust
8 Dawn goddess
9 Important markings on treasure maps
10 Mont ___, highest of the Alps
11 A voice might be heard within this
12 Attorney general under Ronald Reagan
13 Lab simulation
18 Pretend to be, at a Halloween party, say
22 "You should never, ever do this!"
24 Divisions for weightlifters
26 Spot
27 College in New Rochelle, N.Y.
29 Soda can features
33 Best ___ (Academy Awards category)
34 "It doesn't excite me much"
37 Opera set in Egypt
38 "Micro" or "macro" subject, for short
39 Holder of compressed data
40 Stirred up
41 Relevant
44 Portmanteau for a radical environmentalist
45 Like crosswords on Monday vis-à-vis those in the rest of the week
46 Baseballs and basketballs, but not footballs
49 Neglected neighborhood
51 Turn one's attention to
52 Parts
53 Finish by
57 Jazz singer Sylvia
60 In the know
61 Phillis Wheatley wrote one "to Neptune"
62 "Get off the stage!"

by Bruce Haight

ACROSS

1 Chemist's workplace
4 Cousin of "Voilà!"
8 Enjoy a night in Vegas, perhaps
14 Poetic tribute
15 ____ for the long haul
16 Made turbulent, as water
17 "r u kidding me?!"
18 Dalai ____ (Tibetan priest)
19 Alternative to a Tic Tac
20 Earthquakes occur around them
23 "____ Anything . . ." (classic rom-com)
24 Year, in France
25 Tantalizing promos
28 Pretties up
30 Crystal-filled rock
33 Kind of reaction or instinct
36 Fortnite and The Legend of Zelda, for two
38 "Now it makes sense!"
41 Snoozing
42 Construction site vehicles
46 Like some humor and wine
47 Cut wool from
48 Keep time with the foot
51 Early buying opportunity
53 Bundle of paper
57 Of bees: Prefix
59 Eating utensils that might come wrapped in red paper
61 Australian young woman
64 Something to shoot for . . . or shoot at
65 Chart-topper
66 Learn, as a new skill . . . or what can precede the ends of 20-, 36-, 42- and 59-Across
67 Throw in the microwave
68 Siouan language speaker
69 Record holder
70 Online marketplace for artisans
71 Maple product

DOWN

1 Shower scrubber
2 Madison Avenue fellow
3 Underway
4 At an angle
5 Obsessive about little details
6 Anastasia's love in 1997's "Anastasia"
7 No longer happening
8 "Keep off the ____" (park sign)
9 "You've got mail" co.
10 Sch. in Cambridge
11 Came into one's own
12 "Star Wars" character who founded the Resistance
13 Small whirlpool
21 Peaceful pasture
22 Loosen, as restrictions
26 The yolk's not on them, but in them
27 Genuine
29 No longer interested in
31 Animal on an "Xing" sign
32 Outstanding Team award or Best College Athlete award
33 What polytheists worship
34 "Not happening"
35 Watch or clock
37 Brewer's kiln
39 Throw some jabs
40 French for "to be"
43 Home of Salt Lake City
44 Old Spice is a popular one
45 Sign on a moody teen's door
49 Rick who sang "Never Gonna Give You Up"
50 ____ Beta Kappa
52 Ending with sea or land
54 Smart speakers from Amazon
55 Curly-tailed Japanese dog
56 Camera lens setting
57 Snakes by the Nile
58 Singer Collins
60 Nordstrom rival, familiarly
62 1950s presidential nickname
63 Verb on a candy heart

by Rachel Simon

ACROSS

1 Skunk's defense
5 High school exam, for short
9 Reddish-purple salad ingredient
13 Apple TV+ alternative
14 Shakespeare villain who says "I am not what I am"
15 Literature Nobelist Alice
16 They're long for an underdog
17 Steffi with seven Wimbledon titles
18 Church choir accompaniment
19 Temp job?
22 ___/her pronouns
24 Prevailed
25 Necklace that can be made with kukui nuts
26 Prefix with liberal or conservative
27 Union job?
31 Ones potentially contacted in "first contact"
32 Vowel sound at the end of 15- and 26-Across
33 "La Vie en Rose" singer Edith
34 End of a hairy limb
35 Watery or papery
39 Yiddish "Yikes!"
42 Have ambitions (to)
44 Flex job?
47 It sells, it's said
48 MSNBC competitor
49 Chaired
50 Like the opening of Mahler's Symphony No. 9
51 Dream job?
55 It travels at nearly 300 million meters per second
56 Apple Store offerings
57 Story of one's life?
60 "Music is powered by ___": Yo-Yo Ma
61 Olympian's sword
62 Fuzzy bit of car décor
63 Literature Nobelist Morrison
64 Some lab liquids
65 Like Scotch

DOWN

1 "Well, well, well!"
2 Fizzling firework
3 Encyclopedia volumes vis-à-vis Wikipedia, e.g.
4 Deceptive trick
5 Old-fashioned message carriers
6 South Asian wrap
7 Petri dish filler
8 Coming up next
9 Small town
10 Driving force?
11 One might take off a few marks
12 Spanish for "foolish"
15 What may be heard in a herd
20 Exact lookalike
21 Slim and trim
22 Give this for that
23 Lead-in to pad
28 Clear up, as ski goggles
29 Works in a theater
30 Likely to offend, in brief
34 George Eliot and George Orwell, for two
36 Really prosper
37 ___ Man, one of the Avengers
38 Wonkish sort
40 America's Cup vessels
41 Bottleful in un ristorante
42 It was once the world's fourth-largest lake
43 Sch. system with campuses in Buffalo and Binghamton
44 Affirmative reply to "Understand?"
45 Most abundant element in Earth's crust
46 Bullet with a trail
47 Bad break in bowling
52 Spiced tea
53 Scruff of the neck
54 Many a cocktail mixer
58 "Rocks" in a cocktail
59 Big name in online talks

by Dan Schoenholz

ACROSS

1 Scotch ___ (3M product)
5 Olympic martial art since 1964
9 Apt rhyme for "slams"
14 Do as one's told
15 Sailing the ocean
16 Roomba or Automower
17 Go strolling
19 One end of a battery
20 Squirrel's stash
21 Sub at an office
23 Two-finger victory sign
24 Use, as a towel at the shore
25 Outdoor concert stage
27 Doozy
29 Canal to the Red Sea
30 Stiff test
35 Fuss in front of a mirror
38 Legacy I.S.P.
39 Immunity tokens on "Survivor"
41 Genetic messenger
42 Sings out with a lot of power
45 Turnpike feature made obsolescent by electronic passes
48 Sushi bar drink
50 Metal for a girder
51 Gel-filled NyQuil offerings
55 Post-O.R. stop
59 Post O.R. stop
60 Warsaw resident
61 Wildly absurd, colloquially
62 Chef De Laurentiis of the Food Network
64 Unresolved details . . . and a hint to this puzzle's circled letters
66 Subs at a deli
67 Start a poker pot
68 Menu bar option
69 Big obstacles at a golf course
70 Where to buy shares of G.M.
71 Easter egg colorings

DOWN

1 Completely wreck
2 Early calculators
3 Black tea variety
4 "You've got to be kidding" reaction
5 Film with the line "You're gonna need a bigger boat"
6 Miley Cyrus's "Party in the ___"
7 Airline with its main hub in Atlanta
8 Like many chardonnay barrels
9 Brings to a close
10 Sweetie
11 Warmer than freezing, on the Celsius scale
12 One posing for an artist
13 Metal for a girder
18 Declare invalid, as a marriage
22 OB/GYNs and 36-Downs
25 ___ cake (ring-shaped dessert)
26 What's-___-name
28 Garland gift in Hawaii
30 Ride that's hailed
31 Weeder's tool
32 Even-steven
33 Slimy stuff
34 "Black-ish" co-star Tracee ___ Ross
36 Sinus specialist, for short
37 "I don't think so"
40 35mm camera type, in brief
43 Letter after sigma
44 Ticket granting access to the slopes
46 Carried
47 Tournament favorite
49 Green: Prefix
51 Traffic signal
52 Less welcoming
53 Writer Edgar ___ Poe
54 Spring bloom
56 Skillful with home repairs
57 Actress MacDowell
58 One-ups
61 "Gotcha"
63 Stag's mate
65 Tiebreakers in hoops

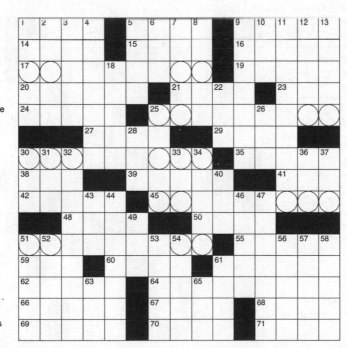

by Carl Larson

ACROSS

1 Get in the game?
5 Home of the comics heroes Asterix and Obelix
9 Month with a so-called "hunter's moon": Abbr.
12 "Let's Make ___"
13 Actor Edward James ___
15 "It's cold in here!"
16 What might be rolled for a strike
18 Put (down)
19 ___ no good (misbehaving)
20 Bud . . . or bait
21 Slightly off
23 Verse in a poem
25 What a clock might strike
27 [A spider!]
28 ___ Fleming, British naval intelligence officer-turned-writer
30 Is on the same page
31 Dexterous
33 Milky gem
36 Put two and two together, say
37 What might strike during a storm
40 Mermaid's home
42 Place for a fork . . . or a jackknife?
43 Cry of pain
46 Popular Nissan model
48 "For sure!"
50 Ctrl-___-Del
52 Who might go on strike
55 Plush fabric
57 Religious believer of a sort
58 Rod between wheels
60 Site for buying and selling crafts
61 Letters on a Forever stamp
62 What might strike you while solving this puzzle
65 6–3 in tennis, e.g.
66 Place to leave one's shoes, perhaps
67 Disney heroine whose name means "ocean"
68 Firefighter's tool
69 Many a big charity event
70 "Bird by Bird" writer Lamott

DOWN

1 Took home a "furever friend," say
2 Fresh spin on a familiar concept
3 Prey-catching claw
4 Inventor Whitney
5 Painter Vincent van ___
6 Lady Gaga's "The Fame" or "Artpop"
7 It's not sweet, sour, salty or bitter
8 Response to a funny text (that usually isn't literally true)
9 Beholden (to)
10 Suddenly stopped working, as a computer
11 Secret meetings
12 Mistreat
14 Sort of language generally found in Urban Dictionary
17 Final Four org.
22 Desert illusion
24 Rigatoni relative
26 Surrealist Salvador
29 Manhattan neighborhood containing some of N.Y.U.
32 Thrashes about
34 Org. that provides chaperones for field trips
35 Name on Woody's shoe in "Toy Story"
38 Overcast
39 Wall Street inits. since 1792
40 Like some couples
41 Atone for
44 Mekong Valley resident
45 Wedding guest's partner, say
46 Only mortal Gorgon in Greek myth
47 Recurring theme
49 Penultimate word in a fairy tale
51 Attempting to, casually
53 G.P.A. booster
54 Kick out
56 Divulge
59 Pre-euro currency
63 Christmastime concoction
64 Doctors' org.

by Olivia Mitra Framke

ACROSS

1 Unit of bread
5 Desensitizes, as with Novocain
10 Prefix with potent
14 Pimply skin condition
15 High-heat oven setting
16 Sizable paper quantity
17 Military leader who lends his name to a Chinese dish
19 Dot on a radar screen
20 Loud and flashy
21 Slenderest parts of Champagne flutes
23 Director DuVernay
24 Cartoon films like "Spirited Away" and "Ninja Scroll"
26 With 49-Across, the face of Kentucky Fried Chicken
28 Bar mitzvah, for one
29 One making a listing on Airbnb
32 Rally around a common cause
33 Clear as ___ (plain to see)
34 Chocolate-and-caramel candy brand
35 Trig ratios
36 Type of battle that 17-, 26-/49- and 60-Across might be engaged in?
39 Desert watering hole
42 Humble reply to "Nice job!"
43 Slump
46 Russian pancakes served with sour cream
47 Mom to Jaden and Willow Smith
48 Walk a ___ in someone's shoes
49 See 26-Across
51 Work in clay or marble
53 U.S. public health org.
54 Puzzle type with pictures
57 Really bothered
58 Touch up before publication
60 Cereal mascot in a naval uniform
62 Nick at ___
63 Bacon or Hamm, e.g.
64 Berry in a smoothie bowl
65 Grammy winner who sometimes sings in Gaelic
66 Something shared on Instagram
67 "And I— / I took the one ___ traveled by": Robert Frost

DOWN

1 Straggling sort
2 South Pacific region
3 Income source for some retirees
4 "I'm hungry!"
5 Where Wizards play with Magic, in brief
6 Web addresses, for short
7 Abolitionist Lucretia
8 Halve
9 Sports replay effect
10 Spherical shape
11 Pigment giving color to skin
12 Gullibility based on inexperience
13 Runs through with a sword
18 Deli bread variety
22 Like winter roads during a thaw
25 "Get outta here!"
27 "You can bet ___"
30 Grayed
31 "Modern Family" actress Vergara
34 More promising
36 Locate
37 "___ be an honor"
38 Mardi ___
39 Shockingly vulgar
40 1992 Disney film with the ballad "A Whole New World"
41 Nickname for Las Vegas
43 Something that may be golden or broken
44 Camel relatives of South America
45 "Here's the best part . . ."
47 Composer of the "Brandenburg Concertos," in brief
48 Held in common
50 Summary of last week's episode, perhaps
52 Electric or hybrid product, maybe
55 No more than
56 Annoying little squirt
59 Pekoe or Darjeeling
61 ___-Magnon

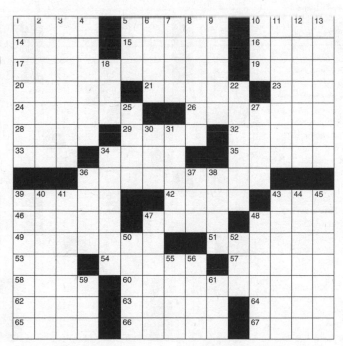

by Li Ding

ACROSS

1 Dance that might be accompanied by a fiddle
4 QB's six-pointer
10 Withdraw from, as a class
14 Laudatory work
15 Forecast provider
16 Judicial cover-up?
17 Under the weather
18 Bros' embrace
19 Supply-and-demand subj.
20 Rainy day savings
22 2005's "King Kong" and 2021's "Dune"
24 Lawyer's title: Abbr.
25 Self-confidence
26 Lingerie material
29 Commando movie weapons
31 Filling station?
34 Neighbor of Afghanistan
35 Musical ability
36 Who might say "Who goes there?"
37 Waste container
38 Put in fancy duds
40 Actor Holland of "Spider-Man" films
41 Freshwater fish with a colorful name
43 Gerund suffix
44 Destination for an Apollo mission
45 Safe havens
46 On a cruise
47 Hypes (up)
48 Good thing to graduate with
50 Dashboard stat
52 They go up and down on a playground
54 Partial floor covering
58 Historical periods
59 "Beats me"
61 Slip up
62 What a tightrope walker walks on
63 Discord
64 Attribute of many celebrities
65 Makes after taxes
66 Greek goddess of the soul
67 Hardly any

DOWN

1 Link
2 Not doing anything
3 Styling products
4 Heavy hardcovers
5 *Trixie Mattel, e.g.
6 Feeling of guilt
7 German interjection
8 Impolite sounds at the dinner table
9 Jason of "Freaks and Geeks"
10 "Oh sure, that'll totally happen!"
11 All-time low . . . or a musical hint to the answers to this puzzle's starred clues
12 Cousin of a bassoon
13 Souvenirs from White House signings
21 Many a high school student
23 Sacred choral work
25 *Contact-free smooch
26 Fair and balanced type, astrologically
27 Strong and resilient type, astrologically
28 *Seasonal confection that may say "I Luv U"
30 Actor Efron
32 Apt rhyme for "group"
33 Songs that might be accompanied by an organ
36 *Sensation after consuming too many Pixy Stix, perhaps
38 "The People's Princess"
39 Early afternoon hour
42 Follows some dentists' advice
44 Bahama ___
46 Fire felonies
49 Admit (to)
51 Pro golfer Calvin
52 Embroidered, e.g.
53 Lake below Huron
54 Knighted actor Guinness
55 Place to find brain coral
56 Prod
57 Get bigger
60 "___ me a river!"

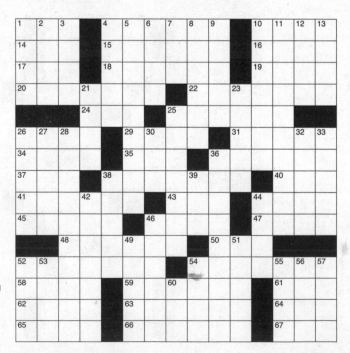

by Simon Marotte

ACROSS

1 Sound of a sneeze
6 Op-___ (newspaper columns)
9 Capital of Oregon
14 Something a mutinying pirate might have to walk
15 December 31, for short
16 Topic in a dictionary or on a utility bill
17 Not in a million billion years
19 Championship mementos
20 Big band ___ (time span after the Jazz Age)
21 Boxing family surname
22 Counterpart of length
24 Beverage often stored in a cellar
26 "Ave ___" (prayer)
28 Term of endearment
29 Document digitizations
31 Utah national monument called Shash Jaa' in Navajo
34 Domain
36 Establish legislatively
37 Soup scooper
38 Small container for carrying a drink when away from home
39 Man's name that's an anagram of ELGIN
40 Rolls-___
41 Be protective of, as a mother hen might
43 Loose, collarless shirt popular in India
47 Feasted
48 Messages that might come with emojis
50 Stuff from a bog
51 Not full, as an effort, informally
54 Sleep briefly
56 Palindromic explosive

57 Run ___ of (come into conflict with)
58 Like some fashion boots
61 Fruit of the Loom competitor
62 Debit inits. on some SNAP cards
63 To whom Alfalfa wrote "You're scum between my toes!"
64 The "A" in WASP
65 Female deer
66 Sugary

DOWN

1 Source of some wire stories
2 Religious official
3 Capital of Cuba
4 ½ + ½
5 Vegetable with pentagonal cross sections
6 Worthy of coveting
7 Easter egg colorer
8 Neighbor of Montenegro
9 "What-e-e-ever you say . . ."
10 China's continent
11 Indigenous reclamation movement
12 Custardy dim sum dessert
13 Breathable fabrics
18 Dutch ___ disease
23 Once in a blue moon
25 Infuriate
27 Sleep phase
30 Passover ritual
32 Nosh between meals
33 Become less harsh
35 Rations out
37 Partner of "prosper" in a Vulcan saying
38 Online game with a Battle Royale mode

39 Opposite of "I love it!"
40 Tyrannosaurus ___
41 "You crack me up!"
42 "By the power ___ in me . . ."
44 End a career
45 Get into a snarl
46 To boot
49 Droop
52 Coal or gas
53 To boot
55 Some advanced degree holders
59 "A Black Lady Sketch Show" channel
60 "Yee-___!"

by Erik Agard

ACROSS

1 Lines at the cinema?
7 Trim, as text
11 What a winner takes, it's said
14 ___ Prize (satirical scientific award since 1991)
16 Seaweed around sushi
17 Oolong, e.g.
18 Mix at a mixer, say
21 Annual video game competition, for short
22 Event first televised in 1953, with "the"
23 Finishes
24 S.U.V. alternative
26 Hoppy brew
27 Gobbled up
29 Texter's "Can you believe it?!"
30 Metaphor for lies, in a Walter Scott poem
35 Pinnacle
37 Took without asking
38 One day ___ time
39 & 43 Historical period found in each set of circled letters
45 Long, long time
46 Add up to
49 Bearded beasts
50 Fit perfectly
53 The first "O" of O.O.O.
54 Fled
55 Cube root of 1,000
56 Intel-gathering mission
59 Opening with leaks?
62 Feature of a deerstalker
64 Baton Rouge sch.
65 Surviving, but just barely
69 A braggart has a big one
70 Opposite of "for here"
71 Humble response to "How do you do it?"
72 "Unbelievable!"
73 Site of a fabled gift horse
74 Snags

DOWN

1 Coins that are 1.35 mm thick
2 "Go ahead, tell me the answer"
3 Latin phrase before a year
4 Yule ___ (Christmas confection)
5 Like kiwis and plum tomatoes, by shape
6 Astonished exclamations
7 Competition participant
8 Homer Simpson's signature cries
9 Vexation
10 The first "O" of O-O-O
11 Gazillions
12 NSFW, probably
13 Young chaps
15 Aboveboard
19 Many California wines
20 ___ Richards a.k.a. Mr. Fantastic
25 "Couldn't have said it any better"
27 Partner
28 "Smells Like ___ Spirit" (Nirvana song)
31 Divine Father
32 Needed further explanation
33 Shakespearean words to a traitor
34 Howls at the moon
35 Terrific, in slang
36 With 52-Down, 39-Across leader from 1949 to 1976
40 Singer James
41 In the near future
42 Greek vowel
44 Feverish symptom
47 "Good going!"
48 Suspicious (of)
51 Class with angles, for short
52 See 36-Down
53 Batman or Harry Potter, e.g.
57 Tributary of the Missouri River
58 Unclothed figures
59 "I'm glad that's over!"
60 Jafar's parrot in "Aladdin"
61 Have memorized
62 Breakfast brand
63 Green dispensers
66 Cousin ___ ("The Addams Family" character)
67 Neither's partner
68 Basis for some vaccines

by Julian Lim

ACROSS

1 Pace set by a metronome
6 Ewe's mate
9 Percolate
13 Measure of gold's purity, not its weight
14 Cause of a laugh
15 Bone parallel to the radius
16 Closing bit of music
17 In memoriam piece
18 Doe or buck
19 "Have another round - my treat!"
22 ___-bitsy
25 Private eye, in old slang
26 C-worthy
27 Gloating words of mock consolation
31 Wretched
32 Amanda of "Sleeping With Other People"
33 Texter's "Hold that thought"
36 Revealed accidentally
39 Once-standard feature not found in most newer vehicles
41 greenpeace.___
42 Trolley
44 Blow, as a volcano
45 Invitation to a prospective waltz partner
48 Actress Rudolph of "Bridesmaids"
50 Feathery accessory
51 Lays down turf
52 Empower a successor, metaphorically
56 "Dagnabbit!"
57 Decorated, as a cake
58 In a good mood
62 Rough patch in adolescence?
63 Rainy day hue
64 Full of fury
65 Bogus
66 Make music on a kazoo, say
67 Sufi poet thought to have coined the adage found at the starts of 19-, 27-, 45- and 52-Across

DOWN

1 Boxing ring ruling, in brief
2 ___ de toilette
3 Mandinka'd star of "The A-Team"
4 Transport built for revelry
5 Tweeter's "alternatively"
6 Title cyborg in a 1987 sci-fi flick
7 Similar (to)
8 Distribute, with "out"
9 Puzzle with a 9 x 9 grid
10 Justice Kagan
11 Foe
12 Peel . . . or, phonetically, a fruit you might do this to
14 ___ K. of Kafka's "The Trial"
20 "___ be a big help"
21 Solaced
22 Author Calvino
23 The ___ of Babel
24 Sound heard twice in "George"
28 Something special
29 Stephen of "The Crying Game"
30 "You bet!"
33 Uncle "we don't talk about" in Disney's 2021 film "Encanto"
34 Bygone music collection from Nas or Lil' Kim
35 Computer memory units
37 Good name for a financial planner?
38 Buddy
40 Sculptures made of found objects and scraps
43 The Reds or the Red Sox, for short
45 The "S" in iOS
46 Folk icon Guthrie
47 Anatomical canal locale
48 1963's ___ on Washington
49 Cat pose or downward dog
52 BlackBerrys and PalmPilots, for short
53 Low's opposite
54 Hosiery shade
55 ___ Pet (onetime fad item)
59 Small butter unit
60 School fund-raising grp.
61 "Oh, quit ___ bellyachin'!"

by August Miller

ACROSS

1 Media player debut of 2001
5 Sacred song
10 Transport between airport terminals
14 Bill of fare
15 Beginning, as of symptoms
16 Marathon, e.g.
17 Air currents from the most typical direction
20 Big part of many kids' cereals
21 Bamboozled
22 Way into a sub
23 Texter's response to a hilarious joke
25 "___ go bragh!"
27 Resorted to good old-fashioned know-who, say
32 Pub order, in brief
33 "The lady ___ protest too much . . .": "Hamlet"
34 Cut, in editing
37 Ice cream brand
39 Survive a round of musical chairs
41 Entrepreneur Musk
42 Some labor leaders?
45 Terse denial
48 Club ___ (resort)
49 Top military leaders in Washington
52 Dutch cheese
53 One may be taken in protest
54 Repeatedly comments (on)
57 Lead-in to "la-la"
59 G-sharp equivalent
63 Rodgers and Hammerstein's "Do-Re-Mi" show, with a hint to this puzzle's theme
66 Not stereo
67 Interrogate
68 Stuff to wear
69 City on the Rhône
70 Good at fixing leaky faucets and creaky hinges, say
71 Crafty website

DOWN

1 Little devils
2 Land in the Andes
3 Universal donor's blood type, in brief
4 "The Shining" actress Shelley
5 Mash prepared for a luau
6 Sketch show V.I.P.s who get a jacket for their fifth appearance
7 The East
8 "Neither a borrower nor a ___ be": "Hamlet"
9 Business appt.
10 Shape describing a complex love relationship
11 Screed
12 Rock band name with a slash
13 Fit together well
18 Packing, so to speak
19 Dog's "Pleeeeze!"
24 Kerfuffle
26 Clear (of)
27 ___ Piper
28 Pageant coif
29 Easy two-pointer
30 "Sure ___!" ("You bet!")
31 Title city in a 2014 Ava DuVernay film
35 Little piggies
36 Ceases
38 Takes overnight to think about
40 Gained influence, as an idea
43 Segue before a conclusion
44 RR stop
46 Spike TV, previously
47 Seat in the iconic photo "Lunch Atop a Skyscraper"
50 Egyptian sun god
51 Haven, as for endangered wildlife
54 Website developer's code
55 Sailor's greeting
56 Janet ___, first female attorney general
58 Thor's father
60 Exam for an aspiring atty.
61 Pretenses one may "put on"
62 Frozen dessert chain owned by Mrs. Fields
64 "Awful, just awful!"
65 Take to the sky

by Lou Weiss

ACROSS

1 Stallions' mates
6 Starting from
10 Inflated self-images
14 Engulfed (in)
15 Roman garment of old
16 Trevor who hosts "The Daily Show"
17 Frank of the Mothers of Invention
18 Humpty Dumpty's perch
19 Cast a ballot
20 Imbibe copiously
23 Tally
24 Snaky fish that can swim backward
25 Middle square on a bingo card
26 Move speedily
31 "The Fox and the Crow" storyteller
34 Depend (on)
35 M.A. applicant's test
36 Go with the ___
37 Persuades
39 "Yay! Tomorrow's Saturday!"
40 Big bird in Liberty Mutual ads
41 Very many
42 Elements that make up the atmosphere
43 Toil arduously
47 Borscht vegetable
48 Pecan or almond
49 Ave. crossers
52 Observe intently
56 Numbskull
57 ___ Grey tea
58 Foxx with an Oscar for playing Ray
59 ___ call (attendance check)
60 Frosty coating
61 Vital part of the stratosphere's protective layer

62 "If all ___ fails . . ."
63 "Shoo!"
64 Beauty's fairy tale suitor, with "the"

DOWN

1 Japanese carmaker with a CX series
2 Oscar, Emmy or Tony
3 Swift
4 "Monday Night Football" channel
5 Drastic reorganization
6 Whenever one wishes
7 Drench
8 Eye rudely
9 Pita sandwiches of deep-fried chickpea balls
10 Regarded with jealousy
11 Big fat zeros
12 Swearing-in pledge
13 "___-Ra: Princess of Power" (1980s animated series)
21 Hall-of-Fame QB Dawson
22 Noisy scuffle
26 Noisy scuffle
27 Boiling mad
28 Piano part
29 One of the Great Lakes
30 N.B.A. whistle blowers
31 Not very many
32 Furry red Muppet
33 Tart hard candies
37 Crawls as a snake would
38 Stir-fry pan
39 Kids' chasing game

41 Actor Guinness who portrayed Obi-Wan Kenobi
42 Found employment
44 Water heater for tea
45 Bit of jewelry to wear with sandals
46 Needing to be paid
49 American ___ (U.S. Pacific territory)
50 Siblings like Jacob and Esau
51 Shooting sport with clay targets
52 Cashmere or angora
53 Nonclerical, at a church
54 Filmdom's la Douce
55 Smoggy overcast
56 Hip-hop's Dr. ___

by Lynn Lempel

ACROSS

1 Kids and their parents
6 Help with a job, in a way
10 Wanted, but nowhere to be found
14 Nickname for Schwarzenegger or Palmer
15 Winged chatterbox
16 Deal (with)
17 Hive minders
19 Having trouble deciding
20 Early-season farming task
21 C, for one
23 Video chat disruption
24 Words before "the stars are brightly shining," in a carol
27 Lute ___, longtime Arizona basketball coach
32 Winged hooter
33 Grind, as one's teeth
34 Second-most-visited website worldwide, after Google
36 Many a Hollywood car crash
38 So as not to stand out
39 Some South Pacific greetings
42 "Skol!," in Sauternes
44 Literally, "on fire" . . . or, metaphorically, excellent
45 "Three coins" fountain location
47 Lip
49 Scatter, as flower petals
50 Drink that comes with a buzz cut?
53 Gently touch, either forward or backward
54 Staples of West African cuisine
55 Frustrate

61 Et ___ (and others)
63 Entranced . . . or what one can do by reading the starts of 17-, 24-, 34-, 44- and 50-Across in order?
65 Neatnik's opposite
66 Palindromic fashion magazine
67 Petulant
68 Line up
69 Ones calling offsides
70 Garlic squeezer

DOWN

1 Yaks
2 Twistable snack item
3 From the top
4 First man, in Polynesian creation myth
5 Observed
6 Rock blaster
7 "Ta-ta!"

8 Prepares to get schooled, perhaps
9 Yummilicious
10 Not just sit around daydreaming
11 Just sit around daydreaming
12 ___ Book Club
13 Yardstick measurement
18 ___ trip
22 Swamps
25 De-weeder
26 West Coast burger chain
27 Cries of dismay
28 "Sweet Jane" songwriter Reed
29 Indented part of an outline
30 ___ rima (eight-line stanza)
31 Invalidate
35 Sch. affiliated with the Latter-day Saints

37 Amy who wrote "The Joy Luck Club"
40 Bouncer's concern
41 Female hog
43 Ride roughshod over
44 911 responder
45 QB's six-pointer
46 In actuality
48 In and of ___
51 Means of tagging in a game
52 Class offered at many Y.M.C.A.s
56 Baking meas.
57 "That's ___ business"
58 Workhorse that's only part horse
59 Tattoo shop supplies
60 Ice cream brand
62 "American Idol" airer starting in 2018
64 "___ Miz"

by Richard D. Allen

ACROSS

1 Musical measures
5 Stats for H.S. students
9 Positive quality
14 Corporate bigwig
15 Figure on a Monopoly card
16 Guy of Food Network fame
17 Additionally
18 Ye ___ Shoppe
19 Pup's peeves
20 Topic of debate regarding online service providers
23 And so forth: Abbr.
24 Arab dignitary
25 Much of a Facebook feed
28 "Ready, ___, go!"
31 "Now I get it!"
33 Evil-repelling trinket
35 Feign sleep
39 Jacques ___, "Mon Oncle" filmmaker
40 Basic trick at a skatepark
41 Eighth mo.
42 Personification of evil
43 Not spoil
44 Helpful feature for tyops . . . um, typos
46 Novelist Hemingway
48 "___ out!" (ump's shout)
49 P, to Plato
50 Its motto is "All the News That's Fit to Print," in brief
51 Stroke on a golf green
54 Product that's often mint-flavored
56 Opposition party group in British politics
62 Created for a certain purpose, as a committee
64 Fish's breathing organ
65 Nativity gift givers
66 Go "Zzzz"
67 Fruit with a cedilla in its name
68 Worshiped figure
69 Pieces that are typically sacrificed in gambits
70 "This email is finished" button
71 Action that can be done to the starts of 20-, 35-, 44- and 56-Across

DOWN

1 Noggin
2 Rod through two wheels
3 Pause, on sheet music
4 British biscuit
5 Mustachioed Marx brother
6 Bombard, as with snowballs
7 Comedian Eric
8 Hot shower emanation
9 Declare confidently
10 Riverbank deposit
11 "Hasta la vista!"
12 Distinctive period
13 "___ the season . . ."
21 French word for a leg of the Tour de France
22 Actor Hemsworth of "The Hunger Games"
26 Unfasten
27 Drunk, in dated slang
28 Like commands given to Siri and Alexa
29 ___ Queen, crime novel pseudonym
30 "The X Factor" or "The Voice"
32 Right away
34 Destination of the Mormon migration
36 Cry of pain
37 Take to court
38 Unattractive
42 Wash with elbow grease
44 Mate for a mare
45 Passport or driver's license
47 What_the_underlines_ in_this_clue_ show
52 Attire on many Roman statues
53 How many times Bette Davis won Best Actress
55 Imitate
57 Common center of a steering wheel
58 Tight-knit tribe
59 Zilch, zip, zero
60 Senses of self-worth
61 Be at an angle
62 Nile serpent
63 23andMe sample

by Simon Marotte

ACROSS

1 Camping trip rental
4 "Me day" destination
7 First in a convoy
14 Devalue
16 Well-informed (of)
17 Material much used for Indian dresses
18 Provider of moral support?
19 What good art can make you do
20 Gave the once-over
21 Creatures in a pod
24 Fish that's an ambush predator
26 Took to an auto impound
30 Wild hog
31 Writer Janowitz
33 Emperor whose mother was Agrippina the Younger
34 Comfort
37 "You must be this tall to ___" (amusement park sign)
39 McKellen or McEwan
40 Kids' party game . . . or a hint to this puzzle's circled letters
43 Asset when playing Skee-Ball
44 Home of Miami University
45 Classic lollipop with a "Mystery Flavor" flavor
47 Hankerings
49 Planets, poetically
51 Trim
52 "Bye Bye Bye" boy band
54 Crunchy, wasabi-coated morsel
55 Wrench handle?
56 "What happened now?!"
58 #carpediem
60 More likely to daydream, say
63 Hold lovingly
67 Place for a poser
68 Announcement upon a late arrival
69 Virtual critters since 1999
70 Belief system
71 Greenpeace, e.g., in brief

DOWN

1 Device associated with the advice "Be kind, rewind"
2 "Gotcha!"
3 Never-been-worn
4 People who might bug others
5 Mononymous "King of Football"
6 Jewelry under a sock, perhaps
7 Bit of gear for a talk show host
8 Online retailer whose first sale was a broken laser pointer
9 Stop, in French
10 Exactly right
11 One getting hailed on Broadway?
12 Silent communication, for short
13 GPS path: Abbr.
15 To the extent that
21 Baby deliverers, for short
22 Some best buds
23 Slander
25 There might be a ring to it
27 Parodist Yankovic
28 Deletion
29 Crime boss
32 Condition that affects executive function, in brief
35 Tech exec
36 Canyon rebound
38 Mer contents
41 Sites of frequent touchdowns
42 Go really, really wrong
43 Writer Rand
46 Boyz II ___
48 Movie theater morsel with white sprinkles
50 Waves, perhaps
53 Doorbell sound
55 Bedside buzzer
57 Like Scotch served without ice
59 Has an open tab, say
60 Dict. listing
61 "The Raven" poet
62 "A long, long time ___ . . ."
64 Cacophony
65 Video call annoyance
66 Angsty genre

by Ella Dershowitz

ACROSS

1 Wizard's weapon
6 Meat in a burger
10 Famous ___ cookies
14 Gem from an oyster
15 Peas, for a pea shooter
16 Tales handed down orally
17 Web company with an exclamation mark in its name
18 Nutty candy offering
20 Mardi Gras city, colloquially
22 Word after game, set or match
23 Ultradense galactic body
29 N.Y.C. airport code
30 ___ Grey (variety of 2-Down)
31 Spot for a mic clip
32 The Bee ___ (music group)
33 Instrument with pipes
35 Deliver a grand message
37 Fresh starts . . . or, when said aloud, what 18-, 23-, 53- and 58-Across all have?
42 Like some sprays and voices
43 Danger
45 "Seven" things for a pirate
48 Construction beam material
51 Part to play
52 Sanjay Gupta's channel
53 Soba servings, for instance
55 Houston baseballer
57 Pollen gatherers
58 Top dog
62 Airplane seating alternative to window
66 It's catchy
67 Picked a card
68 Step
69 Strong desires
70 Wraps up
71 Uses a computer keyboard

DOWN

1 Intel employee?
2 Breakfast beverage
3 Ooh and ___
4 Grassy areas near driveways
5 Each button in an elevator
6 Yellow fruit
7 Music subcategory that's a vowel change from 8-Down
8 Australian bird that's a vowel change from 7-Down
9 Weather phenomenon that London is famous for
10 Judy Garland, voicewise
11 Kind of phone on the coast of Alabama?
12 Fruit with the name of its color
13 Some mattress choices
19 Mo. before May
21 "Haha" alternative
23 Protagonist in "The Matrix"
24 Bring in, as income
25 Strongly suggest
26 This is not good!
27 Arctic ___ (migratory bird)
28 Mathematician Turing
32 Philanthropic quality
34 Org. for the Hawks, but not the Falcons
36 Gratuity
38 Canadian gas brand
39 Cat: Sp.
40 "Money doesn't ___ on trees"
41 Window ledge
44 "___ Misérables"
45 Insufficient in quantity
46 Guarantee
47 Avenger played by Paul Rudd
49 Macaroni shapes
50 Suni ___, Team U.S.A. gymnastics medalist
53 Neither's partner
54 Brutish creature
56 Parts of a gym set
59 Poem of praise
60 Coffee vessel
61 Sansa's father on "Game of Thrones"
63 Source of maple syrup
64 Political fact-checker's verdict, maybe
65 Triage centers, for short

by Alexander Liebeskind

ACROSS

1 Plenty
6 Actor Hemsworth
10 Keep bumping into another punk music fan?
14 Request to someone dressing your submarine sandwich
15 Baby name that had popularity bumps after the releases of "Frozen" and "Frozen II"
16 Not supporting
17 Figure in many hexes
19 Challenge for a plumber
20 Poverty and pollution, for two
21 Scale amts.
22 Discerning
24 Napkin holder
25 Alternative to Huggies or Luvs
27 Prefix with puncture
29 One of two akimbo
30 Stampede
33 Supporting
34 Puts on
38 Suggestion to defer discussion . . . and what might be said of 17-, 25-, 46- and 60-Across
41 Brand with the flavor Cookie Cobblestone
42 Cavernous opening
43 Without leaving crumbs behind, say
44 See 44-Down
45 Place for a royal flush?
46 Place for splits and spares
53 Org. for King James and Dr. J
56 More sore
57 With 64-Across, symbol of coldness
58 Gait that's not as fast as a canter
59 Spot for a guard at the World Cup
60 $$$ dispenser
63 What many do on the Sabbath
64 See 57-Across

65 National Zoo attraction
66 Pseudo-sophisticated
67 Barriers to compromise
68 Teen spirit?

DOWN

1 Heavy chorus "instrument" in "Il Trovatore"
2 $$$
3 Gathering where one might make a splash
4 Tupperware tops
5 Grp. with the 1975 hit "Evil Woman"
6 Prompted
7 "___ It at the Movies" (collection of Pauline Kael reviews)
8 In which "I'm sorry" shows a closed fist, in brief
9 Clumsy
10 Country in the Mediterranean
11 Outdo
12 Word before "of mind" or "of emergency"
13 Many a consumer of trail mix
18 Symbol of wisdom
23 Member of a virtual family
25 Edge
26 Angel's instrument
28 "Ornery" sort
30 Cry at a World Cup match
31 Nickname for Benedict or Edgar
32 Group targeted for destruction in "Independence Day"
33 Hairy hand
34 Classical queen who cursed a Trojan fleet
35 One in a deep-fried side dish
36 Zippo
37 Wreck room?

39 Powder-based beverage
40 Its tributaries are Blue and White
44 With 44-Across, holder for a Thanksgiving dessert
46 Principal Iraqi port
47 Shade of some turning leaves
48 Card game in Austen novels
49 Like some unbrushed suits
50 Competition favoring flexible contestants
51 Zeniths
52 Org. that might give a grant to a sculptor
54 Barry with 12 Silver Slugger Awards
55 Really bothered
58 Less ___ perfect
61 Yank
62 I.R.S. expert

by Sam Buchbinder and Brad Wilbe

ACROSS

1 Kudzu or ivy
5 Alternative to solid, liquid or gas
11 ___ Lanka
14 Celebrity who's adored
15 Coded message
16 Nonhuman member of the family
17 *Secretary of Perry Mason
19 "A" card in the deck
20 Science fiction writer Asimov
21 Variety
22 Do the hustle?
23 *Alcoholics Anonymous program
27 Hosts with mics, for short
30 Call between ready and go
31 Indigenous people for whom a Great Lake is named
32 Trees with acorns
34 Drug also known as angel dust, in brief
36 Measuring instrument that may have a needle
39 *Finish a gymnastics routine perfectly
43 Justice Sotomayor
44 Little rascal
45 Doe's mate
46 Memos
49 Nile snake
51 Pigs' place
52 *Description of a wholesome, clean-cut guy
55 Make ___ meet
56 Letter between oh and cue
57 Element suggested phonetically by NOPQ STUV . . .
62 Hawaiian necklace
63 Cry after navigating the last parts of the answers to this puzzle's starred clues?
66 Sass

67 Similar chemical compound
68 Actor McGregor
69 Chicago trains
70 Big name in small planes
71 Diarist Frank

DOWN

1 "Veni, ___, vici"
2 Midmonth date
3 Mardi Gras city, informally
4 Jazz great Fitzgerald
5 Some laptops, for short
6 On fire
7 Busy month for accountants
8 Table for later
9 More timid
10 "But is it ___?"
11 Attire for astronauts
12 Summary

13 Trinkets, tchotchkes and whatnot
18 "Macbeth" has five of these
22 Places
24 Cried
25 Write on stone, say
26 Road Work Ahead or Dead End
27 Carpet on a forest floor
28 Famed Roman censor
29 Is unsuited to go swimming, but does so anyway?
33 Descendants
35 I. M. ___, Louvre Pyramid architect
37 Swarming pest
38 Like holiday nogs
40 Fashion designer Spade
41 "OMG, that's so funny!"
42 Lhasa ___ (dog breed)

47 Many a newspaper scoop
48 Shorthand writers
50 Baby buggy, to Brits
52 "Beauty and the Beast" heroine
53 Baseball great Buck
54 Considers
58 Perlman of "Cheers"
59 Dress worn to a ball
60 Its capital is Muscat
61 Hawaii's only native goose
63 Juice brand with a hyphenated name
64 Japanese currency
65 Savings plan, briefly

by Michael Schlossberg

ACROSS

1 "Get out" key
4 Rocky outcroppings
9 According to
14 Actor Mineo
15 Watercolor and oil, for two
16 Ingredient in laundry products
17 Make a goofy appearance in someone else's picture
19 Little brats
20 "Nevermore" speaker, in poetry
21 Twins' org.
23 Sitcom ET from the planet Melmac
24 Angers
25 Multipost rant online
29 How tuna or steak may be served
31 Annoying complainer
32 Fancy
34 Existential dread
35 What the "spinning beach ball of death" might indicate
40 Schwarzenegger, familiarly
41 Ingredient in lemon curd
42 Greyhound station freebie
44 Crispy tortilla dish
49 Message sent to many recipients
52 Many a Mideasterner
53 Rank below cpl.
54 Title equivalent to Dame
55 Foamy part of un espresso
56 Bail on plans, with "out"
58 Big times in Silicon Valley . . . or a hint to 17-, 25-, 35- and 49-Across?
61 Actress/model Bo
62 Not deserved
63 Big name in jeans
64 Brief comment to an audience
65 Indiana pro basketballer
66 Throw in

DOWN

1 Vivacity
2 Much of Chad and Mali
3 Honey source
4 "Hurry up!"
5 Basketball stat: Abbr.
6 Tizzy
7 "Ooh, I need that!"
8 Black
9 Six-pack contents
10 Light piano piece
11 Drags out
12 Subway line?
13 Pharmacy pickups
18 Litmus ___
22 "Oh, and also . . . ," in a text
25 Short pants?
26 Mae who said "I'll try anything once, twice if I like it, three times to make sure"
27 Ocean beasts that lack bones, surprisingly
28 Old TV star whose haircut was inspired by Mandinka warriors
30 Take to a higher court
33 "What's the big idea?!"
35 Wads, as paper
36 Watching the big game?
37 Did an impression of
38 Goes bad
39 Coagulate
40 Fiver
43 "Nova" network
45 Tuber type
46 Anatomical ring
47 Blocked, as a river
48 Degraded
50 Suddenly showed happiness
51 Impressive venue to sell out
55 "Good buddy" speaker
56 Public health org.
57 Barely manage, with "out"
59 Public health org.
60 Rose or lilac

by Carly Schuna

ACROSS

1 Like the path of a lob
6 Stand the test of time
10 Newspaper opinion piece
14 Instrument in a string quartet
15 French peak
16 "____, far, wherever you are" (Celine Dion lyric)
17 Applies sloppily, as paint
18 Data graphics with wedges
20 Egyptian queen, for short
21 Stuck ashore, as a whale
22 Cries loudly
24 Air traffic control equipment
28 Dirty dozen?
31 Do surgery
33 Skips over, as a spoken syllable
34 India's smallest state
35 Ambulance specialists, in brief
36 Hot springs resort
37 Sent by UPS, e.g.
40 Baseball's ____ Wee Reese
41 Light white powder
43 ". . . spoon ____ fork?"
44 Existing in hidden form
46 Spotted wildcats of the South American jungle
48 Nuts used to make marzipan
49 Crumple into a ball
50 Princess played by Emma Corrin on "The Crown"
51 Ramadan observers
54 Fill to capacity
58 Garments similar to rompers . . . with a hint to the shaded squares in this puzzle
61 Three-point driving maneuver
62 "Ah, that makes sense now"
63 Fiction's opposite

64 Malodorous
65 Kings of Leon or Queens of the Stone Age
66 "If you ask me . . . ," online
67 Farmer's harvests

DOWN

1 Electrical adapter letters
2 Authentic
3 You're reading one right now
4 Nudged
5 ____ and don'ts
6 Big flaps in the fashion industry?
7 Assumed name
8 Blueprint detail
9 Silicon Valley field
10 How you might walk through the graveyard at night
11 The "p" of m.p.g.
12 Have for lunch
13 Stethoscope users: Abbr.
19 "Present!"
21 V.I.P.
23 Middle ____ (time before the Renaissance)
25 Make slightly wet
26 Go to an event
27 Adjusts, as a clock
28 Confer (upon)
29 Andean herd animal
30 Used a rotary phone
31 Alley ____ (basketball play)
32 Spanish rice dishes
34 4.0 is a great one, for short
38 Org. that won't call to demand payments, despite what its impostors would have you believe
39 "Shucks!," only stronger

42 In a mass
45 Appliance on a kitchen counter
47 Numbered musical work
48 Hopes one will
50 Get rid of, informally
52 Believer in Islamic mysticism
53 Actor Neeson
55 Lead-in to correct or tune
56 Excursion
57 Finishes
58 Triangular sail
59 Land between Can. and Mex.
60 All vice presidents before Harris
61 Colonel Sanders's chain

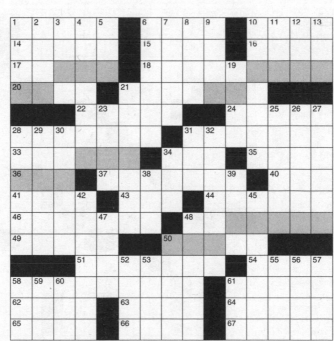

by Hoang-Kim Vu and Jessica Zetzman

ACROSS

1 Hot dish that sounds cold
6 Increase, as a pot
11 ___ Dhabi
14 Composer Copland
15 Feature of five U.S. presidents from Lincoln to Harrison
16 Hummus, for one
17 Easy order for a barista
19 Feminine suffix
20 They play among the reeds
21 Gin flavoring
22 Exclamation of epiphany
25 Not quite ROFL
26 Inventor's protection
28 $, %, & or @
30 "If ___ Street Could Talk" (2018 film)
32 "It is a tale told by an ___, full of sound and fury": Shak.
33 Coil in a mattress
37 Oscar-winning film set partly in Iran
38 Jell-O shapers
39 Slushy summer treat
40 Ocean invertebrate with a round, translucent body
42 Trumpet's sound
43 Furious
44 Prevailing tendencies
45 Sherwood ___
48 Go a-courting?
49 "The Waste Land" author's monogram
50 Big nights before big days
51 Artist Henri Toulouse-___
55 A live one might be hot
56 Genre with a Hall of Fame in Cleveland . . . or what can follow the respective halves of 17-, 33-and 40-Across

60 Card player's call
61 More robust
62 Pisa dough?
63 Kylo ___ of "Star Wars"
64 Serviceable
65 Put down new turf on

DOWN

1 Taxi
2 "2001: A Space Odyssey" antagonist
3 Nest egg letters
4 ___ citato (in the passage quoted)
5 Rorschach pattern
6 Bubbling away
7 Dict. offerings
8 Loopy
9 Overstep one's bounds
10 Verse that exalts its subject
11 "Easy on Me" singer, 2021
12 Plains figure replaced by Monticello on U.S. nickels
13 Surprise win
18 Cucumber-like, maybe
21 Lifelessly dull
22 "Take me ___"
23 Water power, informally
24 Compadre
27 Mont Blanc, for one
29 Outskirts of the outskirts
30 Book-loving Disney princess in a yellow gown
31 Whirlpool
33 Bit of lightning
34 Defeatist's assertion
35 Bookish sorts
36 Flappers in a gaggle
38 Late singer with a food name
41 PSAT takers, often

42 Operator of a stud farm
44 Community card between "flop" and "river" in hold'em
45 It's connected to the tibia
46 Sheepish
47 Intel mission
48 Gawk
52 Rights advocacy org.
53 Some four-stringed instruments, for short
54 Mötley ___
56 Letter after pi
57 Common conjunctions
58 John of Salisbury
59 "Acid"

by Robert Won

ACROSS

1 Tiny unit of matter
5 Singer Paul with a star on Canada's Walk of Fame
9 Leafy fresh herb in a caprese salad
14 Arrived
15 "___ mio!" ("My lord!": Sp.)
16 Tolerate
17 Data sources for Election Day coverage
19 Ringlets
20 "Same here"
21 Accessories that may feature Windsor knots
23 Ships' records
26 Kid-lit classic "Blueberries for ___"
27 "And Still I Rise" poet Maya
30 Three-dimensional
35 Fawn's mother
36 Plead
38 Largest branch of Islam
39 Large props held by contest winners in publicity photos
44 Sticky tree secretion
45 Make a scratch or dent in
46 "Abandon hope, ___ ye who enter here"
47 Mournful, as poetry
50 Anticipate
53 Lady in Progressive ads
54 Nincompoop
55 Late-1950s car stylings designed to look aerodynamic
60 Word with tricks and thrills
64 Opposite of urban
65 D.C. baseball players . . . or what the ends of 17-, 21-, 39- and 55-Across sound like
68 Make up (for)
69 Ireland, in literature
70 Ideologies
71 Small lakes
72 Like moldy basements and some memes
73 Subdermal lump

DOWN

1 Got 100% on
2 Steer a plane toward the runway
3 Forget to mention
4 Test one's ___ (be a challenge)
5 Ballyhoo
6 Zip, zero, nada
7 München : Munich :: ___ : Cologne
8 Subject to a tax, as property
9 Strong negative reaction, as from the public
10 Border on
11 Apple's voice assistant
12 Run in neutral
13 Word sometimes used incorrectly for "fewer"
18 Game with 15 numbered balls
22 Beanie, e.g.
24 Desert on the Silk Road
25 Canal through Egypt
27 Cherish
28 Toni Morrison's "Beloved," for one
29 Plural that makes one wonder why there aren't any meese
31 Mon. follower
32 Early Peruvians
33 Joint just above the heel
34 Cotton fabric named for a French city
37 Beauty
40 18-wheeler
41 Nasal sounds from someone with a slight cold
42 Silly
43 Bird that caws
48 Oscar winner Mahershala
49 Duped
51 Puerto ___
52 Of a shared cultural identity
55 Ensnare
56 What you park in a driveway or drive on a parkway
57 Clothes presser
58 Acquire, as a job
59 Singer Bareilles
61 Beginnerish
62 "___ for the poor"
63 Discreet attention-getter
66 Container for mints
67 Squirt from an octopus

by Christopher Youngs

ACROSS

1 Arid Mongolian expanse
5 Forensics facility at Quantico, Va.
11 Driver's guide, for short
14 Mireille ___, co-star of AMC's "The Killing"
15 Yale, to alums
16 Muscle worked by a kettlebell swing, informally
17 "This is payback!"
19 Manipulate
20 N.F.L. Hall-of-Famer Dawson
21 "Hold your horses!"
22 Cheese in a Greek salad
23 Winning
25 City that's home to the Anne Frank House
27 Teri of "Mr. Mom"
28 ___ punk (fusion genre with Jamaican rhythms)
29 Toilette water
30 Bit of firepit debris
31 Bull with a horn, informally
33 "Silence!"
37 The Thinker and others
39 ___ 500 (NASCAR's "Super Bowl")
41 German bacteriologist who lent his name to a kind of dish
42 "Ripped"
44 Destination on a fast-food lover's bucket list?
45 "Knives Out" actress de Armas
47 Constitutional initiative passed in '72 but never ratified
48 Self-description for many an expert hobbyist
49 Desk item that's shaken
53 Linger
54 Countess's counterpart
55 Actress Bonet
56 ___ House" (1970 Crosby, Stills, Nash & Young hit)
57 Fright ___ (gag item)
58 Instant . . . hinted at four times in this puzzle's circled letters
62 Señora Perón
63 Grimm sister
64 One of 24
65 Kylo ___ of "Star Wars"
66 Bullfighter
67 CPR specialists

DOWN

1 ___-X
2 The Yoko of "Oh Yoko!"
3 Headgear for Laurel or Hardy
4 "Cross my heart!"
5 Jump ___ joy
6 Displayed affection from across the room, say
7 He's got notions
8 Some jeans
9 Small building wing
10 Container for recycling
11 Stuck together, in a way
12 Spaghetti, e.g.
13 Emission from a whistling kettle
18 Bitter ___
22 Peach or persimmon
23 Audibly astonished
24 Undue hurry
26 Rapper on 1988's "Straight Outta Compton"
28 "___ Drives Me Crazy" (Fine Young Cannibals hit)
31 Having misgivings about
32 Shoe insert
34 Part of a house that might have a full house
35 Surmise
36 Exhibiting poor taste
38 Big drag on a fishing expedition?
40 In the style of
43 Place to get a cookie, maybe
46 Yearly honor awarded for each N.F.L. position
48 Lacking grace and refinement
49 Ninja turtle hangout
50 Unwise to the ways of the world
51 Hymn player
52 Edmonton athlete
53 Piggy, in a nursery rhyme
58 Pepper or Friday: Abbr.
59 ___-mo
60 Bolt's counterpart
61 A.M.A. members: Abbr

by Alex Eaton-Salners

ACROSS

1 End of a dorm name, usually
5 Old-fashioned "Jeez!"
10 Huggers
14 Cause for an aha
15 On the up and up
16 One of more than 30,000 in Scotland
17 "A Fish Called Wanda" co-star [7,9]
19 Tapered hairstyle
20 Say "I dunno," say
21 Wolf (down)
23 Female whitetail, e.g.
24 Last ___ (final option)
26 A total blast [8,1]
28 On one side of an outfield pole
30 Sister brand of Crest
31 Pre-weekend outburst
34 Biting remark
37 Ends of mazes
39 "Whew!"
40 Purple Heart honoree, maybe [4,0]
42 Giant in camping gear
43 Reply to "Nuh-uh!"
45 Fully cooked
46 Musician's break
47 Pulse painfully
49 Galifianakis of "Birdman"
51 Eschew scuba gear, say [3,5]
54 Downside of starting a new career path, perhaps
58 Sluglike secretary in "Monsters, Inc."
59 Sulky states
61 Sandwich eaten next to a fire
62 Nano or Touch
64 Some poster-making supplies [2,6]
66 ___ melt
67 Respected person in a tribe
68 Caroler's tune
69 Conform to
70 Landowners' documents
71 Posh shindig

DOWN

1 One often seen wearing boots with shorts
2 Singer with the album "30"
3 ___ Stadium a.k.a. "Field of Jeans"
4 Idled, as workers
5 Animal facing a moose on Michigan's flag
6 Comes together nicely
7 Anti-___ cream
8 Currency of Iraq
9 System that might include a turntable
10 TV ET
11 Impromptu signal to slow down
12 Two-patty burgers introduced in 1997
13 Matte's lack
18 Ruler during the Great Fire of Rome
22 FX series set in the Great Plains
25 Brass instrument with the largest mouthpiece
27 East Asian doctrine
29 Nonkosher cooking fat
31 "Spare me the gory details"
32 Venue for meals with microbrews
33 Acutely focused and attuned
35 Greek "P"
36 German automaker Karl
38 Stand no more, say
40 Tiger on the green
41 Glean
44 Contents of a vein
46 Like 17-, 26-, 40-, 51- and 64-Across, with respect to the numbers in their clues
48 Oversaw?
50 Playbill heading
51 ___-Lay
52 Common city name ending
53 Exercise that works the fingers
55 Hot ___
56 Nerdy "Family Matters" boy
57 Cybertruck maker
60 March Madness datum
63 Word after field or before dreams
65 "For reals," in texts

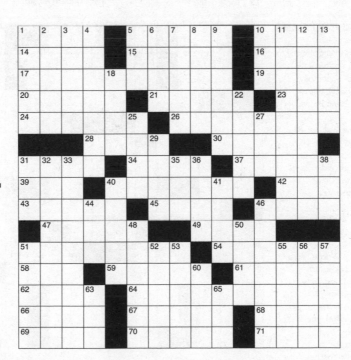

by Adam Aaronson

ACROSS

1 Urgent order
5 Alternatives to dogs
10 Winter hrs. in Seattle
13 "Mas Que ___" (classic Brazilian song from the 1960s)
14 Certain bite risk
16 Quizzical cries
17 Striped polecat's defense
18 ___ pan (kitchen utensil)
19 "The sweetest joy, the wildest ___ is love": Pearl Bailey
20 Important warning before you answer 32-, 40- and 52-Across?
23 Maneuvered (for)
26 Skyline features
27 Skyline feature
28 Top suit
31 Interruption
32 2003 Pixar animated adventure
35 Start to profit?
36 Pad, so to speak
37 Pirates' domain
40 2004 Quentin Tarantino martial arts film
45 Suburb about 20 miles WNW of Boston
47 Low island
48 Birthplace of Pythagoras
49 Petitions
51 "___? We don't need no stinking ___!"
52 1993 Warner Bros. family drama
56 Investment inits.
57 Disinclined
58 Texas is the largest U.S. producer of these
62 Hullabaloo
63 Makes merry
64 Thought
65 Acoustics, for one: Abbr.
66 Striped yellow balls, in pool
67 Stretch in logic

DOWN

1 Year in Brazil
2 Word before case or sack
3 Flurry
4 Chimichurri ingredient
5 Chicks, say
6 Actor Malek
7 ___ Tesfaye, a.k.a. The Weeknd
8 Flooring option
9 Some card readers
10 Standing like Wonder Woman, say
11 They're constantly lapped
12 Kind of fly
15 Jump scares, in horror movies
21 Ideal, informally
22 Gallagher of rock's Oasis
23 Subject line abbr.
24 Home of N.Y.C.'s Public Theater
25 Singer with the 2016 #1 album "This Is What the Truth Feels Like"
28 Apt rhyme for "Rubik"
29 "The ___ Holmes Mysteries," young adult series about a 14-year-old detective
30 Not as expected
33 Kind of branch depicted on German euro coins
34 Formerly known as
38 Political correspondent Mystal
39 [Sigh]
41 Rime
42 Cause to be admired
43 Anachronistic verb in the age of smartphones
44 Lotion alternative
45 Green bugs
46 One of a character class in Dungeons & Dragons
50 Upside-down L, on a calculator
51 Approve
53 Goddess in the Hindu pantheon
54 Small bird with a loud song
55 Man, for one
59 Ending with Gator or hater
60 Rooibos, e.g.
61 Exhaust

by Karen Lurie

Note: This is a "uniclue" crossword, which combines Across and Down. When two answers share a number, they also share a clue.

1 Reposition an icon, maybe
2 Crowd's sound
3 Sub
4 "Check it out for yourself!"
5 Key inspiration?
6 You, in hymns
7 Grande of "The Voice," to fans
8 Alamo offering
9 Kind of fragrant oil in some Asian cuisines
10 Genre with a Hall of Fame in Ohio
11 Daisy variety also called a marguerite
12 Constellation known as the Whale
13 Leslie ___, Amy Poehler's role on "Parks and Recreation"
14 Chocolate-and-caramel candy
15 Number of Brontë sisters or Karamazov brothers
16 Ones with a lot of pull in agriculture?
17 Major crop for Russia and Canada
18 Checks held by Santa?
19 Actor Jared
20 One who wasn't due to arrive, informally
21 Fountain treats
22 Count
23 Poppin', as a party
24 Collect, as profit
25 "___ dreaming?"
26 WNW's opposite
27 Principle of complementary duality
28 Some people bow to it
29 Some protest handouts

30 Did some crunches at lunch?
31 Mass × acceleration, in physics
32 Area near TriBeCa in N.Y.C.
33 Gets comfortable with
34 Chewy Easter treat
35 Plains tribe
36 Bright color in the garden
37 Spoken
38 Italy's Mount ___
39 Things taken in class
40 Mess up
41 Issa of "Insecure"
42 Pleasantly concise
43 Joyful giddiness
44 DC Comics antiheroine a.k.a. Selina Kyle

45 Talk show visitor
46 Loud chewing, for some
47 Id's counterpart
48 Most faithful
49 First vegetable grown in space
50 Lead-in to a culinary attribution
51 Combine, as versatile wardrobe pieces
52 "Veni"
53 Strobe light gas
54 Miracle-___
55 Medieval adventure tale
56 Add fuel to
57 Bears easily
58 Info collected by H.R.
59 Fashion accessories in a 1940s #1 Dinah Shore hit

60 Scholarship consideration
61 PlayStation maker
62 Neutral shades
63 Author of macabre tales, in brief
64 Potpie bit
65 Stackable food item
66 "Let's go already!"
67 Hearty meal options
68 Perceptive
69 Ones tending to brood?
70 Essential ingredient in Welsh rarebit
71 Miniature whirlpool

by Ori Brian

ACROSS

1 It counts on your movements
7 Rev (up)
10 Neighbor for a Syrian
14 Antelope with lyre-shaped horns
15 Loving murmur
16 "Chestnuts roasting ___ open fire"
17 Side Hyde tried to hide
18 TV talent show?
20 Spark of a sort
21 "The Simpsons" character who competed in a crossword tournament
23 Gathering of spies?
24 Ocho ___, Jamaica
26 Eavesdropping on the most conversations, maybe
28 FM band on the radio?
32 Pinkish violet
33 Typical kabuki performer, in any role
34 Round food item with square indentations
38 Blesses
39 Approaches closely
43 Rare tic-tac-toe win
44 Popular samosa filling
46 Aid at a carwash
47 Field of "Mad Men," informally
49 Academy Awards M.C.?
53 "Les Demoiselles d'Avignon" artist
56 Rating one chili pepper, say
57 Ever
58 General meaning
60 Programming language named for a beverage named for an island
64 U.S. symbol?
66 Tied up, as a ship
88 Promotional gift, often
69 Actress Ortiz
70 Mean
71 Minor uproar
72 Place to climb stairs that go nowhere
73 Places

DOWN

1 Many-time "Survivor" locale
2 Invited to chat, in brief
3 Toll rte.
4 Where Silicon Valley is
5 "___ say!"
6 Soap ingredient
7 Deeds
8 Mahatma Gandhi's given name
9 Mascot of the N.F.L.'s Ravens, appropriately
10 Lacking the killer instinct, say
11 Team up
12 Four of the 10 decathlon events
13 Prepared to pray, perhaps
19 Collectible stamp?
22 Prefix with -tonic
25 Hankering
27 Present opener?
28 Complete failure
29 Such as
30 One of two Disney characters singing "For the First Time in Forever"
31 Watch brand for 007
35 Expanse crossed by the Silk Road
36 Enter
37 Exhibit greatly, as charm
40 "The Lord of the Rings" baddies
41 Brownish red
42 It dissolves in H_2O
45 What teaspoons are vis-à-vis tablespoons
48 Many a groaner
50 Setting for Robinson Crusoe
51 Lifesaving inits.
52 Kind of test
53 Sulks
54 "Alternatively . . ."
55 Torch thistles, e.g.
59 Prayer leader
61 Highlight of una scena
62 Sell
63 Goes on to say
65 Give under weight
67 Niagara Falls locale: Abbr.

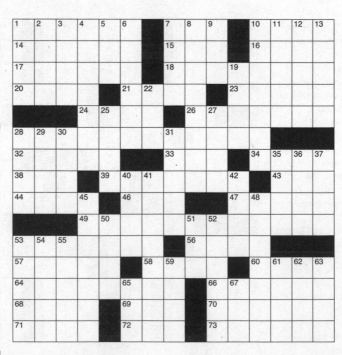

by Howard Barkin

ACROSS

1 Lettuce often used in lettuce wraps
5 Guest essays
10 Major oil acronym
14 Blend of black tea, honey, spices and milk
15 Packed, like a ship with cargo
16 Language of Pakistan
17 First part of a message suggested by this puzzle's circled letters
20 Cloak-and-dagger sort
21 Hypotheticals
22 Wall St. debut
23 Site of a legend
24 One with a venomous bite
26 Many a Jul. 4 party
28 Second part of the message
35 Against
36 Old Toyota coupe
37 Dear's rhyming partner
39 "The Simpsons" prankster
40 Root beer treat
41 Z, in Athens
42 Eldest von Trapp daughter
44 Minecraft block made from gunpowder and sand
45 Sega hedgehog
46 Lead-in to "long"
47 Last part of the message
50 Vegan milk source
51 Plain
53 Genre similar to indie rock
56 Corrects
60 Manhattan district
61 ___ alla vodka
65 Garden hose shape
66 Stratford's river
67 Cinder-to-be
68 Actress Hathaway
69 Parisian papa
70 Furnace/vent connectors
71 Chow

DOWN

1 Includes secretly, in a way
2 Breakfast chain
3 Sacred Indian plant also called the strangler fig
4 Ginormous
5 German chancellor Scholz
6 Caresses
7 End of a college valedictorian's address?
8 Place to nosh on a knish
9 Like some decisions
10 Paris accord?
11 These women "rule" the dance floor
12 Poet ___ St. Vincent Millay
13 Brink
18 Kelly of morning TV
19 Keith of country music
25 Barely rains
27 "Bedtime for ___"
28 Studio sign
29 Beach bottle letters
30 Like pretzels and winter highways
31 Doesn't get fooled by
32 Not as messy
33 Came down with
34 5:1, e.g.
35 Fit
38 Borderline indecent
43 Fallon's late-night predecessor
45 Edible part of asparagus
48 Jabbered
49 Scornful looks
51 Ahead by a run
52 After-dinner coffee order
53 "Stat!"
54 The "heart" of "I [heart] N Y"
55 Avenger with a hammer
57 Taboo
58 Member of the Rat Pack
59 Coaster
62 Member of the ratite pack?
63 43-Down's network
64 Sports barrier . . . or target.

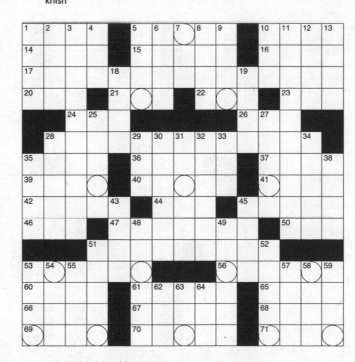

by Michael Schlossberg

ACROSS

1 What hearts and ships may do
5 German physicist after whom a unit of magnetism is named
10 Round houses?
14 "Hmm, OK"
15 Surprise ending, of sorts
16 "I'm starting right now!"
17 Question after a digression
19 Lip
20 Nonkosher lunch order
21 Villain in the DC Universe
22 It can be a show-stopper
24 Foofaraw
25 O.R. staffers
26 "I'm with ___" (2016 campaign slogan)
27 Easy mark
28 Alaskan peak
30 Who wrote "Who controls the past controls the future. Who controls the present controls the past"
32 1970s–'80s Renaults
34 Like a stamp pad
35 Classic John Donne line
38 So-so
40 Republican politico Michael
41 Garden produce named for an Italian city
44 Driller's blowout
48 Grazed
49 Suffer
50 Escort's offering
51 Chopper
52 Young celebrity socialite
54 Something to break at a casino?
55 Be off guard
56 Blacken on a grill

57 Go on horseback à la Lady Godiva
60 "Forever, ___" (1996 humor book)
61 Immobile
62 Wasatch Mountains resort town
63 Tanners' supplies
64 Upstanding fellows
65 Dennis the Menace, e.g.

DOWN

1 Storied mariner
2 Princess in a Wagner opera
3 "Principia" author, 1687
4 London district famous for its botanic garden
5 Picasso antiwar masterpiece
6 Preceder of ski or midi
7 Arenas typically have many of them

8 Finish, with "up"
9 "Fantasia" was the first commercial film shown in it
10 It's measured in feet, not inches
11 Action after a change of mind
12 Rodomontade
13 How mountain roads rise
18 Setting for the 2009 film "Precious"
23 Drop the ball
26 Locale of Wiesbaden, Germany
29 Pearl City greeting
30 Cornmeal dish
31 Red and rosé, for two
33 Adams behind a camera
35 1965 Shirley Ellis hit full of wordplay, with "The"

36 Certain amenities for first-class passengers
37 Michelle Obama vis-à-vis Princeton
38 Cooked slowly in a closed pot
39 Cause for many people to scratch
42 Gob
43 Something well-placed?
45 Take care of
46 Glorifies
47 What two sets of dots within double lines indicate, in musical scores
50 Head off
53 Some long-term plans, in brief
54 It's perfect
58 Like Bach's Partita for Violin No. 3
59 Fist-bump

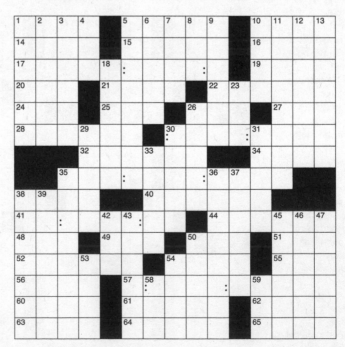

by Lewis Rothlein and Jeff Chen

ACROSS

1 Basis of a trivia question
5 Selects from various places
10 Main component of soapstone
14 Party with poi and poke
15 Threat to the Allies in W.W. II
16 Brouhahas
17 Website links
18 With 20-Across, goes to great lengths
19 Party giver
20 See 18-Across
22 Roll of fabric
23 More reasonable
24 Bottom-first birth position
26 "Scram!"
29 One in peak singing condition?
31 Saint, in Portuguese
32 Pull a fast ___
34 Solidify, as Jell-O
35 With 39-Across, superior
36 See 41-Across
39 See 35-Across
41 With 36-Across, plays dirty
42 "Impressive!"
44 Actress Zellweger
45 "The price is negotiable," in classified ads
46 What might display a little spirit?
49 Airport inits.
50 Prominent Venetian Renaissance painter
52 Particle binding quarks together
54 Like some tales
55 See 60-Across
59 Isolate, in modern lingo
60 With 55-Across, no longer an issue

61 Discovery
62 Notable nights
63 Wear away
64 It might come with breakfast in bed
65 Lead-in to wolf
66 ___-turvy
67 Sources for longbow wood

DOWN

1 Blunder
2 Emanation
3 Class with integrals, for short
4 Walrus weapons
5 Sandwich invented in Florida, despite what its name suggests
6 Took a car, in a way
7 La capital de Inglaterra
8 Fellas

9 Crosswalks cross them: Abbr.
10 Vehicle named after a lake
11 One between 10 and 20, say
12 They're hopeless
13 Winter hrs. in New Orleans
21 Surname of Batman, by day
22 Cold comment?
24 Piano-playing sister in "Little Women"
25 Something brewing
26 Went on a lucky streak
27 Constraining
28 Abstainer from alcohol
30 Tennis call
33 C-section performers
35 "So there you ___!"

37 Pork order
38 Boatload
40 Blunder
43 Style of sneaker
46 Bad, in French
47 Demands blackmail from
48 ___ Beardsley, 19th-century English illustrator
51 Words of concession
53 Dandy
55 Popular boba flavor
56 Grim
57 Chew (on)
58 Brand name in the freezer
59 Do a bit of tailoring
60 Rainy

by Meredith Colton Hazy

ACROSS

1 Aid in woodworking
4 Having excessive pride
8 Neighbor of Francia
14 Chinese "way"
15 Primo
16 Where a sleeping bag may be found
17 Spokeswoman in Progressive insurance ads
18 Warm coals
20 Shakespearean fool
22 Pop singer Jason
23 4G ___ (phone norm)
24 Springs (from)
26 Arnaz of 1950s comedy
27 Sunbeams
28 Hurried home, in a way
30 Beverage brand whose name means "fresh" in Hindi
32 Go for bronze?
33 Walls in a cinema
36 Squeaks (by)
39 Key lime
42 Over again
43 Moviemaker Miyazaki
44 Homophone of a synonym for "obey"
46 Big Board org.
48 Skunk marking
50 1942 romance movie heroine
53 Preceder of Romeo or Bravo
56 Whoop-de-do
57 "Kidding!"
58 "Good enough"
60 Paper view?
61 Proofreader's reminder . . . or some advice for finishing here?
64 Agcy. making lax regs
65 One who makes bail, perhaps
66 Buggy app version, maybe
67 Drink suffix
68 Acquiesce
69 Primer dog
70 Org. Edward Snowden once worked for

DOWN

1 Before knowing more
2 One for whom libel is a major issue
3 Magnifies, in a way
4 Hurl, say
5 Kind of ring or music
6 Nonunion?
7 Sci-fi or romance
8 And so on
9 Dry, as a vino
10 Afg. neighbor
11 Express service since 2000
12 Harebrained
13 Church areas
19 Provide a good reason for
21 King or queen
25 Fibrous
27 IV device found in many homes nowadays
29 Grandma, in Cambridge
31 Beginning of an ordered sequence
34 Game whose board is an 8 x 8 grid
35 Big bygone bird
37 Addis Ababa denizen
38 Goal keepers' kin
40 Suvari of "American Pie"
41 Profs' aides
45 Some of Jordan's border
47 Companions of Dionysus
49 Offspring of Kanga
50 Quechua speakers
51 "___ Doone"
52 Cheap cigar
54 Messes up
55 "Mad Men" worker, in brief
58 "Hmm . . ."
59 Prussia's ___ von Bismarck
62 Foxy
63 Squalled, say

by Adam Wagner

ACROSS

1 & 6 Underwater creature that's not actually a 6-Across
10 "Let's go!"
14 MacDonald's jingle?
15 ___-1 ("Ghostbusters" vehicle)
16 Comb home
17 Part of a palm
18 Reddish-purple side dish
20 Uncle of 1960s TV
22 Security ___
23 & 25 Underwater creature that's not actually a 25-Across
28 Kazakhstan's ___ Sea
31 Conformists, metaphorically
32 Mythical ship that sailed to Colchis
33 Burglarize
34 Lieu
35 Gas brand with a triangular logo
36 & 38 Underwater creature that's not actually a 38-Across (nor a 36-Across, for that matter)
39 Classical performance hall
40 High-ranking Turkish officer
43 ___ Jemison, first Black woman in space
44 Actress Diana of "The Avengers"
45 Arouse, as interest
46 Remain to be seen
47 & 48 Underwater creature that's certainly not a 48-Across
50 Capital that ends with its state's first two letters
52 Yankees' div.
56 They're chucked in a chuck and bored in a board
59 Have a soak
60 Juno's husband
61 Rings at a luau
62 The Ivy League schools, e.g.
63 Gets the picture
64 & 65 Underwater creature that actually IS a 65-Across despite a common misconception

DOWN

1 Actor Goldblum of "The Fly"
2 Cork's land
3 Proud, loyal types, it's said
4 Window frame part
5 Sing in a high range?
6 It changes length every four years: Abbr.
7 It's often made hot and served cold
8 Had the wheel
9 Insight from an insider
10 Latte option
11 Beer o'clock, in commercials
12 Egg cells
13 Leftorium owner on "The Simpsons"
19 Kind of fly
21 Pauses from playing
24 That, in Italian
26 Doctor ___ (Sonic the Hedgehog villain)
27 cc'd, with "in"
28 Equips for battle
29 One who sets the stage
30 Rare blood type
32 Word before drop or ball
34 Virtual city dweller
35 "___-ching!"
37 Barge tower
38 Biblical queendom
40 More difficult to please
41 Like the five animals in this puzzle's theme
42 45, for each row and column in a sudoku grid
45 Southwest settlement
46 "You said it!"
48 Sgt.'s inferior
49 Place to find a crook
51 Corrida cheers
53 Lead-in to girl
54 Author Silverstein
55 French "noodle"
56 45 spinners
57 Preschool group?
58 Org. for retirees

by Grant Thackray

ACROSS

1 Sharp bend
7 Tipping point?
10 Intro course?
13 "Fa-a-ancy!"
14 Heap praise on
16 Home of the Boston Mountains
17 Polite Spanish assent
18 Online fad
19 Pricing word
21 Just the worst, in slang
22 "The time for diplomacy has passed"
24 Women's soccer and gymnastics powerhouse
25 "___ Blues" (song on the Beatles' "White Album")
26 Treatment plants?
28 Letters of qualification
31 Sweet sign-off
32 Trees sacred to Hecate
33 Prey for a heron
34 ___ Poovie ("Gomer Pyle, U.S.M.C." character)
36 Sounds from a pond at night
38 French agreements
39 Stone with "fire" and "water" varieties
43 "Ish"
44 Unspecified ordinal
45 Travelocity spokescreature
46 Make a pick
47 Bird found in the mud?
49 Pea, e.g.
51 "Death of a Salesman" surname
53 It may turn slowly in a horror movie
54 Denny's competitor

58 "What a pity"
60 Liken
62 Attend to details . . . or a hint to entering six Down answers in this puzzle
63 Applies, as lotion
64 [Some of us are trying to watch the movie here!]
65 "Success!"
66 Trickled

DOWN

1 Destine for failure
2 Trickle
3 Rock genre for Roxy Music
4 Southern border city in a Larry McMurtry title
5 Game measured by its number of points

6 Elements No. 7, 8, 9 and 10, e.g.
7 Certain martial arts takedown
8 Word after bad or hard
9 ___ monkey
10 Trendy brunch order
11 Benefit
12 Really hope
14 Proportionate size for some model trains
15 It's a lot to carry
20 Online status
23 1982 film set in a mainframe
25 "It's not hard to guess how this will end"
27 Key to a quick exit?
29 Shark species with the largest brain-to-body ratio
30 Some E.R. cases

31 Strike
33 Underwater weapon-launching apparatus
34 Horror star Chaney
35 Stop start?
37 2003 cult film known as the "'Citizen Kane' of bad movies," with "The"
40 Spotty pattern
41 Modifies
42 Kind of block
45 Afraid to commit, say
48 Actor Bomer of "Magic Mike"
50 Gets a ride, in a way
51 '65 Ford debuts
52 "Me! Pick me!"
55 Locking mechanism
56 Great Plains tribe
57 Await a ruling
59 "Isn't that obvious?"
61 "___ es eso?"

by August Miller

ACROSS

1 Weak hit
6 Big hit
11 Speak disrespectfully to
15 Hindi for "palace"
16 Mischievous fairy
17 "___ Homo" (Nietzsche book)
18 Worker designation coined by Upton Sinclair
20 Key that's never used alone: Abbr.
21 Sign of a packed house
22 "Confound it!"
23 Disney mermaid
24 Traditional folk song played by British and Australian ice cream trucks
28 Devoid of pleasure
32 French trick-taking game
33 Really bothered
34 Doughnut shapes
35 Get ready
38 Envy source in Genesis 37 that hints at 18-, 24-, 49- and 58-Across
42 Steve with eight N.B.A. championships
43 They're placed in locks
44 Signs of saints
45 Cry for help
47 Most likely to preen
49 Upside, when down
52 Characteristic
53 "Understood"
54 "The Problem With ___" (documentary related to "The Simpsons")
57 Letter after theta
58 Some sushi menu fish
62 Tech review site
63 Like prunes vis-à-vis plums
64 Nonstudio film
65 Sedgwick of "The Closer"
66 "The Lorax" author
67 Stun gun

DOWN

1 X1, M2 and i3
2 Cowardly Lion portrayer
3 Lima's home
4 Nondairy milk option
5 Promise that one will
6 Mushrooms produce them
7 Children's author who wrote "People say nothing is impossible, but I do nothing every day"
8 Rose of Guns N' Roses
9 "Cheap Thrills" singer, 2016
10 That ship
11 Scheme
12 Important part
13 Rocky debris
14 What sex does, they say
19 Train units
23 ___ Lingus
25 Highlighter shades
26 Prognosticate with a crystal ball
27 Secular
28 Plug receptacle
29 First Native American tribe to meet with Lewis and Clark
30 After quite some time
31 Verdi opera originally titled "Amore e Morte" ("Love and Death")
34 Foot bones
36 Cherubic god
37 "You there!"
39 Author Jonathan Safran ___
40 Rough up
41 Line when you're late to the punch line
46 Dog doc
47 Features of some bike helmets
48 Freshly
49 Carrot's counterpart
50 Complaining about social media on Facebook, say
51 Frasier's brother on "Frasier"
54 Gives a hand
55 Ballet bend
56 Employer
58 R.B.'s stat
59 Before, to Shakespeare
60 Simu ___, star of "Shang-Chi and the Legend of the Ten Rings"
61 Santa ___, Calif.

by Rich Proulx

ACROSS

1 [I'm speechless!]
5 Float
9 Italian car, informally
13 Northeast Corridor train
15 1934 novel made into a hit 1970s BBC/PBS miniseries
17 Hawaii's "Pineapple Isle"
18 Bus excursions to see homes of celebrities
19 At the party where the scientist was demonstrating her new shrink ray, [ZAP!] the punch ladle turned into a . . .
21 Analogy words
22 West ___ (furniture chain)
25 Family
28 When the appetizers were passed around, [ZAP!] the potato wedges turned into . . .
34 Exaggerate, as a stage role
36 Flag down
37 Sweetheart, in modern lingo
38 When the main course was ready, [ZAP!] the six-foot hoagie turned into an . . .
42 ___ Faire (historical festival, informally)
43 Territory
44 Didn't dive (into)
45 When the dessert was brought out, [ZAP!] the pudding cake turned into a . . .
49 Boris Johnson, e.g.
50 Mum's mum
51 Principal
53 Finally, when the still-hungry guests went back for more, [ZAP!] the additional helpings turned into . . .

61 Language that gave us "aardvark"
64 "Middlemarch" author
65 Prepare for cold weather
66 Dig (into)
67 Taobao, the so-called "___ of China"
68 Citrus drinks
69 Trickle

DOWN

1 Audacity
2 It's berry tasty!
3 On cloud nine
4 Credit card status
5 Domain of Athena
6 Stage opening
7 Tizzy
8 Bit of weatherproofing
9 Devotee
10 ___ Yifei, star of 2020's "Mulan"
11 Something traded at a trading post
12 Ding-dong
14 Isn't well
16 People for whom a state is named
20 Supposed creators of crop circles, for short
23 Longing to go to bed?
24 More grinchlike
25 Bracelet item
26 Triangular sail
27 King of the Egyptian gods
29 Leave in ___
30 Setting for the 1962 hit "Monster Mash"
31 Calculus calculation: Abbr.
32 Scratch or nick
33 Ramshackle
35 A.C.C. team, informally
39 Mongrel
40 ___ Lanka
41 Squalid abodes
46 Hostile state
47 Misses abroad
48 Before, in verse
52 Kept informed, in a way
54 Old presidential nickname
55 Italian term of endearment
56 It's a bust
57 Eleven, to an élève
58 Home for many hippos
59 Magician's bird
60 Put one's foot down
61 Dazzle
62 "You've hardly aged a bit," usually
63 Genetic material

by Aaron M. Rosenberg

ACROSS
1 Common hotel room item
6 Judi Dench, since 1988
10 Bruins' sch.
14 Pinhead
15 Puff piece?
16 Letters after pis
17 Sneaking suspicion
19 "Get ___!"
20 Purl counterpart
21 Pirate whose hidden treasure inspired "The Gold-Bug"
22 Largest city in North Dakota
23 Cozy lodging
24 Farm female
25 Turn down a request
27 Doctrine
29 An ironic punch line
33 100%
35 Word in favor
36 Dynamic start?
37 Accept a package formally . . . or a hint to 17-, 29-, 45- and 62-Across?
42 Burden
43 Reine's husband
44 Parrot
45 Rough flight
48 Get on a soapbox
52 Architect Frank ___ Wright
53 1960s fashion style
55 Dallas player, informally
56 Like almost two-thirds of the earth's population
58 Costa ___
60 Social media-induced anxiety, for short
61 Pint-size
62 Reason to pause a workout
64 First world?
65 Shrek, e.g.
66 Buffalo hockey player
67 Noted enforcer of Prohibition
68 Solutions
69 Strait-laced

DOWN
1 One no longer using a sippy cup, say
2 "Beats the heck out of me"
3 Acerbic
4 Certain overhead apartment
5 When to take a cruise on la Seine
6 Get fuzz out of
7 "Salt Fat ___ Heat" (popular cookbook)
8 Imagination
9 To use this you'll need to get cracking
10 One who recreationally explores sewers and underground tunnels
11 Like Sequoyah, for whom the tree is named
12 The "L" of LP
13 Apropos of
18 Scrape (out)
22 Letters accompanying a tip
24 What 12 is, to this clue's number
26 Mowgli's friend in "The Jungle Book"
28 Speaks patronizingly, in a way
30 Supermodel Gigi or Bella
31 Go astray
32 Family name on HBO's "Succession"
34 Truck, in Tottenham
37 Cry hard
38 Shiba ___ (dog breed)
39 Teeth disappear under them
40 Angry outburst from a bodybuilder, maybe
41 Apple product
46 Over there, quaintly
47 They run the show
49 Simple creature
50 Gluten-free Japanese soy sauce
51 Drew out, as a smile
54 Implement with a flat head
56 "You can say that again!"
57 Faction
59 "Just doing my job"
60 Bunch of brothers, for short
62 Concave cookware
63 Some STEM degs.

by Rose Conlon

ACROSS

1 Parties with smokers
7 "In what universe?!"
11 Positive consideration
14 Make available
15 "Holy cannoli!"
16 Spreadsheet part
17 Wight, e.g.?
19 ___ Productions (company behind the James Bond films)
20 Deployed, as a naval officer
21 Rum drum
22 Soul mates, for short
23 Experienced certain growing pains
25 Emulate the Lonely Goatherd
28 Crunch bar and Cadbury Creme Egg, e.g.?
32 Give it a twirl!
35 Tennis's Nadal, familiarly
36 Test for coll. seniors
37 Word after gay or fashion
38 Thingamajigs
40 One observing the holiday of Arba'een
41 Common Thanksgiving activity
42 Home for the Himalayas
43 When some local news comes on
44 1995's "Johnny Mnemonic," e.g.?
48 With the heels elevated
49 Smash success
53 Landlocked African country
55 Go yachting
57 Medieval club
58 Squirreled away
59 Sloth, e.g.?
62 & 63 Test for pupils
64 Beat overwhelmingly
65 It may be revolutionary
66 Monocle, basically
67 Apartment building V.I.P.s

DOWN

1 What most clarinets are tuned to
2 Became apparent
3 ___ Montgomery, retired W.N.B.A. star
4 Shameless fund-raising drive, informally
5 Who is this in France
6 See 31-Down
7 Handled sharp objects?
8 Deliberately amateurish filming technique
9 Particle with a superscript
10 Flavor of the month
11 When pilots go through their checklists
12 Feature of Arthur Ashe Stadium since 2016
13 Has
18 Youth health and safety org.
22 Resting place
24 Chinese dynasty from 206 B.C. to A.D. 220
26 Keystone Kops, e.g.
27 What makes you unique
29 Band with the first platinum-selling double album
30 Northernmost county of Pennsylvania
31 With 6-Down, former White House press secretary portrayed by Melissa McCarthy on "S.N.L."
32 Donation receptacles
33 Source of a purple purée
34 Washing machine that opens upward
38 Analogy words
39 Window, of a sort
40 Gets foggy
42 Leaf-cutter, e.g.
43 2008 bailout recipient
45 Abolish
46 Leave out
47 Both consonants in "geek," phonetically
50 Celerity
51 Less sympathetic
52 Is prone
53 Mull (over)
54 "Greetings!"
56 Goes (for)
59 Animation frame
60 Eliminate
61 "Rugrats" grandpa

by Jake Halperin

ACROSS

1 The girl next door, for one
6 Polite term of address
10 Claire Dunphy of "Modern Family," for one
15 Act like some poles
16 One joining in the chorus
17 Energy-healing discipline
18 Put in the pot
19 Eager
20 Record of the year
21 Three world capitals (5,4,10)
24 My Chemical Romance genre
25 "Groovy!"
26 "Fancy ___!"
27 Like some meds
29 Hired security guard
32 Sounds of hesitation
33 Pi follower
34 ___ Lovelace, computer programming pioneer
35 Display one's humanity, in a way
37 Visible
38 Three U.S. states (4,4,10)
43 Racing shape
44 Metaphor for many a college dorm room
45 Dug-out material
46 Gun, as an engine
47 Club workers, informally
49 Malt shop selections
54 Sr.'s test
55 "Bummer!"
57 Cow's mouthful
58 Sorrow
59 Three countries (6,4,9)
63 Believe unquestioningly
64 Speaker's quality
65 Going from 0 to 100, say

66 Line to the house
67 Put forth
68 Role once played on TV by Jay Silverheels
69 You, in Uruguay
70 Big name in little gumdrops
71 Spurred (on)

DOWN

1 Post office inquiry
2 Edit, in a way, as a computer file
3 Possibility
4 Jury member
5 Sir Walter Raleigh's goal
6 Manage
7 Longtime "Jeopardy!" host Trebek
8 Wiped out
9 French term of endearment
10 Large expanses
11 Start of a Caesarean boast
12 Cookie with a green creme center
13 "Well, alrighty!"
14 "Cool" amount of cash
22 Colorful parrot
23 Something a coxswain lacks
28 Pro's counterpart
30 Follow closely
31 Annoyance
36 Jean who wrote "Wide Sargasso Sea"
37 Dance element
38 Part of a highway cloverleaf
39 "Dig right in!"
40 Per the preceding discussion
41 "Obvs!"
42 Degree recipient
43 United Nations, e.g.: Abbr.
47 Hung loosely
48 ___ session
50 Stable electron configurations
51 Admitting to, as a mistake
52 Ballet technique
53 Neptune, for one
56 Replay feature
60 Neutral lipstick shade
61 Monogram part: Abbr.
62 Brimming with anticipation
63 ___ de parfum?

by Dylan Schiff

ACROSS

1 Earth and Mars, e.g.
5 "Office-inappropriate" tag
9 1:15 or 1:30, e.g.
13 Part of a comparison
14 Its motto is "Fiat lux"
15 Part of a guitar
16 *Rosh Hashana and Yom Kippur
18 "If you come to___ not understanding who you are, it will define who you are": Oprah Winfrey
19 H.S. class
20 Regarding this matter
22 Trick
23 Rolls follower
25 *The wolf in "Peter and the Wolf"
27 ___ People's Democratic Republic
29 Goddess whose name means "lovely"
30 Airport aprons
34 Representation
35 Simple recipe instruction . . . or a hint to the answers to the four starred clues
37 Measures of cellular strength
38 Counters
39 She met her husband Frank after beating him in a shooting match
41 Not just "a"
42 *Cape Cod retreats
46 It's famous for doing the floss
50 ___canto
51 Actor Jeremy of "The Hurt Locker"
53 "The ___ of Pooh"
54 City on the Rhône
56 *Last possible second
58 Formerly, once
59 Its motto is "Lux et veritas"
60 Make binding, in a way
61 Meeting, informally
62 Feels crummy
63 Not just smart

DOWN

1 [Not shown here]
2 It has Javan and Sumatran varieties
3 Like Hammer pants
4 Show that spawned "Wayne's World," in brief
5 Wearing just a smile, say
6 Accessory for a soccer fan
7 Philadelphia athlete
8 Eggshells and coffee grounds, typically
9 Switch position
10 Some street fights?
11 Soul sucker in the Harry Potter books
12 Western hat
17 Start of some souvenir shirt slogans
21 Small bill
24 Like works of Shakespeare or Frank Sinatra
26 Varmint
28 Ilhan in Congress
30 See red?
31 Punchy ending?
32 AOL freebies, once
33 "M*A*S*H" Emmy winner
35 1847 novel originally subtitled "An Autobiography"
36 Where flotsam and jetsam may end up
37 Talks endlessly
40 It covers 6.8% of the earth's land area: Abbr.
43 "Bye!"
44 China's Zhou ___
45 Fishhook attachment
47 Top story
48 Crack up
49 Lifted
52 Some big nights
55 Advanced degree?
57 Org. whose logo has an eagle grasping a key

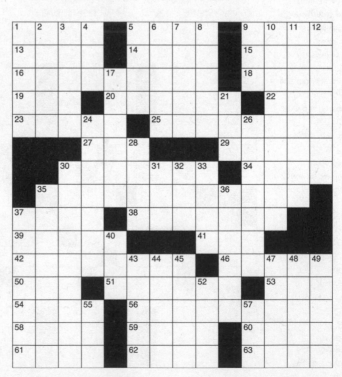

by August Lee-Kovach

ACROSS

1 Italian sauce with meat and tomatoes
5 Person seeking damages
9 Letter that's only 25% of the way through the Greek alphabet, surprisingly
13 Cheers for banderilleros
14 Martial artist/actor who played the emperor of China in 2020's "Mulan"
15 Good name for an ophthalmologist
16 "You and I should eat that"
18 Salmon, e.g.
19 Force out
20 Flowering plants associated with the Augusta National golf course
22 Utter
23 Actress Garr
25 Dating app description
26 Kid at a college bar who seems, to me as a bouncer, too young to allow in
32 Palestinian president starting in 2005
34 Place
35 Calendar box
36 Essential point
37 Bill worth billions
39 When most Geminis are born
40 Spoil
41 Dog breed whose coat resembles dreadlocks
42 Drinks at soda shops
43 Easter item that the woman is going to decorate
47 More, in Mexico
48 Short johns?
49 Nowhere to be found, informally
52 Risk territory bordering Siberia
56 Sponsored boys at baptisms
58 Desertlike
59 What the couple dressed in lupine costumes said
61 It's worth zero in baccarat
62 Gets wind of
63 Land whose prime minister is known as the Taoiseach
64 "For Pete's ___!"
65 Stops waffling
66 Licks, maybe

DOWN

1 Hats, so to speak
2 Siri : Apple :: ___ : Amazon
3 Seat of Pennsylvania's Adams County
4 Losing team in the "Miracle on Ice" hockey game
5 Harsh
6 Shoshonean language
7 Director Kazan
8 Little Nabisco crackers
9 Bag brand
10 Great Lakes port
11 Mother of Beyoncé and Solange Knowles
12 Requests
14 Affected by ennui
17 Most Rwandans and Burundians
21 Member of a support staff
24 Impart, as values
27 Dodgers might not pay it
28 "Jeopardy!" impossibility
29 XXX film
30 Speak hysterically
31 Batiking needs
32 High point
33 Talk big
37 "Tell me if you recognize me from just my voice and the feel of my hands over your eyes"
38 Last word of the Pledge of Allegiance
39 Middle Brady family daughter
41 Cool, in old slang
42 Botch
44 Photocopy flaw
45 Waiters at busy restaurants might be handed them
46 Declares openly
50 Like helium
51 Sure-footed pack animals
52 Sure-footed pack animals
53 Number that's often in Italian
54 Sharp twist, as in a hose
55 Remain fresh
57 Whole bunch
60 Tattletale

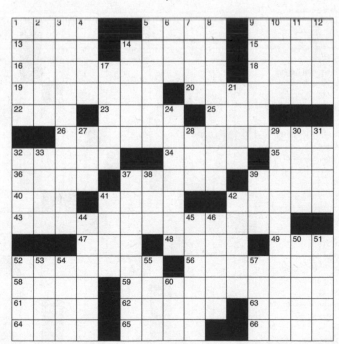

by Peter Gordon

ACROSS

1 "Mad Men" milieu, informally
6 Slammin' Sammy ____
10 33⅓, 45 and 78, for short
14 Sorceress who turned Odysseus' men into pigs
15 Exam that qualifies one for a National Merit Scholarship
16 First name of Time's 2021 Person of the Year
17 Equestrian is wanted to . . . / Experience needed: conducting
19 Smooth over, in a way
20 Prankster's projectile
21 Parches
22 Dummy, in Canadian slang
23 Baseball pitcher is wanted to . . . / Experience needed: negotiating
26 Scintilla
27 Hearing disorder remedy?
28 Movement that began with Stonewall, informally
30 It begins "again"
33 Build
35 Words of begrudging agreement
36 Washington, but not Washington, D.C. (yet!)
38 Tied up
39 "No hard feelings"
41 Número de días en una semana
42 Exclaim
43 End of a trip?
45 Biathletes do it
46 Carpenter is wanted to . . . / Experience needed: flying
51 Places where you might ask for the Wi-Fi password
53 Draws the short straw
54 Yours: It.
55 Drop it!
56 Change careers, or a hint to this puzzle's theme
58 Kicked oneself over
59 What's picked up in a hurry?
60 Basic skateboard trick
61 Online crafts marketplace
62 Member of the "Scooby-Doo" gang
63 Shirts named for a sport

DOWN

1 Showed some character?
2 Somber song
3 Actress Sonia of "Moon Over Parador"
4 "Nous sommes ____!"
5 Youngest person to win the Emmy for Outstanding Lead Actress in a Drama Series (2020)
6 Cocktail made with sparkling wine
7 Willow used in basket-weaving
8 Cause for pity
9 Dug in
10 Collector's item?
11 DC Comics supervillain
12 Museum curator is wanted to . . . / Experience needed: freestyle dancing
13 Mortimer ____, ventriloquy dummy of old TV
18 Brit's bottom
22 Casual greetings
24 Chill
25 Danny who played Walter Mitty
29 Latin for "lust"
30 Plant on a farm . . . or animal on a farm
31 Nurse is wanted to . . . / Experience needed: philanthropy
32 Alarms
33 Bud
34 Human organ with its own immune system
36 Kind of food or music
37 All-out military conflict
40 Steals, slangily
41 Grinder vendor
43 Checked out
44 In ____ verba (verbatim)
45 Alarm
47 "Neat"
48 Volcanic vestige
49 Politician Marco
50 Just what the doctor ordered
52 Swirl in a toilet bowl, say
56 Burn notice?
57 "Hustlers" co-star, informally

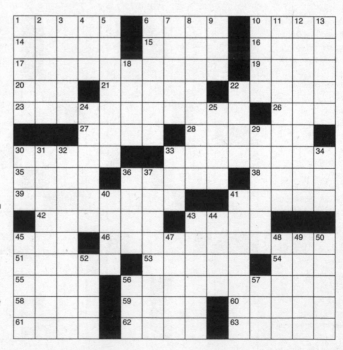

by John Westwig

ACROSS

1 Duck
6 Imaginary ordinal
9 Duck
14 Word of leave-taking
15 Swing ____ (1933–47)
16 Tablecloths and napkins
17 Duck
19 It could be a problem
20 Strategically evasive
21 Handout for a walking tour
23 Cosy "spot"
24 Mike of "Shrek"
25 ____ Duck
27 Total disarray
30 Heavenly: Prefix
32 Attachment for a bit
33 Big snarl
37 Print "oopses"
40 Examine
41 Be in a mood and brood
42 Wet wood woe
43 Largest lake in Ethiopia
44 Average mark
45 Has in hand
46 Duck, e.g.
50 Lightning strike
51 Cotton gin inventor Whitney
52 A chance of a lifetime, say
55 Raphael's weapon in "Teenage Mutant Ninja Turtles"
58 "The Duck Variations" playwright
60 Duck
62 Mexican pal
63 Conger, for one
64 Swiss author of "Elements of Algebra"
65 Duck
66 Pigpen
67 "Duck, duck . . ." follower

DOWN

1 High-rise units: Abbr.
2 ____ parmigiana
3 Like many a barrel-aged wine
4 "Rocks" in a tumbler
5 Molds, e.g.
6 "Henceforth I ____ will be Romeo"
7 Keep close to one's heart
8 No ____, no foul
9 Laceless shoes
10 What a flat "b" palm facing a nearby fellow stands for, in A.S.L.
11 Pic-sharing app, informally
12 The second "R" in J. R. R. Tolkien
13 Prepare to proof, in baking
18 It's mined, all mined!
22 "It's ____!" ("We're on!")
24 Butterfly also called a common tiger or wanderer
26 Perpetual
27 Street ____ (rep)
28 What to call a man in Mannheim
29 Like cheese puffs and rice cakes
31 Tampa Bay pro
34 List ender: Abbr.
35 Transmit
36 Opening on Christmas Eve?
38 In direct confrontation
39 Used as a dining surface
45 Coatroom fixture
46 "Fine, stay angry then!"
47 Mission to remember in San Antonio
48 Skittish
49 Sís and das
50 Scene of pandemonium
53 Editor's "Forget I wrote that"
54 Sanctified
55 Musician's chance to shine, perhaps
56 Flabbergasts or gobsmacks
57 Memo subject header
59 Something a duck lays
61 Bugs and Daffy in "The Iceman Duckoth," e.g.

by Joseph Gangi

ACROSS

1 Something to click
5 Pigeons on a platter
11 ___ trivia
14 Astronomical news
15 Term of address for many a respected elder
16 Strand in a cell
17 Serious schlep
18 *Secure
20 Monstrous sort
21 Nail polish brand with an "I'm Not Really a Waitress" shade
22 Give permission to
23 *Trick
26 Some frozen drinks
27 Global manufacturer of chemical products
28 What Graham Greene called a "failure of imagination"
30 Unflinching
32 Requested pickup time on many online orders
34 "How's it goin'?"
37 What to do before the answers to the starred clues will make sense
41 Boom times
42 Voting bloc
43 Didn't wax, say
44 Incense, in a sense
46 Senate majority leader from 1996 to 2001
47 Like men's double-breasted suits, e.g.
50 *Speck
55 Destination of the first marathon (490 B.C.)
57 ___-roaring
58 Words that may scare off a buyer
59 *Riot
61 Afflictions
62 Number of a certain rear bowling pin

63 The hair of one's chinny chin chin, maybe
64 Get on board
65 Neighbor of Bolivia: Abbr.
66 ___ manual
67 Optometrist's offering, casually

DOWN

1 Being pulled along
2 Short-legged herding dog
3 Totally misses . . . or totally surveys
4 Uncouth untruth
5 Watering hole in many westerns
6 Wisecracks
7 Leave with no strings attached?
8 QB stat: Abbr.
9 Bitter feeling
10 Words repeated while scrolling through a Netflix list, perhaps
11 Voyager 1, for one
12 Cry to end a pin
13 Makes, as cakes
19 ___ to the bottom
24 Having mucho dinero
25 "___ of Sunset" (Bravo series)
29 Galoot
30 Disco-dancing enthusiast on "The Simpsons"
31 Select
32 Company whose name comes from a term in the game of Go
33 Farm outbuilding
34 Popular site for holiday gift orders
35 Application
36 Many a prof has one

38 ___ Attack (card game variant)
39 Uncommon bills
40 Some hairstyles in punk fashion
44 ___ O's
45 "Wait!"
46 Expires
47 Certain Pan-Africanist, informally
48 Air up there
49 Flip-flop
51 Keynote, e.g.
52 Car part that moves rhythmically
53 What a jalapeño has that a habanero lacks
54 One of England's so-called "home counties"
56 Boat that's good in shallow water
60 Took off

by Daniel Bodily and Jeff Chen

ACROSS

1 Quite dry, but sparkling?
5 Swallow or duck
9 Instrument with 47 strings and seven pedals
13 ___ fide
14 Proven
15 Hummus, e.g.
16 FLIP
18 Paperless return option
19 Altercation
20 FLOP
22 Itsy-bitsy biter
25 Volunteers
26 FLIP-FLOP
30 Metonym for the U.S. Congress, with "the"
31 Cheney in the House
32 Matches up
36 Mathematician Lovelace
37 Rock band that memorably played Carnegie Hall on 2/12/1964, with "the"
40 One of the Manning brothers
41 Verboten
43 Polish off
44 Goal of philanthropy
45 FLIP-FLOP
49 Dr. Montgomery on "Grey's Anatomy"
52 Fancy pillowcase
53 FLIP
55 Doesn't buy, say
59 Make a knot not?
60 FLOP
63 Education professional
64 Drink of Athens
65 Asics competitor
66 Famed English boarding school
67 Stepped
68 Andrew who ran for president and mayor of New York City

DOWN

1 Cookouts, for short
2 Cad
3 Newton, for one
4 Like whatever comes after "How should I put this?"
5 "Dynamite" boy band
6 Part of a nest egg, in brief
7 Word that may be defiantly rhymed with "schmool"
8 Intensify
9 With a chip on one's shoulder
10 Challenging soprano pieces, say
11 Kindled anew
12 Pre-pares potatoes?
15 Place to play dodgeball, informally
17 Caffeine nut
21 Many a swing voter: Abbr.
23 Magazine that sponsors Women in Hollywood awards
24 Home to more than 2,300 languages
26 Zoom window
27 Verdi opera set in ancient Egypt
28 It's a piece of cake!
29 Culture that introduced popcorn to the world
33 Light element
34 One of a pair in the mule family?
35 Pro or con
37 Third shot, for many
38 Big name in chips
39 Make one's mark, in a way
42 Polling subject
44 Time for tailgating
46 ___ roll (Brits' term for toilet paper)
47 Where the cool kids go
48 "Listen!"
49 Less than right
50 Food with a hole
51 "So do I"
54 Curved line over a series of notes, in sheet music
56 Flare up?
57 Single bed, curiously
58 Cause for a run, maybe
61 Emmy-winning actress Aduba
62 Wordlessly agree

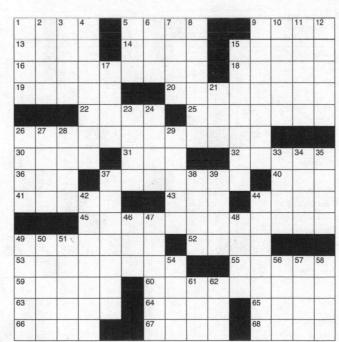

by Barbara Lin

ACROSS

1 Big position for an M.B.A.
4 Email folder
8 ___ buddy
13 Language that gave us "pajamas"
15 ___ Minor
16 Emcee's warm-up
17 Sustainable water receptacles
19 Sports-star-turned-model Gabrielle
20 Place to order sake and sashimi
21 Where values may be taught
23 Summer setting for Toronto: Abbr.
24 Where the tibia is
26 Attention-getter
27 "Mr. Roboto" band
28 Banned from trade or commerce
31 Sound check sound
34 Strip of computer shortcuts
35 Brita competitor
36 Revered figure
37 Half of an old movie duo
39 Machu Picchu locale
40 Have a little lamb?
41 Elvis Presley's middle name
42 Seasonal drink
44 Get off
46 New York City's ___ Delano Roosevelt Park
47 Where you might find very little liquor
48 Marvel mischief-maker
49 East Coast and West Coast educational inits.
52 Like many endangered species
55 Fastest of three famous ships
57 Many Bhangra dancers
58 Heighten expectations, say . . . or a hint to entering four answers in this puzzle
60 Some nasty weather
61 "The jig ___!"
62 Shabby establishment
63 Towel cloth
64 "Goodness me!"
65 Stroke . . . or the object of strokes

DOWN

1 Malediction
2 Credit card issue
3 Poet who's full of praise
4 California's Big ___
5 Blend before use
6 Lion of Narnia
7 Overseas post?
8 Traditional canoe material
9 What a pirouette is performed on
10 Secretly unseal, in a way
11 Tolkien monsters
12 Homer's local watering hole
14 Home of some N.C.A.A. Wildcats
18 One with the grounds to serve you?
22 Nonkosher entree
25 Like oxygen therapy chambers
27 Subway stop: Abbr.
28 Word with dog or elephant
29 100-cent unit
30 Acetaminophen, for one
31 Even
32 Bowl berry
33 High-minded sort?
34 Part of a royal flush
38 ___ choy
39 Org. for paid drivers
41 Official pardon
43 Complaint
45 This or that
46 About 40% of table salt
48 Lead
49 Not cool
50 "Stone Cold" ___ Austin (TV host/wrestler)
51 Club with dinner and a show
52 Attention-getter
53 Provoke, with "up"
54 The good fairies in "Sleeping Beauty," e.g.
56 "___ be great if . . ."
59 Person with intelligence

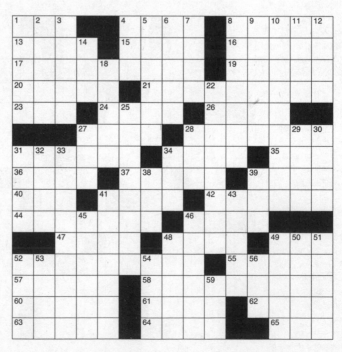

by Jess Shulman

ACROSS

1 They may be switched while cycling
6 Shorthand pro
11 Crossword solver's cry
14 Deity with 99 names
15 Raphael, Gabriel or Michael
17 Cradlin' a Salinger protagonist?
19 Preserve, as ashes
20 Vodka brand
21 "Footloose" star cookin' a fresh batch of brownies?
26 "Need an ark? I Noah guy," and others
27 Blond at the bar, say
28 Letters on a luxury handbag
29 Chips brand
31 Sentence . . . or something found in a sentence
33 Did so-so at school
34 The Great Emancipator sharin' URLs on his blog?
40 Cover for illicit activity
41 "Right on!"
43 "I don't want to hear the gory details"
46 ____-C.I.O.
49 Strands in a cell
50 Four-time Grammy winner India.____
51 Bein' in debt to a "Wedding Crashers" co-star?
54 Some burrowing mouselike rodents
56 One-point Scrabble draw
57 Massachusetts senator wagin' conflict?
63 Houseplant that some think brings luck and prosperity
64 One in 1,000?
65 Beat it!
66 Bee teem?
67 Internet admin

DOWN

1 Cry of frustration
2 Chess rating system
3 ____ fours
4 Minute hands, essentially
5 Climb (up), as a pole
6 Related to religious rites
7 Sedative in a blowgun dart, informally
8 Old French coin
9 Org. for Ducks and Penguins
10 Bunglers
11 Get too old to qualify
12 "Over my dead body!"
13 Hugo-winning "Hothouse" author Brian
16 Particularly particular
18 Pencil remnants
21 Actress Dennings
22 Philosopher Zeno's birthplace
23 Crow, but not magpie
24 "American ____"
25 "Moi? Never!"
30 Went on, as an errand
32 Gotham City supervillain in a cryogenic suit
33 Intl. standard used by many astrologers
35 Amount to
36 Our genus
37 Freshly
38 Roadside bombs, for short
39 One-billionth: Prefix
42 Solo in spaceflight?
43 "I need a hero!"
44 Computer language that sounds like a literary intro
45 Under the weather
46 "Ode to Joy," for the European Union
47 Texter's "I think"
48 New Hampshire state flowers
52 Bury
53 The "L" of Samuel L. Jackson
55 Declares
58 As an aside, in a text
59 The "E" of B.C.E.
60 Info in an apt. listing
61 Texter's "I think"
62 Catch some Z's

by Jack Murtagh

ACROSS

1 Beat in chess
5 Astronomer who lost part of his nose in a sword duel
10 Classic Jumbotron shout-out
14 Frost
15 Takes a bit off
16 Certain newspaper column
17 Boot
18 Sorna y Nublar, en "Jurassic Park"
19 Long locks
20 Educator in a smock
22 Figure seen on Athena's shield
23 Thumbs-up
24 Skim
26 Bit of letter-shaped hardware
28 Rangers' domain
32 Thoroughbred, e.g.
36 FedEx Cup organizer
37 ___ of war
38 Bluish hues
40 Muslim leaders
41 "A Promised Land" author, 2020
43 Get into trouble, in a way
45 Grassy expanse
46 Some drinking vessels
48 Kind of zone in a city
50 1948 Literature Nobelist
52 Youngest player to score in the FIFA World Cup (age 17)
53 Two-word tribute
55 Bottle topper
59 Profession in an O'Neill title
62 What "should be made by filling a glass with gin, then waving it in the general direction of Italy," per Noël Coward
64 Declare
65 Kid-lit character with a green suit and gold crown
66 Midrange club
67 Award-winning Ward

68 Chess : check :: go : ___
69 "Pretty please?"
70 Geekish
71 Fixes
72 Big name in printers

DOWN

1 Now: Sp.
2 Talks up
3 Some bridge positions
4 Leader of the house band on "The Muppet Show"
5 Low-budget feature
6 Like decisions made on a dare, typically
7 "Stormy Weather" composer
8 Learn secondhand
9 Either end of a school bus?
10 Side that usually has the most supporters
11 Device used in interactive museum displays
12 What a "hamburger button" opens
13 Dedicated works
21 Reader's jotting, e.g.
22 Reader's jottings . . . or a hint to this puzzle's theme
25 Fancy-pants
27 Title derived from "Caesar"
29 Most of a sugar cane
30 Marisa of "In the Bedroom"
31 Writer Sontag
32 Underway
33 Some salads
34 French "equivalent"
35 Gusto

39 Dot on a subway map
42 Dissolve
44 Scan options for the claustrophobic
47 Kind of milk or sauce
49 Put on sale, say
51 So far
54 Densely packed, in a way
56 Under-the-sink fixture
57 Animals depicted on the Ishtar Gate
58 Film composer Morricone
59 Tried something?
60 At any time
61 The blue part of blue cheese
63 About .914 meters
65 "Pow!"

by Oliver Roeder

ACROSS

1 *Leave briefly
6 Follow
10 Colorful freshwater fish
15 Midwest hub
16 Mystical character
17 Celeb with a good friend named Gayle
18 World leader born Vladimir Ilyich Ulyanov
19 Hankering
20 Subdued hue
21 Seriously vex
22 *Final say
24 Aromatherapy provider, perhaps
25 How best to determine consent
27 Coral-based ecosystems
28 Went the distance
31 Pioneer in color TV
32 Start of all Washington, D.C., ZIP codes
35 Contingent of like-minded voters
37 Nation on the Gulf of Oman
39 Like some Quad Cities residents
41 *All for one
45 Louvre Pyramid architect
46 Witty Mort
47 Mulligan
48 ___ Wee Reese
49 Fund-raising group for the G.O.P.
52 Didn't fail
54 Subs
56 Bit of body ink
57 TV screen type, for short
60 *Flies frequently
64 She released "30" in '21
66 Broadcast again
67 Farming prefix
68 Word with wave and pool
69 "___ luck!"
70 Political commentator Joy
71 Arctic people
72 Get-go
73 Monopoly holding
74 Punctuation mark missing in "Let's eat people!" (at least one would hope!) . . . as well as from the starred clues

DOWN

1 Animals that become different animals when their first letter is changed to an "M"
2 Oodles
3 Fruit often served in ball form
4 "Brava!" elicitor
5 Busybodies
6 Underhanded tactics
7 Not manually operated
8 Bring on
9 Longtime news anchor Jim
10 "Seeing the other side of the matter . . ."
11 Blunted blades
12 Cereal "for kids"
13 Musical form heard in some Bollywood films
14 [Don't forget about me!]
23 Fleeting moment
26 Move about
29 Doxycycline target
30 Some playground attendants
32 Wonderland twin
33 Pixie stick?
34 Not conned by
35 Minor anomaly
36 Shiny fabric
38 Spring's opposite
40 Brutish sort
42 No-good, backstabbing scoundrel
43 "How bizarre"
44 Disney's Queen of Arendelle
50 Pedagogic org.
51 Unfounded rumor
53 Unchanging
54 State capital in the so-called "Treasure Valley"
55 "Me and Bobby ___" (posthumous #1 hit for Janis Joplin)
58 Something staked
59 Difference symbol, in math
60 Singer/songwriter Guthrie
61 Blindingly bright
62 D.C. nine
63 Buffalo's county
65 Pet in the town of Bedrock

by Damon Gulczynski

ACROSS

1 Beginner, in lingo
5 Beaten via a referee's decision, for short
9 Menial position
14 Words sung twice before "A pirate's life for me"
15 Pint-size
16 Where the terminal dash in "Home Alone" takes place
17 Organized workers
19 Mythical lion's home
20 Apt name for a worrier
21 One driving kids to a rink, say
23 "Roger that"
26 Sticking points?
27 Hindi for "reign"
28 Honor student's pride, for short
29 Put up with
30 Accustoms (to)
32 Like planes and flags
33 Kind of lily
34 Fuel for a mustang?
35 Lucky hit for a Ping-Pong player
39 Non-starters
42 Successfully study
44 Impostor syndrome feeling
45 The Heat, on scoreboards
46 Catch
47 Prefix with sexual
48 Jailers . . . or a hint to "unlocking" four answers in this puzzle
50 Vie to get
52 Sound of a mouse pointer?
53 Skirt
54 She played Billie Jean King in 2017's "Battle of the Sexes"
58 Formal decrees
59 "___ Creator Omnium" (ancient hymn)
60 Biblical son of Seth
61 Raring to go
62 Francis Drake and Ernest Shackleton, for two
63 Community served by Lambda Legal, in brief

DOWN

1 Sch. with the Elmer Holmes Bobst Library
2 Seemingly for-ev-er
3 Moonshine container
4 Plunder
5 "You shoulda kept that to yourself"
6 Stuffed Jewish dish
7 How some ballet is performed
8 ___ golf
9 Jordan Peele's production company, named for a classic horror short story
10 Natives of the Great Plains
11 Like some signals and traffic
12 Their name has the "re" of "cream" and the two o's from "chocolate"
13 Big smile
18 "Psst!" alternative
22 Certain high-fat, low-carb diet, informally
23 Treasures buried in the hills
24 Bob ___, co-creator of Batman
25 Photo ___
29 Calculating
31 Purchases for a high-tech hobby
32 Peeps, so to speak
34 Solution to a bad hair day, maybe
36 1981 video game that featured the first appearance of Mario
37 Age, in a way
38 Moves out to sea
40 Thanksgiving
41 Gen-Z style with emo and anime influences
42 Go public with
43 Bugaboos
44 Boil down
45 Soothing sound
47 "___ On Up" ("The Jeffersons" theme)
48 Marisa of "My Cousin Vinny"
49 ___ One (vodka brand)
50 Actress ___ Pinkett Smith
51 Gangbusters
55 Word with bad or smart
56 Head, slangily
57 The "e" of i.e.

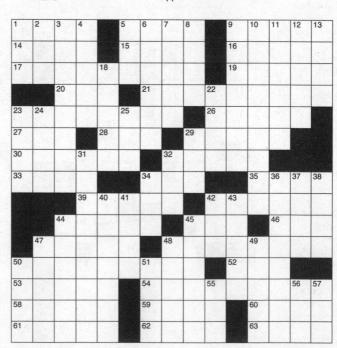

by Lucy Howard and Ross Trudeau

ACROSS

1 Ending with walk or run
4 Grape group
9 Exude irrepressibly
13 Poppable muscle, informally
14 Popular Japanese brew
15 Experts
16 Scorpion's stinger
18 Ikea department
19 Polo of "The Fosters"
20 "Don't worry"
22 Less soaked
24 .com alternative
25 Lose
27 "Already?"
29 Likely answer to "Who wants ice cream?"
30 Festival, in Arabic
31 Awe and Tay, for two
32 One to tip
34 Breading for tonkatsu
35 Tortilla dough
36 Bring stress or agitation to
37 ___ large
41 South American capital with the world's longest urban gondola
44 Nuclear codes?
46 Zero out
47 Plead
48 Therein lies the rub!
49 Bit of metadata
51 Wet weather wear
53 Poet's sphere
54 Coverer
56 Portion
57 Word with sitter or steps
59 Good name for a black cat with white feet
61 Commander, in Arabic
62 Mt. Fuji setting
63 1990s TV nerd
64 Is that what ewe said?
65 Uber-enthusiast
66 Part of a child's bedtime ritual
67 Stale

DOWN

1 "That's good" thinking
2 "That's good thinking!"
3 Cutter
4 Rotten
5 Something heard secondhand?
6 Mother of pearl
7 "Parasite" actor Woo-shik
8 Adds to the team, so to speak
9 Go (for)
10 Cookie-flavored cereal
11 Fictional character partially inspired by Mexican folklore
12 Provide digital approval
17 Apt rhyme for chop and crop
21 Artist who said "A line is a dot that went for a walk"
23 Breaker
26 The "A" of A.Q.I.
28 Exhibited
31 Hardly strict
33 One to tip
34 Candy once marketed as a smoking cessation aid
36 Big tub
38 One name for the game depicted in this puzzle
39 Like Rome starting in the first century B.C.
40 Promo
42 "Rush!"
43 Perseus' horse
44 Mousse alternative
45 Bigwigs may have big ones
46 Actress Margot of "Bombshell"
47 Carnival hypeman
49 Case of emergency?
50 Clear
51 Geico "spokeslizard"
52 "Nevertheless, ___ persisted"
55 Dessert wine
58 Himalayan ox
60 Foxy

by Rebecca Goldstein

ACROSS

1 Tour de France leg
6 Showbiz grand slam
10 Potential con
14 Keen
15 Kin of King Kong
17 Homer's self-satisfied assertion?
19 Aurora's counterpart
20 Multinational insurance inits.
21 Kind of nut
22 Feasts, e.g.
25 Pours from one container to another
29 Bums, for example?
31 Court org.
33 Spanish article
34 Bug that no one likes
35 Yam source, historically?
40 Québec street
41 Egg: Prefix
42 Some raw materials
43 Place to find a comet?
48 Does the watusi, say
49 Laundry leftover
53 Steps on a scale?
54 That there
55 Sweetheart
56 Thoroughly . . . or a hint for parsing some lowercase letters in four of this puzzle's clues
62 Sensed without being sure
63 "Woo-hoo!"
64 Arabian port
65 Critical time
66 It may come in shells

DOWN

1 Waste line
2 Lake in the Sierra Nevada
3 Sounding shocked
4 Grok
5 Jazz Age, e.g.
6 Self-seeker
7 Subject of rationing in the old English navy
8 Work started by London's Philological Soc.
9 Wood shop tool
10 Discriminatory compensation practice
11 Water monitoring grp.
12 Band with the 4x platinum albums "Out of Time" and "Monster"
13 Pitchfork-shaped letter
16 Affect emotionally
18 Cat, in Córdoba
23 Bubbly source
24 Peruse
25 [Correct!]
26 Like some checking accounts
27 Poker snafus
28 Name that's an alphabetic trio
30 Caesar dressing?
31 Shark's racket
32 Pickle unit
36 Certain facial decoration
37 Currier and ___
38 Feature of many a Druid's robe
39 Sea eagles
40 Onetime inits. on the Supreme Court
44 King of Saudi Arabia beginning in 2015
45 Hide away
46 Like a wide grin
47 Info on a security badge, for short
50 Falls into line
51 Diamond figure
52 Home country of the two-time Olympic marathon winner Eliud Kipchoge
54 Facility often referred to by its first letter
56 Mortgage org.
57 "Sweet!"
58 It's an honor
59 Derrière
60 Drench
61 "J to ___ L-O! The Remixes" (2002 album)

by Ashish Vengsarkar and Narayan Venkatasubramanyan

ACROSS

1 Congratulatory gestures
6 Div. of the Treasury Department
9 "Murder Mystery" or "Roaring Twenties," for a party
14 "Todo Sobre Mi ___" (1999 Almodóvar film)
15 Stick on a rack
16 Like some legs and mustaches
17 Aptly named Olympic sprinter
19 Epic poem written in dactylic hexameter
20 It's multifaceted
21 Rudely arrogant
22 "___ no sin to cheat the devil": Daniel Defoe
23 The Cowardly Lion, back in Kansas
24 Aptly named six-time All-Star first baseman
30 Bread with a palindromic name
31 Cry for assistance
32 Hold up
34 Actor Elgort of "Baby Driver"
36 "___ queen!"
37 Mist a spot?
39 Animal that symbolizes good fortune in Chinese culture
40 Mushrooms found in ramen
43 Shake, as a tail
44 Aptly named tennis great
47 Behind, in England
48 Football carriers: Abbr.
49 Listen to gossip, in slang
52 What driver's licenses serve as
57 Writer Nin
58 Aptly named N.B.A. M.V.P., in a manner of speaking
59 Period of work
60 Plastic ___ Band

61 "Later"
62 Album makeup
63 Gives the nod
64 Legally prohibit

DOWN

1 Self-satisfied
2 Use a beam on, as for cutting
3 Apple consumer with an unhappy story to tell?
4 Mint
5 Submitted
6 Tiny floppy disk, for "Save"
7 Reign
8 Decided
9 Puts out light, as a star
10 Angelic, in a way
11 ___ strategy
12 Most substantial part
13 Small vortex
18 Painter of "The Garden of Earthly Delights"

21 "Be as you wish to ___": Socrates
23 Shuts up
24 Bygone airline with a logo nicknamed the "Blue Meatball"
25 One who may use the pronoun "I and I" (meaning God-in-me)
26 Children's character who says "It's not much of a tail, but I'm sort of attached to it"
27 Unreliable sort
28 Statistical calculation
29 Event for a Comedy Central special
30 Capture
33 "Later"
35 They allow you to kick back and relax
38 Unnamed guests
41 Org. behind the Artemis program

42 New England seafood staple
45 Five stars, maybe
46 More than right
49 Give attitude
50 Digging
51 Bread: Fr.
52 Pop star whose name is stylized with an exclamation point in place of its second letter
53 Insurance grps.
54 "O.G. Original Gangster" rapper
55 Word before ". . . wanna go home," in calypso
56 Instant, as a decision
58 When doubled, excessive

by Joseph Greenbaum

ACROSS

1 Rounds out, as an event
5 Sound of a cake hitting the floor, frosting first
10 Gush (over), as to gain favor
14 Plant watcher, for short
15 Reluctant
16 Designer Saab
17 Wins the Hunger Games, e.g.
19 Young newts
20 Annual pageant winner
21 -
22 Maker of Z-cars, once
23 Hoover rival
25 Online handle
28 Like the "5" of "5 & 10"
33 Maine university town
34 Repellent spray
37 Coleridge's "The ___ Harp"
39 One requested by disgruntled customers: Abbr.
40 Bard's "before"
41 See 30-Down
42 Common street name in suburbia
43 Fish with a long snout
44 Mexico has 31 of these
45 "The Sleep of Reason Produces Monsters" artist
46 Go haywire
48 Have as a tenant
50 One of the Eternals, in Marvel comics
52 Insurance giant acquired by CVS in 2018
56 Followers of the largest denomination of Islam
57 Labor group for athletes
62 -
63 Top-shelf
64 Supersharp
66 Actress Kunis of "Family Guy"
67 "Thumbs up from me!"
68 Sea eagle
69 Rustic verse
70 Steady looks
71 Wine category

DOWN

1 Classic pink cocktail
2 Up and about
3 Terrible twos, e.g.
4 Surrenders
5 Ukrainian, for one
6 Neighbor of a Ukrainian
7 Hideout
8 Off-roaders, for short
9 Grp. established by 1992's Maastricht Treaty
10 Bottom ___
11 Car whose logo features a coiled green serpent
12 With full knowledge
13 Puccini aria popularized by Pavarotti
18 "Only joking!," to a texter
24 -
26 Acoustic measure
27 -
29 Result of a rift
30 With 41-Across, a celestial event . . . or a hint to four squares in this puzzle
31 Top-shelf
32 What avocados don't do until they're picked
34 Catastrophic weather event potentially caused by a meteor crash
35 Spiderlike
36 "Yes, of course"
38 Brief second?
41 Bruins legend, to fans
45 Receives an anesthetic, perhaps
47 Open, as a tomb
49 Button on a scale
51 Herb unit
53 Un gato grande
54 Incessantly
55 Much of Chile
58 ___ land
59 Ansari of "Master of None"
60 Harness
61 You are, in Spanish
63 -
65 -

by Max Chen Lauring

Note: The circled letters, reading clockwise starting at the bottom, will reveal a hint to this puzzle's theme.

ACROSS

1 One inclined to go in and out
5 "Peace out"
10 Certain vipers
14 Where one may purchase a sectional with a side of meatballs
15 Cover story
16 "Star Wars" general with the line "If you see our son, bring him home"
17 Stuff
18 Deals with fries and a beverage, maybe
20 Hornswoggle
21 County north of the Firth of Forth
22 Three or more on a semi
23 It may lead to a "no catch" ruling
27 Not square, in a way
28 Screen, as a potential running mate
29 What's often kept undercover?
30 Cygnus constellation, with "the"
32 Put (down)
36 Fight a needless fight, metaphorically
39 Thrill-seeker's acronymic motto
40 Top 40 songs
41 Ring around a lagoon
42 Hairstyle that sounds edible
43 Swings around
44 One with a quintessential McJob
49 "Same with me"
51 Director Kazan
52 Bruce on the Hollywood Walk of Fame
53 Extra-bountiful harvest
56 Two in a two-car garage

57 Singer Rexha
58 Community far from a city's center
59 Playing extra minutes, briefly
60 Parched
61 "___ on the igpay atinlay!"
62 Heater meas.

DOWN

1 Christina of 1991's "The Addams Family"
2 City nicknamed "Rubber Capital of the World"
3 Has the best intentions
4 Actress Grier
5 Pretty trim
6 Up in the air
7 Hourglass, e.g.
8 Flow back
9 2016 Olympics host, informally
10 Name often called in a smart home
11 Tuft & Needle competitor
12 Stack
13 'Tude
19 Type of shake
21 Fruity soda brand
24 Hook up with
25 Jazz pianist Bill
26 Be in limbo
29 Place for mucking around
30 29-Down residents
31 Drollery
32 Like festive houses during the holidays
33 Potted succulent
34 "Until we meet again"
35 Cable alternative
37 Rap's Young ___

38 Onetime presidential daughter with the code name Radiance
42 Cheeseboard staple
43 Evade capture
44 Thumper's forest friend
45 Cried foul?
46 Any "Scrubs" or "Friends" episode, now
47 Regional greenery
48 Takes time off
49 Group with the tribute band Björn Again
50 One alleging injury, perhaps
54 Big retailer of camping gear
55 Roman numeral equal to 12% of M
56 Chest protector

by Alex Bajcz

ACROSS

1 Thumbnail, e.g.
6 "No worries"
11 Guts
12 Wordle, e.g., in 2022
13 Lies ahead
14 What's in the stars
16 Titular Disney protagonist of 1942
17 Ranch dressing?
18 Boxer's warning
19 Hosp. hookups
21 Letters before an alternate name
22 Adding purpose?
24 Backing
25 How many reprimands are issued
27 "Double Fantasy" Grammy winner
28 Many attachments
30 Postponed
31 ___ B'rith
32 Novelist Jennifer
33 Enlightenment, in Buddhism
34 Hamilton producers?
35 Illinois city that was the first home of the Chicago Bears
37 Send beyond the baseline of a tennis court, say
39 Plans for some seniors, in brief
40 Kid
41 It begins with "In the beginning . . ."
44 Video game with a "rosebud" cheat code that grants free money
47 :-O
48 Potato-stuffed pastries
50 Struggle

51 Zippo
53 When el Día de los Reyes is celebrated
54 Pole, e.g.
55 Utah's ___ Canyon
56 Flavor
57 Home to Caesar's palace
58 2018 Literature Nobelist Tokarczuk
59 Do nothing
60 Mating call?

DOWN

1 Part of a sun salutation, in yoga
2 Title with an apostrophe
3 Outs
4 Cut the small talk
5 "Grey's Anatomy" settings, in brief
6 ___ factor
7 Concept in Reaganomics
8 Walk like you own the place
9 Princess in L. Frank Baum books
10 Handles discreetly
13 Trim
15 Seismologist's concern
18 Hung open
20 Title for Don Quixote
21 Pepper used in mole sauce
23 Dewy
26 Purge
29 Part of a drum kit
31 Pound sounds
36 Item on a list
38 Sight seers

41 Muppet whose self-identified species is "Whatever"
42 "This meeting could've been an ___"
43 Biblical mount
44 Pulsate
45 Only U.S. city bordered by two national parks
46 Nitrogen, on the periodic table
49 46-Down, in French
52 Filmmaker ___ Lily Amirpour
54 Honorific from Sanskrit

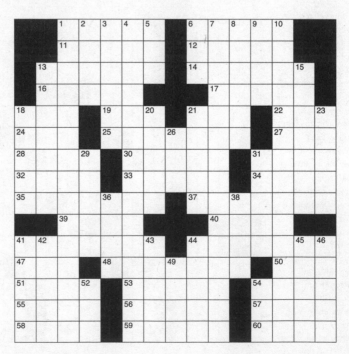

by Pao Roy

ACROSS

1 Quickly microwave
4 Stock index founded in 1885, informally
10 Cooler in glasses
13 Afflictions
15 Elder Levy in "Schitt's Creek"
16 Islanders' grp.
17 People who acknowledge when they've been verbally bested?
19 Berkeley, familiarly
20 Paper opener
21 Two for a basket: Abbr.
22 "Sweet!"
23 Ruins a shiny fabric, as a pet might?
27 Stratovolcano in Sicily
28 Shot taker
30 Computer scientist Turing
33 "Should that be true . . ."
36 Determined to do
37 Power, as an engine
38 Embassy staffer . . . or a hint to 17-, 23-, 49- and 59-Across?
40 "S.N.L." alum Gasteyer
41 Colosseum country
43 Lead-in to girl
44 Skating jump
45 Numb, as a foot
47 MCAT subj.
49 Bad advice from grandpa?
54 Without
55 Desire
56 Spammer's medium
58 Parabola piece
59 Managed to stomach a cracker spread?
62 Undefined ordinal
63 Feared fifth-century ruler
64 Diez menos dos
65 Turn red, maybe
66 Summit attendee
67 Corral, e.g.

DOWN

1 Cylindrical pasta
2 ___ the way
3 Dog owned by a talking mouse
4 Equipment not needed in miniature golf
5 Cabana
6 King Tut's land
7 Profundity
8 "Be right with you"
9 Director Anderson
10 Payroll deduction
11 Parent on a field trip, often
12 Woman's name that sounds like a letter of the alphabet
14 Vet
18 Run the show, say
22 Maggie Smith, for one
24 "I'll do that right away!"
25 International pact that ended in 2020
26 Blast with a beam of photons
29 Fussy in the extreme
30 Handel's "La giustizia," for one
31 Bacchanalian cry
32 Overwhelming amount
34 Took a load off
35 Group of eight
38 "The ___ have it!"
39 Suspend
42 Without
44 At the original speed, in scores
46 Psychoactive drug from a cactus
48 "So true!"
50 Volkswagen compact
51 Reversed
52 Org. co-founded by W. E. B. Du Bois
53 10% offering
54 Castle material
57 Revolutionary Trotsky
59 Eight pts.
60 Fútbol cry
61 Game with the objective of winning all the cards

by Eric Bornstein

ACROSS

1 Little 19-Across
4 Units on Czech checks
11 Student-led LGBTQ+ grp.
14 "Just as I suspected!"
15 Common recipe step
16 What psychotherapy can treat, in brief
17 Someone well versed in this puzzle's theme
19 Many people do this about their height
20 Opining opening
21 James of "Carpool Karaoke" fame
23 Turn on the stove?
24 "The wait's almost over"
28 Hammer part
29 Sugar
30 When preceded by [the circled letters], natural shape said to be seen in 61-Across and 27-Down
32 First word of Poe's "The Raven"
34 "Cat"
36 King of ancient Rome
37 Pupil of a cat's eye, often
38 ___ jacket (formal men's wear)
39 Duke's grp.
40 Much-desired
41 Uses psychedelics
42 Terence ___, noted expert on combinatorics and analytic number theory
43 Lid seen in a kitchen?
44 Polynesian performance
45 Foolish person
46 Slip past
47 Prefix with glottis
48 Some convertible choices
49 John of "Monty Python" fame
51 Source of much early immigration to the U.S.: Abbr.
52 When doubled, not-so-subtle nudge
53 Judgment days?
60 They seem to believe otherwise
61 Classic van Gogh subject
62 "What'd I tell you?!"
63 A bygone age

DOWN

1 Starve
2 "You gave me no choice"
3 Brings home
4 Perry who used to have the world's most-followed Twitter account
5 Written honor
6 Nutritional fig.
7 Where second gentleman Doug Emhoff got his J.D.
8 "Pass"
9 "Smart" name
10 Razor sharpener
11 Numerical constant associated with [the circled letters]
12 Summer learning opportunity for students
13 Mideast's Gulf of ___
18 When doubled, sarcastic laugh
22 ___ Speedwagon
24 Dilemma
25 Word with snake or salad
26 Diner cry after a bell is rung
27 Certain cephalopods
30 Some shindigs
31 Parkinson's treatment
33 Many security guards
34 ___ Colvin, civil rights pioneer who refused to give up her seat on a segregated bus nine months before Rosa Parks
35 Nav. rank
37 When preceded by [the circled letters], progression starting with 0 and 1
40 Warehouse store equipment
41 An alternative?
43 Computer pros
45 Like some horse bedding
48 Queen Mary or Queen Elizabeth
50 Crafts site
51 Fanning of film
54 Regret
55 They might help you get a job
56 Sternward
57 Propper noun?
58 Bygone ___
59 Kazakhstan, e.g., formerly: Abbr.

by Adam Wagner

ACROSS

1 Drops the ball big-time
8 Home to about 60% of the world's population
12 One with a whistle . . . who sometimes 1-Across?
15 Soccer superstar Cristiano
16 Sporty car roof option
17 Genre of Death Cab for Cutie
18 Tot's mount
20 Cold War jet
21 Cover, as tasks
22 Connecticut Ivy Leaguer
23 Willy Wonka prop
24 Practically forever
25 Jim Beam competitor
28 Gun
29 Auction action
30 Thinks the world of
31 Hard to swallow, in a way
34 Shake a leg, in Shakespeare
35 Chinese poultry dish marinated in wine
40 ___-fi
41 Torments
43 Residents of ancient Minos
47 PC key
48 Windy City rail system, in brief
49 1980 boxing film for which De Niro won Best Actor
51 Criticize harshly
53 "Couldn't agree more!"
54 Name, as a price
55 ___ bear
56 Flat refusals
57 They're always ready for a good time . . . or a description of 18-, 25-, 35- and 49-Across?
61 Tree creature of Middle-earth
62 Brothers Grimm villain
63 Legislative bodies
64 Marx's "___ Kapital"
65 Cherry or walnut
66 Recliner feature

DOWN

1 Remark from one having cold feet, perhaps
2 Bit of unfinished business
3 Cursory appraisal
4 Rouse
5 Pita pocket cuts, e.g.
6 Passport fig.
7 Dress (up), quaintly
8 Island like Kiritimati
9 Jazz piano style played by Fats Waller and Mary Lou Williams
10 Siri's platform
11 Copy
12 Fresh take on a classic, perhaps
13 Slim Shady, by another name
14 Some old-timers
19 Eric ___, 1980 Olympic speed skating gold medalist
23 Streaming sites?
24 Cardinals' home, in stats
25 Illusionist's skill
26 Part of a casual layered look
27 College city in upstate New York
29 Blues legend with a guitar named Lucille
32 Hoffman who played Captain Hook
33 Early quinoa cultivator
36 Like chewable calcium, often
37 Place for a concert or lecture
38 Get really serious really quickly
39 Pitching statistic?
42 Rode the bench
43 Stretched to get a better look, say
44 ___ Quimby, Beverly Cleary heroine
45 Discharges
46 Pizzeria chain
50 Formal "you," in Spanish
51 Sound of spring?
52 Former L.A. Laker Odom
55 Banjo spot, in song
57 "Right in the kisser!"
58 Fourth word in the "Star Wars" prologue
59 Communication method in much of the 2021 film "CODA," for short
60 Bygone Mach 1 breaker, in brief

by Michael Paleos

ACROSS

1 Locale for part of Dinosaur National Monument
5 ___ Geo
8 Birthplace of the 44th U.S. president
14 Singer Simone
15 Comment from a klutz
16 Changes to survive
17 ___ State (Big Ten school)
18 Nietzschean ideal
20 Document for returned goods
22 "I'm such a bozo!"
23 Fortune 100 company with a heart in its logo
24 Site with selfies, familiarly
26 Produce, as an egg
27 Tree under which Siddhartha attained enlightenment
28 Feeling at Victoria Falls, say
31 Scent of an animal
33 Harden
34 "No worries"
36 Trait of a babe in the woods
38 Noted literary sisters
39 Like many Bluetooth headsets
40 Spanish for "Listen!"
41 Second
42 Director Craven
43 Buffalo ice hockey pro
45 It sees right through you, in brief
46 "The Handmaid's Tale" author
47 One who whistles while working?
48 Six-footer Down Under
50 Ice cream brand whose first storefront was in Brooklyn Heights
55 Activity at singles bars
57 Popular cake topping ingredient
58 Diacritical mark resembling a dieresis, both of which are represented in this puzzle
59 Celebration six days after Xmas
60 Bit of smoke
61 Tributes containing insults
62 Ending with rip or whip
63 Results in

DOWN

1 Not acceptable, in a way
2 Mezzanine, e.g.
3 Youngest of the 38-Across
4 Whittle, e.g.
5 Inning-beginning stat
6 Some messages on old radios, for short
7 Poet who wrote "Do I dare / Disturb the universe?"
8 One of the "Five Colleges" of Massachusetts
9 End of a block?
10 Comedian Sykes
11 Lhasa ___
12 Ski suit wearer's annoyance
13 "Kinda sorta"
19 Uneaten part
21 Brown, for one
25 ___ Puente, a.k.a. El Rey del Timbal
26 Sarges report to them
27 Where one might sit for a spell?
28 When Macbeth slays Duncan
29 Serenaded, maybe
30 Instead
31 Kind of globe
32 It's framed
33 Beachcombers' headwear
35 Inhale
37 90°
38 "Peace"
40 Confers holy orders on
44 Greet with derision
45 All U.S. vice presidents until 2021
46 Vibes
47 Affirm again, as vows
48 TV character originally called "Baby Monster"
49 Kunis of "Black Swan"
51 "Saturn Devouring His Son" artist
52 German opera highlight
53 Relish
54 Soaks (up)
55 Lab coat
56 Ruler with a famed golden mask, informally

by Ross Trudeau

ACROSS

1 Sleeper, e.g.
5 Suddenly spoke (up)
10 Winner's gesture
15 Apple product since 1998
16 Grassy plain
17 "Here we go again . . ."
18 Confess one's true feelings . . . or Step 1 for solving a jigsaw puzzle?
21 Eventually
22 Dirty money
23 Holiday celebrating the first day of spring
24 Lowdown
26 Stop texting after a first date, say
28 Recover after a heartbreak . . . or Step 2 for solving a jigsaw puzzle?
34 Gift of ___
35 Plethora
36 "Again!"
37 N.B.A. star Westbrook, to fans
39 Long, loose hood
42 Word before loose or tight
43 Div. for the Tampa Bay Rays
46 Tiny bit
49 Screening org.
50 Look for an ideal partner . . . or Step 3 for solving a jigsaw puzzle?
54 Eat dirt?
55 Cold-weather cryptid
56 One volt divided by one ampere
59 Performer's comment to the audience
61 Tree that's a source of salicylic acid, a precursor to aspirin
65 Get some perspective . . . or what you do once you've solved a jigsaw puzzle?
68 Animal that wears red pajamas in a popular children's book
69 Porter alternative
70 Residents of Splitsville?
71 Choose to participate
72 Run into a hitch?
73 "The ___ is silence": Hamlet

DOWN

1 Something that may be raised on a farm
2 Nation bordering the Arabian Sea
3 Dunaway of "Mommie Dearest"
4 By no means basic
5 Like a frisky puppy
6 Feeling crummy
7 Gloomy atmosphere
8 "Quit it!"
9 Medicinal rinse
10 Elects
11 "This is a library!"
12 "Yeah, right"
13 Vice president in the 1990s
14 Opposite of "da"
19 Some scuba gear
20 Evil clown in a horror film, e.g.
25 Intl. group with members on three continents
27 ___-savvy
28 St. ___ Girl (beer brand)
29 Playwright whose work inspired the Peer Gynt Sculpture Park in 56 Down
30 Number of hole cards in Texas hold'em
31 Relative of a raccoon
32 Dada pioneer Max
33 Dreamcast console maker
34 Steffi who achieved a Golden Slam in 1988
38 "The Sweetest Taboo" singer, 1985
40 Console whose name sounds like a pronoun
41 Sluggish
44 N.F.L. Hall-of-Famer Michael
45 Word that might be said while pointing
47 TV series named second-best of all time by Rolling Stone, but which never won an Emmy
48 Story used for storage
51 What skullcap mushrooms aren't
52 Call back
53 Instagram effect
56 See 29 Down
57 "A little ___ ?"
58 Charcuterie selection
60 Brand originally called Froffles
62 Sumptuous and expensive
63 Minerals ending in -ite, often
64 Mae who said "To err is human, but it feels divine"
66 "All right, I've heard plenty"
67 Vim

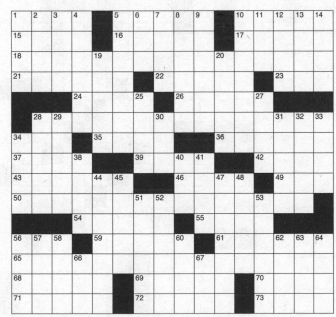

by Andy Kravis

104 Medium

ACROSS
1 Fuel efficiency letters
4 They may join in a circle
8 Big-box hardware chain
13 "That's it!"
14 Model Campbell
16 Cricket fields and badminton racket heads, for two
17 Punishes
19 Interrupt . . . or what to do as you enter the answer to the previous clue
20 Aptly named ski town in Utah
21 Stop the clock
23 Compact disc?
25 Hot spot in the afternoon, say
26 I.C.U. specialists
29 Backed financially
31 Prep for surgery . . . or what to do as you enter the answer to the previous clue
34 Multiple of one?
36 City whose name is Siouan for "good place to dig potatoes"
37 Primitive kind of diet
41 Subject of job offer negotiations
43 They get high twice a day
44 Actress Munn
46 One of Alcott's Little Women
48 Workplace with no commute
50 Leave . . . or what to do as you enter the answer to the previous clue
55 Constellation next to Ursa Major
56 Prefix with skeleton
58 Hagia ___ (World Heritage Site in Istanbul)
59 Concession stand morsel
63 One of the pounds in a pound cake
64 Brazenly disregarding

66 Flail at home plate . . . or what to do as you enter the answer to the previous clue
68 "Heaven forbid!"
69 Pledge drive bags
70 Gold in them thar hills, e.g.
71 Promise
72 Home to the oldest continuously operating university in the Americas
73 Retreat

DOWN
1 Sophisticated ladies
2 Queen Elizabeth's husband
3 Prefix with -pod
4 Alex and ___ (jewelry brand)
5 Affiliated group of M.C.s, as for Death Row Records
6 Rum mixer
7 Refine, in a way
8 Plot points?
9 Fallopian tube traveler
10 Something to sleep on with no springs
11 Country's ___ Young Band
12 Only four-ninths of it is usually shown: Abbr.
15 Lands in the ocean
18 Media journalist David
22 It's said to be "the art of recognizing when to be big and when not to belittle"
24 Holy Roman emperor beginning in 973
27 Quickly heat up, in a way
28 Yellow Pages section after "Sound Systems"
30 Dramatic tango move
32 Abstract Expressionist Mark
33 News inits. since 1958
35 Snag
37 Four-time Hugo Award winner Frederik

38 Potted ornamental
39 Prom night booking
40 Biblical progenitor
42 "And ___ . . ."
45 Super-duper
47 Better prepared, perhaps
49 Just be oneself
51 Sport in which you could use some pointers?
52 "Great to hear!"
53 Reckon
54 Secure
57 In first place
60 Psychoanalyst Freud, daughter of Sigmund
61 Marty Feldman's role in "Young Frankenstein"
62 Big name in Art Deco
64 N.F.L. three-pointers: Abbr.
65 Temperature extreme
67 Sch. 50 miles west of 36-Across

by Alex Rosen

ACROSS

1 Green spot in a city
5 Top dog
10 ___ threat
14 Monopoly token replaced by a cat in 2013
15 Like the boondocks
16 ". . . ___ the twain shall meet"
17 Group of winners at a film awards show?
19 Reminder of a past injury
20 Discharges
21 Not real royals, maybe
23 Executed, as a program
24 Team ___
26 Something to take up or let out
27 Target for William Tell?
33 Singing Crow
36 Cause of some breathing problems
37 F–, for one
38 Command-C, on a Mac
39 Turn into a film, e.g.
41 To boot
42 Comedian Wong
43 Personification of Earth, in Greek myth
44 Tiny parts of archipelagoes
46 Where séance leaders get their degrees?
49 Unfinished crusade of the 1970s, in brief
50 Inning : baseball :: ___ : curling
51 Eggs in a lab
54 Art of bone carving
59 Green spot in a desert
61 Actors who don't play their roles subtly
62 Lo-o-ong lecture from a parent?
64 Early Ron Howard role
65 "___ you a little short for a stormtrooper?": Princess Leia
66 Do more than just check out
67 Fling
68 The Rockies, e.g.
69 Drink from a Viking's goblet

DOWN

1 Itinerant musician with a flute
2 Patisserie allure
3 "The Kiss" sculptor
4 Heal, as a broken bone
5 Word after long or strong
6 One-named ancient satirist . . . or a Pokémon character
7 Baby buggy in Piccadilly Circus
8 Hinged bit of hardware
9 Cher, voicewise
10 Part of a foot
11 Convert into a higher-level language, as computer code
12 King of English theater
13 Muffs
18 Crime of great interest
22 Carpet type
25 Arabic "peace"
27 Alan Paton's "___, the Beloved Country"
28 Oscar ___, player of Poe Dameron in "Star Wars" films
29 One who calls people out
30 Statement to a chair of a meeting
31 In need of directions
32 Grandson of Adam and Eve
33 Almost every get-rich-quick scheme
34 Spot in a green
35 Outer layer of skin
40 Throw shade at
41 Monopolist's portion
43 Territory ceded by Spain to the U.S. in 1898
45 Vice city
47 Van Gogh work that in 1987 became the most expensive painting ever sold
48 Chopping
51 ___ orange
52 Home on the Riviera, say
53 Didn't contain one's curiosity
54 Attempt
55 Aria da ___
56 Symbol on an "8" key
57 Juno's Greek counterpart
58 Mideast's Gulf of ___
60 Itsy-bitsy bit
63 Tribe for which the 45th state is named

by Christopher Youngs

ACROSS

1 "The Winner Takes It All" group
5 Singer Diana
9 Radiate
13 Hardly a jaunt
14 Ready to go
16 Central points
17 Tolled time
18 "Byeee!"
19 One having a turn at a roast?
20 You've got to know when to hold 'em
23 Worrier's words
24 Former queen of Jordan
25 Good cheer
26 What do ewe say?
27 Spice ___
29 Often-changed item of wear
31 Know when to fold 'em
35 ___ Mode, animated film character who says "Words are useless! Gobble-gobble-gobble-gobble-gobble-gobble!"
36 It might be in the form of a thumbnail
37 "The Music Man" locale
41 Know when to walk away
46 Famed designer whose career was boosted by "American Gigolo"
49 Small batteries
50 Butter, e.g.
51 Concern for a tailor
52 ___ facto
55 Box markings
57 And know when to run
60 Moistens
61 Water nymph
62 Earnest request
64 Pueblo people
65 "The Child," also known as Baby Yoda
66 Snack, as on a knish
67 Places with springs
68 Exclamation after a witty comeback
69 ___ Major

DOWN

1 Bit of air pollution
2 Gasbag
3 Anthony of "Parts Unknown"
4 Concur
5 Speaker's platform
6 Scott Turow memoir
7 Gertrude who wrote "We are always the same age inside"
8 "___ to This" (song from "Hamilton")
9 Jewelry designer Peretti
10 Mod do
11 It comes to a point when it's too cold outside
12 One who gives one-tenth
15 Tiered temple
21 Actress Gilbert
22 Hosp. scans
23 Light wind?
28 Lettuce wrap lettuce
30 "Yeah, suuuure"
32 Event with a dress code
33 Snoopy grp.
34 German film award akin to an Oscar
38 Risqué
39 "What is your greatest ___?" (interview question)
40 Section of a Sunday newspaper
42 "Wilco!"
43 Erasing, as data
44 Prepared to skate
45 Org. with thousands of inspectors
46 Forty winks
47 Provoke
48 View from Catania, in brief
53 Shoots up
54 Whopper ingredient
56 College sports channel
58 Print collectors, for short
59 "A Song of Ice and Fire," e.g.
63 "Why, that's it!"

by Jonathan M. Kaye

ACROSS

1 "Damn right!"
5 What a lizard's tail can do
11 Word with snow or bank
14 Holiday trio, with "the"
15 Mark in the World Golf Hall of Fame
16 Kerfuffle
17 Info typically not found in the Yellow Pages
19 Become one
20 Like produce in the produce aisle, often
21 Washington post?
23 Surreptitiously say "26-Across," say
26 See 23-Across
27 Railroad stops: Abbr.
29 Creative activity for grade schoolers
34 Neighbor of Sudan
35 Aspect
36 "Back to the Future" actress Thompson
37 Can type
39 Instinctive behavior for a mother-to-be
41 Arafat's grp.
42 Writer Gay
44 Tiny salamanders
45 Reason to sleep with a night light
47 Spell-offs
48 Org. in "The Bourne Identity"
49 Positions
51 Full of noxious vapors
55 Pop singer Simpson
59 "Catch-22" character
60 Prized possessions for numismatists
63 Prefix with century or sentence
64 Just one little bite
65 David Ortiz had 1,768 of them, for short

66 Jerk
67 Unknown people, in slang
68 Not yet completed

DOWN

1 Digital clock toggle
2 When doubled, seafood burger choice
3 Some causes of stubbornness
4 Switch maker
5 Sonata finale, often
6 Only living creature in the genus Dromaius
7 Little treasure
8 Broccoli ____
9 City near Provo Bay
10 Vintage military planes
11 Rescue tool at a crash site
12 Lines that lift

13 Main section of text
18 Some reef dwellers
22 Mathematician Lovelace
24 Rice dish infused with saffron
25 Neighbor of Ire.
27 ____ life
28 The Hanged Man and The Chariot, for two
30 Scandinavian-inspired shoe brand
31 Language spoken in the Canadian Prairies
32 Farmer's market sights
33 Droops
34 Guitar clamp
35 Shoulder's place
38 Early vehicle that could take up to minutes to start
40 One might be graphic
43 Screw up

46 What's-____-name
47 "Yours truly" alternative
50 Assails, with "into"
51 Place to see a Matisse in N.Y.C.
52 Biometric scan identifier, maybe
53 Smidge
54 Rap's Wu-Tang ____
56 Gray wolf
57 Children's author Blyton
58 Italian for "it"
61 Psilocybin alternative, for short
62 W.W. II zone: Abbr.

by Chase Dittrich

108 MEDIUM

ACROSS

1 What a left arrow might mean
5 Setting for much of "A Farewell to Arms"
10 Convalescent's need, for short
13 Where Ulysses encountered the Cyclops
14 Saw
15 Blacken
16 With 1 Across, warning at sea
18 Accrue in large amounts, with "in"
19 "Aww"-inspiring one
20 Small batteries
21 Feature of the Devil
23 Capital city with three consecutive vowels
25 "Bad Guy" singer Billie
26 With 1 Down, like a free-for-all fight
30 Dostoyevsky novel, with "The"
33 Air alternative
34 1930s Depression-fighting org.
35 Dings
36 Otoscope-using M.D.
37 Scales on a pangolin, e.g.
39 Farm delivery letters
40 Hero feature, often
41 They're attached to many houses
42 With 1 Across, charity event involving a coast-to-coast human chain
46 Besmirches
47 Cheese often mixed with Monterey Jack
50 It's funky
51 Death Valley's is −282.2 ft.
53 Glass part
55 "Houston, ___ had a problem" (message misquoted in "Apollo 13")
56 With 1 Down, dessert sometimes made with pineapple

59 Father of Phobos and Deimos
60 Tennis star Osaka
61 Hula accompaniers, informally
62 Web portal with a butterfly logo
63 Three-time Emmy winner Cicely
64 ___ Myerson, only Jewish woman crowned Miss America

DOWN

1 Outdo
2 Malkovich's role in "The Man in the Iron Mask"
3 Benjamin
4 ___ Chow, author of 2021's "Seeing Ghosts: A Memoir"
5 Hawaiian "thanks"
6 "You have no ___"

7 Places to find dishes of different cultures
8 Fifth word of "American Pie"
9 Zooey Deschanel sitcom
10 "I take the blame"
11 Great place to visit near Michigan?
12 Largest First Nations group
15 "Brooklyn Nine-Nine" actor Robinson
17 Baits, in a way
22 Greeting in Portuguese
24 "Enough already!"
25 One behind The Times
27 Some Sephora purchases
28 West of Malibu
29 Ones on the briny
30 The "i" in p.s.i.
31 Worst-case scenarios

32 Words from the "speechless"
37 Nook
38 Yemeni money
40 Much of "The Fugitive"
43 Some Nordics
44 [not a typo]
45 Stuck until a thaw
48 Mini freezer?
49 "Oh no!"
50 Made a bank getaway?
51 Those, in Spanish
52 Stretch for the stars?
54 Tinker (with)
57 Word before "a fine" or "a visit"
58 Ursa minor?

by Michael Lieberman

ACROSS

1 Plate appearance
6 Short break?
11 Director Brooks
14 Some Kiwis
16 Love, in Livorno
17 Fútbol cheer
18 Doth choose a comedy routine?
20 Routing word
21 Author of the "Letter From Birmingham Jail," in brief
22 Two-way
23 Memoirs and profiles, informally
24 Citizenry doth work hard?
29 Upstage, say
32 Fastball, in slang
33 Watery
34 Locale for drawers in the study?
37 Subject of many a funny TikTok
38 Once-popular activity hath no more fans?
41 Golf variable
42 They may be close to reception
44 Post-boomer cohort
45 Title 6-year-old of 1950s children's literature
46 Schuss with a chute
49 Doth apply graffiti?
52 Goes out
53 Grains in some milk
54 Rim
57 ___ Simbel (Lake Nasser landmark)
58 Runway walker hath megatalent?
63 Record
64 Be on the hunt
65 Blown
66 A and B, in D.C.
67 Whammies
68 Some boards

DOWN

1 Day and night?
2 Follow closely
3 Strong German brew
4 Months-long couples retreat?
5 Busy
6 Frankie of the Four Seasons
7 "___ the only one?"
8 Fool
9 "___ we good?"
10 OK
11 Things cast for films
12 "Middlemarch" novelist
13 Setter fetter
15 Well-used pencils
19 Robust
23 "Yecch!"
24 It may burst your bubble
25 Rock with four Emmys
26 Mal de ___
27 Hop kiln
28 Rash sensation
29 Chisel
30 Elaine ___, labor secretary under George W. Bush
31 They may leave a lengthy paper trail
34 Job in the TV biz
35 Sound heard "here" and "there" on Old MacDonald's farm
36 L.P.G.A. star Thompson
38 Ice ___
39 Somewhat
40 Small amount in a recipe
43 Fraternal order
44 Boyle's law subject
46 Jack of 1950s TV
47 Character ___
48 Bail out
49 "Square" things
50 Monastery figure
51 Relaxes
54 Horne with a sultry voice
55 Thingy
56 Many profs
58 NASCAR stat
59 Deposit of a sort
60 Publish private info about online, in modern lingo
61 Sheepish one?
62 Breakfast cereal with little balls

by Bruce Haight

ACROSS

1 Some sleeveless undergarments, informally
6 It may result in damages
10 Hip-hop subgenre in Lil Nas X's "Old Town Road"
14 Creature whose saliva acts as a blood thinner
15 One side of a bet
16 [giggle]
17 "Queen" of 40-Down
18 CeeLo Green's "Forget You" and the Black Eyed Peas' "Don't Mess With My Heart"
20 Egg holder
21 Shade
23 Distribute, as pineapples?
24 "Rugrats" dad
25 Scatter
27 Irene of old Hollywood
28 Trace
30 Sanctuary scrolls
32 Place for a hammer and anvil
33 Christmas display
35 Wheelhouses
37 & 39 Some Sundance submissions . . . or a hint to four squares in this puzzle
41 Comedian who said "Embrace who you are. Literally. Hug yourself," familiarly
43 Popular urban hangouts
46 Cold War inits.
49 Sappho, for one
51 Spiritual teacher
52 Steamed
54 Best Actor winner for "Bohemian Rhapsody"
56 Grist for a mill
57 Sisterly
59 Journalist ___ B. Wells
60 Underground N.Y.C. group
61 Increasingly common weather event akin to a hurricane
63 One with Windows
65 Come out of one's shell, say
66 Word after G
67 One-named former wrestler who twice won the W.W.E. Divas Championship
68 "A Day Without Rain" singer
69 Genderqueer identity
70 Like a comet's path

DOWN

1 "Old Coke" vis-à-vis New Coke, in marketing
2 Faucet accessory
3 Rom-com staples
4 I, to Einstein
5 Bygone rulers
6 One wearing a traje de luces ("suit of light") in the ring
7 Eggs
8 Star with low luminosity
9 The Minutemen, e.g.
10 What Britain left in 2020, in brief
11 Fixed up
12 Ingredient in sushi rolls and poke bowls
13 Bother persistently
19 Seasoned sailor
22 Ridiculous introduction?
26 ___ Now (onetime political button)
29 Place for icing
31 Did a job on
34 Calls
36 Urban ill
38 Bank offering with a fixed payment schedule
40 Otis Redding's genre
42 Actress Long
44 Mentored one
45 Powdered, in a way
46 Words on a candy heart
47 E-commerce site with a portmanteau name
48 By a narrow margin
50 By a narrow margin
53 Mexican sandwich
55 Italian sportswear brand named after a Greek letter
58 "Look ___!"
62 Bone to pick at dinner, say
64 Tesla, for one

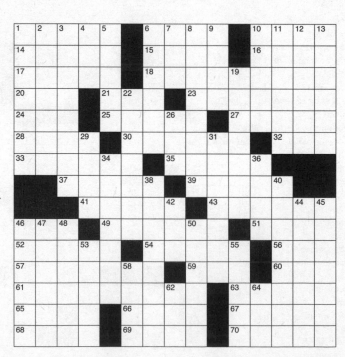

by Dan Ziring

ACROSS

1 Buds
5 ____ Empire, a.k.a. the Realm of the Four Parts
9 Word with bar or bowl
14 Pizazz
15 Cup-and-saucer luncheons
16 Hot apple pie has one
17 Start of a punny quip with two correct answers
20 Step up or down
21 Phnom ____
22 Oversight
25 Aloof with
30 Peter Sarsgaard's role in 2016's "Jackie," for short
33 Part 2 of the quip
34 Traveled to an island, in a way
35 Children's author Carle
37 Squid predator
39 Wanting no more, say
40 Part 3 of the quip
43 Disoriented
44 Cry at the end of a big job
45 Files a petition
46 Continue with
48 Part 4 of the quip
50 Lunar New Year
51 Play around
52 Philippine coins
54 Drop a line?
56 Devise, as a plot
60 End of the quip
66 Where shampoo was invented
67 Home of 66-Across
68 Stumble
69 ____ footage
70 Many a driver's ed enrollee
71 Regarding

DOWN

1 Writes
2 Slews
3 Tibetan spiritual leader
4 Epitome of slowness
5 Cousin ____ ("The Addams Family" member)
6 Agatha Christie ____ Miller
7 ____ diem
8 Arthur ____, 1975 Wimbledon winner
9 Woodcutter's prop
10 Spot for many a "mom" tattoo
11 Singer Rawls
12 Theater chain or cable channel
13 Dit's counterpart
18 Aid in busing
19 Back in the day
23 Fictional character who dreams about Heffalumps
24 Positive response to "Agree?"
26 Some exams
27 Skedaddled
28 Conical shelter
29 Most unusual
30 Meal
31 Tutti-____
32 "____ Cousins" (1964 Elvis film)
34 ____ Mae (mortgage company)
36 "10-4!"
38 Head to the office?
41 Come under fire, literally or figuratively
42 Ones ordering lab tests?
47 Heroine Prior of the "Divergent" series
49 London's ____ Square
52 Terrible twos, e.g.
53 Ed Asner role in 2003's "Elf"
55 "Right now!"
57 Rips [five letters]
58 Lit ____
59 Shot, for short
60 Certain sib
61 "Explosive" cable channel
62 Prelude to a kiss
63 New driver's acquisition: Abbr.
64 Something dispensed with in "business casual"
65 Actor McShane

by Rob Baker

ACROSS

1 Good or bad vacuum review?
6 Psych (up)
9 Provides a hideout for, maybe
14 ". . . but it seems like you hate the idea"
15 Round figure?
16 "Well, imagine that!"
17 One performing a palm print analysis
20 Some strays
21 Essence of a good roast
24 Ones playing cornhole, e.g.
25 Core assets?
28 Wedding speech opener
30 Sonny and Cher, e.g.
32 Trochee's counterpart
33 Country bumpkins
37 Tots (up)
38 One of the pounds of a pound cake
40 Something used to improve one's English?
41 Informal term of affection
42 Grain
43 Downed
44 ___Car Series
45 Repeated Warhol subject
46 Tree in the etymology of "gin"
49 Leads, as a D&D campaign
51 "I'll take that as ___"
52 Worries
53 Common scat syllable
54 Setting for the memorable cable car scene in "Moonraker"
55 First-aid item
57 TiVo, e.g.
58 Desktop array
60 Factory vessel
61 Singer Gorme
63 Setting of 2019's "Parasite"

64 ". . ." equivalent
65 High number?
66 Together
67 ___ degree
68 In a lather, say

DOWN

1 Luke, to Darth Vader
2 Catering vessel
3 "Facts First" sloganeer
4 Hawaiian coffee
5 Features of some beach houses
6 Features in some houses of worship
7 New York City store with 1.2+ million square feet of retail space
8 Something that's asked
9 "That's a goldang lie!"
10 Lunch orders often served hot
11 Biblical patriarch with a two-syllable name
12 "Full Frontal With Samantha Bee" airer
13 Stand-up comic's material
18 Clergy, metaphorically
19 Three fighters at the O.K. Corral
21 Thin, unhealthy-looking sort
22 Treats usually served in miniature cups
23 Pizzeria supplies
25 Eventgoers
26 "Booksmart" and "Dumb and Dumber," e.g.
27 Uninspiring
29 Be up against
31 Hassle

34 "This is just . . . too much"
35 Adorable sweethearts
36 Stand guard
39 "The Big Bang Theory" role
41 Cassis cocktail
45 Actress Tomei
47 College inits. on both the East and West Coasts
48 Bailout button
50 One way to be missed
55 Man is one
56 Florida has some
59 Sister
62 Solver of this puzzle

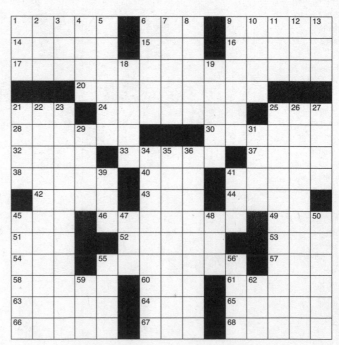

by Parker Higgins and Ross Trudeau

ACROSS

1 Word before bar or party
7 Athena's winged companion
10 Hype (up)
13 Diamond official
14 Sulk
16 "___, fi, fo, fum"
17 *Drivers' process when two lanes of traffic become one
19 Antitrust law enforcement org.
20 Sick
21 Bizarre
22 Ancient Greek market
24 The windows to the soul, it's said
26 *Garden plant that opens and shuts its "mouth" when squeezed
28 Pony up
30 Brand of sunglasses
31 Syria's Bashar al-___
34 French word after "vous"
36 When you're on it, you're en pointe
38 *White pizza toppings
42 Sacramento-to-San Diego dir.
43 Long stretches
44 What you've got going for you
45 Threaten, as a cat might
48 Puncher's tool
49 *Design on some baseball uniforms
52 Bus driver for Lisa and Bart
56 Darkest part of a shadow
57 They're sworn
59 Burgle
60 Brown who wrote "Bury My Heart at Wounded Knee"
61 Accept and let go of something . . . or a hint to the starts of the answers to the starred clues

64 Vitamin supplement retailer
65 Munich Mrs.
66 Official declarations
67 Laugh sound
68 ___ mode
69 Major-leaguer who wears 49-Across at home

DOWN

1 Q preceder, in song
2 Poet Dickinson
3 Jobs creation
4 "Let 'er ___!"
5 Gaffer, best boy and others
6 Inquisition charge
7 Work from Bellini or Rossini
8 Popular blogging platform
9 Tote
10 Espresso-over-ice cream desserts
11 Time keeper
12 Pie nut
15 Like some people at weddings and funerals
18 Lowest part of a range, for short
23 Chitter-chatter
25 Old-fashioned shoe cover
27 Inexact recipe amount
29 Hubbub
31 They can be sculpted and chiseled
32 You might order ahi tuna or yellowtail from it
33 "East of Eden" author
34 Moving
35 Wine vessel
37 Abbr. on a cornerstone
39 Close by
40 Uncooked
41 Home of the Viking Ship Museum
46 Azerbaijan or Lithuania, once: Abbr.

47 Wizard's accessory
48 Daughter of Joe and Jill Biden
49 Chubby
50 Italian city in a "Kiss Me, Kate" song
51 [waves hand in a circle]
53 Something weighed at a weigh station
54 Linzer ___ (pastry)
55 Very corpulent
58 Pop
62 Glass of "This American Life"
63 Missing letters in "transgre_s_o_," appropriately

by Kate Hawkins

ACROSS

1 South Asian, informally
5 "Imperial gem" mined as early as 6000 B.C.
9 Supplier of iron carrots in old cartoons
13 Islamic scholar
14 Make some cuts, perhaps
15 Tender feelings
16 Mood setters for a romantic dinner
18 Samples
19 What may be traded for tat
20 Comic actress Kristen
21 "My Friend ___" (classic of children's literature)
22 Captain Marvel, for one
24 Actor Cooper
26 Duck color
27 Ancient dweller of Central Asia and Eastern Europe
28 Some hesitations
29 There are 30 on an icosahedron
31 Bounds
34 Photosynthetic process "inflating" 16-, 24-, 46- and 56-Across
37 Author of "The Bonesetter's Daughter," 2001
38 One of two in 2/22/22
41 Things "said" in doctors' offices
44 Texter's "hold on a sec"
45 Repellent
46 Torn and ragged clothing
50 Feminine name that anagrams to another feminine name
51 Is behind
52 "___ one teach one" (rhyming proverb)
54 Prez who founded the March of Dimes
55 His first initial stands for "Ieoh"
56 Quarter-pound things at McDonald's
58 The Ark of the Covenant, e.g.
59 Fake coin
60 "Popular Fallacies" writer, 1826
61 Adam's apple locale
62 Sprites, but not Pepsis
63 Controvert

DOWN

1 Call the shots
2 Corresponded with, in a way
3 World capital on the so-called Pacific Ring of Fire
4 "You didn't ask, but . . ." to a texter
5 Force-ful character
6 Wing it
7 Soccer star Maradona
8 Mars rovers, in brief?
9 Like burning plastic
10 Early chewing gum ingredient
11 More submissive
12 60-Across output or 18-Across synonym
15 Where Aquaman reigns as king
17 Biting remarks?
21 Carnivorous : meat :: carpophagous : ___
23 Echo speaker
25 Often-uttered lead-in to "That's gotta hurt!"
30 Like Canada's maple leaf
31 Leave alone
32 ___ moment
33 Unravel
35 Street food favorites topped with tzatziki
36 It may be applied to a single digit
39 Sit after everyone else scooches over
40 Grist for the rumor mill
41 It may get worn out
42 In a position to sue, say
43 Readers may flip over it
47 Movie-themed Happy Meal, e.g.
48 Sphere
49 Took notice, in a way
50 Comedian Margaret
53 Peons, metaphorically
56 Letter resembling Indiana University's logo
57 ___-Ed (animated talks for kids)

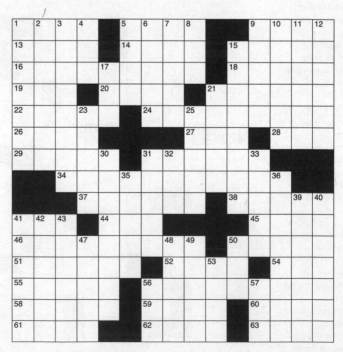

by Jeff Chen

ACROSS

1 Cardamom-infused tea
5 Not give up, say
10 Pronoun before "it may concern"
14 Partner of raised
15 China's Zhou ___
16 Place that generates buzz
17 Ate and ran, say
19 Almost closed
20 ___ on actual events
21 Fit to live in
23 "The Goldfinch" writer Donna
25 Some E.R. cases
26 Make a scapegoat of
28 Kigali resident
32 Title of respect
33 Unclear mental state
36 Throw with force
37 Legendary Himalayan humanoid
41 Capacious
42 Not falling for
43 Play for a sucker
44 Place to pitch a product
46 Entice
49 Amber quaff
50 Catherine of "Beetlejuice"
52 The magic word?
56 Japanese automaker
60 Jabba the ___ ("Star Wars" meanie)
61 Core exercises . . . or a hint to eight squares in this puzzle
63 Relative of a cor anglais
64 Consumes, in a way
65 Sharer's word
66 Tear to bits
67 Food service giant
68 Norse god of thunder

DOWN

1 N.Y.C. venue for the Ramones and the Cramps
2 Sesenta minutos
3 Certain horses
4 Still being debugged
5 Gave sustenance
6 "Not right this second"
7 Flicker of light
8 "Thirty days ___ September . . ."
9 Finish gift-wrapping, say
10 "How've you been?"
11 Muslim headscarf
12 The earth's path around the sun, e.g.
13 Little more than
18 Dutch cheese
22 Neighbor of Montana
24 Fix up again, as a house
26 Hen's hatchlings
27 V.I.P. conveyances
28 Staff break?
29 Block, as a stream
30 "Stop!," at sea
31 State bird of Hawaii
32 Hummus brand
34 Prickly plant with healing qualities
35 ___ garden
38 Affected
39 Spiral-horned antelope
40 The "N" of N.B.
45 Aromatic everareens
47 Dublin's land, to poets
48 Poppin' Fresh or Tony the Tiger
50 Arctic predators
51 Cool head?
52 Dislike with a passion
53 Cartoonist Goldberg who drew contraptions like the "Self-Operating Napkin"
54 Gobs
55 Friar's home
57 "Think again!"
58 Bit of binary code
59 Geographical inits. until 1991
62 Troop troupe, for short

by Jared Goudsmit

ACROSS

1 It may be mined or crunched
5 Night lights, of a sort
11 ___ card (auditioner's need)
14 Suit
15 Documents
16 Actress Mendes
17 Mechanical
18 Snack
19 Dispensers
20 An official language of the Northwest Territories
22 Go ashore
24 French
27 Cake
30 Advocate?
31 Word with sing or string
33 Green hazard
35 A word before we forget?
36 Loud firework
38 Catherine of "Schitt's Creek"
40 Warning before a gory movie scene . . . or a phonetic hint to answering four rows in this puzzle
44 Thoroughly enjoyed
45 Somber rings
47 Burn a bit
50 Fictional Christian of books and films
52 Sussex smell
53 Atlantic
55 Division
57 Skaters
58 Tries to please, with "to"
60 Host that preceded and succeeded O'Brien
62 Home
63 Office
66 Convenience
70 "Didn't I tell you?"
71 Game 1 in a playoff series
72 Jolly season
73 Poet's palindromic preposition
74 More than a hypothesis, but not quite a law
75 PlayStation rival

DOWN

1 Part of R&D: Abbr.
2 Big name in body sprays
3 Face value?
4 "Thunderstruck" band
5 Sleeper's problem
6 !, in emails
7 ___-com
8 Some cryobank deposits
9 Accounting dept. stamp
10 Vampiric in appearance
11 House that's not the House
12 Turns away
13 "Blown" seal
21 Facepalm emotion
23 Fixed, as a climber's rope
24 Guide showing relief, maybe
25 Smart ___
26 Kind of scoring in fantasy sports leagues, informally
28 Speeder stopper
29 American home of a royal palace
32 Pamplona's province
34 Top gear?
37 Last little bit
39 Celebrity
41 Mongolian tent
42 University near Greensboro
43 Counterfeit token
46 G.R.E. takers, usually: Abbr.
47 Obsolescent music holder
48 Revival figure
49 P.M. preceded and succeeded by Churchill
51 Modern food critic
54 ". . . but perhaps I'm wrong"
56 City in Northern Ireland
59 Former frosh
61 Mineral with parallel bands
64 Meghan Mountbatten-Windsor ___ Markle
65 Composer Brian
67 Butter purchase
68 "Turn to Stone" band of 1977, for short
69 Playmate of Fido and Rover

by Samuel A. Donaldson and Doug Peterson

ACROSS

1 Repair bill segment
6 They may be checked at the door
9 Have being
14 Essential ___ acid
15 Siesta
16 Big name in rental trucks
17 Plant used as ground cover
18 Did or didn't agree to end the illustrators' strike?
20 Did or didn't dilute the prom bowlful?
22 Whirling water
23 Rumple, as hair
24 Suffix with Marx
26 Like the base-8 number system
29 Dean's domain: Abbr.
30 Apr. workhorse
33 Did or didn't perform a New Year's ceremony?
37 Butt out?
38 Org. based in Langley, Va.
39 Fox talent show, for short
40 Did or didn't surpass a D.J.'s mark for accident-free days?
45 Set, as a price
46 Pal
47 Earns the booby prize
48 Part of a terza rima rhyme scheme
49 Corner Monopoly square
51 Gem for some Libras
54 Did or didn't play a good round of golf?
60 Did or didn't participate in the Boy Scouts outing?

62 Dinero
63 With 44-Down, features of some Greek architecture
64 Pro vote
65 Zaps, in the kitchen
66 Ream unit
67 Ready for war
68 High, pricewise

DOWN

1 Source of pumice
2 In the thick of
3 Tight spot
4 In a past life
5 Item in a gas station kiosk
6 Pakistan's chief river
7 Works on socks, say
8 Design detail, briefly
9 Disco ___ (1970s)
10 Woody tissue
11 Reply of confirmation

12 Email command
13 Long basket, in hoops lingo
19 "This or that?"
21 Orange juice option
25 Cow or sow
26 Landfill emanations
27 Shepherd's aid
28 Honky-___
29 Sirius, e g
30 Core group
31 Moves laboriously
32 Detergent brand
34 Lover of Narcissus
35 Thing with pips
36 Head shot accompaniers, maybe
37 Wall St. hire
41 Fall back
42 Wreck, as a hotel room

43 Bush 41 and Bush 43, for two
44 See 63-Across
48 DTs sufferer, for short
49 One of a deck pair
50 Mr. T TV group
51 Singer Redding
52 Milne's bear
53 Super-duper
55 Casual greeting
56 Ring contest
57 Elbow
58 On the sheltered side
59 Stereotypical mobster's voice
61 Insincere display

by David Ben-Merre

ACROSS

1 One of a popular TV game show duo
6 Not present when expected, for short
9 Block
14 Many a "Today" show sign
15 Goof
16 Silly
17 Predecessor of Ariel Sharon
19 Number of days in una semana
20 Questionnaire response column
21 Practiced
22 Queen of Denmark, 1947–72
23 Moravian capital
24 Object
25 Request that would complete 42-Across
31 One looking down
32 Some fuzz
33 ___weekly
35 When a right is sometimes allowed
36 Rocky peak
37 Novelist whose first wife had the same first name, curiously
39 Vet, e.g.
40 Boxer's response
41 Title figure in a Mitch Albom best seller
42 When completed, popular TV program starting in 1975
46 Man's name meaning "young man"
47 Black
48 Meeting place for mathematicians?
51 Linear, in brief
52 Confusion
55 Erase
56 Military protection
58 Thunders
59 Suffix with winter
60 A long time
61 Yes or no follower
62 Land once partly held by the Crusaders: Abbr.
63 One of a popular TV game show duo

DOWN

1 "Say ___"
2 Longtime Ritz competitor
3 "___ in the Morning"
4 9-Down fox
5 Made a start
6 Certain red
7 "Dies ___"
8 Couples cruise locale?
9 See 4-Down and 36-Down
10 It's a mystery
11 Heavyweight champ after Carnera
12 Fighting
13 Crumhorn, e.g.
18 Commander of Saul's army, in I Samuel
22 Live ___
23 Dentist's directive
24 Construction beam
25 Mini, for one
26 "What should I ___?"
27 Clumsy move
28 Kind of switch
29 Pacific nation
30 The British Museum's ___ Marbles
34 Something to fill in
36 1982 9-Down movie
37 You might go to bed early before these
38 Like many gallerygoers
40 "Family Ties" boy
41 Some Monopoly game equipment
43 Sign of an absent mind
44 Nonrhyming poetry
45 One earning a fee, maybe
48 Devices with spools
49 Wells race
50 Raise
51 Like mud
52 Key with three sharps: Abbr.
53 Seven-year-old explorer
54 Ural River city
56 Ones sexually flexible, for short
57 Actor Stephen

by Kevan Choset

ACROSS

1 [5]
5 [1]
10 Word on either side of "à"
13 Sporty auto, for short
14 Call to mind
15 Asteroid area
16 Stand up to
17 In an intellectual manner
19 Pointy-eared TV character
21 [25]
22 Polished off
23 Couldn't help but
27 Feudal lord
28 With 49- and 69-Across, a hint to the meanings of the bracketed clues
31 [10]
32 Spoken for
33 Climber's goal
34 Giga- follower
35 Creator of Oz
37 King of tragedy
39 Dud's sound
42 Caramel-filled candy
44 Prom, e.g.
48 Cyberaddress
49 See 28-Across
51 [30]
53 Combine name
54 Free pass, of sorts
55 Some locker room art
57 Garden pest genus
59 Ones whipping things up in the kitchen?
63 Sci. branch
65 He and she
66 Like some checking accounts
67 Sportsmanship Award org.
68 Bourbon and Beale: Abbr.
69 See 28-Across
70 [50]

DOWN

1 Crumple (up)
2 Faux fat
3 Like late-night commuter trains
4 Harry Belafonte catchword
5 Eat like a bird
6 Alternative to Ct. or La.
7 ___ favor
8 Squeeze (out)
9 Gen. Beauregard's men
10 Soft and smooth
11 Dishonest, informally
12 Compound in disposable coffee cups
15 "South Pacific" setting
18 Small brook
20 [20]
22 Court fig.
24 [60]
25 Do better than
26 Bob Marley classic
29 Red ink
30 Let go
34 Support providers
36 Barista's container
38 Seller of TV spots
39 Some children's show characters
40 Rig contents
41 Projecting wheel rims
43 Links concern
45 Fig Newtons maker
46 [15]
47 Check out
49 Mont Blanc, par exemple
50 Clears the board
52 [40]
56 Turned state's evidence
58 Pal around (with)
60 Parisian pronoun
61 Gee preceder
62 Emeritus: Abbr.
64 "Awesome!"

by Michael David

ACROSS

1 Knock on wood, say
7 Arizona product
14 "Gotcha"
16 "Hoo-oo-ey!"
17 "No clue"
18 One who made the crew cut?
19 Locational nickname with origins in horse racing
20 Amount to be divvied up
21 Operation time
23 Christian of film
24 Antarctic body named for an Englishman
28 Ring
31 Raid target
32 Noted series of paintings by Andrew Wyeth
36 Face seen on many T-shirts
38 500, e.g.
39 Preparing to be shot, say
40 Capital of Australia: Abbr.
41 Googly ___
42 Medical subject of Time magazine covers of 1967 and 2010
44 Wear down
47 Échecs pieces
48 Symbol of might
49 Dweller on the Straits of Johor
55 Shipwreck cause, perhaps
57 Let up on
60 Melancholy, say
61 Private business, in slang
62 Tube warning . . . or an apt title for this puzzle?
63 Manages

DOWN

1 Lightly roast
2 Enzyme suffix
3 One encouraged to drink on the job
4 Midsize moon of Saturn
5 "As I Lay Dying" father
6 Dead center?
7 "Come hungry. Leave happy" sloganeer
8 Kentucky export
9 Being, in Bordeaux
10 License to drill?
11 Battle of Fort Brooke locale, 1863
12 Text alternative
13 "Bonne ___!"
15 Chinese dynasty during the Three Kingdoms period
21 Bummers
22 Food with an inedible center?
23 Censor, in a way
25 Inconclusive
26 Like some extreme coincidences
27 Composer Menken and others
28 Loop of lace
29 Bitcoins, e.g.
30 Stuck, after "up"
33 Top-of-the-hour broadcast, maybe
34 Reason for a food recall
35 Emulates a bear
37 Menu with zoom options
43 Encomium
44 Automaton of Jewish folklore
45 Feminist Wolf
46 City intersected by I-76 and I-77
49 Cut open
50 Architect ___ Ming Pei
51 Lucky figure in Chinese culture
52 Ball
53 Roger of "Cheers"
54 Gen. Robert ___
56 It's about when you leave: Abbr.
58 Brewery sight
59 Prefix with thermal

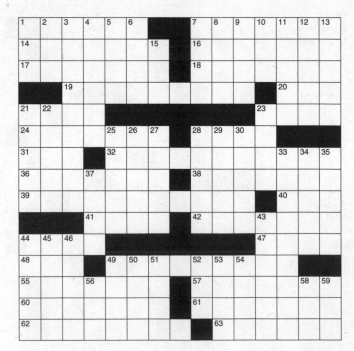

by Milo Beckman

ACROSS

1 Deal
5 "Fine ___"
9 "Stop!," at a checkpoint
13 Finito
14 Balkan native
15 Jackie Robinson's alma mater
16 It might start with "Starters"
17 2003 OutKast hit that was #1 for nine weeks
18 Bumpkin
19 Po boy?
22 Female kangaroo
23 & 24 Like Edward Albee's "The Zoo Story"
25 Teen heartthrob Zac
27 To a greater extent
29 L.A. woman?
32 N.L. team with a tomahawk in its logo
33 Notable 2012 Facebook event, for short
34 Artist Rembrandt van ___
35 In person?
38 Obama education secretary Duncan
40 Draw
41 Chow line?
42 P.R. man?
44 Pushover
48 Detergent brand
49 Apt name for a chef?
50 Turn___
51 Not funny anymore
52 It girl?
57 Natl. Merit Scholarship earner's exam
59 Give or take
60 Antioxidant berry
61 Lucky Charms ingredients
62 Steak cut
63 Scandal suffix
64 Rung
65 Went under
66 Quelques-___ (some: Fr.)

DOWN

1 It might be shaken next to a field
2 Johnson & Johnson skin-care brand
3 Tallest member of a basketball team, often
4 "You make a good point"
5 "Rush Hour" director Ratner
6 It has its ups and downs
7 Tuna salad ingredient
8 List ender
9 "Come again?"
10 Environmental problem addressed in the Clean Air Act
11 Rapper on "NCIS: Los Angeles"
12 Fooled
14 Like many éclairs
20 Guy in dreads, say
21 Pickled delicacy
26 Way in the distance
28 Stands in a studio
29 Fourth-anniversary gift
30 Donkey Kong, e.g.
31 The Cyclones of the Big 12
35 Overwhelm
36 "Homeland" org.
37 Rainbow ___
38 Suitable
39 Harangues
43 Person in un palais
45 Amazon flier
46 Cell body
47 Spots
49 One raising a stink?
53 Tanks
54 "Mamma Mia!" group
55 When shadows are shortest
56 Sauce brand
58 Recipe amt.

by Joel Fagliano

ACROSS

1 Chiquita import
8 Sailor's heavy jacket
15 1968 to the present, in tennis
16 Gathers on the surface, as a layer of molecules
17 Small image displayed in a browser's address bar
18 Quick break
19 Subject of a 2010 biography subtitled "The Voice"
21 Marie Antoinette's loss
22 Title boy in a Humperdinck opera
26 Forearm bones
30 Word before and after "yeah"
32 "Whoa, baby!"
33 It may have one or two sides
35 Part of a baby's daily schedule
37 Port ___
38 City that's home to three Unesco World Heritage Sites
39 Tabloid TV show once co-hosted by Mario Lopez
41 Atomic
42 "Broccoli again?," e.g.
43 Tale
44 Put on guard
46 Hollywood's Roberts and others
48 Part of P.S.T.: Abbr.
50 Several "Boris Godunov" parts
51 Lapsed
53 Back
55 Compact since 1982
61 Bordering state
64 Two

65 Line of Porsches whose name is Spanish for "race"
66 Decorative melody added above a simple musical theme
67 With 47-Down, popular hotel chain
68 Goddess with a golden chariot

DOWN

1 Sockeroo
2 On ___ with
3 Gulf of Finland feeder
4 Have ___ with
5 Unimaginative gift, maybe
6 Sprang
7 "Madness put to good uses," per George Santayana
8 Nickname for Haydn
9 First lady of the 1910s
10 Off course
11 Dangerous family
12 Meal morsel
13 Type letters
14 Medicine amt.
20 Colorful fish
23 Country lads
24 Newsweek and others
25 She was on the cover of back-to-back issues of Time in September 1997
26 Metalworker's tool
27 Sweater material
28 It stops at Manhattan's Washington Square and Rockefeller Center

29 Affair of the 1980s
31 Bygone political inits.
34 Sushi fish
36 Part of the Iams logo
40 Fraternity letters
45 Side by side
47 See 67-Across
49 "You're welcome, amigo"
52 Line that ended in 1917
54 Consistent with
56 Leave rolling in the aisles
57 "Good job!"
58 Ride in London
59 Rice-A-___
60 Talk show times: Abbr.
61 Pal
62 "Kapow!"
63 City community, informally

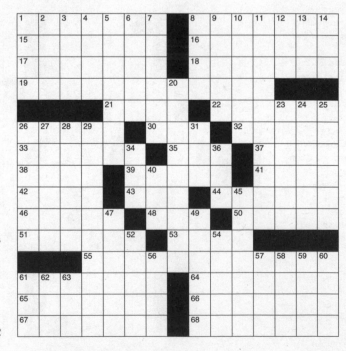

by Michael Shteyman

ACROSS

1 Muscles strengthened by squats
6 Shul attendees
10 Easy-to-spread cheese
14 Zac of "High School Musical"
15 "Don't worry about me"
16 Course list
17 Coming on to a patient, perhaps?
19 Way off
20 Piltdown man, for one
21 Deny membership to skater Starbuck?
23 Agree to
26 Kedrova of "Zorba the Greek"
27 Genre that includes freestyling
28 Up time
29 Cyberspace 'zine
31 Less-than sign's keymate
33 First name in scat
34 "Make my ___!"
35 Shiverer's sound
36 Dictator's directive at a dance club?
42 Seek pocket change, say
43 Itinerary word
44 Close to closed
45 "Taras Bulba" author
48 Marijuana, informally
49 Seeker of illicit 48-Across
50 Hollywood's Gardner
51 Cowardly Lion portrayer
53 New York site of Mark Twain's grave
55 Bad-mouth designer Chanel?
57 "Mon ___!"
58 Radio City's architectural style
59 "Strive for medium quality on this one"?
64 Cheese that doesn't spoil
65 Painter Nolde
66 Muslim woman's veil
67 Idiot
68 Onion rings, e.g.
69 Potentially dangerous strain

DOWN

1 Proof letters
2 Area 51 craft, supposedly
3 Part of a curve
4 Dance to Tito Puente, say
5 Buttinsky
6 Give bad luck
7 Rock subgenre
8 Hit the jackpot
9 Toast word
10 Key using all the black keys: Abbr.
11 Go straight
12 Facing big trouble
13 Moon of Jupiter
18 Suitable for most audiences
22 Decorative inlay material
23 First fratricide victim
24 Nat or Natalie
25 Gelding-to-be, maybe
26 Break between flights
30 Fannie ___
32 Sunday hymn accompaniment
35 2002 sequel starring Wesley Snipes
37 Mello ___ (soft drink)
38 Budget chart shape
39 City near Santa Barbara
40 Teri of "Tootsie"
41 Ocean predator
45 Traipsed (about)
46 City of northern Spain
47 Often-removed car part
48 Amnesiac's question
52 Topmost points
54 Hades' river of forgetfulness
56 Command to Fido
57 Editorial strike-out
60 Give a ribbing
61 Spanish eye
62 ___ ammoniac
63 Geisha's accessory

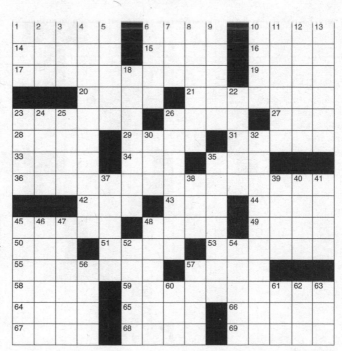

by Will Nediger

ACROSS

1 Toon/live action film of 1996
9 Typewriter's spot
13 Tool for the scatterbrained
15 Thereafter
16 Tragedy-stricken
17 "Three Sisters" playwright Chekhov
18 Torpedo detector
19 Trademarked Intel chip
21 "This Little Girl of Mine" country singer ___ Young
23 Take
24 Telegraph suffix
25 Told to come
26 Tripp's rank on "CSI: Miami": Abbr.
28 True: Ger.
30 Tear up
31 Tetley products
32 Twit
34 Tiger's bagful
35 Taoism, e.g.: Abbr.
36 Technical work requirement
37 Total
38 Tense, maybe
42 TV channel with "Style Report" and "Beauty Report"
44 Tsars and others
45 Tide's ebb, e.g.
48 Threaded across and down
49 Texas hold'em action
51 Text you might R.S.V.P. to
52 Thing that's highly explosive
56 Trig functions
57 Treating all fairly
58 Toboggan
59 Taxed

DOWN

1 Tosses, as seeds
2 Theorem work
3 Titan booster
4 The Café Carlyle and others
5 Times to start new calendarios
6 "The ___ is up!"
7 Type of dye
8 Target audience of Maxim
9 Ten-spots and such
10 Taken
11 Traveled by Vespa
12 Ted and others
14 Third way, maybe
15 "The House of the Seven Gables" locale
20 Towering tree
22 Tadpole's later form, perhaps
23 This puzzle's theme
26 Turn a blind eye, say
27 Turkey or chicken dish served cold
29 Taste authority
31 Toned quality
33 Tunnel effect
34 Trumpet blares
39 Treated for preservation, maybe
40 Touchdowns : football :: ___ : rugby
41 "That's terrible!"
43 Tec group in old France
46 Terri with the 1980 country hit "Somebody's Knockin'"
47 Tenor standard "___ Mio"
50 Took (out)
53 Test figs.
54 Tough ___
55 Theater head: Abbr

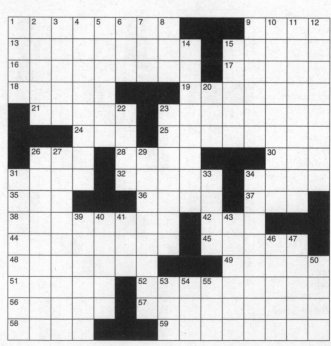

by Mike Buckley

ACROSS

1 Espousing crime?
7 Custard need
10 Michigan college or its town
14 Baby attire with crotch snaps
15 Pistol PAC-ers?
16 Luau handouts
17 Respiratory woe
18 1/sec, in trig
19 Green sci.
20 Graduation requirement, perhaps
23 Some 'Vette roofs
24 "The Wiz" director
25 Org. that negotiates with G.M.
28 Matures
30 Athlete Jim whose Native American name was Wa-Tho-Huk
32 High-pitched cry from an ump?
36 Scarf down
37 Signs to heed
38 Cooked, as Swiss steak
40 Fiancée of Napoleon
42 Singer Eydie
43 ___ Lanka
44 Anastasia's father was one
45 Hullabaloo
47 Island off the coast of Scotland
49 Napoleonic marshal Michel
50 Dance for two
52 Big shot
57 Result of not following through (of which there are four examples in this puzzle's grid)
60 Part of 39-Down
62 "___ had it!"
63 "Für Elise" key
64 Sportscaster Albert
65 Finalized
66 Model Bündchen
67 Portend
68 Shop window posting: Abbr.
69 Sonnet's finish

DOWN

1 Toot one's horn
2 Cartographer's blowup
3 "I don't ___ respect!"
4 "I saw ___ a-sailing . . ."
5 Brunch libation
6 Classic car datum
7 Coat, in a way
8 "I do" sayer
9 Pilot light, e.g.
10 Baldwin of "30 Rock"
11 Some college staff
12 See 55-Down
13 Nonverbal communication syst.
21 Seek mercy, say
22 Guiding beliefs
26 Sleep problem
27 "The Pied Piper of Hamelin" river
29 "I didn't know that!"
31 Exclude
32 Toy you can "put somebody's eye out" with
33 Soap-on-___ (bath buy)
34 Last Celtic to wear #33
35 Bride's ride
39 1954–77 defense grp.
40 Lose tautness
41 Austrian "a"
43 Official seals
46 Jaunty in appearance
48 Societal breakdown
51 "Over my dead body!"
53 Out of kilter
54 I.Q. test pioneer
55 With 12-Down, classic Neapolitan tune
56 Army Ranger's topper
58 All-night bash
59 Threadbare threads
60 U.N. figure: Abbr.
61 Saint, in Rio

by Peter A. Collins

ACROSS

1 Suitable company?
7 Model behavior
13 Veteran
16 Those created equal, per Jefferson
17 Regular in Judd Apatow comedies
18 Sheer, informally
19 "Cómo ___?"
20 State that is home to the Natl. Teachers Hall of Fame
22 Promises to pay
23 Came across as
25 It can be raised or folded
28 Flimsy, as stitching
34 Tinseltown terrier
38 "Sprechen ___ Deutsch?"
39 Keys on a keyboard
40 "Geez!"
41 Home of the Azadi Tower
43 Rice quarters
44 Composer Shostakovich
46 Extreme soreness
47 Alternatively
48 Kidney doctor
51 Some pokers
52 Gently pulls
57 Tiny fraction of time: Abbr.
60 "Little" name in 1960s pop
63 Divine dish
64 Bacteriologist Paul who coined the word "chemotherapy"
67 Subject of the Final Jeopardy! question that knocked out Ken Jennings after a record 74 wins . . . or a hint to this puzzle's theme
69 Borrower

70 Like Ziploc bags
71 Clay targets, informally
72 Fouled (up)

DOWN

1 Boobs
2 Teammate of Robinson of the 1940–'50s Dodgers
3 Dull
4 Religious retreat
5 Props used in "The Good, the Bad and the Ugly"
6 Gerund's end
7 Pops
8 "Hip, hip, Jorge!"?
9 Winter jaunt
10 "If ___ believe . . ."
11 Prime minister who gave his name to an article of clothing
12 Lion prey
14 Cartoonish cry
15 Test subj.
21 Texans are part of it, for short
24 Concentrate
26 Lowest in fat
27 N.L. East team
29 Never, to Nietzsche
30 Baseball's Iron Horse
31 Global warming subj.
32 Pretense
33 Julie Andrews, for one
34 Wing: Abbr.
35 Equal
36 Spill
37 Mineral with high carbon content
42 N.L. West team
45 Ticket info
49 Verb ending?

50 Spill
53 Big bashes
54 Ones who may annoy hoi polloi
55 Tante's husband
56 In the flesh?
57 Flanders and Kelly
58 William Steig book on which a hit 2001 film was based
59 North Sea feeder
61 Kind of tape
62 Big source of reality TV
65 Barracks bed
66 Smash hits: Abbr.
68 Butt

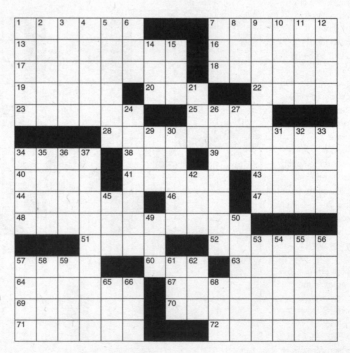

by David Levinson Wilk

ACROSS

1 Blood bank supplies
8 Foliage-viewing mo.
11 Welcome sign for a B'way angel
14 Dental deposits
15 P, to Pythagoras
16 Pricing word
17 Senior softballers, e.g.?
19 LAX monitor info
20 "The Turner Diaries" conflict
21 ___ Flux (Charlize Theron role)
22 Star in Cygnus
25 K-9 Corps member?
27 Gooey camp fare
29 CNN's Barnett and others
30 Counterpart of long.
31 Had down cold
35 Descartes's "sum," translated
36 Former first lady sporting a different outfit?
41 El Al hub city
42 Tries to win
43 Make "it"
45 Greyhound lookalike
48 Magician's hiding spot
51 Small-screen performance of "Hamlet," e.g.?
55 Missed the mark
56 Thai currency
57 Broadway title character who sings "Tea for Two"
59 Vacation time in Versailles
60 King, queen or jack?
64 Lineage-based women's org.
65 Ore suffix
66 Sparkly component of face paint
67 'Fore
68 Leftorium owner on "The Simpsons"
69 Teeter-totters

DOWN

1 Fig. on an I.R.S. schedule
2 "Well, ___-di-dah!"
3 Barley wine, really
4 Fun-house worker, maybe
5 Zimbabwean strongman Robert
6 Author Waugh
7 Lesser-played half of a 45
8 Nymph of Mount Ida, e.g.
9 Use plastic
10 Certain turkey
11 Dash component
12 Prepare for next year's models, say
13 Cousins of chimps
18 Pan Am rival
21 "What ___" ("Ho-hum")
22 Cable alternative, for short
23 Mus. key with four sharps
24 A few bricks short of a load
26 CNN's Burnett
28 One of a biathlete's pair
32 Common packaging word
33 "The Name of the Rose" author
34 "___ knows?"
37 Try to win
38 Pittsburgh radio station since 1920, said to be the world's first
39 Fool
40 Humorist Barry
44 Many a H.S. dropout's goal . . . and what's added to 17-, 25-, 36-, 51- and 60-Across
45 "Venerable" monk of old England
46 First movie to gross more than $2 billion (2009)
47 Put a match to
49 Allow to expire
50 Puts up
52 Relaxed
53 Paternity suit evidence
54 Safecrackers
58 Prefix with cast
60 Rouge or blanc selection
61 ___ crossroads
62 FF's opposite, on a VCR
63 "ER" personnel

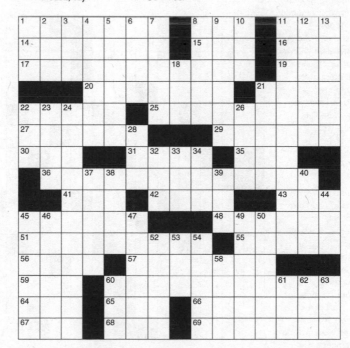

by Richard and Judith Martin

ACROSS

1 Tow job, maybe
5 Saturn or Mercury
8 Best buds?
13 Stylishness
14 ___ canto
15 A Jackson
16 *Comfy place
18 Rick who sang "Together Forever"
19 PayPal money
20 *Alternative to a Crock-Pot
22 Clear
23 Oahu-to-Molokai dir.
25 Truly
26 Prefix with thermal
27 *Metaphor for a sharp mind
30 Make lean
32 Woman in a garden
33 American Heart Mo. (appropriately)
35 Pitcher Hideo ___
36 *Gathering spot for the upwardly mobile?
39 Turn about
41 Discernment of a sort
42 Enumeration follower
43 What George lacks?
45 *Campaign from town to town
50 Return address for many absentee ballots: Abbr.
51 Wall St. insider, maybe
53 Like some stocks, for short
54 Weak ___
55 *Where a cast may be found
58 Skater ___ Anton Ohno
60 Garment with buttons on the left
61 Welcoming symbol . . . or what each part of the answers to the six starred clues can do?
63 Compounds with nitrogen
64 Where a cast may be found
65 Jai ___
66 Sharp tastes
67 Big do
68 Filibusterers, e.g.: Abbr.

DOWN

1 Directs
2 Draw
3 Detour-causing event
4 Some poor Olympic scores
5 Eastern wrap
6 Like Texas vis-à-vis New York, politically
7 ___ cheese
8 Four-time Pro Bowler Ahmad
9 "Beetle Bailey" dog
10 Algebra problem directive
11 Test with letters
12 Refuse
15 Some frills
17 Put off till later
21 Universal donor's classification
24 Case who co-founded AOL
28 Caught fish in a pot, say
29 Broadcast workers' union
31 Pass
34 Gen. Scowcroft who advised Ford and Bush
36 New mintage of 2002
37 Limerick scheme
38 Oncology procedure
39 Day of rest
40 One of the Canary Islands
44 Dangerous buildup in a mine
46 Onetime Ebert partner
47 Eight-time Oscar nominee who never won
48 Advance again
49 Hunters of the now-extinct moa
52 Shippers' plans: Abbr.
56 ___ fu
57 "An expensive way of playing marbles," per G. K. Chesterton
59 P.R. agents' aids
62 Massage target, maybe

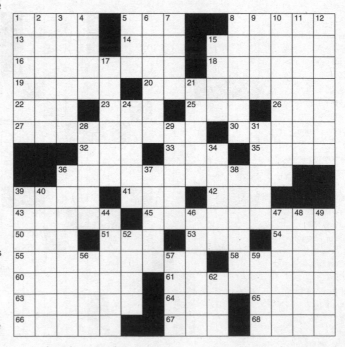

by Jules P. Markey

Note: The answer to each starred clue is a compound word or a familiar two-word phrase. A certain four-letter word (spelled out clockwise by the circled squares) can follow the first half and precede the second half of each of these answers, in each case to complete another compound word or familiar two-word phrase.

ACROSS

1 Balkan land
7 Semi compartment
10 Former Chevy subcompact
14 Countenance
15 Burmese P.M.
16 Classico rival
17 *Approval indicators
19 Calendario spans
20 Sharp-eyed sort
21 *Ban
23 Greenish shade
26 Legion
27 "Public Enemies" officer
31 Repeated cry in the Ramones' "Blitzkrieg Bop"
34 "Honor Thy Father" author
35 Shape of the Aleutian Islands, on a map
37 Miles away
38 Tulsa sch.
39 *December 31
42 H.I.V. drug
43 Old
45 Capital of 58-Down, briefly
46 Some navels
48 Places for judokas
50 Mail that isn't opened
52 H-dos-O?
54 Striking part
55 *What a "forever" stamp lacks
59 2007–08 N.B.A. M.V.P., to fans
63 "___ Dinka Doo"
64 *Union supporter?
67 Manhattanite, e.g., informally
68 Figure who works with figures, for short
69 On
70 Kit ___ (candy bars)
71 City ESE of the 10-Down
72 Managed

DOWN

1 Bond girl Barbara
2 Watchdog org.
3 Expel forcibly
4 Accessory for Annie Hall
5 ___ factor
6 $$$ source
7 Make waves?
8 1950s heartthrob Paul
9 ___ Gardens
10 Kazakh border lake
11 *Magazine with an annual Hollywood issue
12 Inflated things?
13 Boot
18 Competent
22 ___-i-Noor diamond
24 "No sweat"
25 Arthur and his family in "Hoop Dreams"
27 Coen brothers film
28 *Sailor
29 Deal breaker?
30 Number of colors on the Italian flag
32 Tormented, as pledges
33 Scraps
34 Lowly sort
36 Big bill
40 Jungfrau, e.g.
41 Il ___
44 Place savers of a sort
47 Ale vessel
49 Santa Fe or Tucson, in brief
51 Short detail?
53 Car repair chain
55 Informer
56 Author Seton
57 Sitting spots on Santas
58 See 45-Across
60 Steinbeck character
61 Distort, as the truth
62 "In which case . . ."
65 It often gets cured
66 Wartime stat

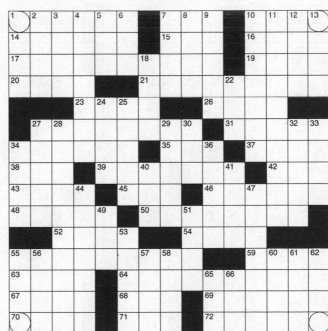

by John Farmer

ACROSS

1 Dust Bowl phenomenon
8 Word with oyster or rose
11 Chatter
14 "Verrry interesting!"
15 Facebook co-founder Saverin
17 Total
18 Shades, e.g.
19 Travel option
20 "Grand, ungodly, godlike man" of fiction
22 Latin lover's whisper
23 It might avoid a collar
24 "No ___!"
26 Biblical hunter
27 Last Pope Paolo, numerically
29 Goose : gaggle :: ___ : knot
30 Hotel room option
31 Be off
33 Press
35 Hierarchical level: Abbr.
36 Charmin and others, for short
39 Started
41 Hi-___
42 Move like a 29-Across
43 Stipend source
44 "Bewitched" wife, familiarly
46 Norway's patron saint
48 Skedaddles
50 Spin-heavy shot
54 Spin-o-___ (360-degree hockey maneuver)
55 Commercial snack cakes
57 Unbelievable, say
58 A satellite may be kept in it
60 First name in the 2012 Republican primary
61 Enterprise counselor
62 Private performances?
64 Discuss in detail
66 Pull in the driveway, say
67 Orchestrate
68 Suffers from
69 What cats and waves do
70 Seafloor features

DOWN

1 Overshadows
2 Traditional Irish brew
3 Radio format
4 Howl
5 Econ. stat
6 ___ blazes
7 ___ wonder (Tone Loc or Crowded House, e.g.)
8 Apiarist's facial display
9 Big name in ice cream
10 Offenbach's "Belle nuit, ô nuit d'amour," e.g.
11 Like frying vis-à-vis baking
12 Unwillingness to yield
13 New York City composition
16 Every seven days
21 & 25 See 32-Down
28 "Carmina Burana" composer
32 With 21- and 25-Down, lacking refinement . . . like this puzzle's grid?
34 Cracker topper
36 Leaving no stone unturned
37 One is named for the explorer James Ross
38 Mass junk mailers
40 Worker's advocate
45 "The Bad News Bears" actor
47 Islam, e.g.
49 "Who cares?"
51 Unisex wrap
52 Shed, with "off"
53 In groups
56 "Octopus's Garden" singer
59 Utility belt item
63 Actress Thurman
65 Sign of a hit

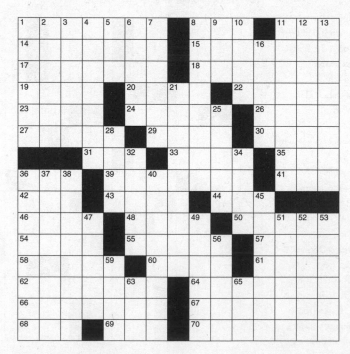

by Paul Hunsberger

ACROSS

1 Sing the praises of
6 Online party reminder
11 Josh
14 "The Family Circus" cartoonist
15 Corral
16 Surgeon's org.
17 Yellow-eyed birds of prey
20 Apple products since 1998
21 Solemn column
22 Part of a fraternity ritual, perhaps
28 energystar.gov grp.
29 Sound of delight
30 Spectrum start
31 Traces of smoke
34 Dr. Seuss's surname
37 Decision reversal . . . or, literally, what can be found inside 17-, 22-, 49- and 58-Across
41 Church laws
42 Model's asset
44 Counselors' org.
47 It's hot, then it's not
48 Web video gear
49 Cybermenaces
56 Pants, slangily
57 Hunter in the night sky
58 How children should be, in a saying
65 Eye, to a bard
66 Apple products since 2001
67 Blast from the past
68 Code-cracking org.
69 Guitar accessories
70 Place to schuss

DOWN

1 Hosp. readout
2 Gen ___
3 ___ Bo (exercise system)
4 How elated people walk
5 "I want to try!"
6 Geologic span
7 Vice ___
8 Room offerer
9 Homophone of 3-Down
10 Maze's goal
11 Where to order oysters
12 "My answer was . . . ," in teen-speak
13 Whacked good
18 Magician's prop
19 Sound of delight
22 Embroider, e.g.
23 Movie that might have a cast of thousands
24 Transaction option
25 Unworldly ones
26 Gauge site, for short
27 Docile sorts
32 Pre-election ad buyer, maybe
33 Chaotic situation
34 Crystal-filled rock
35 Seemingly forever
36 Southeast Asian tongue
38 Swarming annoyance
39 Major Thai export
40 Late 19th-century anarchist's foe
43 Ambulance letters
44 Pursues, as a tip
45 Wood-damaging insects
46 Simple creature
50 Wordplay from Groucho
51 Sonata finale, often
52 ___ Perot
53 River islet
54 Some Pacific salmon
55 Belfry sound
59 Razor brand
60 ___ creek
61 Blouse, e.g.
62 Hoo-ha
63 Letters on Halloween decorations
64 Near-failing mark

by Daniel Kantor

ACROSS

1, 4 & 7 Both sides . . . or the missing starts for all the remaining Across answers
10 Plot
12 Stops working
14 For free
15 Manuscript reviewer
16 Talk
17 Disclose
18 Walks
20 Like some explosions and substances
22 German toast
23 Bowl-shaped part of the ear
24 Moral sense
28 Traffic
32 Atom parts
33 Ban
35 Study of verse
36 Some golf events
37 Family name on "Roseanne"
38 Singer Stevens
39 Characterized by
41 Solidifies
43 Be made up (of)
44 Hinders
46 Squeezes
48 Iran-___
49 1997 Nicolas Cage/John Malkovich thriller
50 Ones jacking up prices, maybe
54 Declared publicly
58 Bit of mountain flora
59 Introduction
61 Signify
62 Big shells
63 Associates
64 Show
65 For a while
66 French tales
67 "Now!"

DOWN

1 ___-Penh
2 Rampant
3 Something you might get your mitts on
4 "___ Death" (Grieg work)
5 Conjunction that's usually part of a pair
6 Tidy up, in a way
7 Cobra's shape, at times
8 French wave
9 Declined
11 Clears the board
12 Complain
13 Group of three rhyming lines
14 They're a couple short of C notes
19 Cacophony
21 Quaker cereal
24 Laurel and Lee
25 Astronomer's sighting
26 Orch. member
27 German article
28 Ladies in waiting?
29 Like some columns
30 Keats, for one
31 Some Security Council votes
34 "___ pal"
40 Pictures of the Old West
41 Twists into a knot
42 Loses freshness
43 Fathering
45 Dander
47 Narrow waterway
50 Half of a best-seller list: Abbr.
51 "___ hollers, let . . ."
52 Overflow (with)
53 Shade of black
54 Skips, as class
55 Early time
56 Conseil d'___
57 Show, informally
60 Test for an M.A. seeker

by Joe Krozel

ACROSS

1 Whitewater craft
5 Chews the fat
9 "Nothing but net" sound
14 She sang with Duke and Dizzy
15 Instrument called "an ill wind that nobody blows good"
16 Ionian Sea vacation isle
17 Out there
18 Lacks pizazz
20 Former Haitian leader Duvalier
22 Clothing, slangily
23 Radio host who often wore cowboy hats
25 Got hitched
26 Overly partisan
31 "Uncle" on a food package
34 ___ Mountains
35 Sen. Biden represented it: Abbr.
36 Jam session feature
37 Doesn't fight back
40 Failed to show up for, informally
42 A lot of a flock
43 "Major ___" of 1990s TV
45 Shire of "Rocky"
46 Roseanne's husband on "Roseanne"
47 Animal on display
50 Filming site
51 Roe source
52 Casual eateries
56 Put up
61 Inuit, maybe
63 Leander's love
64 Téa of "Spanglish"
65 Prefix with plane, to a Brit
66 Calif. neighbor
67 Three-star rank: Abbr.
68 Amount between some and all
69 High roller's pair

DOWN

1 Realize, as profit
2 Sporty auto, for short
3 Try to get airborne, maybe
4 Setting in a Mitchell novel
5 "Get lost!"
6 Ancestor of a calculator
7 Fenway nine, on scoreboards
8 Email folder heading
9 Ruined a shutout
10 Tried to win
11 Rombauer of cookery
12 "Bullitt" law enforcement org.
13 Confused responses
19 Words said with a shrug
21 Light tennis shots that fall just over the net
24 Caesar of old TV
26 Brought along on a hike, say
27 2000s Vienna State Opera conductor
28 Like some heavy buckets
29 Assaying samples
30 Cotillion V.I.P.
31 Yalie's cheer word
32 Like Keebler workers
33 Low-cal yogurt descriptor
36 One-for-one transaction
38 "Same with me!"
39 Confucian principle
41 Chopin piece
44 Built-in feature of the Apple II
47 Focus (on)
48 "Bottoms up!"
49 Stick's partner, in an idiom
50 Soup ingredient in an old folk story
52 Legislature's consideration
53 The Beach Boys' "___ Around"
54 Walk wearily
55 Did laps, say
57 Landlocked African land
58 Hatcher who played Lois Lane
59 Spy novelist Ambler
60 Go out for a short time?
62 Prefix with natal

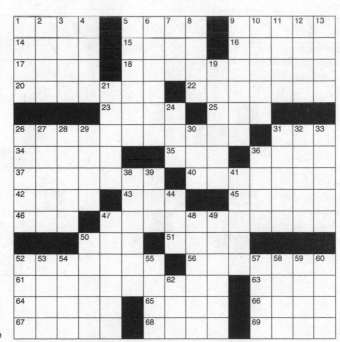

by Richard Chisholm

ACROSS

1 Result of a rise, perhaps
8 Other half
14 One of the Balearic Islands
15 Dessert order at a Mexican restaurant
16 Quirky sort
17 Life-form led by Optimus Prime in the "Transformers" movies
18 Monthly expense
19 Ballpark figure
21 ___ Lonely Boys, group with the 2004 hit "Heaven"
23 Button for enlarging an image
24 Mark of perfection
25 Expose
28 Really, really
31 Gender-___
34 T-Bird alternative
36 Cabbage alternative?
37 "This isn't a trick question"
40 "___ c'est Paris" (French soccer club slogan)
41 Vibe
42 Airs during the holidays
43 Jimmy of high-end footwear
45 Made it through
47 Pro in D.C.
49 Exaggerated
50 "The Bachelorette" network
53 Deli lunch options
57 Sound after a sip
59 Midcruise milieu
60 Where Bill and Hillary first met
62 In
63 Budgeting class?
64 Automotive amenity that offers an annual Santa Tracker
65 Stingrays, often

DOWN

1 Emissions concern
2 Like some pools
3 "Thus . . ."
4 What something bacillary is shaped like
5 Word with wonder or designer
6 Protest movement launched in 2011, familiarly
7 Peace slogan
8 Barricaded
9 To ___ mildly
10 Cry from a balcony
11 Big adventure through the concrete jungle
12 Emissions concern
13 Ciudad del ___, Paraguay's largest city after Asunción
15 Sound investment in the 1980s?
20 Follower of Jesus Christ?
22 Paper cut, e.g.
26 Troubles
27 ___ power
29 Sovereign land, so to speak
30 Excuses
31 It has a $100 billion line of credit with the Treasury Dept.
32 Cousin of a firth
33 Ones calling the strikes?
35 Zwölf minus elf
38 Chill
39 "___ problem"
44 Acorn, by another name
46 Fine wool source
48 Cybertruck maker
51 Mowgli's teacher in "The Jungle Book"
52 Belt wearer, perhaps
53 Lead-in to -graphic
54 Keeping current with
55 Graduation class
56 This is taking fore-e-ever
58 Many start with "I": Abbr.
61 Sinus doc

by Joseph Greenbaum

ACROSS

1 Trash
5 Kind of rock
9 Toni Morrison title character who lives in the Bottom
13 Lower-cost option at a supermarket, usually
15 Fresh
16 Furry creature that Wallace becomes during the full moon, in a "Wallace & Gromit" film
17 Bio subject
18 "___ changed"
19 Feature of the inner planets
20 Thread count?
21 Facebook allows for more than 50
23 Reciprocal of a siemens
24 Sharon Olds's "___ to Dirt"
25 Hush puppies alternative
27 Restaurant starter, informally
30 Prominent attire for Jr. Pac-Man
35 Assumes
36 Grande and others
37 Actress Susan
38 Order at a lodge
39 It's sold by the yard
40 Good things to have for a private party
41 What a trip!
45 Alliterative partner of 45-Down
48 Proceeds smoothly
50 Creature whose male incubates the eggs, during which it won't eat, drink or defecate for 50+ days
51 Trails
52 New York City setting of the "Eloise" books
54 It may be bonded
55 "Much obliged!"
56 Whom to call "maman"
57 Guard, perhaps
58 Current

DOWN

1 Martin or Harvey
2 Actress with an Academy Award for 1960's "Two Women"
3 Amount to
4 Maker of the world's first diesel-powered passenger car
5 Photographer Diane
6 Pickup line?
7 Still alive, so to speak
8 Noted organochloride, in brief
9 Boston exurb
10 Bell Labs development of the 1970s
11 Took off
12 Floors
13 Amount from a flask, maybe
14 Amounts from a distillery, maybe
20 Program replaced by "CBS This Morning"
22 Olympics rule-breaker
23 Like Tony-winning plays
25 Brightens, with "up"
26 ASCAP and A.S.P.C.A.: Abbr.
27 Lead-in to date
28 Walk on water?
29 Disposable shoe liners
30 What cognitive behavioral therapy might treat, in brief
31 Grade
32 "Capisce?"
33 Sure thing
34 Home of the two deepest canyons in the Americas (each 11,500+ feet)
40 Response at the door
41 Gave off, in a way
42 ___ Hall
43 Change in writing
44 'Tis the season to be jolly
45 Kind of rock
46 Behind
47 2008 animated film with the tagline "He's got a monster of a problem"
48 Barents Sea sight
49 Quad part
52 Stone
53 "Absolument!"

by Brooke Husic and Will Nediger

ACROSS

1 San Francisco or Fire Island
9 Lift one's spirits?
15 Brutish boss
16 Unnatural
17 Orthodontist's recommendation
18 Lengthy Twitter post, often
19 Not take for granted
20 Units equivalent to ⅙ of an inch
22 Hosp. diagnostic
23 Throw or shoot
25 Imitation
26 Primed (for)
30 Serving with shawarma
31 Shrimp in a shell, maybe
32 Interminably
34 Tusked beast
37 Movie series set inside a simulated reality, with "The"
38 Home to Mayan ruins like Caracol and Lamanai
39 Many a bill's name in Congress
41 Spare clothes?
42 Young stud
43 Troubadour
45 Actress Amanda
46 Cherry-pick
47 Subscripts on Scrabble tiles
49 C, for one
50 International cricket matches
51 Neat and clean
56 Heartburn reliever
58 Focus of the 2009 Lilly Ledbetter act
60 Dot-com whose name is stylized with two converging arrows

61 Prepare on short notice
62 Greek locale once described as "the island of overmastering passions"
63 Hunter of fish

DOWN

1 Hiker's handful
2 Swear
3 "Monsters, Inc." character who loves snow cones
4 Jason with the 2008 hit "I'm Yours"
5 Architect Saarinen
6 Fan gathering, informally
7 Entered quietly
8 Purposeless
9 "Imagine a case in which . . ."
10 Soft shoes, informally
11 Zero reaction?
12 Hotel hummer
13 Covering for a cold one
14 Bauer of leisure apparel
21 Arcade game feature
24 Miniaturist's supply
25 Accompanier of a black eye
26 2018 film for which Alfonso Cuarón won Best Director
27 Off the mark
28 Copper containers?
29 Commit to a course
31 Long way to go
33 By ___ of (due to)
35 Countenance
36 Heroic exploit
40 Ones who'll manage somehow?

41 Succinct, if nothing else
44 Changes
46 Leviticus calls it "unclean" and not fit for consumption
47 Puzzles
48 Be found not guilty, shockingly
50 Rumpus
52 Civil rights activist Baker
53 Video file format
54 Name of six popes, including one in the 20th century
55 Info described on a Tinder profile
57 Where to fill a flask with alcohol
59 2026 FIFA World Cup co-host

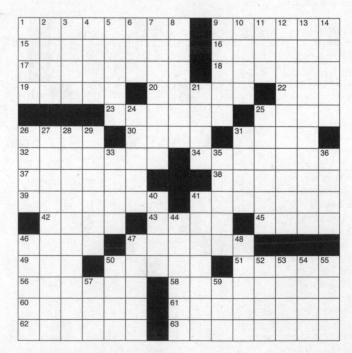

by Patrick John Duggan

ACROSS

1 Maker of the Karma quadcopter drone
6 East Timor's capital
10 Call to a mate
14 Like white-eyes and wheatears
15 River that's a letter off from 20-Across
16 Default result, maybe
17 Chilling
18 Capital whose name means "smoky bay," referencing the steam from its hot springs
20 Sea that's a letter off from 15-Across
21 Hockey star Patrick
22 ____-friendly (ecolabel)
23 Netflix series that caused a 2017 surge in Eggo sales
26 Stadium refrain
27 Palme d'Or field
28 Groups with lots of issues to talk through
31 Not-so-big shot
34 Needing to be charged
35 Donnie ____, title role for Jake Gyllenhaal
36 "Slick"
37 Monitor of a tap
38 Activity with a drawing of names
40 Car music player button
41 Epitome
42 Something good eaters "join"
47 Passages in a long story?
48 ____ Parker (handbag retailer)
49 Suddenly show (up)
51 "Ah, yes, of course . . ."
53 Director Sam
54 Lead-in to medicine
55 Savory sauce made with chocolate
56 Most likely, in a text
57 Home of the Sultan Qaboos Grand Mosque
58 Got rid of
59 Collection of brains

DOWN

1 Mother (and wife!) of Uranus
2 Stay out for too long?
3 Notorious online hub for illegal file sharing, with "The"
4 Reading, for instance
5 With 39-Down, "Wait!"
6 "Anyone who has ever worn a ____ spells it '____,'" per a 2018 New York Times article
7 Nobel-winning daughter of Marie and Pierre Curie
8 What bakers might do their level best to make?
9 Sort
10 "Prego" preceder
11 County that's home to Plymouth, England
12 Mocking, maybe
13 Joins
19 Heads
21 Heavily engaged (in)
24 ____ country
25 Chalamet of 2021's "Dune"
26 9-to-5, e.g.
29 You might take the bait from one
30 Foul up
31 Eponym of Israel's largest airport
32 Scented products that cause underwater "explosions"
33 "Don't wait!"
36 You might have a file for this
38 Word with talking or horse
39 See 5-Down
40 Shade of pink
42 Casual pants material
43 2019 Super Bowl loser, for short
44 Lead role in "The Vampire Diaries"
45 First person to appear simultaneously on the American and British covers of Vogue (Oct. 2021)
46 Played out
50 Site of a famous tilt in European history
52 Sport with a big pay-per-view audience, in brief
53 Spinning inits.

by Adam Aaronson

ACROSS

1 Phrase popularized by Long John Silver of "Treasure Island"
16 It's "on a dark desert highway," in song
17 Ways in which different cultures interact
18 Le Dakota du Sud or le Dakota du Nord
19 Like some traditions
20 Listens, old-style
21 Have that *wow* factor
22 Name ending for Mari- or Rosa-
23 Things people often claim to have read when they haven't
24 Typesetting unit
27 Funky stuff
29 N.B.A. M.V.P. of 2015 and '16, familiarly
31 "I don't do ___. I am ___": Salvador Dalí
32 Eponymous instrument inventor Adolphe
35 Smaller than usual, endearingly
37 "What do you call cheese that isn't yours? Nacho cheese!," e.g.
39 Periods that aren't usually added, for short?
40 "Live in ___" (clothing slogan)
42 Water colors
43 Japanese camera
44 Protagonist of "The O.C."
45 What may be thrown down for a duel
47 Popular video game series with cars, for short
49 Nickname that drops "An-"
52 Show petulance, in a way
53 Former-Yankee-turned-broadcaster, to fans
54 Clean, as decks
55 "Don't sweat the naysayers"
58 Opening statement of an appeal?
59 Digs near a flower bed, say

DOWN

1 Black ___
2 "Too ___ Handle" (Netflix reality show)
3 "We've all been there"
4 Let it all out
5 Hebrew name meaning "my God"
6 Pioneering brand of caffeine-free soft drink
7 Combine
8 Longest-serving U.S. first lady, informally
9 One might be open for business
10 "___ tree falls . . ."
11 Big time for long-distance calling
12 Prickly shrubs
13 Vast, poetically
14 Places for curlers
15 Be wise to
23 Apparel often worn with sandals
25 Computer addresses, for short
26 Green stew
28 Outfit
29 NorCal airport
30 Syllable of disapproval
31 "Whip It" rock band
32 It travels at Mach 1
33 Black sorority with 300,000+ members, in brief
34 Marks, as a survey box
36 The Cowardly Lion's counterpart in Kansas
38 Presidential monogram of the early 1800s
41 The cool kids, e.g.
43 "That really isn't necessary"
44 Original "S.N.L." cast member
45 Home to Lake Volta, the largest artificial reservoir in the world
46 Volume measure
48 Island nation near Fiji
50 Betray, in a way
51 Critic who said "Art is the closest we can come to understanding how a stranger really feels"
52 Daniel Webster or Henry Clay
53 Sheik's peer?
54 Part of a fancy bedding set
56 ___ Juan
57 Like the mizzenmast

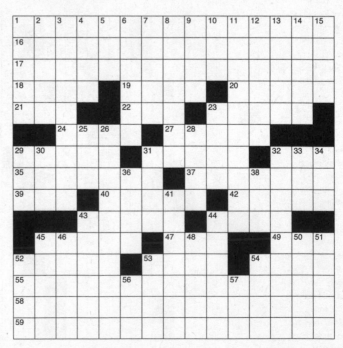

by John Hawksley

ACROSS

1 Sassy
6 Drink with a shot balanced on chopsticks over a beer
14 Meredith's half sister on "Grey's Anatomy"
15 Pack man
17 Certain record
18 Gracious words when accepting an honor
19 Eroded
20 Exhibition that might attract eye rolls, for short
21 Went quickly
22 Third-most popular baby girls' name in 2020, after Olivia and Emma
23 Serengeti grazer
25 Make out
26 Joint winner of Time's Person of the Year for 2020
30 "Incorrect!"
31 "Intolerable Cruelty" director, 2003
32 Org. associated with the note series G-E-C
35 Author who referred to his works as a "legendarium"
37 More vexing
39 Word before now
40 Scoop often used in Indian cuisine
42 Ship on which Darwin collected material for "On the Origin of Species"
43 Encouraging words
45 "Mmm hmm . . ."
48 Ingredients for pastry cream
49 Gumshoe
50 Term of address for a noble
53 Mass Appeal Records co-founder
54 Sheltered place

55 French phrase in many bistro names
57 Daughter of Elrond in "The Lord of the Rings"
58 Fearless
59 Like the flame between exes, sometimes
60 Century of note
61 Examinations

DOWN

1 Played in the wind, say
2 Fixer-upper
3 Above and beyond, with "the"
4 Part of an equine bloodline
5 Song word sung twice before "goodbye"
6 Opened up during an examination
7 The first one printed in America was in 1639
8 Metric speed meas.
9 ___ Olmert, former Israeli P.M.
10 Foe of the Fighting Tigers
11 Multicolor hair effects
12 Fountain fare
13 Censor
16 Whirl
20 The highest form of flattery?
23 Pacific Ocean phenomenon
24 Lemon ___
27 Query
28 Running gear named after running animals
29 Legends, often
32 Ones late to work?
33 "Seriously!"
34 Symbols on the flags of Algeria and Azerbaijan
36 Kind of blue

38 Kit ___ Club ("Cabaret" locale)
41 Genre for "The Dark Knight," appropriately
43 Medieval servant
44 Secretive things?
45 One-named model and philanthropist
46 Storage units prone to explosion
47 Lift a lot
51 Tennis star of the 2000s, familiarly
52 It covers a lot of ground
54 Native of central Canada
56 Word in some South American city names
57 Refined oil product?

by Mary Lou Guizzo and Jeff Chen

ACROSS

1 Small headache
5 Onetime chain that offered Free Battery Club memberships
15 10-Down highlight
16 Best-selling heavy metal band named for a torture device
17 Big ol' mouth
18 Brushing, e.g.
19 TV character who said "I am so smart! I am so smart! S-M-R-T!"
21 Old worker with pads
22 Big ol' mouth
23 Pine product
25 It's flat on a snapback
26 Coin-___
27 8 vis-à-vis 2
29 Aimee ___ McPherson, evangelist behind America's first megachurch
34 Vulnerable newcomers, in slang
37 Field
38 Duo in an ellipse
39 Intoxicate
41 They might be gathered by the pound
42 Bio subj.
43 Labor union offering, perhaps
45 More than dangerous
48 Part
49 Banned Books Week org.
50 ___ Yaga (folklore villain)
52 Release
54 Its structure was evidenced by Photo 51, an X-ray captured in 1952
57 Several Russian czars
59 Cocktail tidbit
61 Going from 99 to 100, say
64 Archer of note
65 In hot pursuit
66 See 60-Down
67 Experts in English?
68 Sharp, in a way

DOWN

1 Trail
2 Like a butterfingers
3 Bucky in the comic strip "Get Fuzzy," e.g.
4 Patches up, in a way
5 Clear
6 Foe of Wonder Woman
7 "Stay in touch!"
8 Place underground
9 Subjects of a certain sultanate
10 Strauss work with the "Dance of the Seven Veils"
11 Flashin' Fruit Punch brand
12 #1 dad?
13 Michael who played George Michael Bluth on TV
14 Was aware
20 Like angel investors and devil's food cake
24 Not sensitive (to)
26 Viscera
28 Queen's subjects
30 Not natural
31 The art of politics?
32 Entitled sort
33 Desire of a quick study?
35 Emperor's order in "Star Wars"
36 Fatty tuna in Japanese cuisine
40 Register
44 Stay good
46 Goes along with
47 Extravagant
51 Where to get money in Milano
53 Bit of a character
54 Go down
55 You shouldn't do this
56 What you might unthinkingly be on
58 Gone down
60 With 66-Across, "Good thinking!"
62 Senators' org.
63 Three for a trey: Abbr.

by Kate Hawkins

ACROSS

1 Act the cynic, maybe
6 Embarks on a newly righteous path
13 Felt off
14 "This is no laughing matter!"
16 Operative
18 Realizes
19 Where Jesse Owens ran college track, in brief
20 Kitchen extension?
21 Soirée invitee
22 Big gun, you might say
24 Brilliant display
25 Small boat of East Asia
27 Draft letters
29 Spot early on?
30 Gardening practice that minimizes the need for water
34 The book of numbers
36 Low member of a marine ecosystem
38 Symbol on an ancient sarcophagus
41 People credited with discovering mechanoluminescence, using quartz crystals to generate light
42 More like mud
44 Savage
46 Something out standing in its field
49 Head of Hogwarts?
50 Bit of hunting gear, for short
51 Today preceder
52 It started smoking again in 2021
53 "You can come out now"
58 Those tending to the fallen warriors called einherjar, in myth
59 Collage application
60 Dangerous place for a leak
61 Put up

DOWN

1 Hot spots
2 Channel owned by HBO
3 Prompting nostalgia, say
4 Schedule listings
5 Who famously offered this speaking advice: "Be sincere, be brief, be seated," in brief
6 Variety offering
7 Sri Lanka-to-Singapore dir.
8 ___ curiam (by the court)
9 Reconstruction, e.g.
10 Man's name that's an African country if you change the last letter
11 Maneuver in dancing or football
12 He wrote "Appear weak when you are strong, and strong when you are weak"
14 Anjou alternative
15 Rather inclined
17 It welcomes change
22 Rescue
23 England's Middleton, younger sister of Kate
24 The world's most-visited city (20+ million travelers annually)
26 5-Down, e.g., in brief
28 Self-playing instruments
31 Deals
32 Tool with an eye
33 Jazz great Stan
35 One might determine fertility
37 Newborn
38 Where "Lost" could be found
39 Foe of Popeye
40 Emmy-winning actress Adlon
43 Didn't just tee-hee
45 Hits hard
47 One in a one-on-one session
48 Unchanged
52 Vivacity
54 Castor ___ (old cartoon character)
55 Lennox of R&B
56 Vice principle
57 Book reviewer?

by Trenton Charlson

ACROSS

1 This and that
5 God of fertility, agriculture and the afterlife
11 "Love Life" network
14 Cassowary kin
15 Doing something wrong
17 Objectives
18 Fresh burst of energy
19 Five-star
21 Class structures?
22 Makeup palette assortment
23 Coruscates
25 Less likely to happen
27 You might seek forgiveness for this
28 Scans, say
29 New parents' purchases to block off staircases
34 Actress Mara of "Pose"
35 Empanadas and patatas bravas
36 "Happy to help!"
37 Nice position to be in?
39 Kind of cup
40 Just gets (by)
41 Go to bat for
42 San ___, seat of California's Marin County
45 Not expired
46 Everything one could possibly offer, with "the"
47 Mariah Carey and Madonna, for two
50 "Later, dude!"
53 ___ oil, extract obtained from the Amazon rainforest
54 Reverent
55 Pirate's activity
56 "Five Guys Named ___" (1992 Broadway musical)
57 Back-combed
58 Oh, to be in France!

DOWN

1 Challenge while sitting
2 Answer to the old riddle "What's round on the ends and high in the middle?"
3 Play with fire
4 Blanks
5 Out-of-office procedure?
6 72 answers and 34 black squares, for this puzzle
7 Hankering
8 Quintana ___, Mexican state that's home to Cancún
9 Spot for the night
10 Covering some ground?
11 Vertical dimension of a flag
12 Bops
13 "___ are . . ."
16 Longtime newswoman Ifill
20 Gender-neutral possessive
23 Holder of emergency supplies
24 Giant in chip manufacturing
25 Gets to
26 Many a Guinness Book record
27 Shade akin to royal blue
29 6–0 set, in tennis slang
30 "Whatever!"
31 Pet that's mostly black with a white chest
32 Ellie Kemper's role on "The Office"
33 ___ money
35 Kid
38 Firmly fixed
39 Offerer of fresh cuts
41 Made last night, say
42 Its participants are in for a wild ride
43 Pop up
44 Completely bomb
45 Fuzzy
46 Not cool—not cool at all!
47 Some Twitter postings
48 Brand that offers "Leg Mask" products
49 One of nine for a traditional Baha'i temple
51 Pro
52 Org. at Grand Central Terminal

by Claire Rimkus

ACROSS

1 [Perfection!]
10 Face to scale
15 Some exercise wear
16 Artist _____ de Toulouse-Lautrec
17 What the name "Renée" means
18 List of pointers
19 Pull (out)
20 Overdrawn account?
21 Actress MacDowell
22 Classical music tradition from Hindustan
24 "Dear future me . . ."
27 Nest egg yield
29 He's been called the "Father of Science Fiction"
30 Pastoral sound
31 Quarters
33 Bit of mayo?
34 Scuttled
35 Taps
37 With some side-eye
39 Some transcript omissions
40 Strips
42 Home to the three highest capital cities in the world
43 March alternative
44 Big inits. in admissions
45 Alternatives to toilet paper
48 "Can we chat real quick?"
52 Nose-crinkling
53 They rate very high on the Scoville scale
55 "I got you"
57 Food truck output
58 Fictional Harvard Law student played by Reese Witherspoon
59 Favored, with "with"
60 Artful
61 Like many apartment rentals
62 Bash

DOWN

1 Connection point not seen much anymore
2 Establishment where indoor smoking is permitted
3 Beyond the pale
4 Deadly household appliance, according to Korean urban legend
5 Sterilize, in a way
6 First female dean of Harvard Law
7 Straight
8 Wasn't generous
9 Digits on a paper card, for short
10 Trousers named for an Asian country
11 Gives, as credence
12 They don't have a major-label contract
13 Like many jobs in the gig economy
14 Make whole
21 Book with scales
23 Rock group whose name came from letters found on a sewing machine
25 _____ Sports Bureau (official 32-Down keepers)
26 Mountebanks
28 Stay quiet
32 See 25-Down
34 Minimalist style
36 Polite form of address, abroad
38 Blades used in "Kill Bill"
41 Masked warning?
43 Notre Dame setting
44 Follower of an "I'm late" text, in brief
45 They might be loaded with singles
46 Poker declaration
47 Deadpan
49 Like Falstaff
50 Take the edge off?
51 One might fly close to the sun
53 Printmaker?
54 "No Ordinary Love" singer
56 Pastoral sound

by Nam Jin Yoon

ACROSS

1 Ensemble purchase that includes sheets and pillowcases
10 Cheek-related
15 Heading for
16 Set apart
17 Skew conservative
18 "___ boogie!"
19 Meat
20 Period at the beginning of the Stone Age
22 Value
24 Wilson on the Hollywood Walk of Fame
25 Back on board
26 1968 Peace Nobelist Cassin
27 Garments that sound like you'd exercise in them
30 "Let's ___!"
31 California setting of several Steinbeck novels
32 I, for one
34 At a discount
38 Big brass
40 ___ fever, a.k.a. allergic rhinitis
41 Have a natural interest in gambling?
44 Wear out
45 Company that helped launch TMZ
46 Spot
47 Spots for dips
48 Japanese dish of raw fish and vegetables over rice
51 Kind of limit
52 Was peripatetic
53 Untrained, perhaps
57 Up
58 Ignored protocol
59 House of ___
60 Beat reporting?

DOWN

1 ___ esprit (gifted person)
2 Suffix with acetyl
3 Involve as an unwilling participant
4 Charge, in a way
5 Many a frontline worker
6 Words after keep or going
7 Importune
8 Albert Camus or Isaac Asimov, religiously
9 What over 40 million U.S. adults do annually
10 They're known for their holiday gifts
11 2019 rap hit whose title follows the lyric "How much money you got?"
12 Mandrake the Magician's sidekick
13 Modern protest movement
14 Jerks, say
21 Rightful praise
22 School for the college-bound, informally
23 Bench warmer?
24 Rush while racing?
27 Springs
28 Ones using a x-walk
29 One side of a coll. football "Holy War" rivalry
31 Vintner Claude
33 Intl. Rescue Committee, e.g.
35 Largest college sorority by enrollment (380,000+ members)
36 Noble title
37 Goes green, say?
39 Golden Ball winner in 2019's Women's World Cup
41 Of holy rites
42 Christmas cheer?
43 Twist in a story
44 Lethargy
47 Neil ___, drummer/lyricist for the rock band Rush
49 Inbox category
50 Puts on
51 Level
54 Subj. of supercoiling
55 Same old, same old
56 "Let's ___ . . ."

by Joe DiPietro

ACROSS

1 Producer of inflation
4 Ranking no.
7 Confront, in slang
13 Some origin stories
16 "Rumors are carried by ___, spread by fools and accepted by idiots" (old saying)
17 Moles are found in it
18 1991 platinum debut album by a female singer
19 Fantastic voyage
20 Collaborative resource
22 React to a baby, maybe
23 Promulgate
25 Food often served with plastic grass
27 Onetime Mughal capital
29 Dirt farm?
32 Ran
33 Army ___
34 Befuddled
36 Ushered
38 Medalla material
39 "Ain't gonna happen"
40 Country rocker Steve
41 Small-batch publication
43 It's often framed
44 Treatment for jet lag
46 One of the Scooby-Doo gang
47 Elder brother of Moses
48 Like talk, they say
50 Pentagon inits.
52 "It would ___ . . ."
54 Elizabeth of cosmetics
56 Question that introduces doubt
58 Something a judge might show
61 "It's nothing," in Spanish
62 Where some unsolicited advice comes from
63 Course challenge
64 Black ___
65 "Cool, dude!"

DOWN

1 Prone
2 Where the Noah's Ark story is thought to have occurred, today
3 Essential work
4 One might be educated
5 Unsettle
6 Subject of David Remnick's "King of the World"
7 "All Eyez on Me" rapper
8 It's thought to ward off bad energy
9 H
10 One making good points in the classroom?
11 Something no two people can be
12 ___ buco
14 17-Across offering
15 Spotted
21 Kind of muscle contraction
24 Tender union?
26 Cousins of crew cuts
27 Fit
28 Twinkle
30 San Rafael's county
31 Director Sergio
35 Struck dumb
37 One face of the moon
42 Bolster
45 Identifier seen in the "Six Feet Under" title sequence
49 Actress Alexander of "Get Out"
50 2010's ___-Frank Act
51 Name for a Dalmatian, perhaps
53 Card games are played in it
55 Grp. with much-discussed amateurism rules
57 Spanish seasoning
59 Have
60 Paycheck abbr.

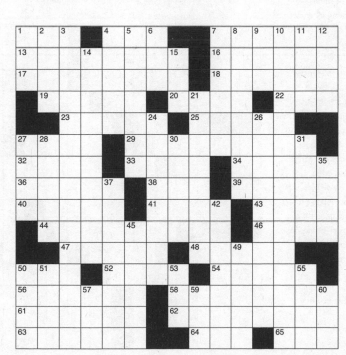

by Hal Moore

ACROSS

1 Popular Korean rice dish
9 Facial expression
15 Bach's "Christmas ___"
16 Offline activity?
17 Towered over
18 Sugar in one's coffee, e.g.
19 Ancient land that included parts of modern Iraq and Turkey
20 Place to buy overpriced drinks
21 Keane who drew "The Family Circus"
22 Do some light cardio
23 Ink
24 Quarters feed into them
27 Kind of salami
29 His debut album was 1987's "Rhyme Pays"
30 Tears
35 "Ahhh!"
37 "Wow, wow, wow!"
38 It's made by coagulating soy milk
39 Mammal with four toes on the front feet and three on the back
40 Pleasantly flavorful
41 Financing figs.
45 C'est un article défini
46 Certain judge's ruling
47 Portmanteau for a dumpster-diving anti-consumerist eater
49 One might be offensive
53 Just peachy
54 Deliberately damage
55 Possible cause of fatigue
56 Mean figures
57 People people
58 Milky Way and others

DOWN

1 Bubble tea
2 Ticks off
3 Amp knob
4 Minute
5 Northern New Jersey county
6 Oven setting
7 Sophia Loren title role of 1953
8 He once wrote "I became insane, with long intervals of horrible sanity"
9 Fifth-century invaders
10 "That's my cue!"
11 Challenge in an alley
12 Dutch-speaking Caribbean island
13 Insinuated
14 Wisconsin governor Tony
20 The original Frankenstein wasn't one, despite popular belief
22 Competes in the Aquabike World Championship
24 Jedi foe
25 Second
26 Fast finish?
27 Shook one's defender, in sports lingo
28 "___ You Experienced" (Jimi Hendrix album)
30 It's all downhill from here
31 Passing financial concern?
32 Per
33 First name in U.N. diplomacy
34 Draw counterpart
36 Follower of F.D.R.
40 Madame, across the Pyrenees
41 It has a duck float in the Macy's Thanksgiving Day Parade
42 Inclined
43 Have a ball
44 Directive to talk
46 Some smears
48 A little too slick
49 It's hot stuff!
50 Noted gift givers
51 He won a posthumous Pulitzer Prize in 1958
52 Adjective-to-noun suffix
54 Slump

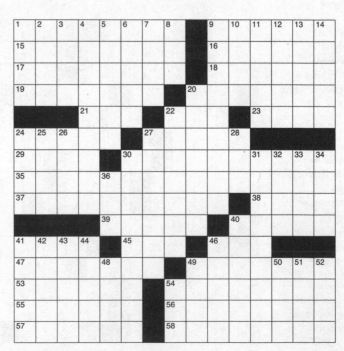

by Evans Clinchy

ACROSS

1 Two things in Broadway's "Dear Evan Hansen"
5 Goes off
10 Puts on
14 Wonderful review
15 ___ Stadium, longtime home of college football's Hula Bowl
16 Spree
17 Scratch-off success
19 Princess ___, main role in Pixar's "A Bug's Life"
20 "Didn't expect that to happen!"
21 Treats often topped with caviar
22 The point of writing?
23 Modern-day put-down popularized by a 2019 TikTok video
25 Flavor similar to fennel
26 Vintage eight-track purchases, maybe
27 Stress specialist?
28 "Britain's first family of harmony," per Brian Wilson
29 With 51-Across, package recipient's cry
30 Terrible review
31 Kind of exam with an "Auditing and Attestation" section
34 "Hey man, listen up . . ."
35 Speak loudly and harshly
36 What's at home on the range?
39 Pieces together?
40 Doesn't delete
41 Sires
42 Heavens
43 Kids might make a stand for this
45 Top-___
46 Something promoted on the front of a magazine

48 Challenge for a free soloist
49 Unit of firewood
50 Main ingredient in the Japanese dish tekkadon
51 See 29-Across
52 Visibly shows embarrassment
53 Opposite of ginormous

DOWN

1 Actress Nicole ___ Parker
2 "Let's stop. Is this really necessary?"
3 "Dallas" or "Atlanta"
4 Info for a group of performers
5 Industrial dept.
6 Resort locale east of Snowbird
7 Lead-in to a grave pronouncement
8 "Not so fast!"
9 Eastern honorific
10 Buffaloed
11 Complete a sentence, say
12 Not-so-common extension
13 One way to the top
18 What may come as a relief?
21 Basic framework
22 Champagne ___, one of Drake's nicknames
24 Funeral fixtures
26 Firsts in flight
28 Wade in the Baseball Hall of Fame
30 Colin Kaepernick was one, familiarly
31 Hollered
32 Crop circles, e.g.

33 Pro group?
34 Separate
35 Alternative to a Lamborghini
36 Furnish with feathers, as an arrow
37 Go out of business?
38 "Capeesh?"
39 Biden and Harris, once: Abbr.
41 Nowhere near engaged
44 English adjective that becomes a French noun when an accent is added
46 Print examiner, for short
47 "___, me!"

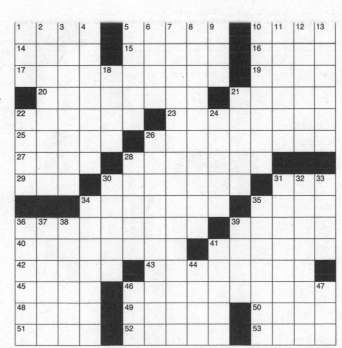

by David Distenfeld

ACROSS

1 Retreated
9 Drop
13 Artificial intelligence system modeled on the human brain
15 Something that gets passed around a lot
16 Golfers Ernie Els and Retief Goosen, for two
18 So much
19 All the king's men?
20 Simple and glib
21 School with the slogan "Ex scientia tridens," familiarly
22 Ancient symbols of life
23 Velcro alternative
25 Democratic leader?
26 Recipe direction
27 Strong, dark quaff
28 The British royal family has one called the Cambridge Lover's Knot
30 Some abbey attire
31 Up
32 "I wasn't going to say anything, but since you brought it up . . ."
36 Crew
37 Many a confession on a theater stage
38 Throws, informally
39 "I'm game"
40 Last ___
44 ___ Miguel Island, largest of the Azores
45 Currency units in Peru
47 Puccini opera . . . or the first five letters of the maestro who conducted its La Scala premiere
48 What Twix bars are sold in
50 Companion of the droid BB-8, in the "Star Wars" universe
51 Ear hair?
52 Calculus calculation
53 Gained some courage
55 What Shøp on "The Simpsons" is a parody of
56 Agronomic analyses
57 A cold wave can produce one
58 Yule log?

DOWN

1 Sequencing locale
2 Polish
3 Triumphant shout
4 "Black Boy" memoirist Richard
5 Gets the batter out, say
6 "___ poor Romeo!": Shak.
7 Wolf's home
8 Monitor
9 Besides Brunei, the only current sovereign sultanate
10 Creation date, file size and location, for an iPhone photo
11 "That doesn't bother me anymore"
12 Like an F.B.I. director's term
14 Fast fashion?
17 Office address abbr.
23 Ones making insulting offers
24 Part of many university names
27 Flamboyant prop
29 "Black" follower
30 "The gymnasium of the mind," per Blaise Pascal
32 Question that cannot be answered if its answer is "no"
33 Two-wheeler at a charging station
34 "___ away!"
35 Cardinal points?: Abbr.
36 Alternative to litmus paper
40 It's the truth!
41 Noted basilica town
42 Things picked up on a trail
43 Most likely to burn, maybe
46 Kind of chart, informally
47 Decorum
49 Underground band
51 One end of the Mohs scale
54 GameCube successor

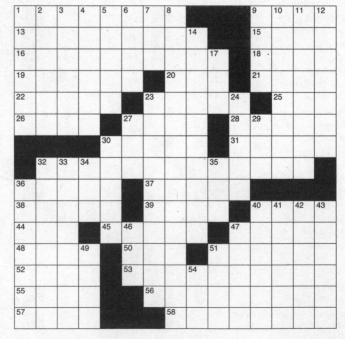

by Evan Kalish

ACROSS

1 Things you might snap on, nowadays
10 Something suddenly fashionable
12 Welcome sign of spring
14 Bases of support
15 Writer whose initials, when doubled, become another answer in this puzzle
17 Charge
18 Fly far, far away?
19 More familiar name for hydrated magnesium silicate
20 Sam who directed "A Simple Plan"
24 Ball ___
25 Body opening?
26 Stuff
28 Subject of some MK-Ultra experiments
29 "Let's pray it never comes to that"
31 Sarcastic response to an attempt at intimidation
33 Java has a rare species of one
34 "What ___?"
36 Members of filmdom's Breakfast Club
37 The oldest known one was found carved into a mammoth tusk (~25,000 B.C.)
40 Battery type
42 They're filled with dough
43 Aquaman portrayer
45 Side (with)
46 Listing in the Fortune 100
49 W.N.B.A. M.V.P. in 2015 and 2019
50 Jumper, e.g.

DOWN

1 Relating to sound
2 One cycle per second
3 1979 Donna Summer hit . . . or where it was heard
4 Model and body positivity activist Holliday
5 Pained expression
6 Help lift something, maybe?
7 Checkout choice
8 Some spreads
9 Lug
10 Bad way to be disguised
11 "Bad Lieutenant" star
12 Dulcé ___, correspondent for "The Daily Show" beginning in 2017
13 Classic "I messed up" gift
14 Souvlaki go-with
16 Be behind bars?
21 Switch letters
22 Some news on Wall St.
23 Linguist Okrand who created Klingon
26 21 popes
27 Japanese beer
29 Lose it completely
30 One straying from the norm
31 "No way!," spelled out in a text
32 Refuse
33 Pass on
35 Places to get waxed
36 Reins in
37 Spongelike delicacy
38 Enough
39 Cannonball targets
41 Units equal to 10 micronewtons
43 Manner
44 Father of many children with Aphrodite
47 Ohio pro athlete, informally
48 Kick in

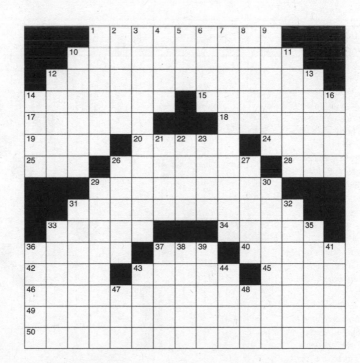

by Johan Vass

150 HARD

ACROSS

1 Colorful custardy confection
10 Sudden inspirations
15 Waltz onomatopoeia
16 Love
17 Classic diner orders
18 Apply, as ointment
19 Kitchen brand whose name is an ambigram
20 Pit-___
21 More might come before it
22 Its employees might get under your skin
24 Thing with rings
25 Legal action
28 Some Disney-inspired Halloween costumes
30 "___ me!" (request to a fridge-goer)
31 Like blue and green ski trails, vis-à-vis black diamonds
33 Pep
36 Looks the other way
39 Modern ___
40 "A ___ place is in the House, and in the Senate" (bumper sticker)
41 Actress Kendrick
42 Sharon's predecessor as Israeli P.M.
43 One of the Blues Brothers
45 One of the Coen brothers
48 Relative by marriage
50 Where to do as others do, it's said
52 Stain
53 Sprinkling
56 Canon competitor
57 Street featured in Fellini's "La Dolce Vita" (that's also 50-Across)

59 Still sticky
60 Make thin
61 Crushes it
62 Couple in the back of a car

DOWN

1 Snap
2 Component of three of the five French "mother sauces"
3 "That's . . . never gonna happen"
4 "Double" or "triple" drink
5 Actress Taylor of TV's "Bones"
6 Agatha Christie novel named after Death's mount in Revelation
7 Make ___ for
8 Danger for desert hikers
9 Ending with four or six, but not five
10 Teri of "Mr. Mom"
11 Does laundry or pays bills, in modern lingo
12 Clearheaded
13 Novel content
14 Tell
21 Couldn't let go of
22 Group portrayed in "Slacker" and "Reality Bites," familiarly
23 Straighten
25 Proficient
26 ___ review
27 One quadrillion: Prefix
29 Trio of horrors?
32 Target
33 Rosso o bianco
34 Driver's license fig.

35 Ren Faire concession
37 United competitor, once
38 "Heavens!"
42 Squarish
44 Not yet manifest
45 Spurns
46 Longtime "Inside the N.B.A." commentator
47 Writer Jong
49 South America's Río de la ___
51 Eponym of the World Series M.V.P. award
53 "Have no ___ of perfection ___ you'll never reach it": Dalí
54 Suffix with towel
55 Melancholiac's list
57 Dictionary abbr.
58 Rapa ___ (Easter Island)

by Meghan Morris

ACROSS

1 First person?
7 Backups
13 First name in daytime talk
14 Red Guard's attire
15 Like "To be or not to be"
16 Baking aisle mascot
17 Smart device feature
19 Ice Breakers alternative
20 Aftermath
21 Engagement calendar info: Abbr.
25 "That's so not the case!"
26 Fodor's listing
27 Assembly at a camporee, perhaps
28 Anti-trafficking org.
29 Comic strip with the 1998 collection "I Am Woman, Hear Me Snore"
30 Skylar of the "Pitch Perfect" films
31 Start of many a Google search
32 Line just before a comma
34 "Anything to ___ ?"
35 Brand with an iComfort line
37 Leporine creatures
38 Bags one might have when tired?
39 Tanks and such
40 Botched
41 "Got it"
42 Intersections requiring a turn
43 Singing duet?
44 Bartolomé de las ___, social reformer during Spain's colonial era
45 Coin featuring Lady Liberty and a bald eagle
48 Part of a forecast without clouds
51 Colonnade sight
53 Pirates, in old slang
54 Rumpled, say
55 "Yeah, sure"
56 Like some fruits and tennis players

DOWN

1 Setting of the Robert Graves memoir "Good-bye to All That," in brief
2 Mopey teen's lament
3 "Can't eat another bite"
4 "I don't want to hear any excuses!"
5 Some major productions
6 Oil-___
7 Press "K" while on YouTube
8 Jordan is found on one, notably
9 Yoga retreat locales
10 Central point
11 Lead-in to diversity
12 Home for a farrow
14 Pastry that gets pulled apart
16 Where scenes on Tatooine were filmed for "Star Wars"
18 They're full of twists and turns
19 Feverishly tries to open
22 Cookout dish
23 Big outdoor June event
24 Length of a president's veto window
26 Adolphe who invented a musical instrument
27 Costco rival, familiarly
29 Titan
33 Still in the box, say
36 Beyond what's needed
41 Phone line?
43 Goes on
44 Singer with the 1962 album "Sentimentally Yours"
46 Aces have low ones, for short
47 Major production
48 "___: Vegas"
49 One of a piano trio
50 ___ oxygénée (hydrogen peroxide: Fr.)
52 Like diamonds

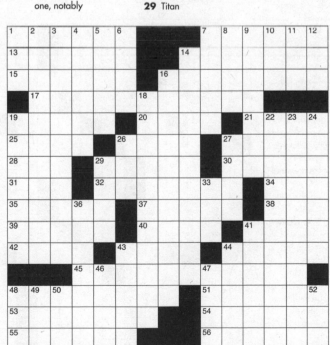

by Peter Wentz

ACROSS

1 Something you may want to clear up
5 Othello, for one
9 Loses sheen, perhaps
14 One of the Aesir
15 Uncovered
16 ID seen at the post office
17 Nobel winner Morrison
18 Dressing room encouragement
20 "Stop trying to help!"
22 A counting job?
23 Own up (to)
24 Purpose
25 Eva Perón was one: Abbr.
26 You can bet on it!
28 Simple matter of probability
33 Numbers not meant to be shared
34 Speedy sci-fi technology
35 Secretly unionize?
36 Drop the ball
37 With 11-Down, kids' party activity
38 "Peter Pan" princess
40 Lashes makeup
41 Look that might freeze you in your tracks
42 Martini option
43 Subj. of international treaties
44 Bon ____ (high society: Fr.)
45 Friendly introduction?
47 Cause of weakness
51 What Babe aspires to be in "Babe"
53 Romantic bunch
55 ____ Mountains, range crossed on the Trans-Siberian railway
56 What "he" and "do" don't do
57 Biblical preposition
58 Terpsichore or Calliope
59 Strategic bodies of water
60 "Out of Africa" author Dinesen
61 Little drones

DOWN

1 Story that goes over your head?
2 One constantly craving kisses?
3 "It was not my intention to make anyone upset," often
4 CNN's Burnett
5 Scavenger hunt cry
6 Little sucker
7 Substance
8 Towering figure in "The Two Towers"
9 "Wake up, sleepyhead!"
10 Kake ____ (Japanese dish)
11 See 37-Across
12 Biblical pronoun
13 ____ vide (culinary technique)
19 Substitute for legal tender
21 Ports, e.g.
25 Pathetic
27 Metaphorical knowledge
28 Eric who wrote "The Very Hungry Caterpillar"
29 Accomplice in "Romeo and Juliet"
30 Broadway show where everyone knows the ending?
31 Country named for a now-banned trade
32 They can be felt
33 Org. for Carl Sagan
34 "That's odd . . ."
39 Rapper/producer who won the 2018 Pulitzer for Music
42 Gets by
44 Letter in the Greek spelling of Athens
46 Looks like a jerk
47 Driver in "House of Gucci"
48 Canceled
49 Book after II Chronicles
50 Runners' event
51 Figs. assigned randomly since 2011
52 Animal also known as a catamount
54 Air France confirmation

by Robyn Weintraub

ACROSS

1 Number pattern named after a 17th-century French mathematician
16 Teddies and such
17 Exhausted beyond belief
18 Certain acct. info
19 Diatribes
20 Longtime distributor of James Bond movies
21 Immersed in
23 Business ___
24 Lot
25 Maipo Valley exports
27 Pings, maybe
28 ___ Gervasi, director of 2012's "Hitchcock"
29 Union IDs, for a performer
31 Basic analysis?
32 Market debuts, in brief
33 Mini-___ (small retailer)
34 One way to manage expectations
37 Eschew Uber, say
41 More steadfast
42 "For once maybe someone will call me '___,' without adding, 'You're making a scene'": Homer Simpson
43 ___ Player, first Black woman to become president of a four-year college
44 Taking off
45 Setting for "La Bohème"
47 Calm
48 Hominid
49 Some stylish suits
51 Measure of volume
52 Do some modeling
55 "Life is short. ___" (Jacques Torres quip)
56 Captain's phrase

DOWN

1 Two-person log cutters
2 Loss of smell
3 Biblical punishment
4 Loc. ___
5 Marcello, Rodolfo, Colline and Schaunard, dans "La Bohème"
6 Turpentine-yielding conifer
7 Certain anti-inflammatory medicines
8 Hymns of thanksgiving
9 Yelp reviewers, say
10 Shuffles and such
11 Rental units: Abbr.
12 "Don't reckon so"
13 Reaction to a really bad pun
14 Stretches
15 Lean protein
22 Tenths, in statistics
24 Increased likelihood of extreme scenarios, in statistics
26 Taste
28 Mammal in the Soricidae family
30 Spreadsheet specification
31 Golf Hall-of-Famer Se Ri ___
33 Only M.L.B. team never to have played in a World Series
34 National geographic books?
35 "Again ..."
36 Small knapsack
37 Diatribes
38 Certain sports instructor
39 Whatever's left
40 Works that may require leaps of imagination?
42 Savory Indian pastry
45 Uninspired, as writing
46 Like the most recent Pope Paul among all popes named Paul
49 Seasoned
50 Jewelry store?
53 Canine protection org.?
54 Russian fighter jet

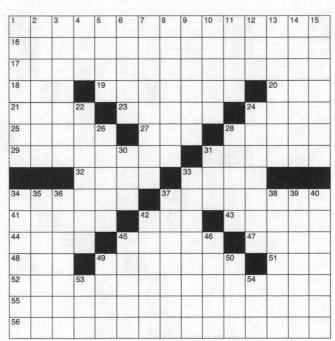

by Freddie Cheng

ACROSS

1 One playing second fiddle, perhaps
9 St. Louis clock setting, briefly
12 Move a cursor across
13 Burn
14 Where to try out some gunpowder?
15 Italian verse form
16 "Cars 2" competitor ___ Bonn
17 ___ Academy, organization for self-paced education online
18 Kicked butt
19 They can be friendly while patronizing
21 Not allowed to go back, say
23 Author of "What I Know for Sure," familiarly
24 Place of rest away from everything
26 ___ Jones
27 What purple prose and technical jargon have in common
29 Donations for life?
30 Modern source of juice
34 Summer sip suffix
35 Build-your-own IHOP order
36 "Coolio!"
37 Responds to an alarm, in a way
38 They outrank viscounts
42 Dandy accessories
44 Stir-fry recipe step
45 "Cool it!"
46 Abbr. near zero
49 Doing
50 Assents asea
51 Sith superpower
53 Stronghold
54 "This better not get out"
55 When repeated, an expression of disapproval
56 Playing God?

DOWN

1 Headwear for many a barbershop quartet singer
2 Google Docs feature
3 Org. whose initials are found in "unsafe," ironically
4 Hotels have ones in front
5 One who's light-headed?
6 Footwear brand
7 Osaka and others
8 Bit of work
9 Hybrid fair fare
10 2013 Macklemore/Ryan Lewis hit with the lyric "And I can't change, even if I tried"
11 Conflict that may involve sanctions
12 Got together
13 Heart
14 DoorDash designation
18 Shifted in a theater, say
20 Once-ler's opponent in a Dr. Seuss book
22 When repeated, call to someone going to bed
24 Go gaga for
25 Choice in a cabin
28 "Please ___" (printed request)
30 World of ___
31 It's a challenge
32 "Warning!"
33 Study
39 Skill event that might follow barrel racing
40 Bath water unit
41 Blackthorn
43 Like the universe
44 Fail to be
47 Accumulation
48 "___ Enchanted" (2004 romantic comedy)
51 . . . : Abbr.
52 Miroir image?

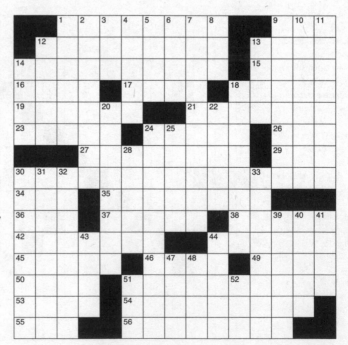

by Matthew Stock and Sid Sivakumar

ACROSS

1 Squarely
9 Not straight up
15 Old World bird with distinctive ear tufts
16 Baby's barnyard bovine
17 Sympathetic response to dissent
18 A-to-Z
19 Crashing an online meeting
21 One might be loaded
22 Creatures whose newborns have striped bodies
23 Prattles
24 Watch here!
26 All ___
27 Boxy delivery vehicles of old
29 London's ___ Square
31 Make slicker, maybe
32 Wined and dined, say
35 Spiritual object
37 Wiped out
39 W.W. I, W.W. II, etc.
41 What rotates throughout the office?
46 Gold units: Abbr.
48 Any of the Seven Dwarfs
49 Something you might raise a flap about
50 ___ tide
51 Kind of drive
52 Locale 60 miles south of the California/Oregon border
55 Creator of the first pumped-up athletic shoe
57 Catchphrase of Winnie-the-Pooh
58 Popular typeface similar to Bauhaus
59 "To be honest with you . . ."
60 Out of it
61 Date format on digital forms

DOWN

1 Gets stuck, as an engine
2 Youngest-ever QB to be named Super Bowl M.V.P. (2020)
3 Grow too old for
4 Simoleons
5 Spot for a bus stop, in Bristol
6 Get into a pose, perhaps
7 What God is, per an Ariana Grande hit
8 Cold weather layer
9 Eye-opening declaration?
10 One jotting down a few notes?
11 Area for development
12 Like apples and oranges
13 Safe
14 Some brief updates
20 Locale for a castaway
25 Stick around school
27 2010s fansite craze whose members joined Hogwarts houses
28 Start of many a criticism
30 "Ho" preceder
33 Main ingredient in hitsumabushi
34 Mirabile ___ (wonderful to say: Lat.)
36 Takes advantage of a situation, so to speak
38 How things typically are
40 Majestic
41 Blue-nosed sorts?
42 Get smart
43 Like many apps with faulty features
44 Country song
45 "Things aren't looking so great"
47 Dalmatian mascot of the National Fire Protection Association
50 Well-suited?
53 Response akin to "So what?"
54 Word after foot or before hands
56 2021 Super Bowl champ

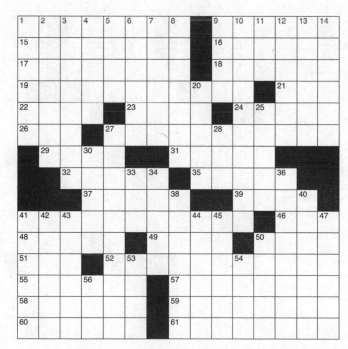

by Sam Ezersky

Note: This puzzle has four different solutions. When you're done, read the circled letters from top to bottom to find another one.

ACROSS

1 You might bid on it
5 First man, in Maori mythology
9 Lead to
14 Plant
15 Encumbrance
16 It makes il mondo go 'round
17 Bathroom cabinet item
19 More than flirt with
20 Vegas machine with the best odds?
21 A head
22 "American ___" (Neil Gaiman novel that won the Hugo and Nebula)
23 Japanese electronics brand
24 Brain freeze cause
27 Product often advertising 99.99% effectiveness
31 "Headliner" of the first Warner Bros. short to win an Oscar
32 ___ Ren of "The Force Awakens"
33 Big 12 sch.
36 Makes a small, plaintive sound
37 K.C.-to-Detroit direction
38 Ad Council output, for short
39 Grp. that advertised in "The Book of Mormon" playbills, surprisingly
40 Command after mistakenly pressing Ctrl+Z
42 Spicy kind of seasoning
44 It might help clear things up
47 Nocturnal marsupial
49 Event with Easter eggs
50 Runs
51 Behind
52 Where the cucumbers are not for eating
55 Play matchmaker for
57 Sound filler
59 Upper atmosphere
60 Little rascal
61 Damage
62 Authority
63 Federation formed in 1922, for short
64 Like many college film projects

DOWN

1 ___ Raducanu, 2021 U.S. Open winner
2 Kick hard
3 Who might be asked for a donation, in brief
4 "___ again . . ."
5 Illegally parked car, maybe
6 How some pet food is sold
7 Potent marijuana
8 Suffix with bull or bear
9 Cry of contempt
10 Citizenship test taker, perhaps
11 Get put away
12 Eat at
13 It may be perfect for writing
18 Job at a bank, say
23 Some sources of vitamin C
24 Ocular affliction
25 Wee
26 Emmy winner Aduba
27 Code inits.
28 How you might feel looking at the Northern Lights
29 Fit for a big write-up, say
30 "Right?!"
34 Closing activity
35 ___ interface
37 Biblical land near the kingdoms of Judah and Moab
38 Scotch flavorer
40 E.R. staffers
41 Brown. follower
42 Mess
43 Get more 45-Down
45 See 43-Down
46 Gets ready, as a cue stick
47 Fertile spots
48 Masterwork completed in 1499
51 Snack brand owned by PepsiCo
52 Holiday cookie shape
53 Sassy
54 Drove
56 Whiz
57 Nickname that's an alphabet trio
58 "I've got it!"

by Evan Mahnken

ACROSS

1 Office held five times by Julius Caesar
7 Not physically, say
15 Program commemorated on the back of the Eisenhower dollar coin
16 Do some wedding planning
17 Withdraw
18 Preposterous
19 Word with club or queen
20 Stuff, but not junk
21 Where "the cheese stands alone," in a classic song
22 They're tops to Scots
23 Lug
25 Faulty: Prefix
26 Grow up
27 Color not generated by light
29 Very nearly resemble
31 Livened (up)
35 Picked up
36 Sushi chef's tasting menu
37 Literally, "substitute"
38 Midwife's focus in the third stage of labor
39 Dazzling skill
41 2019 World Series winner, in brief
42 Org. with clubs, in two senses
45 "Anything!"
46 Veronica ___, author of the "Divergent" trilogy
47 Orange candleflower, for example
49 "Mastering the Art of French Cooking," for one
50 Expert with picks
51 "Whatever you say . . ."
53 ___ chai (Indian beverage)
54 Short hooking pitch
55 Eventually
56 Herbalists' panaceas
57 Muscle connectors

DOWN

1 Setting for drinks and deals
2 Met someone?
3 Policy around the publicity-shy, say
4 In-verse functions?
5 It runs up the arm
6 Offering for a developer
7 Capital of ancient Persia
8 In an elegant way
9 Canny
10 Campaign fund-raising letters
11 "That ___ love thee, Caesar, O, 'tis true": Shak.
12 Tore
13 Where 23-Down was coined
14 Flushes, e.g., in poker
20 Gloucester catch
23 The art of appearing effortlessly nonchalant
24 Institution roughly two millennia old
27 Submitted
28 It started in 1964 as Blue Ribbon Sports
30 Allure
32 Salvo from Old Ironsides
33 Acts of will?
34 Sci-fi effects that are beyond stunning
36 Source of some nostalgia
38 Many human anatomy students
40 Unlikely to pontificate, say
42 Some ribbons and shells
43 Congee, e.g.
44 Coming in waves, in a way
46 Up now
48 Barrier against burrowers
50 Digital job, in brief
52 Match
53 1–12: Abbr.

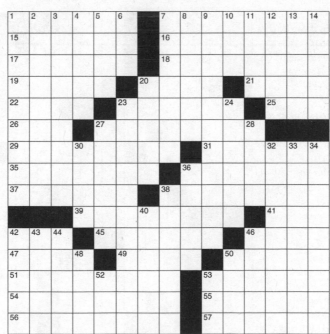

by Kyle Dolan

ACROSS

1 Setting for "A Few Good Men," informally
6 Hang (around with)
9 Frustrated outburst
12 Nubian Museum locale
13 "Gotcha," in a groovier era
15 Start to a logical conclusion
16 That's the spirit!
17 Revealed all
19 Tiny seeds of green fruits, technically
21 Expert problem solver
22 Sign of fall
25 Like refrigerators at night, sometimes
26 Key element of opera seria
27 Subjects of Monet paintings "in Venice" and "at Lavacourt"
30 SeaWorld roller coaster ride
32 ___ bar
33 "Shameless" airer, for short
36 This isn't what it looks like!
39 Jenny, for one
40 Really, really fancy
41 In and of itself
42 Boost someone's signal, in a way
44 In and of itself?
45 Go back to see again, maybe
48 Hardly worth mentioning
50 Biggest stars
53 A bunch of crock?
54 Raw footage?
56 Off the chain, say

59 Ammonia has one
60 ___ brilliant (diamond cut)
61 Musical based on a comic strip
62 Mint
63 Letters on some foundations
64 Grand

DOWN

1 ___ order
2 Ending with freak or fool
3 Safety net?
4 GranTurismo maker
5 At the ready
6 Insta post
7 Levine of pop music
8 Pacific Coast capital
9 Love of lucre
10 5.5-point type size
11 Refined
14 "Puh-lease!"
15 Actress Tracee ___ Ross
18 Woos with words
20 Nuclear unit nickname
22 Where lavalava skirts are worn
23 Shooting game
24 Wanted one
28 Easily had
29 Pique
31 Gives some stress
33 Fatal attraction?
34 Popular leafy perennial
35 Former center of Los Angeles
37 Like Los Angeles's Griffith Observatory

38 Increment on a scale
42 Stage support
43 Number 1, with "the"
45 Was fueled by
46 Escape
47 Black ___
49 Toddler's eruption
51 Makes purr, maybe
52 Speak sharply
55 2003 film in which the title character exclaims "Son of a nutcracker!"
57 Mononymous singer of "Alive," 2015
58 Sushi fish that's not served raw

by Caitlin Reid

ACROSS

1 "Wish I could live like that . . ."
11 Some radio announcements, in brief
15 First winning presidential ticket to alternate vowels and consonants
16 Schmooze
17 Where the entirety of the "Lord of the Rings" trilogy was filmed
18 Folderol
19 Common Italian verb ending
20 Brewery supply
21 Amoeba feature
23 Michael of "Superbad"
25 Shake hands, perhaps
26 Many jingles
30 People of Burundi
31 Huffing and puffing, e.g.
33 Spread out at a party
34 Free
37 Bishop's group
39 Some fridges
40 Deadlines?
42 It might be captured on a safari
44 Who famously said "I really didn't say everything I said"
46 Some seaside gatherings
50 "In the end . . ."
52 Rear guard?
53 Drink that comes with a wide straw
54 Chinese ___, food also called nagaimo
57 Approval inits.
58 Like much of Sudan
59 One with news to share, often

62 Musical Case
63 Counter request
64 Sharp
65 People might have personal ones for what they do

DOWN

1 R&B artist with the 3× platinum 1995 debut album "Miss Thang"
2 Went for a ride, in a way
3 Carpenters, at times
4 Website with a "Got a Tip?" page
5 Boxing champ Max
6 Site for a snipe
7 It turns red in Exodus
8 B.C. neighbor: Abbr.
9 Gathering that occurs once per decade
10 Call everything off
11 Caused a ruckus
12 Poor cell connection?
13 What you find kitsch in
14 Sources of some tips
22 Line on a map: Abbr.
24 Land on the Med.
25 Alternative to a Gallup survey
27 "Utter your gravity ___ a gossip's bowl": "Romeo and Juliet"
28 Tennis great with the most consecutive weeks ranked #1 in the world (377)
29 Devices used to sterilize medical equipment
32 Racket
34 Take the money and run, say

35 Rule that's often broken
36 Kawasaki offering
38 Cold War inits.
41 Walk all over
43 Put down
45 Word with fair or film
47 Garment of the Middle East
48 Like Meg among the March sisters
49 Close calls
51 CVS Health acquisition of 2018
54 Subject of numerous hoaxes
55 Tablet collection
56 Grow out of something, say
60 Doctor's orders, for short
61 Mens ___

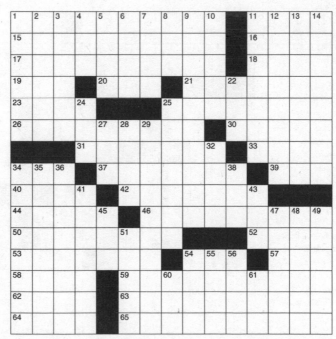

by Sam Buchbinder

ACROSS

1 Means of supervision?
9 Co-winner of the 1994 Nobel Peace Prize
15 Kisses and hugs
16 "I can ___"
17 What can strike up a tune?
19 Tiny bit of concern
20 Saint associated with the Russian alphabet
21 ___ jure (by the law itself: Lat.)
24 Discover fortuitously
26 Rail construction
29 "Buzz off!"
30 Florida city in the middle of "horse country"
31 Soft shade
32 Pioneer in instant messaging
33 Fire (up)
34 Watch from the shadows, say
35 Industrial support
37 Easy mark
39 As it happens
40 Critical
41 Silent ___
42 Small grouse
43 Refreshers
44 Unlike filibusters
47 Shelter from a storm, perhaps
48 Negotiation site that led to the 1994 Nobel Peace Prize
49 Appropriate
50 Draft teammates?
51 Mythological lyrist
53 Fictional narrator whose first name is a fruit
55 Epitome
61 Wireless network necessity
62 Toon with a brother named Castor
63 Oxford pad, e.g.
64 Locale in SW France

DOWN

1 Beyond steamy
2 Boy's name that means "king"
3 Rose by another name?
4 "Anybody there?!"
5 Fair
6 Accompaniment for a bottle of rum
7 Beautiful and rare
8 Chaz, to Cher
9 ___ Game, annual event on the second Saturday of December
10 Raise
11 Everything considered
12 Occasion for Druids to gather at Stonehenge
13 Absorbed
14 Winter festival
18 Grandes ___, part of France's higher education system
21 Reiterated refusal
22 Admissions to a counselor
23 Network of nerves in the abdomen
25 Rarer than rare
27 Keep on keeping on
28 Stop for a bit
36 Employ for lack of better options
37 Place to pick up litter?
38 Comeback that sounds like a "Star Wars" character
45 Without incident
46 Alchemist's offering
47 Flimflammers
52 His brother was no keeper
54 One end of the narthex
55 Prefix with -assic
56 Countless lifetimes
57 Keystone figure
58 Who wrote "All that we see or seem / Is but a dream within a dream"
59 Pipe cleaner
60 High rails

by Trenton Charlson

ACROSS

1 Like much White House press
8 Stick with
14 Social elites
16 Susan who wrote "The Orchid Thief"
17 Line of Pokémon
19 Actor James of "The Fresh Prince of Bel Air"
20 ___ Who Code (nonprofit)
21 Forerunner of rocksteady
22 Bad thing to miss
23 Native Costa Ricans, informally
24 Something that might be raised in a fight
25 Amount to
26 Locales for the Jets and the Sharks
27 Like wicker chairs
28 Daisy Dukes, e.g.
30 Draft status?
31 Excessive coverage, perhaps
32 Mounted
33 Daylight saving time adjustment: Abbr.
34 You might have one on the side
37 Roaster
38 Sound of the West Coast
39 What stamens are, in botany
40 Word with change or color
41 Unmasked, say
42 Swears at
43 Travel around the world
46 Stuck in the Middle Ages?

47 Summer cooler
48 Early Macedonian capital
49 Divinity

DOWN

1 Famed Portuguese explorer
2 Good luck with that!
3 "Oh, get outta here!"
4 Lead-in to physical
5 Suspension of a sort
6 Onetime trade org.
7 Sue
8 Target alternative
9 "De dónde ___ ?" (Spanish 101 query)
10 ___ borer (beetle)
11 Russian Revolution figures
12 Silent counterparts, once
13 Where cruise passengers end up
15 Propensity for pilfering
18 Practice that yields mixed results?
23 New York county near Pennsylvania
24 Big name in crackers
26 1998 Robert De Niro crime thriller
27 The heart of Paris
28 Try to win, in a way
29 Author/screenwriter Ben
30 "Drink marvelously" sloganeer

31 Trailer
32 Look up, in a way
34 Something a 38-Down likes to eat
35 Current weather concern?
36 Tried-and-true
38 An adult one can spend up to 16 hours a day eating
39 Footslog
41 Contests in which the competitors are eliminated one by one
42 Pulitzer winner Maureen
44 Syringe amts.
45 Soft-spoken words

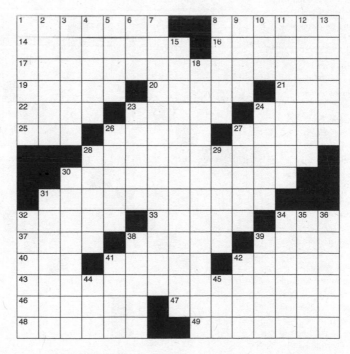

by Hemant Mehta

ACROSS

1 Cheap trick, perhaps
9 Apply pressure to
15 "Stupid me!"
16 Recherché
17 Food, water, a place to live, etc.
19 Decreases?
20 Who wrote "The poetry of earth is never dead"
21 Drawing method
22 "___ I do!" (informal assent)
23 Rivals of the 1980s "Showtime" Lakers, to fans
24 Part of a pool
25 Regulation followers, for short
26 Cuts (down)
27 "Wassup, my dude"
28 Intended
29 Winter slopes activity
30 One born in the wrong generation, maybe
33 Expands
34 Works with 17 units
35 Like speeders, often
36 Features of some glasses
37 Wade in the Baseball Hall of Fame
38 Manhattan campus around Washington Sq. Park
41 Where to set une couronne
42 Name spelled with six dashes and six dots
43 Air
44 Where Wonder Woman first worked: Abbr.
45 Words of agreement
46 "Gotcha"
47 Soak up the sun, say
50 What I might be in a lab?

51 Multiheaded dog guarding the gates of the underworld, in myth
52 Features of some accents
53 James Baldwin, e.g.

DOWN

1 What an aphrodisiac boosts
2 Eastern lodging
3 North Atlantic island group
4 Tweak
5 Sweeties
6 Modern "art"
7 Young male chicken
8 Prepared to propose, perhaps
9 Holds up
10 Greek counterpart of Discordia

11 See 18-Down
12 "Perfect!"
13 Dealing directly (with)
14 They're saved for a rainy day
18 High school alternatives to the 11-Down
23 After Kipling, the youngest-ever Literature Nobelist (1957, 44 years)
24 Turn
26 Reverential
27 Historically Germanic observances
28 Offer to help
29 Shade
30 "You're such a tease!"
31 It ends after midnight in New York, with "The"
32 Pepsi Max, e.g.

33 Spots for archaeologists
35 As an exception
37 Word with shop, shot or shape
38 Sushi variety
39 2013 #1 album from Kanye West
40 Civil disturbance
42 Biblical figure with a large staff
43 Walk in a leisurely way
45 Track, say
46 "___: Duets" (2007 country album)
48 Main component of britannium
49 Invoice info: Abbr.

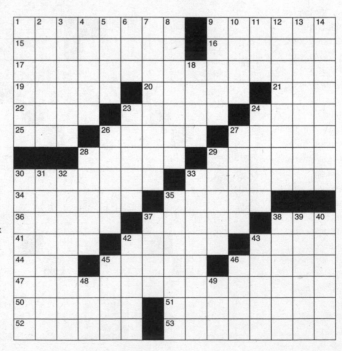

by Daniel Sheremeta

ACROSS

1 Colorful warning
8 Freedom cry, for some
12 Material for a child's necklace
13 Rapper with the 2001 hit "Superwoman Pt. II"
14 They've got their own problems
15 Off the mark?
16 Plus ___ (Spain's national motto)
17 Software engineer's presentation
19 "I ___ you!"
20 Consolidate
21 Shot, e.g.
23 Departure announcement
24 Much
25 Clodpole
27 Word with hot or fly
28 Flexible positions
30 Modern initialism for one skimming text
31 Something of miner interest
32 Theia or Rhea
33 Joe carter?
35 Lacks for nothing
37 Like some gallery displays
38 Molten pools
40 Peter Pan competitor
42 Flavor of many Anglo-Indian chutneys
43 1978 hit whose title is spelled out in its chorus
47 "That's enough out of you!"
49 Spiritual wanderer
51 Aid for a breakfast chef
54 Kelley of the U.S. women's national soccer team
55 Blow up

56 Step two in many skin-care routines
57 Right on
58 Gram alternative
59 Twitch

DOWN

1 They might smell fishy
2 Hue made from Ilmenite
3 What's spread on a spreadsheet
4 Palindromic preposition
5 Baseball team announcement
6 Step in
7 Game with baskets
8 Beat
9 All made up, perhaps
10 "How awful!"

11 Other side
12 Land once known as the "peninsula of gold"
13 Drove
14 Where to get down and dirty
18 They can have you going the wrong way
20 Some advanced degs.
22 Setting of the first panel in Hieronymus Bosch's "The Last Judgment"
24 Orange refreshment
26 Part of la famille
29 Digital tool
30 Turnpike feature
33 It goes hand to hand
34 Online seller of specialty crafts
36 Pop singer ___ Max

39 "___, I cannot be" (Emily Dickinson poem)
40 Block
41 Like a schlemiel
44 Disney title girl
45 Fixes
46 Part of some drills
47 Thing: Sp.
48 Bird with a forked tail
50 Playground denizens
52 Org. offering traveler's checks?
53 Fix

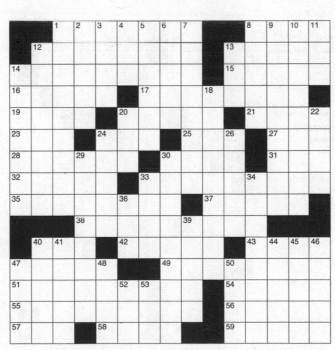

by Matthew Stock

ACROSS

1 Clean
5 Brims
10 Peak also known as Mongibello
14 Big brand of kibble
15 Anthony of "In the Heights"
16 He called Hulk a "friend from work," in a Marvel movie
17 Dalliance
19 Victor ___, Nobel winner for the discovery of cosmic rays
20 Romeo and Juliet, e.g.
21 Reverential term of address
22 Show featuring Bowen Yang, for short
23 Item at a T.S.A. checkpoint
24 Symptoms of stress, it's said
26 Montreal's Côte Saint-___
27 Largest city in the U.S. that's not a county seat
29 "O patria ___" ("Aida" aria)
30 It's just you and me, baby
33 Rhetorical question of self-deprecation
34 They promise no hurt feelings
35 Goof
36 ___ + anais (baby care brand)
37 "___ sleep comes down to soothe the weary eyes": Paul Laurence Dunbar
38 "Doesn't matter to me"
40 "What do we have here!"
41 Schedule abbr.
44 ___ Chen, member of the girl group S.H.E.
45 Apple counter
48 Unoccupied
49 Score keeper?

50 Repeated cry in aerobics
51 Marc or Pau of the N.B.A.
52 Cher, but not Sonny
53 Dance wildly
54 Tea party serving
55 Haze

DOWN

1 Floats
2 Klein who once managed the Beatles and Rolling Stones
3 Pitch
4 Cape ___, place where the Pacific and Atlantic meet
5 "Waiting for Godot," e.g.
6 Put down the hatch
7 Sheik's peer
8 Stock exchange?
9 Bit of info for an accountant: Abbr.
10 Guiding principles
11 Eerie-sounding instruments that are played without physical contact
12 Item of punk jewelry
13 ___ Technica (website)
18 An infant's mind, according to John Locke
21 False and malicious
24 It's on the road again
25 Org. that merged with AFTRA
26 Diving bird
27 "___ Whoopee" (jazz standard)
28 Where Oliver Hazard Perry said "We have met the enemy, and they are ours"

30 "Will You Love Me Tomorrow" group, with "the"
31 Bundle
32 Wear (out)
33 Grew in appreciation for
34 One of the Maritime Provinces: Abbr.
39 The "a" of Torah?
40 Cause of bad breath
41 Intro to America's pastime
42 Tonal language family
43 Fervor
45 Chips go-with, for short
46 Bygone U.S. fuel brand
47 Try
48 End of class?
49 Tiny dosage units: Abbr.

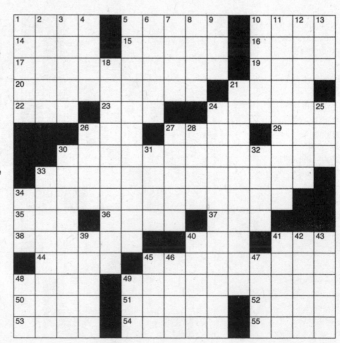

by Erica Hsiung Wojcik

ACROSS

1 Certain archaeological site
4 Received, as a guest to one's flat
9 Felicity
14 Flying start?
15 Olds that was once in the news
16 Make altogether
17 Cheerful response to "How're you doing?"
20 Faded
21 C_6H_6
22 "Guess again"
23 Bachelor, e.g.
24 Amused reaction
25 31-syllable Japanese poem
27 Heavy shoe
29 Women's soccer powerhouse
30 Poorly written words
32 A mighty long time
36 Its slogan "Get Smarter Now" matches its initials
39 Writing is sometimes done on it
40 Looking wise?
41 Part of some after-work plans, in brief
42 Comment after clumsiness
44 John Steinbeck's middle name
46 Burning issue
49 Top
50 E.P.A. concern
51 Playroom?
53 Buffaloed
56 People may never get over it
58 Halfway between yellow and orange
59 Musical segment
60 Auto shaft, informally
61 Tries out
62 Claudio or Gio, father-and-son players for the U.S. men's national soccer team
63 1977 Sex Pistols song written after a record-contract termination

DOWN

1 When doubled, attention-grabbing
2 During
3 It's first among Americans
4 "That's a big 'no thanks'"
5 Michael Caine film
6 Regard
7 Address in a bar
8 Delectable made with grass
9 Actress Fricker of "My Left Foot"
10 Leap with a twist
11 Dossier contents
12 One working for a dictator
13 Philosopher Georges
18 Sci-fi's Chief Chirpa, e.g.
19 Relatives of foxhounds
23 String of typographical symbols, like @%$&!, to represent an obscenity
25 Jerks
26 "Step on it!"
27 Navigator was in the first one
28 Sticks nix
31 Did some prep work in the kitchen
33 About to be sold
34 Has things backward, say
35 Game with matadors and schneiders
37 Energy-saving mode in some hybrid cars
38 Soprano's group
43 Cowboy features
45 Lead, e.g.
46 Up
47 "For ___!"
48 Components of a bouquet garni
50 A toaster might hold one
52 Give some bad assistance
53 Affected
54 Hustle
55 Final precursor
57 Composition of some sheets

by Joe DiPietro

ACROSS

1 Blue print?
7 Water wings, for example
13 Toasted treat
15 Japanese for "teacher"
16 Skating expos
18 Bearing
19 Paragon
20 Suck up, in a way
22 Author of "The Kitchen God's Wife" (1991)
23 There's no coming back from this
26 Initialism that might have a ring to it?
27 1000 hrs.
28 Scale notes
29 Agent of immunity
31 "Did I just hear him say that?!"
34 Principle indicating "No second chances"
35 Outer border for 36-Across
36 See-through items
37 Two-time Olympic gymnast Raisman
38 Male's name hidden backward in this clue
42 Barely make, with "out"
43 Whet bar?
45 Make lace
46 Longtime Disney chief Michael
47 Big __
48 Hair holders
50 Descriptor for a champion
53 Half-page, perhaps
54 Fatherly tips, to use a portmanteau coinage
55 Decks with major and minor arcana
56 Lean against

DOWN

1 Turn-on for a bartender?
2 Big epoch for mammals
3 Hypothetical missing links
4 Chain parts: Abbr.
5 "This is the life!"
6 Lacking literary sparkle
7 Setting for a shot
8 Historic kingdom of Spain
9 Most populous Canadian prov.
10 So to speak
11 Sound
12 Traffic light
14 Some social media back-and-forths
17 Short relationship
21 One who loves to bring up the past
24 Surfer girl
25 Doctors
29 Poet who wrote "A Child's Christmas in Wales"
30 Firmly bond
32 Court
33 "___ Carter III" (best-selling Lil Wayne album)
34 Napa excursion
35 Fictional African country of film
36 Took care of a dog or cat, maybe
39 "Alrighty then"
40 "Romanian Rhapsodies" composer
41 Like the days following Mardi Gras
43 Cruxes
44 Gloomy, poetically
46 Sub text, maybe
49 Hawaiian fish also called the wahoo
51 Juice suffix
52 Some Best Buy buys

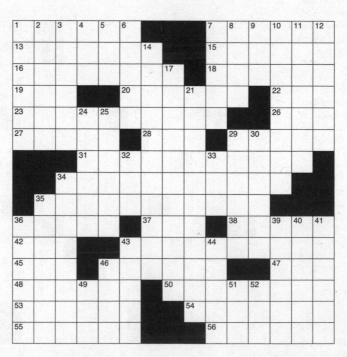

by Aaron Ullman

ACROSS

1 750-milliliter bottles
7 ___ C. J. Walker, first American woman to become a self-made millionaire, per Guinness
12 Pretend
13 Flowers known botanically as Leucanthemum vulgare
15 Lady Gaga album named for her aunt
16 Stops being stubborn
18 "There's no accounting for taste"
21 Birthplace of Buddha
22 More spacious
23 Walks in the park
25 Carries on
26 Up
27 Compliment to a chef
29 Tartarus, by another name
30 Prefix with night or day
31 Mimicked
33 Tepid assessment
35 Actress whose nickname derives from her middle name, Stamatina
36 Family prefix
38 Make it, gamewise
40 Eponym of a red-and-white heraldic rose
42 Decorated athlete whose name could be parsed as "zero" + "loss"
44 Nikkie ___, beauty vlogger with more than 13 million followers on YouTube
46 "Way to go!"
48 Replenish
49 Eliminate from contention
54 More affected
55 Outfit with flaps and snaps
56 Pays in the Alps?
57 Move around
58 "The Divine Miss M"
59 Thought and thought and thought (about)

DOWN

1 Challenging setting for the 2020 Olympics men's road cycling course
2 Playing past regulation, informally
3 ___ house
4 Letters
5 Had a craving
6 Take time to think about something
7 By ethical standards
8 Cousin of a lutz
9 Reese in "Touched by an Angel"
10 Affirmative on the U.S.S. Enterprise
11 State emblem of Israel
14 Target
17 Member of the A.F.C. team with most division titles
19 ___ y pimienta
20 "4 real?!?"
23 Lesser-used passages
24 Total
26 British singer with the hits "How We Do (Party)" and "Your Song"
28 They may be mixed
30 Network with Joy Reid's "The ReidOut"
32 "I like telling ___ jokes. Sometimes he laughs!"
34 French Calvinist
37 Check attachment
39 Escape
41 Sap
43 Longhaired star of 1950s TV
45 Quickly put down
47 Give a lift
50 Suffix akin to "-o-rama"
51 "You don't have to tell me!"
52 One of the few places where traffic is appreciated
53 Ticked (off)

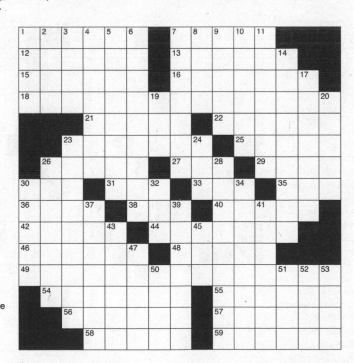

by Rachel Fabi

ACROSS

1 Billboard magazine feature
6 Abbr. in skin care
9 Creatures with asymmetrical ears for accuracy in hunting
13 Facts-as-fiction work
16 Some summer arrivals
17 "Join the club!"
18 World's best-selling contemporary female artist of all time, per Billboard magazine
19 "Who ___ ?"
20 "So . . . who wants in on this deal?"
22 Snag
23 Alongside
24 Children in Vienna
26 Costume that might start with a cardboard box
28 Two cents for a paper, perhaps
30 Body with a floor
31 Orchestral instrument that doesn't make a sound
32 Extension ___
33 Pass (out)
34 Trinket
36 Unpolished
37 One might be chosen for its perspective
38 Loafers
40 Like hair at salons
42 Bad side
43 Data head?
44 Drummed-up measures?
47 Seasoned rice dish
50 Make a big stink
52 Blue book alternative
54 Actress Sink of "Stranger Things"
55 Say goodbye to many a 34-Across à la Marie Kondo
56 Prunes
57 Destiny's Child's "___ My Name"
58 Was appealing?
59 Some time

DOWN

1 Newmark with an eponymous list
2 Series of stakes
3 "Truer words were never spoken!"
4 Word from the Dutch for "talk nonsense"
5 "Claws" channel
6 Trail
7 One way to avoid a lecture
8 Experienced
9 Bygone
10 Makes very uncomfortable, informally
11 They may be tied up in a sequel
12 W-2 ID
14 Are in store
15 Didn't come through as promised, in slang
21 Not be serious
23 Given (to)
25 Garden tool
27 Summons before congress?
29 More sententious
31 Group with the 2020 #1 album "Be"
32 Country whose official languages are French and Arabic
33 Be superinfatuated with someone
35 Jazz great Laine
36 What a bee may be
39 "To All the ___ I've Loved Before" (2018 film)
41 Hoist, redundantly
44 Given a number, maybe
45 Press, e.g.
46 Oozing smarm
47 Fills with fluff
48 One may be floated or rough
49 Liu of "Why Women Kill"
50 Coronation, e.g.
51 -
53 Card display?

by Brooke Husic and Nam Jin Yoon

ACROSS

1 Stagger
9 Incomplete Wikipedia entry
13 Part of many a software demo, informally
15 Former Philadelphia mayor Wilson
16 Unanticipated deficit
17 Bug
18 Piercing tool
19 Children's toy that's sprayed from a can
21 Informal pronoun
23 Prefix with pronoun
24 You ___ (words before an amount after discount)
25 Tautological words of resignation
31 Something to take home
34 [not our typo]
35 Advisor, e.g.
36 Room where a Peloton may double as a clothing rack
38 Literally, "guilty mind"
40 Codeshare partner of American Airlines
41 Make a quick visit, with "in"
43 Most alert to social justice issues
44 "Let's move on"
47 Broadway star Phillipa
48 "Was ist ___ ?"
49 Renders
53 They're not always free with their advice
58 "That'll be the day!"
59 "Mae alsalama," across the Mediterranean
60 Tex-Mex brand
62 Writer of the line "Did you ever stop to think, and forget to start again?"
63 Extent of a commuter rail system, perhaps

64 Gender-neutral pronoun
65 "This stays between us"

DOWN

1 Test for purity
2 Either side of Alaska?
3 Online heckler
4 "The Strife Is ___, the Battle Done" (Easter hymn)
5 Table tennis equipment
6 Luxury home installation with a vanishing edge
7 Horoscope symbol
8 Makes sacred
9 "Oh, never mind—you clearly don't want to talk about it"
10 Amos with the 1994 hit "Cornflake Girl"
11 Soba alternative
12 Icy detachment
14 Practice
15 Try to say
20 Genre for "Cowboy Bebop" and "The Mandalorian"
22 Subjects of some parental speeches
26 Comedian Notaro
27 "What's eating ___?!"
28 Exhaust
29 Day after Pi Day, e.g.
30 Parking spot?
31 "That was a close call!"
32 Ensemble part
33 One member of Congress's "Squad"

37 Part of many a three-day weekend: Abbr.
39 Here-there connection
42 Biked
45 Put out
46 Give in person
50 United hub
51 Stand for something
52 Large mass of swimming fish
53 Purchase at a military supplies store, informally
54 Anthony Hopkins's character in the Marvel Universe
55 Shade of green
56 ___ yum (hot-and-sour Thai soup)
57 Blank on a sign-up sheet
61 Down ___

by Ada Nicolle

ACROSS

1 Prefix with directional
5 Border
9 Sort who refuses to answer
13 A sumo wrestler's is called a mawashi
15 Catherine of "Schitt's Creek"
16 Spot remover?
17 Candle holders, sometimes
18 Close
19 Prophetic
21 ___-jongg
23 U.S. locale that, when said quickly, sounds like a cheer
24 Highway exit sign
25 As seen in chemistry class?
29 Velvet-voiced Mel
31 Word with happy or rush
32 Causing a boom, maybe
36 Pokémon that ultimately evolves into Alakazam
37 Digital alternative
38 ___ of Citium, philosopher who founded Stoicism
39 Vulnerable area
41 Keen
42 Monster's opposite
43 Doctrines
45 ___-term test for divergence (calculus concept)
47 Improvise on stage
49 San Francisco's ___ Hill
50 Grammy winner for 1983's "Flashdance . . . What a Feeling"
53 Small flaw
56 Ambulatory aids
57 Manet called him "the painter of painters"
60 Cousin of an aardwolf
61 Unlikely match
62 ___ noche (tonight: Sp.)
63 Source
64 Its website has a "Fantasy" page

DOWN

1 Up there, you might say
2 Stock exchange?
3 Close
4 Unable to perform operations
5 Weisshorn, e.g.
6 Astronomer Thomas for whom a comet is named
7 Not yet delivered, after "in"
8 Status on a conservationist's "Red List"
9 Non-coffee Starbucks order
10 Germans call it Genfersee
11 Political ___
12 They're rigged
14 Board game set on an island
15 "It ___ to me . . ."
20 Unit equal to 907.2 kilograms
22 Like only one member of the Supreme Court in its history (Sonia Sotomayor)
25 Solvers' reactions
26 Lead-in to call
27 Browse, say
28 Seek advancement through flattery
30 Only one-word country that contains all five vowels
33 Literature's Napoleon, e.g.
34 Contending
35 Best Picture winner in 2022
40 W.N.B.A. great Weatherspoon
44 Highly exaggerated and subjective, as journalism
45 Specialization
46 High-chair features
48 Italian nickname that omits Al-
51 "99 Luftballons" singer
52 Big name in fashion footwear
54 Holds gingerly, maybe
55 Underwater forest
58 Charade
59 Kind of garden

by Hal Moore

ACROSS

1 Rolls dough, perhaps?
11 Roll an ill-timed seven, with "out"
15 It's all black and white
16 Veg out
17 Che Guevara, when he wrote "The Motorcycle Diaries"
18 Private org. involved in the most Supreme Court cases
19 Chic
20 Some Yamaha products
22 Settled down
23 Selena's "Baila ___ Cumbia"
26 Zoo heavyweight
27 Didn't play, say
28 What a duck might be
30 Actor Levy
31 Climb the social ladder, in a way
32 Function
33 It nowadays offers streaming recommendations
36 Common pharmacy orders
38 Purchase at a pro shop
39 Barbecue coating
41 Spanish diminutive suffix
42 Schedule with little room for spontaneity
43 Go back
46 ___ Gabler, Ibsen title character
48 Kind of sheet
49 Catherine, e.g., in "Jules et Jim"
50 NyQuil shelfmate
52 Doles out
54 ___ rage
55 Ventriloquist's prop, maybe
58 Names
59 Makes clearly understood
60 Editor's overruling
61 Like some cookie cutters

DOWN

1 They can lead to long sentences
2 Nipple ring?
3 Website with the slogan "Dive into anything"
4 Put forward
5 Isn't oneself?
6 "Yeah, that's right!"
7 Admin on 3-Down, e.g.
8 Barely make do, with "by"
9 Michelangelo, e.g.
10 Word before and after "à"
11 Look bad together
12 Many a Rolling Stone cover subject
13 At the end of the day
14 What some invitees bring to parties
21 "___ me!"
24 Opposite of dewy-eyed
25 Lord's Prayer possessive
28 Antioxidant drink brand
29 Luxury attire for white-tie events
31 Feature of many a military obstacle course
32 Lightly roast
33 Devotees of Team Edward and Team Jacob, in fandom slang
34 Unseated
35 Positive impression
37 "Sounds like a good time!"
40 "There's an ___ for that"
42 ___ Minella (monkey Muppet)
43 Genre for the All-American Rejects
44 Rude refusal
45 Outshone
47 Accomplished, old-style
49 Early software version
51 Results of some successful defenses
53 Verdant
56 Long of "The Best Man"
57 Save for later, in a way

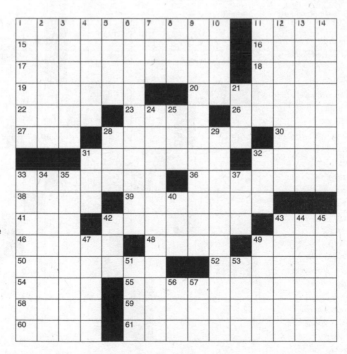

by Ryan McCarty and Yacob Yonas

ACROSS

1 Lures into a relationship by using a fictional online persona
10 Occasion for a high flute?
15 Like households with stay-at-home spouses, typically
16 Like many spiral notebooks
17 It may be taken for dramatic effect
18 World record holder?
19 "Do the Right Thing" pizzeria
20 Get around
22 Giant mfr. of industrial machinery
25 5/15, e.g.
27 Hawaiian chorus
30 ___ job
31 Onboardee
33 Follower of many state names
34 Really dry
36 Season ticket holder, maybe
38 Pond blossom
40 Rockets can be found in it, in brief
41 Infiltrates
42 Dealing with technical details, say
45 Blowout
46 Put away
47 Herbal infusions
49 Do-over
50 "Psycho" psycho
52 First name in gossip
53 Some SAT takers
54 Not be completely accurate with
56 Spanish key
58 Kind of cake with layers of coffee and chocolate
60 Where to find 55 and over?

65 Resource in the game Catan
66 Film technique that accommodates wide- and full-screen display
67 Act crabby?
68 Parents obsessed with play dates?

DOWN

1 Mustard, for one: Abbr.
2 "Is that ___?"
3 Start of a count
4 Some pudding ingredients
5 Hurting
6 Like the milk in café au lait, sometimes
7 Improbable orders for oenophiles
8 Myanmar has two of them
9 Matches

10 They're used during film production and promotion
11 The one in "Layla" lasts 3 minutes 48 seconds
12 Mixed emotions, so to speak
13 Jacques Cousteau's milieu
14 Parts of some bowls, in brief
21 Journalist Swisher
22 Dressing option
23 Home of the largest street fair in North America
24 Modern-day scroll, of a sort
26 Mama grizzly
28 Item to pack for a trip abroad
29 Down times?
32 "Really? Wow!"

35 "Thanks, Captain Obvious"
37 Telephone trio
39 Prepared to end an engagement
43 Buffalo ___
44 Picking up
48 Oscar Wilde tragedy
51 Many a work by the artist Banksy
55 Mythical archer
57 Driver in Hollywood
58 Reactions to strikes?
59 Letter after upsilon
61 Suitable
62 "Was ___ blame?"
63 Source of withdrawal?
64 Article in a French newspaper

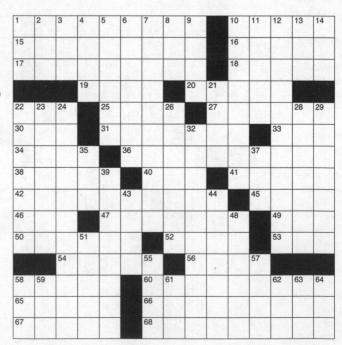

by David Distenfeld

ACROSS

1 Order with four periods
5 Relative of mustard
10 Worked a reception, say, informally
14 What might be followed in an investigation
16 Kind of pants
17 It's often found on bow ties
18 Booted up, say?
19 Nickname in 1950s–'60s TV
20 Some members of a blended family
22 River of Hades
24 Buck
25 "___ America (And So Can You!)" (Stephen Colbert best seller)
28 Name names
29 Salon offering
30 Tease, with "on"
33 Flew private, for instance
37 Is super-punctual
38 Make no plans
39 It traditionally starts with a strophe
40 Saucer contents, for short
41 Terence ___, Fields Medal-winning mathematician
42 Prefix with cortex
43 Things sometimes named after scientists
45 Secret ___
47 Loves, and then some
49 Cusps
52 Low joint
53 In a manner of speaking?
56 Company that uses about 1% of the world's wood supply annually
57 It ends with a big splash
58 Distinguished fellows

59 Mortimer ___, famed ventriloquy dummy of old
60 Longevous

DOWN

1 Twitch, say
2 Onetime subsidiary of G.M.
3 Word that sounds like a plural of 1-Down
4 Corolla part
5 Decisive periods, in brief
6 Activities for dummies
7 High-end
8 It may be served in a bed
9 1980 black-and-white film that was nominated for Best Picture, with "The"
10 Maker of the Supersonic hair dryer
11 England's first poet laureate (1668)
12 They're big in Hollywood
13 TV's "American ___"
15 Glowing things
21 Staples of old westerns
23 Gifts are displayed in these
25 ___ disco (European music genre)
26 Secret alternative
27 Look at with awe
29 Port authority?
31 Uniquely
32 Reach
34 Focus of une biographie
35 Oafish outburst
36 Pro follower
44 Spots

45 Avalanche
46 St. Teresa's birthplace
47 It means "be quick" in Hawaiian
48 Where zardozi embroidery is prevalent
50 Juul, e.g., informally
51 "Soldier of Love" singer, 2009
52 An opening to "closing"
54 Chi-Town airport code
55 Championed

by Joseph Greenbaum

ACROSS

1 Puzzle genre
6 Company with the motto "When you rise, we shine"
10 Arcade game ender
14 Jimi Hendrix vis-à-vis the Monkees, in 1967
16 Eastern leader
17 Supplied with dough, as a bakery
18 Giving chocolate to the dog, e.g.
19 "Woo-hoo!," in Oaxaca
20 Proceed during rush hour, say
21 It's down in France
22 Totals
23 Graham of "Gilmore Girls"
25 Plant with oily seeds
28 Give and take
29 African river with a notorious name
30 "Well, who'da thunk it!"
33 Actor Burton
34 Hot flash?
35 One of three brothers in a Puzo best seller
36 Employer of Kirk and Spock
38 Like O negative vis-à-vis O positive
39 Hucksters have them
40 Dressed, so to speak
41 Went up
42 Magazine with the slogan "All you need to know about everything that matters," with "The"
43 The average American spends over four hours a day on it
44 All 12 Disney princesses, e.g.
46 Small-business partner, perhaps
49 Clip
50 Period before a big deadline
52 It's not good
53 Buildings with many wings
54 Ingredients in mattar paneer
55 Place to park
56 Hoi polloi

DOWN

1 Endangered Western wolf
2 Olympic Australis is a noted one
3 Tiny inheritance
4 It commonly comes in black and blue
5 Trash can, jocularly
6 Looks like a jerk
7 Chronicle
8 Hoth, in "The Empire Strikes Back"
9 Regular: Abbr.
10 Path at a university
11 Comment made while waving in a crowd
12 Wrinkle-prone fabric
13 Parade, with "out"
15 Designer Kamali who made Farrah Fawcett's iconic red swimsuit
21 Non-taxing part of airline travel?
22 They work using photovoltaic cells
24 Bow
25 Images of Pluto, perhaps
26 Assist on the job
27 Part of Canada named for part of Europe
28 Shows
30 Reason some kids won't go to class
31 Yemeni seaport
32 It may be part of a suit
37 Abstract artist Krasner
40 Actress who played Queens Elizabeth and Victoria in film
41 Take a plane to
42 "Cheers" actor George
43 Gear up
45 Dollar alternative
46 Paste in soup
47 Dark clouds, e.g.
48 Private dining room
50 "The Carol Burnett Show" network
51 Day associated with Mars, in astrology: Abbr.

by Robyn Weintraub

ACROSS

1 Senator after whom Honolulu's airport is named
7 Mag, e.g.
10 No longer available, in a way
14 The burger chain In-N-Out has a famous one
16 Transport unlikely to operate in the summer
17 Play it cool
18 Like muesli
19 Formal name for 11-Down, in brief
20 March word
21 Savanna and tundra
23 Sets of closing notes
25 Area near a stage
28 Museum pieces you might find to be moving?
29 Personal identifier in the Deaf community
32 Actual employer of some "government consultants," in brief
33 Mentor to a queen
36 Right this way?
37 Muscle-relieving tools for runners
38 Source of oils used in wellness
40 Source of oils used in wellness
41 Trio in some bios
43 ___ chem (101-level course, familiarly)
44 Course you need a compass to navigate?
45 Lowest-ranking member of a group
47 ___ & Roll (punny name for a sushi bar)
48 "I'll ___ it"
52 Kind of motel
54 Gram alternative
56 "___ Sleeps Over" (classic children's book)

57 L.G.B.T. rights activist Windsor
58 "Sigh . . . never mind"
62 Beauties
63 Playground "immunization"
64 ___ club
65 Partner of 53-Down
66 Rocky Mountain National Park sights

DOWN

1 His burial place is said to be in Israel's Cave of Machpelah
2 Onetime candy maker based in Revere, Mass.
3 The bits in a byte, e.g.
4 Vote holder on "Survivor"
5 "Me, too"
6 "You, too?!"
7 ___ year

8 Spanish article
9 It may be screwed up
10 Lower oneself
11 Major legislation of the 111th Congress
12 Sleepyhead, maybe
13 All 48, following the Volstead Act
15 Popular half-hour sketch comedy of the 1970s–'80s, with "The"
22 + or – something
24 It's a matter of degree
26 Sort of
27 Become one
30 Inspector of British fiction
31 Salute, say
33 It gets hatched in a fantasy novel
34 One to follow

35 Aid in avoiding distractions
36 ___ alcohol
39 Categorizes
42 Post-punk genre
44 Partner in a barn dance, maybe
46 Silly sorts
49 Like yoga instructors
50 Constellation with Betelgeuse and Bellatrix
51 Radio broadcast units
53 Partner of 65-Across
55 What might be a strain in a theater?
59 One starting a row?
60 Actress Claire of "The Crown"
61 Medium strength?

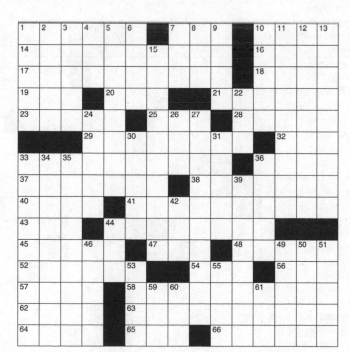

by Scott Earl

ACROSS

1 Puzzling start?
7 Like some rum
13 Where catalysts produce reactions, informally
15 "Sounds good, but . . . huh-uh"
16 Root vegetable with stringy stalks
18 Offset
19 B preceder
20 Painter's protectors
22 Blogroll assortment
24 Pretense
25 Roll
26 Show of authority, metaphorically
27 Apple ___
28 After beginning?
29 Like Gen-Z fans of classic rock, seemingly
33 Things often controlled with remotes
34 Guaranteed success
35 The Rolling Stones' "___ a Rainbow"
36 Ride, in a way
37 Some sneaks
41 Quaint confirmation
42 Scientist for whom a part of the brain is named
44 Skimpy
45 With sauce
48 Swenson of "Benson"
49 Fresh start
50 Gets a late start?
52 "Get out of here!"
53 Birthplace of the Black Panther Party
54 Bad things for a lecturer to hear
55 "There's no wrong way to eat a ___" (classic tagline)

DOWN

1 Buttonhole
2 Parisian sweets?
3 Get it
4 Parts of many breakfast buffets
5 Pick for pics, in brief
6 Hypothesized
7 Harmonizes
8 Key partner?
9 "I, ___," Shakespeare-inspired novel written from the villain's perspective
10 Some customer service agents nowadays
11 Gush
12 "___ matter"
14 Rudely interrupting
17 Offsets
21 Common condiment with fajitas
23 Support against collapse, with "up"
28 Something past or present
30 W.W. II Dambusters grp.
31 "That's a good one!"
32 Butcher shop choices
33 Question asked by a surprise caller
34 Try to persuade through lies
35 Smarts
38 Home of the continental U.S.'s geographic center
39 Road runner?
40 Foul ball's place, maybe
42 Finger
43 Día de los ___ (Spanish holiday)
46 What someone with anosmia cannot detect
47 Vintage, e.g.
51 Just get (by)

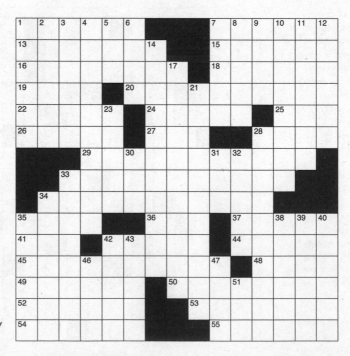

by Blake Slonecker

ACROSS

1 Travel aid in science fiction
9 Classic musical with the song "If He Walked Into My Life"
13 Some spandex garments
15 The Midwest's so-called "Queen Wheat City"
16 No-fuss
18 Teen issue getting much topical coverage?
19 "Weird . . ."
20 Button on a Facebook post
22 Copy room supply
23 Vehicles in "The Phantom Menace"
24 Comic Notaro
25 Drawings with lots of little blocks
26 Ollas, e.g.
29 What might collect a lot of checks
30 Ironic word before an expletive
31 Rapper Fiasco
32 Planks can strengthen it
33 Walk or run in a showy way
37 Mega-celebrities, so to speak
39 Black bird
40 Writer of the autobiography "Freedom in Exile"
41 Game of manual dexterity
43 Willingness to listen
44 Enclose
45 Paul ____, pet food company founder
46 Drink with dry vermouth, paradoxically
48 What has new seeds every spring?: Abbr.

49 Intervals represented by adjacent frets on a guitar
50 Millennials, by another name
51 Jumble

DOWN

1 They can be graphic
2 [grimace]
3 Pressure treatment?
4 Where The Oaks is run
5 Joins a heavy metal band, say
6 Thunderstruck
7 Authority in the field, informally
8 They don't know what they're talking about
9 Some supermarket displays
10 Long gone
11 AA and AAA
12 Shangri-las
14 Like much marshland
17 Study buds?
21 Ruler chosen through the Islamic process of shura
23 Ache for, in a way
25 One side of a fast-food restaurant
27 "It's anyone's guess"
28 Certain crossbred lap dog
31 Currency depicting the Persian poet Rumi
32 Big brand of camping gear
33 ____ wheel
34 Abrupt change in tone, perhaps
35 Inventions of Karl Benz and Rudolf Diesel

36 One sitting on the bench, maybe
37 Noomi ____, lead actress of 2009's "The Girl With the Dragon Tattoo"
38 Wrapping weights
40 Undertaking
41 Banned backyard game
42 N.B.A. general manager Brand
44 "Whoa, whoa, whoa!"
47 Sport with hits and strikes, for short

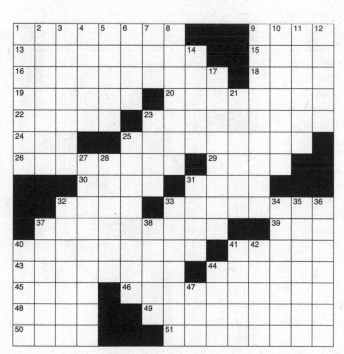

by Sid Sivakumar

ACROSS

1 It was all a dream, maybe
10 File type used in paper-to-digital archiving
13 It helps keep your head above water
14 ___ League
16 Popular poster
17 Tahoe or Winnebago
18 "Catch my drift?"
19 Nonbinary pronoun
20 Mass agreement
21 Key that closes a window
23 "I'm there!"
25 Free educational spots, for short
28 Zelle or Zillow
30 Costa ___
31 The Rockets, on a sports ticker
32 "Incidentally . . ."
36 Like some Marcel Duchamp works
38 Not numb
39 Spread some dirt
41 Pro's opponent
42 Measure (out)
43 Shaft
44 ___ sum (leafy vegetable in Chinese cuisine)
45 "Shush!"
48 Pittance
50 Grayish
51 Round and round and round?
53 Comic who said "I'm not addicted to cocaine. I just like the way it smells"
57 On trend
58 At one's best
60 1987 Lionel Richie hit
61 They're rolled out once a year at the White House
62 Taken care of
63 Sneak off somewhere

DOWN

1 Southern cornmeal dish
2 Artist's pad, maybe
3 Skateboarders' stunts
4 Workshop fasteners
5 One out of 10
6 Refuse
7 Aids in recovering lost pets
8 Runway hazard
9 Lengths of rulers, maybe
10 Heroic knights
11 Whose work may be all play?
12 "Mom" for a day, say
13 Babe, for one
15 "Molto ___"
22 Art capable
24 Team building?
25 Many college profs
26 Shower stall accessories
27 One with sound judgment?
29 Way to go
32 Like many baking sheets before baking
33 What a colon might mean
34 Mr. of film
35 Wee, informally
37 Urban scavenger
40 Certain essential worker, for short
44 Time to go in
45 Campaign grps.
46 Theater props?
47 Succeeded in
49 Word with light or space
52 "Peace!"
54 Literally, Sanskrit for "joining"
55 Bacchanalia
56 Hotel offerings: Abbr.
59 Genealogical listing: Abbr.

by Pao Roy

ACROSS

1 Queer heroine in the DC Universe
9 Minor deviation
13 Literally, "high city"
15 2002 art biopic starring Salma Hayek
16 Star of "12 Years a Slave"
18 Set
19 19th-century activist Dorothea
20 Only person to win a Nobel Prize in two scientific fields
21 French, to the English?
23 It's hot right now
25 Noggins
28 Prey for some hyenas
30 Tide type
32 ___ cat
33 Solving crosswords with a bunch of friends, say
36 Close a tab
37 Morning ritual for some
41 Prefix with sexual
42 Big name in English tea
43 Brownie, e.g.
44 It's nothing
45 See 59-Across
48 Warwick with 12 top 10 Billboard hits
51 Crafty
53 Salon sound
55 Make fun of
57 " ___-hoo!"
59 With 45-Across, performance in Studio 8H
60 "We don't need to rush"
64 Bouquet
65 Inkling
66 Some audio downloads, informally
67 Barkeeps

DOWN

1 Supports
2 Lovesick, perhaps
3 Son of Poseidon
4 Word before and after "just"
5 Opinion offerer
6 Prophecy or hallucinations, in "Macbeth"
7 City with a famous library
8 It's nothing
9 Oven setting
10 Best-selling novel that begins in Pondicherry, India
11 "Yes, ___!"
12 6 is a rare one
14 Brief bit
15 Passion
17 Quickly mounts
22 Anna with two Emmys for "Breaking Bad"
24 Supports
26 Peshwari ___ (raisin-filled fare)
27 Bump on a lid
29 Dissenting group
31 Fitness activity done while suspended from a hammock
34 Result of chafing
35 Some harbor sights
37 Hurtled
38 Master of death, in Hinduism
39 Abreast
40 Audible finger wags
46 Umpire's call
47 Match point?
49 Some holiday deliveries
50 Get exactly
52 Late-night query
54 Petitions
56 What's good in Jerusalem?
58 Galena and cinnabar, for two
60 Small dose: Abbr.
61 Initialism to which an "h" is sometimes added
62 Jazz trumpeter Adderley
63 Not play, with "out"

by Brooke Husic

ACROSS

1 Source of the quote "It is more blessed to give than to receive"
5 Creator of terraced agricultural fields known as andenes
9 Not alcoholic
13 Wig (out)
15 Place to slurp ramen
17 Meghan Markle's "something borrowed"
18 Cheesesteak topper
19 Good auto for an L.A.-to-N.Y.C. road trip?
21 R.N.'s insertion
22 Queen's protection
23 Fermented beverage
24 Frequent maid of honor, in brief
25 Writers' org. with apt initials
26 Alternative to blinds
28 Mortgage offering
30 Historian Schomburg of the Harlem Renaissance
32 Literally, "skewer"
34 Group photo pose during a rush
38 Flip
39 Jeep successor
41 Leak (through)
43 BART : San Francisco :: ____ : Philadelphia
45 Chemical suffix
46 "The Simpsons" character with an 18-letter last name
47 Record label co-founded by Drake
49 Longtime NPR call-in show
51 Home to California's Limekiln State Park
53 Cheese from the south of Italy
54 Numbers that come after 1
56 Renée ____ Goldsberry of "Hamilton"
58 Kind of architectural movement with the philosophy of living with less

59 Author Mario Vargas ____
60 Part of a French 101 conjugation
61 "Wuthering Heights" setting
62 Impertinent sort

DOWN

1 Toward the tail
2 Polecats, raccoons, squirrels, etc.
3 Dress down
4 Brand once produced by Dow Chemical
5 Somewhat
6 Summer temperatures of 120° F, in Death Valley
7 Say "You're so-o-o cute!," e.g.
8 "Stronger than pain" sloganeer
9 Persuade

10 Uncommon member of a high school band
11 Civil rights activist ____ Lou Hamer
12 Things that parks and families have
14 Marsupium, by another name
16 Cause of a breakup
20 Title for Frida Kahlo
22 Brazilian's place
23 Pallid
27 Signature scent introduced in 1968
29 Alive with excitement
31 Itch
33 Mesopotamian goddess of love and war
35 ____ facto
36 Ohio claims to be its birthplace

37 TV character who said "I do love a locker room. It smells like potential"
40 High-pitched cry
41 Christmas ____
42 ____ Gant, protagonist of Thomas Wolfe's "Look Homeward, Angel"
44 Windows might be opened by one
46 Ease
48 When doubled, racing sound
50 They're denoted by T's, for tees
52 States
53 X, maybe, in Spanish
55 What Salt-N-Pepa were not, despite their name
57 Gobble up

by Sophia Maymudes and Margaret Seikel

ACROSS

1 Texter's preamble
5 Branch of the U.S. military launched in 2019
15 Soft-soap
16 Soap in Mexico
17 Coveted object
18 Best Actor nominee for 2019's "Marriage Story"
19 "A Dream Within a Dream" writer
20 Provider of a lift
21 ___-purpose
22 King in "The Return of the King"
24 Rapper with the 1999 #1 album "I Am . . ."
27 What investigators might do
28 Surname of a star-crossed lover
29 "What they said"
31 Slayed
33 Apple selection?
35 Stretches for a swimmer
36 Camp sight
38 Squabble
40 Singer/actress Carter
42 Talk, talk, talk
45 Lectern locale
47 "Why, yes indeed!"
48 Where snorting isn't rude
51 Supermodel Alek
52 Standing at home, say
53 Course pro?
55 What comes before a bet
57 Classic Vans sneaker model
58 "Oh, grow up"
61 Abandon ship
62 Comment from one who's moved on

63 Brand name on Cakesters snack cakes
64 They include satellite cities
65 Poke alternative, maybe

DOWN

1 Cold case?
2 Line at Disney World
3 Go in prepared
4 Competitor of Stridex
5 Like some book reviews
6 Like the grammar police
7 "Succession" co-star Ruck
8 Place for a handprint, maybe
9 Heel, e.g.
10 Kind of loop in programming
11 Pioneer of elegies
12 Gun
13 Unblocked
14 ___ voting
20 In Germany it's "Krautsalat"
23 Chugged, with "down"
25 Source of protein in a poke bowl
26 Pop singer who came out as nonbinary in 2019
30 Stick on, in a way
32 Mess around (with)
34 Playthings with "belly badges"
37 Place where shells are put away?
39 Chains of churches

41 Bit of mendacity
43 Rowlf the Dog and Robin the Frog, for two
44 Few
46 Performer in both the Winter and Summer Olympics, in different sports
48 Certain curtain
49 Party consideration
50 Cause of an uprising?
54 Violeta o rosa
56 Draw
59 Low call
60 2020 thriller in which Jessica Chastain plays the title role
61 Catchy song, in modern slang

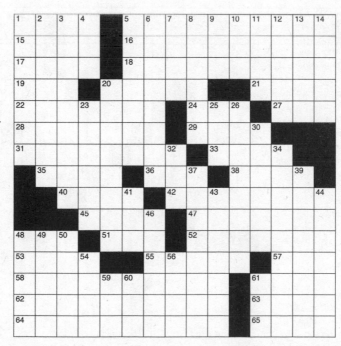

by Adam Aaronson

ACROSS

1 Professional wrestling program since 1999
10 Orion : Hunter :: Cetus : ___
15 Southwestern casserole with a cornbread crust
16 Comfortable
17 Part of Wagner's "Ring" cycle, with "The"
18 The "she" in the line "To Sherlock Holmes she is always THE woman"
19 "All ___ is autobiographical": Fellini
20 Rank below marquis
21 "What a shame"
22 "That hurts!"
24 One up?
26 "Tommyrot!"
28 Little sandwiches for dessert
29 Coppertone no.
32 Activity next to a bar
35 Fund
37 Just for the fun of it
39 Popular beer pong container
40 Cry at the end of a family trip
42 Game you never want to get your fill of?
43 Milk source
44 Ricochet
46 "Get it?"
47 Email button that moves a message to one's inbox
49 "On the double!"
52 Villain
55 Fat, to François
57 Radio station call letters that ask a question?
58 ___ State (Rhode Island nickname)
59 Hunt for treasure, in a way
61 Revolution
62 Chocolate source
63 Old newspaper photo sections, informally
64 Crustacean in Creole cuisine

DOWN

1 Drift
2 1980s skiing champ Phil
3 Question of responsibility
4 Heinie
5 Bauhaus figure
6 "Dancers at the Bar" painter
7 City north of Lisbon
8 Captain in "Apocalypse Now"
9 Homer's neighbor
10 Traditional January events
11 Play (around)
12 Actor Leon of "The Postman Always Rings Twice"
13 "Girls" creator/star Dunham
14 Sized up
21 Defensive retort
23 When repeated, a Northwest city
25 Modernists, briefly
27 Attendance inventories
29 Staple feature of Groucho Marx's "You Bet Your Life"
30 Spittoon sound
31 Dandies
32 Heavyweight champ Riddick
33 Over
34 Accord
36 Completely, in modern slang
38 White wine cocktails
41 Popular BBC car series
45 Hand-held percussion instrument
47 Mystery writer Marsh
48 Colorful talker
50 "Arabian Nights" prince
51 Actor Maguire
52 Yahoo
53 Prefix with phobia
54 Economic concern
56 No longer barefoot
59 Include discreetly, in a way
60 "L" overseer

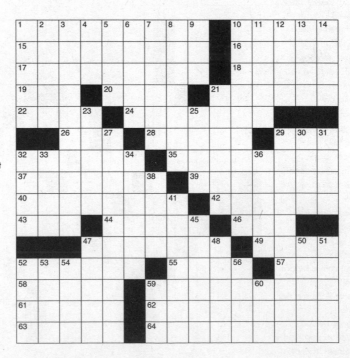

by Ned White

ACROSS

1 Champion's accessory
5 What you can do to "Moon River"
10 Follower of John
14 "Don't rush in!"
16 One of the initial anchors of CNN's "American Morning"
17 Something that might be replaced during car servicing
18 Event in every Summer Olympics since 1900
19 Rhythmic
20 Conflict
22 Chaser of un trago de tequila
23 Determines (if)
27 Misanthrope
28 Lacking in passion
30 Garden sight
32 Block between shows
33 Universal, Sony and Warner
36 Have high hopes
37 Kitty-corner things?
38 Lowly worker
39 Something good for Charlie Brown?
40 Internal rule
44 Writing form even more constrained than a tweet
46 Results of some scans
48 City at the foot of the Sierra Nevada
49 Recite
51 Popular pricing game on "The Price Is Right"
53 Chesterfield, for one
54 Sticking point?
58 Noted Brit in the news
59 Strength rating in video games
60 Teeny
61 Black piano key
62 Promising

DOWN

1 Ohio University player
2 Tee off
3 Prelim
4 Put in one's sights
5 Moves lightly through the air
6 Home of the world's busiest airport: Abbr.
7 Actress Lucy
8 "Did not need to know that"
9 Terminals at London Heathrow?
10 High-end Hyundai
11 Main feature of the Gmail logo
12 National force, informally
13 Mocking responses
15 Blue-striped ball
21 English channel
24 Something only I can go on?
25 In vestments
26 Liquidated
29 Park ranger's weapon
31 Who said "Revolutions are the locomotives of history"
34 Foul call
35 1960s movie with the tagline "A man went looking for America. And couldn't find it anywhere"
36 Devices that hurt sales at Kodak
37 Give for a bit
38 Precious
41 Dell competitor
42 Places for braces
43 Like some caterpillars
45 Sagal of "Futurama"
47 Friendly term of address
50 What suggestive dialogue may result in
52 Response to a joke, maybe
55 "You got me good!"
56 "Wide-staring" one in a Wordsworth poem
57 Deal breakers, for short?

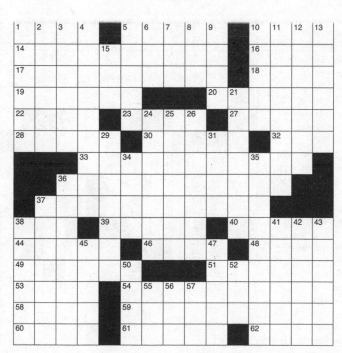

by Peter Wentz

ACROSS

1 "You might be asking too much"
16 Rhyming educational proverb
17 Classic 1959 drama with characters from Chicago's South Side
18 Begin all over
19 Tillis or McDaniel of country music
20 Meditation utterances
21 "The Waste Land" poet's inits.
22 Went back for more, in a way
26 Blew the budget
34 Llama, for one
35 Pastries similar to long john doughnuts
36 Attending a lecture, say
37 Daily
38 Big brand of kitchenware
39 Cough syrup amt.
40 Big Apple?
43 Iridescent material
47 Golfer Aoki
51 African capital where Berber is spoken
53 15 years before the Battle of Hastings
54 Coped (with)
55 Where people may order push-ups
58 D.C. thoroughfare with the Smithsonian's National Air and Space Museum
59 Must
60 Freddy Krueger, e.g.

DOWN

1 Squad
2 Not halal, in Arab cuisine
3 Follower of "pat" in Mother Goose
4 Peter ___, co-founder of PayPal
5 One of Sports Illustrated's two Sportsmen of the Year in 1998
6 "It's not ___, it's a when"
7 Length of the final fight in "Rocky Balboa"
8 On time, in Tijuana
9 Stat for a photographer
10 Wooden strip
11 Phil who described himself as a "singing journalist"
12 "Gone With the Wind" name
13 South Indian pancakes
14 Accustom
15 Dollars for quarters
22 "It's not the end of the world"
23 Motion picture pioneer
24 Pump up
25 Bad mark
26 Lab subj.
27 Attracted to people of all genders, in modern lingo
28 Rival of Regal Cinemas
29 Made a move
30 Some Secret Service wear
31 Writer who said "Living never wore one out so much as the effort not to live"
32 Mrs., abroad
33 Non-Anglophone's course, for short
40 N.F.L. Hall-of-Famer Michael
41 New Brunswick neighbor
42 Choices on a standard Scantron test
44 ___ acid
45 Decked out
46 Hillocks
48 Woman's name meaning "princess"
49 Motrin alternative
50 Weasel family member
52 ". . . max"
54 Numerical prefix
56 Out of the game: Abbr.
57 Show once featuring Leslie Jones, for short

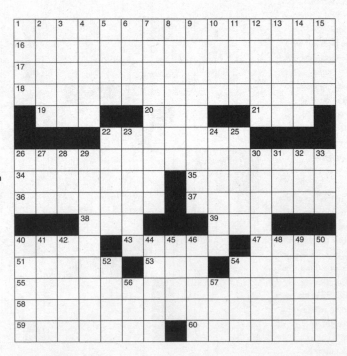

by Erik Agard

ACROSS

1 What a physiognomist studies
6 Palma's island
13 Christopher Paolini best seller
15 Hope was once its driving force
16 Sluggishness
18 Act
19 "Well done!"
21 Something with "three deuces and a four-speed" in a 1964 hit
22 30, on a table
23 God
24 Golfer Mickelson
25 Dryish
27 ____ facie (legal phrase)
28 Former Ecuadorean "dollars"
29 London or Manchester
30 Chicken characteristic
31 Charles of "Hill Street Blues"
32 ____ stick
35 Measure of data transfer speed, for short
37 With nothing on top
38 Touchy subject
40 Successor to Churchill
41 Noted blind mathematician
42 Noted boxing family
44 Blackguard
45 Alliance of groups against a common enemy
47 Measures of sharpness

49 One-named singer with the 2016 #1 album "A Seat at the Table"
50 Parts of pit crews
51 Throw a bomb
52 "You don't have to explain"
53 Like an eisteddfod festival

DOWN

1 Hernando's "happy"
2 A Musketeer
3 Foxes, e.g.
4 Croissan'wich alternative
5 Make more powerful, with "up"
6 Rumpled
7 Bloom that's often white or lavender
8 1940 Fonda role
9 N.H.L. Eastern Conference team, on scoreboards
10 Camp out in the wilderness, say
11 2/2, in music
12 Pertaining to colored rings
14 Field work
17 Parent, e.g.
20 Does some runs
24 Annual June celebration
26 Strand during a storm, maybe
27 Stuck-up sort
29 Newfoundland or golden retriever

31 Staff additions
32 Spell out
33 Nickname for baseball's Orlando Hernández
34 Shakespearean fencer
35 Leave in a hurry
36 Fast-food icon, with "the"
38 Neighbor of Allemagne
39 Hints
41 ____-deux
43 Curry of the N.B.A.
45 A smartphone has lots of them
46 Go smoothly
48 Country music's Mike ____

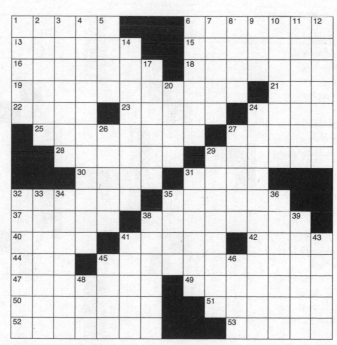

by Alan Derkazarian

Note: The completed puzzle conceals the name of a famous composer, along with something that might help you listen to him. Who and what are they?

ACROSS

1 Help during the fall?
8 Spanish hotel
15 Venting, e.g.
16 Hardin-Simmons University setting
17 N.L. East city
18 Branded
19 Neo-___
20 Touching things in competitions
22 Web developer's development
23 Shipload
24 Like some veal chops
26 Hardly fresh
27 It's not on the level
29 Ed basics
30 Give a kick?
32 Small grouse
33 Wiretapper, e.g.
34 Specifies
35 Healthful juice source
36 Kind of mitt
37 Thrill-seeker's appurtenance
38 Nap sack
41 Girl in a gown
42 Fluff
43 Stuff of life
44 Virtual connection?
47 ___ Lan (giant panda born at the 17-Across zoo)
48 Soaked (in)
51 The Eagle, e.g.
52 That right introduction?
54 Third-largest city of Switzerland
55 Car once advertised with the slogan "The relentless pursuit of common sense"
56 Bubkes
58 Cabinet part

60 Last new Beatles track before their split in 1970
61 Loose, in a way
62 Wraps around the shoulders
63 Big name in shoe stores

DOWN

1 Accords
2 Update at the factory
3 Home office convenience
4 Difficult thing to do, informally
5 Smoking ___
6 Flower whose name derives from the shape of its cluster
7 Some farm equipment
8 Light-colored and medium-sweet
9 Mortify
10 Leaf part
11 Stout cousins?
12 1966 Pulitzer-winning Edward Albee play, with "A"
13 Common rating scale
14 All-nighters?
21 Role in 1993's "Tombstone"
24 Those who may accept tips
25 Figured out
28 Renaissance artist ___ della Francesca
31 Kept going
35 Tedious

37 Expressive and quick-witted sorts, they say
38 Fashions
39 Much of binary code
40 Like a boxer's hands during sparring, maybe
45 Beguilers
46 Sets securely
49 Something to gnaw on
50 "The Vampire Diaries" protagonist
53 Writer Janowitz
55 It makes an impression
57 Place for a piercing
59 Work, as a proposal

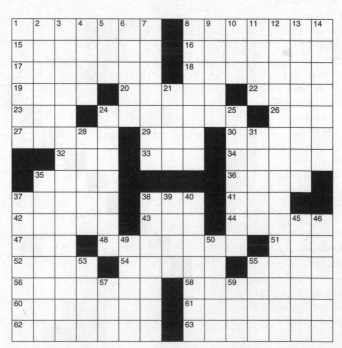

by David J. Kahn

ACROSS

1 Blondie's maiden name in "Blondie"
10 Post something
12 One taking a lot of credit, maybe?
14 Sly remarks?
15 Many necklines
16 Spot for Spot
18 Abbr. on a foundation stone
20 Mosaicist
21 Pomeriggio follower
22 High-grade?
24 Novelist who wrote "I have no fear of depths and a great fear of shallow living"
25 Hamburger order
26 Nocturnal predators of fiction
28 "Because I said so" is not one
29 Tony ____, official character voice of Donald Duck
30 Spartan, e.g.
31 Land north of England, in poetry
32 Turned sickly yellow
33 Aligns
34 Song royalties org.
35 Pasquale ____, baritone at the Metropolitan Opera
36 Meals for seals
37 Standard & ____
39 In ____ (untouched)
40 "The Big Bang Theory" character
41 Like certain ecclesiastical councils
43 Critically examine
44 Democratic principle
47 Setup for a Netflix film, say
48 Gigantic

DOWN

1 Canine command
2 Airing
3 William Wordsworth, e.g.
4 Its player may have a yen for gambling
5 Things that cover all the bases?
6 Grow, as sympathies
7 Whiskered, fish-eating creature
8 Maker of thousands of cars annually
9 Term of endearment
10 Hip-hop icon born Lisa Williamson
11 Paper signed before filming begins
12 Kind of pie that's actually a cake
13 Howdy Doody and others
14 Toadyish response
17 Was successful in the end
19 Files away?
21 Doesn't go straight, in a way
23 Sparta, e.g.
25 Big name in windows
27 Nashville awards org.
28 Subj. of tax exemption
30 Changers of locks
32 Sands
34 Beautiful, in Bogotá
37 Material for a baking vessel
38 Name changed in Genesis 17:15
41 A taste
42 Turn on the ice
45 Tiny amount
46 Gray head?

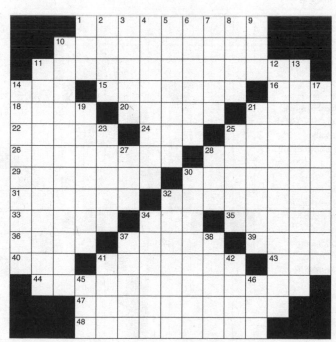

by Alex Vratsanos

ACROSS

1 Source of embarrassment for some public officials
10 Skedaddled
15 How buzzkills end things
16 Golfer's collection
17 Numismatist's collection
18 Mexican sandwich
19 ___ sample
20 One-named singer with the 2007 #1 hit "Don't Matter"
21 Building block makeup
22 Essential
24 First U.S. team to win the N.H.L. Stanley Cup (1928)
26 Diner order that gets filled?
28 Life instinct, in psychology
29 Reverses course
32 Ceiling
35 "___ said . . ."
36 Write a think piece, say
37 Drifter
38 ___ Mosby, main role on "How I Met Your Mother"
39 Some polygamous figures
41 Niche form of architecture?
42 Many workers in Japan's Lake Hamana
43 Sharp-looking footwear?
48 "The Yankee Years" memoirist
49 Home of the first known pizza parlor
50 Certainty
52 Some undergrad degs.

53 Not just in one's head, say
54 Kamehameha Day observers
56 Little buddy
57 From that point on
58 Simplifies
59 Cozy curl-up spots

DOWN

1 Verbal outpouring, in slang
2 Dead
3 Sobriquet for filmdom's Daniel LaRusso, with "The"
4 Common suffix for 7-Downs
5 Areas
6 Ursine sci-fi creature
7 Atom with an electronic imbalance
8 G in jazz

9 Students with 300 and 400 classes: Abbr.
10 Audit, as a class
11 Sticking points
12 One-named singer with the 2013 #1 hit "Royals"
13 Bury
14 Bulgaria's Simeon I and Simeon II
21 Actress Tia of "Wayne's World"
23 They have hops
25 Get back together
27 Ones who know the way?
30 Underdog victory
31 "Blue" or "bearded" bird
32 Act without originality
33 Deviation

34 Has hold of
37 Stud poker variation, informally
39 Skimpy swimwear
40 Sloppy planting job?
41 Refer (to)
43 Backstabber
44 ___ al Ghul (Batman foe)
45 Devices that introduced the click wheel
46 Norwegian king until 1000
47 One spreading seed
51 Something that people wish you would take when you leave
54 Noted mansion man, for short
55 Jr.'s son

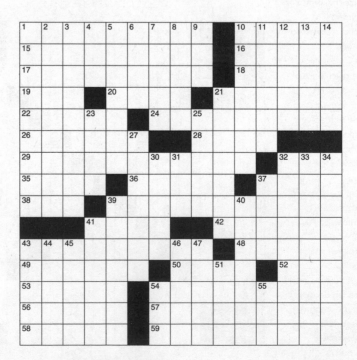

by Caleb Madison

ACROSS

1 When St. Patrick's Day is celebrated
9 Side with?
13 First two-time Nobelist
15 Deep red pigment
16 Slice, e.g.
17 Place for a big wheel
18 Company that launched the game FarmVille
19 Insignificant one
21 A lot of Top 40 music
22 Space race?
24 Word with mother or sharp
26 Call of the wild?
27 One spewing obscenities
31 Wine container
32 Things with pods
33 Ingredient in a Caesar cocktail
34 Like the hepatitis B and C pathogens
36 LinkedIn listing
39 Be open-minded, maybe
40 Trigger-to-cylinder connection
41 Kept close to one's chest?
42 Twain of note
44 Hellenic character
45 Make no effort to stop something
49 Make right
50 Bad way to get to work
52 Extra leaf in some books
54 Freshly
55 Curling and rugby, but not boxing, in the Olympics
56 Hard to get around, say
57 Radio option with improved sound quality

DOWN

1 Title girl in a 1961 Ricky Nelson hit
2 Resident of Isfahan
3 Home run, in slang
4 Actress Boone of NBC's "The Blacklist"
5 Nickname for a pal
6 Feature of many a jalopy
7 The bird in Hitchcock's "The Birds"
8 Palm, in a way
9 "That's the spot!"
10 Woe of a bar habitué
11 Some high points of Mötley Crüe?
12 Relative of tofu
13 ___ Effect (supposed I.Q. boost from music)
14 Opposite of 22 Across
20 Pulpy refuse
23 Coconuts, to a maroon on an island, maybe
25 Fourth little piggy's share
28 Macho type
29 Green-skinned fruit
30 Reject
32 Chaps
33 D.C. body
34 Native of Thimphu
35 Tied up, in the operating room
36 Witty Garofalo
37 Because of
38 Barbershop assortment
39 Something you may lay down or break
40 Baby
43 Not just fling
46 Forbidden, in a way
47 First name in horror
48 Vegetables high in vitamin C
51 Pecorino cheese source
53 Holiday abroad

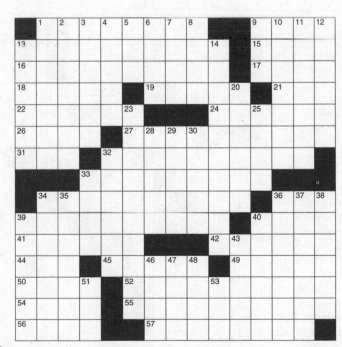

by Mark Diehl

ACROSS

1 Biased investigation
10 Showing shock
15 Hospital sign
16 Total
17 What the British call a station wagon
18 Parting words
19 Laura of "Star Wars: The Last Jedi"
20 Hot dogs
22 Positions
24 Charlotte ___, capital of the U.S. Virgin Islands
25 Iraq War danger, for short
26 Sellers at a craft show
28 Symbol of strength
31 Taunts
32 Twice, musically
33 Some baseball stats
34 Foreshadowed
35 Well-known speaker
36 Boomer baby
37 Charlatan
38 Smarts
39 Some marbles
41 Word on all U.S. coins
42 Show allegiance
43 Upscale kennels
47 Author much used by other authors
50 Word after who, what or anything
51 Get ___ of reality
52 Mid-19th-century czar
54 Robert who played filmdom's Mr. Chips
55 Yosemite attraction
56 Long-running pop culture show
57 Pointing of fingers

DOWN

1 Policy details, metaphorically
2 "No more for me, thank you"
3 Prefix with fluoride
4 Narrow openings
5 6 ft., maybe
6 Followed
7 Last of the Mohicans
8 Member of the C.S.A.
9 Part of a 17-Across
10 Sister of Apollo
11 Sources of jam, jelly and juice
12 Union-busting, say
13 Like the 1930s Soviet Union
14 Has
21 Stale
23 Disney collectible
26 Right hands
27 KOA customer
28 Portmanteau for lovers
29 Trampled
30 Brown family member
31 Complete embarrassment
34 Pharmacy brand
35 Commissioner inducted into the Baseball Hall of Fame in 2017
37 Uncovers, with "out"
38 Monopolize
40 Vacillate
41 Police commissioner Gordon's turf
43 Bing Crosby's record label
44 Montana motto word
45 Silk center of India
46 Subject for Raoul Dufy and Henri Matisse
48 Spoiler of a perfect report card
49 Breathing aid
53 Unseal, in poetry

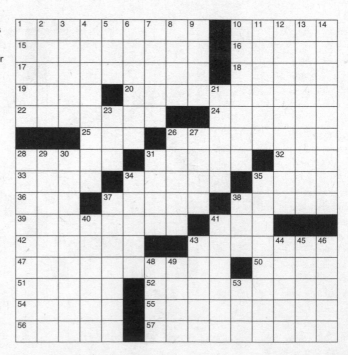

by Randolph Ross

ACROSS

1 Toilet paper?
9 Having many openings
14 Powerful Russian
15 Fancy affair
16 Coca-Cola product since 2001
17 Cafe chain
18 "O.G. Original Gangster" rapper
19 Overly sentimental writers
21 Junípero ___, founder of San Francisco
23 Arizona athlete, for short
24 Media co. led by the Sulzberger family
25 Events with tents
27 Really bugged
29 Airer of Neil deGrasse Tyson's "StarTalk"
30 Become edible
34 Kind of coordination
36 Be charged
37 Touristy area on the Irish coast
39 Wiccan groups
40 Balkan capital
41 Things held in a cannonball
42 Place to watch a race, for short
45 Tony once nominated for an Emmy
47 ___ May Lester of Erskine Caldwell's "Tobacco Road"
49 Vitamin-rich green side dish
52 Setback
53 ___ center
54 Popular vodka brand from Holland
56 Front spoiler on a car
57 Like many people on January 1
58 Fancified
59 Spaces out

DOWN

1 Pueblo Revolt participants
2 1930–'40s film star with the signature song "You'll Never Know"
3 Unshackles
4 Cause associated with the rainbow flag
5 ___ Americana
6 Newspaper section
7 Provincetown catch
8 Weekly Jewish observance
9 Request for backup?
10 Isn't bad?
11 Fancify oneself
12 Commodore in Sondheim's "Pacific Overtures"
13 Passover no-no
15 Thyme keeper?
20 Suddenly took notice
22 Feature in a telephone directory
26 Any man or boy, biblically
28 Collection of posts about a trip
29 Part of 24-Across
31 Million-selling 1977 Donna Summer song
32 Many a British retiree
33 Some tech grads, for short
35 Sombrero, e.g.
38 Ethnic group whose name means "wanderers"
42 The planets, e.g.
43 Gateway of a Shinto shrine
44 Get on
46 Fox Islands resident
48 They have big mouths
50 Spiral-horned antelope
51 Italian source of smoke
55 ___ salad

by Sam Ezersky and Byron Walden

ACROSS

1 "No, really"
8 Sort
15 Carpet cleaner
16 High-minded sort?
17 Give a flat fee?
18 Back in the stadium
19 [Can you believe they wrote this?!]
21 TV commentator Navarro
22 Abbr. in math class
23 Stock at a wine bar
27 Off the wall
30 Battle of Soissons setting
32 Place for a miniature flag
33 Goon
34 Weapon with a rope and balls
35 Literary nickname for Dolores
36 One of the Smithsonian buildings
39 What "they" can only be, to grammar sticklers
40 Enliven, with "up"
41 Signal
42 Iowa town where Grant Wood's "American Gothic" is set
43 Shade of red
44 Word with chicken or news
45 Go here and there
46 Tight spot
47 Scare quote?
49 Pitch to a publisher
55 Paper that runs mots croisés
58 Seeing someone, say
59 When Caesar says "Yond Cassius has a lean and hungry look"

60 Prized sheep
61 1831 Poe work
62 Prizes

DOWN

1 Carnival Cruise stop
2 Twosome
3 ___ tide
4 Walk alluringly
5 "Well . . ."
6 Aspires to do something
7 "Star Trek: T.N.G." role
8 Mount near Haifa
9 Like a squashed circle
10 Peugeot symbol
11 It may come long after the play
12 Gangbusters, for short?
13 "___ soon?"
14 Go astray
20 Exercise started by crouching
24 Per
25 Not stray
26 Did phenomenally onstage
27 Debugging tool?
28 Cyclops killer of myth
29 Poet who wrote "Tonight I can write the saddest lines"
31 Ayaan Hirsi ___, Somali-born advocate for women's rights and religious freedom
32 Online hilarity

34 Healthful breakfast choice
35 Do-nothing
37 Ska band instrument
38 Be garrulous
43 Make hand over fist
44 Epicure
46 "Doctor Who" actress Whittaker
48 Good genre for a maze maker
50 Intro to Torts student
51 "The Bicycle Thief" setting
52 All together, so to speak
53 Bond collector?
54 Not so great
55 W.W. II craft: Abbr.
56 Pro-sustainability, in lingo
57 "It doesn't excite me"

by Brendan Emmett Quigley

ACROSS

1 Player in a baseball stadium
6 Kind of system in which 64 is 100
11 "Hold on ___!"
14 "Serial" podcast host Sarah
16 "Far out!"
18 ___ Panza, sidekick of Don Quixote
19 Not go out to dinner
20 . ÷ 40
22 Jesus, with "the"
23 Went to bat (for)
25 Adjective on Tex-Mex menus
26 "Seriez" is a form of it
28 Things with microgrooves
29 Winner of the 2016 Pulitzer Prize for Drama
38 Almost certainly
39 Backdrop to AMC's "The Walking Dead"
40 Remote area?
41 Letters on some bulletproof vests
42 Mass-produce, with "out"
45 Big name in mops
50 One of a kind
54 Beer pong receptacle
56 Seemingly expressing
58 Wife in F. Scott Fitzgerald's "Tender Is the Night"
59 Fugitive's destination, maybe
60 Painter's undercoat
61 Sly chuckle
62 Newspaper divisions
63 Group of near nobodies

DOWN

1 "Your point being . . . ?"
2 Mounts with a little white on top?
3 French novelist/dramatist associated with the Theater of the Absurd
4 Dried chili pepper on Tex-Mex menus
5 Greeting in Guangzhou
6 Fall behind
7 Scorch
8 Home to Rodin's "The Kiss," with "the"
9 Slightly
10 When Taurus begins
11 Oenophile's criterion
12 Copied
13 Word with space or rock
15 British writing award
17 Region near Mount Olympus
21 Bauhaus-influenced typeface
24 Hospital sections, for short
27 Nudges
28 Celebratory round
29 Tracy and Jenna's boss on "30 Rock"
30 Odysseus' rescuer
31 Marvel series depicting the Tet Offensive, with "The"
32 Annual June sports event, informally
33 Cut off
34 Colorful birds
35 Bite
36 Letters that come before AA?
37 House call?
42 Not stay awake any longer
43 "Manners require time, as nothing is more vulgar than ___": Ralph Waldo Emerson
44 ___ the Hittite, soldier in King David's army
46 Popped (out)
47 Main
48 C.D.C. concern
49 Game sheet
51 Burrowing animal
52 Pompeii's Temple of
53 Made, as a putt
55 Fresh
57 Shortest Magic 8 Ball response

by Finn Vigeland

ACROSS

1 Sci-fi character who graduated from Starfleet Academy in 2359
5 What Iran and Iraq do
9 "Purgatorio" poet
14 Brownie, for one
16 Primitive kind of poker?
17 Dangerous cocktail
18 "___ fine"
19 Luxury hotel option
21 Name related to Rex
22 Wednesday, e.g.
24 Insurance company whose logo contains a bill
27 Tudor house feature
30 Vegan protein source
31 Pot-making supply
32 Like a mythical lion
33 Recipe directive
34 Put away the dishes?
35 Memorable White House Correspondents' Dinner host of 2006
36 You might click it open
37 "Eww, stop!"
38 Singular thing
39 Requiring immediate attention
40 Hebrew : ben :: Arabic : ___
41 "Stop playing" symbols
42 Optimistic
43 Strained, at the bar
45 Dash device
46 Creamy, fruity drink
53 One who's frequently in the dark

54 Fiancée, say
55 Brief bridge opening
56 Like privates, often
57 Part of a pound?
58 Recipe directive
59 Cameos and others

DOWN

1 1/256 of a gal.
2 Plastic Clue weapon
3 Strong team
4 Cube holder
5 South ___, N.J.
6 Boy with a bouquet
7 Surfing destinations
8 Something to spin
9 One who's 60-something?
10 One with a plant-based diet
11 Spotless

12 London museum whose oldest piece is from 1900
13 Some TV drama settings
15 Provisional
20 Sensitive figure, for many
23 Most populous city in Oceania
24 ___ acid (dressing ingredient)
25 Attention-grabbing
26 Epitome of romantic passion
27 Fixes
28 Bounds
29 Natural food coloring sources
32 Rejection of a honey-do list
35 Its ribs stick out

39 Cleaning cloth
42 Wind or unwind
44 It was boosted by Atlas
45 Cloddish sort, in slang
47 Things waiters wait for
48 Huff
49 Long dress
50 "I ___ quotation": Emerson
51 Amazon unit
52 James B. ___, diving bell inventor
53 Secant's reciprocal: Abbr.

by David Steinberg

ACROSS

1 Sport with stunt riding, informally
4 "Heck if I know"
9 Big difference
14 Axe product
16 Goes on and on
17 Reflective stretch
18 Item checked at an airport
19 Misses overseas
20 Gone
21 Trio in a children's rhyme
22 Three-lobed design
25 Roughly 37% of U.S. immigrants
28 Personal bearing
29 Jung ___, author of the 1991 best seller "Wild Swans"
30 It's generally up and running within a few hours
31 "Breaking Bad" protagonist
32 Lead-in to sat
33 Aquarium performer
36 Like a happening party, in slang
37 Olympic Australis, for one
39 Suffix with Jumbo
40 North Carolina home of Appalachian State University
42 Brand with the slogan "Fill your glass"
44 What makes a possum play possum
45 A-number-one
46 Fifth-brightest star in the night sky
47 Part of a pod
48 Author who wrote "Show me a woman who doesn't feel guilty and I'll show you a man"
53 "The Cocktail Party" dramatist
54 Model company?
55 Book in which the Israelites are rebuked for idolatry
56 Common board requirement, in brief
57 Vamooses
58 Winner of nine Grand Slam tournaments in the 1990s
59 Components of many free apps

DOWN

1 Summer outdoor events, informally
2 Manifestation of sulkiness
3 Chose at the ballot box
4 Almost nothing on?
5 Public perception
6 Worn-out
7 2Pac's "Dear ___"
8 Result of prolonged screen time, maybe
9 "Golly!"
10 Threw some back
11 Celery sticks topped with peanut butter and raisins
12 Fixed cord for a paratrooper
13 One source of the umami taste
15 Title figure in a Gilbert and Sullivan opera
23 Quick move?
24 Word with fan or form
25 Come right up to
26 One who always has time to spend?
27 2007 satirical best seller
28 Tops in athletics
30 Professional feeders
34 Constantly updating GPS figs.
35 Widely followed court battles
38 You might experiment with this on
41 Bingeing
43 Ends
44 Crack, in a way
46 Like some very important signs
49 Carny's target
50 Plant also known as ladies' fingers
31 Grant consideration
52 E.T.S. offerings
53 Middle of summer?

by Peter Wentz

ACROSS

1 Matchmaking services?
8 Co-star of "The Office" who played Ryan Howard
15 In a classic form of diamond
16 Victor's gloating cry
17 Rust
18 Technophobe
19 They may be fluid: Abbr.
20 Banished
22 Smidgen
23 Shepherd's pie ingredients
25 Venture a view
26 Miss
27 Radiates
29 "No __ can live forever": Martin Luther King Jr.
30 Street hustler's game
31 Many a corny pun
33 Bravado
35 Lord Tennyson's "The Eagle," e.g.
36 Shaker's cry?
37 Speed of sound
41 Baker's shortcut
45 Certain Bedouin
46 Aladdin's simian sidekick
48 Looks
49 Defeats by a hair
50 Dumps
52 Auto parts giant
53 "The enemy of __ is the absence of limitations": Orson Welles
54 Vehicle used by the police to catch thieves
56 "Delta of Venus" author
57 Mob law?

59 Like many screenplays
61 "The Call of __" (short story by H. P. Lovecraft)
62 Creamy Italian dish
63 Colorful display in a weather report
64 Places in the field

DOWN

1 Slumped
2 Cream in a cobalt blue jar
3 "Once again . . ."
4 Trailblazed
5 Four-letter fruit pronounced in three syllables
6 "Au contraire . . ."
7 The point of church above all?

8 Ghostwriters lack them
9 Unit of energy
10 Like Rodin's "The Thinker"
11 Dated
12 Rendering useless
13 Phoenician goddess of fertility
14 Snack company that's a subsidiary of Kellogg's
21 Top part of a face
24 Capital of Newfoundland and Labrador
26 Reduce one's carbon footprint
28 Copycat's comment
30 Targets
32 Comprehension
34 Ring letters

37 One referred to as "the crown"
38 "You all agree with me, yes?," in one word
39 Modern screen test
40 Savor the praise
41 Stage holdup?
42 Had it in mind
43 Sacrilege
44 Tic-tac-toe plays
47 Smidgen
50 __ Baron Cohen, player of Borat
51 Title woman of a Beatles song
54 Lip __
55 Scrape
58 Published
60 Party person, for short

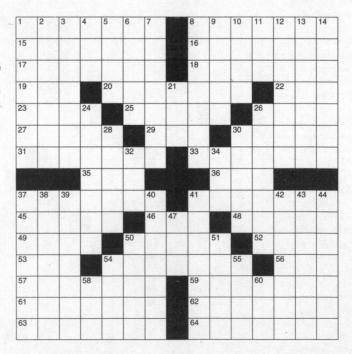

by Trenton Charlson

ACROSS

1 Blogs, social media and other nontraditional outlets
12 Enlightened responses
15 Option when changing jobs
16 ___ Irvin, early cartoonist/designer for The New Yorker
17 Dirt spreader
18 Roam (about)
19 Winter Olympics sights
20 Italian sculptor ___ Lorenzo Bernini
21 Section of a Crayola box
22 ___ talk
23 Campaign supporters
24 ___ Park
25 Words of explanation
27 Pennsylvania city where the Delaware and Lehigh Rivers meet
28 Exhibiting a modern form of obsession
31 Quick way to end a sentence?
32 "Where does it all end?" argument
33 Socket for setting a gem
34 Food preservers
35 "Any ___?"
36 Dolphinfish, informally
38 Flavor additive, in brief
41 It goes clockwise or counterclockwise depending on the hemisphere
42 Legend says it arose on Palatine Hill
43 Search for prey
45 ___-con
46 Offshore waves?
48 Grade of wine
49 Projecting beams on a bridge
50 Cornerstone abbr.
51 Reading and writing, for most jobs

DOWN

1 Guinness Book adjective
2 "Go, me!"
3 Of renown
4 Stepped
5 Start of a start of a menu?
6 The Liberty Tree, for one
7 Ad agency specialist
8 Picker-upper
9 Fuel for planes
10 Follower of four or six, but not five
11 Mess up
12 Containing silver
13 Without deliberation
14 Breakup tune
21 Forwards
23 Little squealer
24 Hollande's successor as president of France
25 Factor in Billboard rankings
26 Buster of myths
27 Latin list ender
28 Extricated from a jam
29 Reason
30 Concept of beauty
31 Slow and steady types
32 Prestigious academic journal
36 When cock-a-doodle-doos are done
37 Italian known for pulling strings?
38 Paradigm
39 Ice cream choice
40 Part of a makeup kit
42 Org. fighting copyright infringement
43 Like very early education, for short
44 ___ Shankar, influence on George Harrison
46 Chemical contaminant, for short
47 High ways?

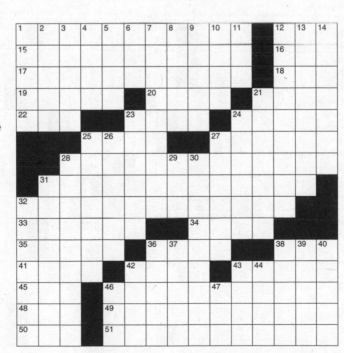

by John Guzzetta

ACROSS

1 Hosp. units
4 ___ peas
10 Basics
14 Kind of flour
15 1965 Michael Caine spy thriller, with "The"
17 ___ grano salis
18 What might help a hacker go undetected?
19 Deride
21 Kentucky's northernmost county
22 Abbr. in an auction catalog
23 Gambling card game
24 "Doctor Faustus" novelist
25 Part of an oven
27 Similar (to)
28 Actor with seven Primetime Emmys
30 Greek cheese
31 Tennis player, to sportswriters
33 Op-ed, e.g.
35 Cocktail with rye whiskey
37 Sean Hannity and Chris Hayes
41 Quarry of cartoondom's Gargamel
43 Pope when Elizabeth I took the throne
44 Virus in 2003 news
47 Cellphone component
49 Do some programming
50 Stud of the sports world?
52 Walked over
53 Hard ___
54 Footwear brand since 1978
55 Hollywood agent Michael
57 Military gathering?
58 Journalist's tool since '67

61 Home of Sen. Mike Crapo: Abbr.
62 Political leader?
63 Sister
64 Elate
65 Like baking dough
66 Big mean on campus

DOWN

1 Those who've seen both Europe and Asia, say
2 Home to Lake Waiau
3 1928 Winter Olympics site
4 Keeper of the flame?
5 Mil. address
6 Dives with a tank
7 W.W. I battle locale
8 "Give it to me straight"
9 Jacket letters

10 Behind, at sea
11 "Kiss my grits!"
12 You're not in it if you're out
13 Car model originally called the Sunny in Japan
16 Tallow source
20 Rosina Almaviva, in "Le Nozze di Figaro"
24 Go pirating
26 "Unless it's impossible"
29 Got back (to), in a way
32 "Uhhh . . ."
34 "Eureka!"
36 Review
38 Programming manager's specialty
39 Did a bit of cleaning
40 Only daughter of Joseph Stalin

42 Typeface that shares its name with the Roman goddess of luck
44 Marks on shoes
45 Who said "Take it from me, every vote counts"
46 The Midwest or the South
48 More than half of scores
51 Ralph Nader's American Museum of ___ Law
56 So
57 "Just doin' my job"
59 Furthermore
60 Fixed

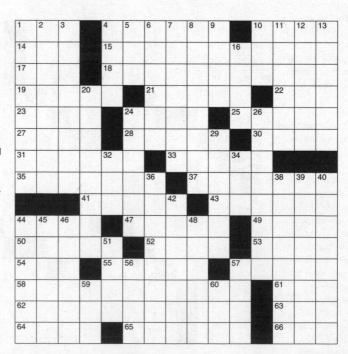

by Rachel Maddow and Joe DiPietro

ACROSS

1 Display, as an image, using only a small number of different tones
10 Goes on
15 Way out in space
16 Enlightened sort
17 "Further . . ."
18 Site of a 1974 fight won by 40-Across
19 Ron ___, nine-time All-Star from the 1960s–'70s Cubs
20 Kid with a moving life story?
22 "The Wire" stickup man .
25 Become completely absorbed
26 G.I. garb, for short
29 Strike out on one's own
32 Staples competitor starting in 1988
34 Swell
39 Put away
40 See 18-Across
41 Many a private investigator
42 Try
43 Hot take?
45 Like many shorelines
47 Car lot designation
48 Philosopher who said "A journey of a thousand miles must begin with a single step"
52 Puzzle (out)
54 "We're done here"
57 "Enough!"
61 Restraint
62 1983 #1 hit with the lyric "Take, take, take what you need"
65 Co-star with Shatner and Nimoy
66 So-called "Father of Zoology"
67 Cinemax competitor
68 Common business attire

DOWN

1 Bible supporters, often
2 Org. with inspectors
3 Good look
4 One who might needle you?
5 With 59-Down, spa supply
6 Band with the monster album "Monster"
7 Market event, briefly
8 Novelist ___ Neale Hurston
9 Linda of Broadway's "Jekyll & Hyde"
10 Slugabed
11 Ishmael's people
12 Ending with Oxford or Cambridge
13 Gogol's "___ Bulba"
14 Correction corrections
21 Chem. unit
23 Questionnaire info
24 Parmesan alternative
26 ___ analysis
27 Men's grooming brand
28 Dramatists' degs.
30 "Gesundheit!"
31 Lime and others
33 Popular cracker topper
35 "How rude!"
36 Crackerjack
37 Shade
38 Piece of punditry
44 Email address ending
46 1921 play for which the word "robot" was invented
48 Airs
49 Plagued
50 City at the mouth of the Yodo River
51 Real stunner
53 Improvises, in a way
55 [Can't wait!]
56 Brief researcher, briefly
58 Riesling alternative, familiarly
59 See 5-Down
60 Intel satellites, metaphorically
63 Dark side
64 High-speed inits.

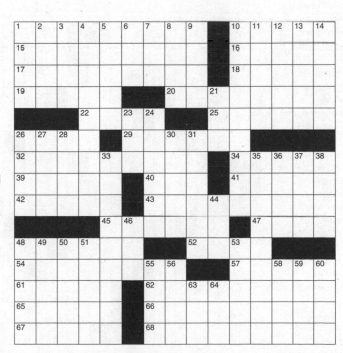

by Damon Gulczynski

ACROSS

1 Group in the original "Ocean's 11"
8 Classic arcade game with lots of shooting
14 Like Istanbul
16 Emphatic admission
17 First world capital, alphabetically
18 Like clothes buttons, generally
19 Unexciting poker holding
20 2008 Bond girl Kurylenko
22 Bedevil
23 Car once promoted with the line "The thrill starts with the grille"
25 Speaker units
27 Prefix with -gon
28 Nocturnal acronym
29 Strange things
32 Super 8, e.g.
33 Group of female seals
34 Powerhouse in Olympic weightlifting
36 Gradually
39 Animated character who graduated from Dogwarts University
40 The "R" of 28-Across
41 Circular parts
42 Formidable opponents
44 Campaign aid
47 "The Old Curiosity Shop" girl
49 Touched
50 Rail center?
52 Express stress, in a way
54 Gulf of ___
56 Santa ___, Calif.
57 Juiced (up)
59 Jacob's partner in "A Christmas Carol"
61 City nicknamed "The Old Pueblo"
62 So-so, as support
63 Acropolis figure
64 Spots

DOWN

1 One going against the grain?
2 Poem greeting the dawn
3 "What's past is past," e.g.
4 Giant competitor
5 Last name of cosmetics giant Mary Kay
6 "See ya"
7 Bad way to go
8 Buffalo's home: Abbr.
9 Has-___
10 Source of stone used to build the ancient Egyptian pyramids
11 Flag-waving and such
12 Musical "girl who cain't say no"
13 Joe known as "The Comeback Kid"
15 Cause of bad dreams, in modern lingo
21 Follower of bon or mon
24 Show immediately preceding another
26 Scuffle
30 For adults only
31 Special-education challenge
33 Bottom line?
35 Tom Sawyer's half brother
36 Request for food delivery
37 Someone who's pretty darn good
38 It could be on the tip of your tongue
39 ___ rap
43 More, in México
44 O.C.D. fighter, maybe
45 Put forth
46 Enamors
48 Small slip
51 "___ done now?"
53 Superbright
55 "The Wizard of Oz" farmhand
58 Helicases split it
60 Court divider

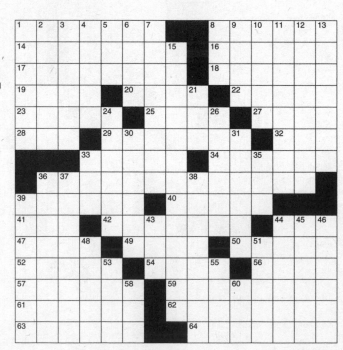

by Neville Fogarty and Doug Peterson

1

```
QUEEN  PACTS  CSI
EDDIE  AMAHL  ETC
DONNASUMMER  RYE
 NAS ALOOF TEXT
 TIS    LISA
 ARETHAFRANKLIN
AVOID DRESS BRO
CAPN SMITH LOKI
HIE AKITA NEWER
ELLAFITZGERALD
 ACTS   GAS
MADE LASSO HES
OLD LORETTALYNN
JOE OPERA WARIO
OER LEAFY SWEPT
```

2

```
PARSE  FIEND  NBA
EMOTE  ANWAR  ELM
TOTELLUSWHY  WII
SKIP ONE  EARNS
  ORISTHEYLEGS
CANNES  IDEAL
AVOID AIRED EAR
NEWT OGDEN MANE
ERS AURAS POSTS
 EDUCE  FACEIT
THEOTHERMILK
YAHOO  HER TUBE
PIE BECOMESACAT
ERR OLINE PILLS
AYE TIDES FLAKY
```

3

```
BUS  BCCS  SILOS
ASEC OAHU ACING
ANCHORLEG GENET
 ROCKMEAMADEUS
ADEPT TRI TAP
SITU SPA SEERS
HELPMERHONDA
EDY UAE BAG SUM
 TICKLEMEELMO
OPERA AYE NFNA
CAN VAT ADDON
FEEDMESEYMOUR
ILLBE IFEELSICK
NOLAN CEOS EDIE
STARS SEWS  EGG
```

4

```
TAB SAPS ATTACKS
ISE IMON FIRTREE
THATSALL FAILURE
ARTOIS OAR  SAT
NANO SYLVIAPLATH
IMING MOOR AUDIE
ASK ARCS HELEN
 ANNASEWELL
 SERTA REEL PHD
MOLAR BAIL AURAE
EMILYBRONTE SOSA
NET EEL  ITSBAD
DOICARE SHEWROTE
ENSURED ARIA WIN
DETESTS LEOS LTD
```

5

```
SOLE WORE  AGENT
OPUS AXEL PATIO
FANTASYBASEBALL
ALKALI OIL SLED
 BUTTONUP
UPC MYSTERYMEAT
PROS OAS RANDY
BUSTOUR OPENSUP
ONTAP ALI YULE
WESTERNWALL ETA
 COIFFEUR
FLAG TCU INEVER
ROMANCELANGUAGE
OPERA SLOT SIGN
GENRE TYCO ELSE
```

6

```
ABBA THUGS  AJAR
SLAB RETRO DOLE
AURA ARIAL WHEN
PERSONALFINANCE
 YEAS  DARN
TAB FINALLY YDS
ATOM TODAY ICET
CONAN TAS INANE
INDIA AMT MASSE
TESLA CSI ASHED
 ONTHINICE
CZAR WALLS COWS
HELD ANVIL OVEN
ARSE SCENE NERO
POOR ERE  DREW
```

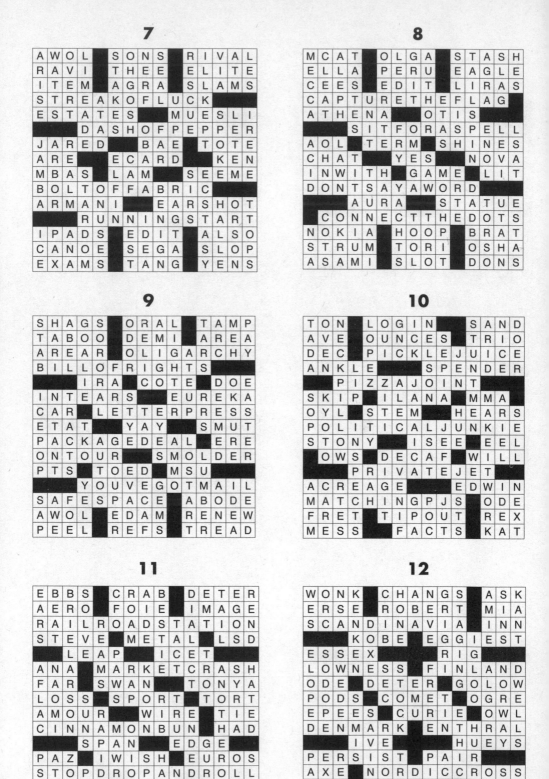

7

A	W	O	L		S	O	N	S		R	I	V	A	L
R	A	V	I		T	H	E	E		E	L	I	T	E
I	T	E	M		A	G	R	A		S	L	A	M	S
S	T	R	E	A	K	O	F	L	U	C	K			
E	S	T	A	T	E	S			M	U	E	S	L	I
		D	A	S	H	O	F	P	E	P	P	E	R	
J	A	R	E	D			B	A	E		T	O	T	E
A	R	E			E	C	A	R	D			K	E	N
M	B	A	S		L	A	M		S	E	E	M	E	
B	O	L	T	O	F	F	A	B	R	I	C			
A	R	M	A	N	I			E	A	R	S	H	O	T
		R	U	N	N	I	N	G	S	T	A	R	T	
I	P	A	D	S		E	D	I	T		A	L	S	O
C	A	N	O	E		S	E	G	A		S	L	O	P
E	X	A	M	S		T	A	N	G		Y	E	N	S

8

M	C	A	T		O	L	G	A		S	T	A	S	H
E	L	L	A		P	E	R	U		E	A	G	L	E
C	E	E	S		E	D	I	T		L	I	R	A	S
C	A	P	T	U	R	E	T	H	E	F	L	A	G	
A	T	H	E	N	A			O	T	I	S			
		S	I	T	F	O	R	A	S	P	E	L	L	
A	O	L		T	E	R	M		S	H	I	N	E	S
C	H	A	T		Y	E	S			N	O	V	A	
I	N	W	I	T	H		G	A	M	E		L	I	T
D	O	N	T	S	A	Y	A	W	O	R	D			
			A	U	R	A			S	T	A	T	U	E
C	O	N	N	E	C	T	T	H	E	D	O	T	S	
N	O	K	I	A		H	O	O	P		B	R	A	T
S	T	R	U	M		T	O	R	I		O	S	H	A
A	S	A	M	I		S	L	O	T		D	O	N	S

9

S	H	A	G	S		O	R	A	L		T	A	M	P
T	A	B	O	O		D	E	M	I		A	R	E	A
A	R	E	A	R		O	L	I	G	A	R	C	H	Y
B	I	L	L	O	F	R	I	G	H	T	S			
		I	R	A		C	O	T	E		D	O	E	
I	N	T	E	A	R	S		E	U	R	E	K	A	
C	A	R		L	E	T	T	E	R	P	R	E	S	S
E	T	A	T		Y	A	Y		S	M	U	T		
P	A	C	K	A	G	E	D	E	A	L		E	R	E
O	N	T	O	U	R		S	M	O	L	D	E	R	
P	T	S		T	O	E	D		M	S	U			
			Y	O	U	V	E	G	O	T	M	A	I	L
S	A	F	E	S	P	A	C	E		A	B	O	D	E
A	W	O	L		E	D	A	M		R	E	N	E	W
P	E	E	L		R	E	F	S		T	R	E	A	D

10

T	O	N		L	O	G	I	N		S	A	N	D
A	V	E		O	U	N	C	E	S		T	R	I	O
D	E	C		P	I	C	K	L	E	J	U	I	C	E
A	N	K	L	E			S	P	E	N	D	E	R	
		P	I	Z	Z	A	J	O	I	N	T			
S	K	I	P		I	L	A	N	A		M	M	A	
O	Y	L		S	T	E	M		H	E	A	R	S	
P	O	L	I	T	I	C	A	L	J	U	N	K	I	E
S	T	O	N	Y		I	S	E	E		E	E	L	
	O	W	S		D	E	C	A	F		W	I	L	L
		P	R	I	V	A	T	E	J	E	T			
A	C	R	E	A	G	E		E	D	W	I	N		
M	A	T	C	H	I	N	G	P	J	S		O	D	E
F	R	E	T		T	I	P	O	U	T		R	E	X
M	E	S	S		F	A	C	T	S		K	A	T	

11

E	B	B	S		C	R	A	B		D	E	T	E	R
A	E	R	O		F	O	I	E		I	M	A	G	E
R	A	I	L	R	O	A	D	S	T	A	T	I	O	N
S	T	E	V	E		M	E	T	A	L		L	S	D
		L	E	A	P			I	C	E	T			
A	N	A		M	A	R	K	E	T	C	R	A	S	H
F	A	R		S	W	A	N			T	O	N	Y	A
L	O	S	S		S	P	O	R	T		T	O	R	T
A	M	O	U	R		W	I	R	E		T	I	E	
C	I	N	N	A	M	O	N	B	U	N		H	A	D
		S	P	A	N			E	D	G	E			
P	A	Z		I	W	I	S	H		E	U	R	O	S
S	T	O	P	D	R	O	P	A	N	D	R	O	L	L
S	T	O	O	L		N	I	L	E		U	N	D	O
T	A	S	T	Y		S	N	O	W		S	E	E	P

12

W	O	N	K		C	H	A	N	G	S		A	S	K
E	R	S	E		R	O	B	E	R	T		M	I	A
S	C	A	N	D	I	N	A	V	I	A		I	N	N
			K	O	B	E		E	G	G	I	E	S	T
E	S	S	E	X					R	I	G			
L	O	W	N	E	S	S		F	I	N	L	A	N	D
O	D	E		D	E	T	E	R		G	O	L	O	W
P	O	D	S		C	O	M	E	T		O	G	R	E
E	P	E	E	S		C	U	R	I	E		O	W	L
D	E	N	M	A	R	K		E	N	T	H	R	A	L
			I	V	E				H	U	E	Y	S	
P	E	R	S	I	S	T		P	A	I	R			
A	X	E		N	O	R	D	I	C	C	R	O	S	S
L	I	L		G	R	E	E	N	E		A	R	I	A
S	T	Y		S	T	E	W	E	D		H	A	M	M

13

```
W E L C H   D A M P   A N A L
O M A H A   A M I E   C U R E
R O Y A L   R E S P E C T E D
S T I T C H I N T I M E
T E N   Y E A   T U S H I E
    H O E   S E A   S E N T
H E M A N D H A W     L A H
A L A S   S O L E S   U G L Y
R I D     D A R N I T A L L
S T A R   W A D   O D E
H E T E R O     A R T   P H I
    C O M M O N T H R E A D
T H R O B B I N G   E E R I E
H O U R   A L E S   F L O R A
O P E D   T E S T   T O N Y S
```

14

```
T S A R   K I S S   N A S A L
O T T O   I N C H   Y E T T O
G R A B   A J A R   C R O O N
A E R I E   U R A L   A P P
  W I N T E R S P O R T S
      S A T E   N O T E D L Y
S P O O L S   B E T S   E Y E
E A R N   M E L   B A R N
E A R   W E E D   S P A D E S
K R I S H N A   D O O R
  S P O O N B E N D I N G
  U R L   S T A B   S T O R E
S P O I L   I R O N   O V E R
T O O N S   M E N U   N E E R
A N T E D   E D E N   E L K S
```

15

```
I L L S A Y   S T I R   C O Y
P E O P L E   A R S E   A V A
A A B A T T E R I E S   P E N
S P F C   A A M E E T I N G
    E M I T       N I T
A L E K E G   A A R D V A R K
T A X   T U S S L E   O L I N
R U G   A A M I L N E   O V O
I R O N   N O D S T O   N A B
A A V E R A G E   A N G E L S
    E R A     E L S A
A A R O N P A U L     S H E A
S U N   D O U B L E A T E A M
I D O   O G R E   P H R A S E
A I R   S O A R   S H O R T S
```

16

```
Z E S T   C H A P   C H E S T
A R T Y   H A R E   L O N E R
G R I P   I B A R   U L T R A
    L O G C A B I N S Y R U P
A L E   P A N   S O T   E M S
C O T T A G E C H E E S E
T O T E   O R U   S R O
S T O R M   A B C   S A T U P
      R I N   E E R   K A L E
    R A N C H D R E S S I N G
C H E   D A Y   A P P   L A S
H O M E M A D E M E A L S
A N O D E   R A I N   A P E S
N O V E L   A S S T   R I G A
T R E N D   S E T S   K N O X
```

17

```
H A R M   N O M S G   E A S E
O R E O   A R E N A   G R A M
M I N D R E A D E R   G E R I
E S T E E   S E T S B A I L
Y E S L E T S   Z E T A
    S L E E P E R A G E N T
A A A   T E A   M E T E R
A L L O V E R T H E P L A C E
H I P P O   I O S   S K Y
S T O P I T Y O U T W O
    O C H O   R A I N M A N
B A D S E E D S   L E O N I
A C A I   G U T F E E L I N G
L I N T   A D I O S   A R I E
E D G E   P E R O T   P E E L
```

18

```
E S C   C R A M P S   S B A
G E L   R E G A L E   T O P
O X O   O C E L O T   E X T
  Y O U C A N T T H I N K
V E N N   P T A S   A C I D
S L E D S       S M I T E
O F Y O U R T R O U B L E S
      L O V E Y A
  W H I L E S O L V I N G
P H O N Y       E C A R D
B O G S   S U N S   E M I R
J A W   O H N E A T   E D Y
    A C R O S S W O R D
M A R G A R E T F A R R A R
A N T I   T A L I   S O D A
C D S   S T E T   P O P
```

19

```
C O P S _ Y O G A _ B E S T
D R A W _ A R O S E _ M Y T H
C E R E A L B O W L _ W E A R
_ G E E S E _ E A T _ S R I
P A N T S _ B I L L Y J O E L
A N T _ P A L L _ R U R A L
L O S T S O U L _ V A L E T S
_ H E L M _ A O N E _
E M B E D S _ E X I T P O L L
S O R T A _ C R E D _ R E P
C L E A N C O A L _ S C A T S
A D A _ S A P _ H O O T S _
P O K E _ P I G E O N H O L E
E V I L _ S E A L S _ E R I N
D A N K _ S P I T _ N Y P D
```

20

```
P R O T O N S _ S T A V I N G
G E N E R I C _ O U T C R O P
A M E R I C A _ F E R R E R A
_ N O E L _ I S I S _
P B J _ L I E _ A D A _ C A M
E R O D E D _ A L G O R E
T O R I _ E D I F Y _ R U E S
E N D S _ A N N U S _ A N Y A
_ Z A H N _ A D D _ I N T O _
M E N _ O N S I G H T _ R U M
U M P _ D A T A S E T _ Y A O
F E E _ R E R A I S E _ S L R
A D E L A _ A R C _ A R T O O
S A L E M _ N I L _ M E A N S
A L E X A _ D E E _ S P R E E
```

21

```
U P S _ A D A M S _ W A C K O
N H L _ G I J O E _ I L H A N
J O A N O F A R C _ C L I N E
A N N O _ R E T I C E N T
M Y G O S H _ S C A R _
_ B O O B Y _ E N G E L S
W I G _ A L O E S _ I K E A
A D R O P I N T H E O C E A N
R E A L _ D I A N A _ S H E
M A D D O W _ S M O K E _
_ S P A S _ W Y V E R N
_ S U P E R P A C _ A C A I
S A R I N _ A S I F I C A R E
T R A C E _ S I T A R _ R E C
P A L E D _ M A I N S _ D R E
```

22

```
O H S O _ M I S T _ A C H Y
F O W L _ L A K E _ T R E E
T W O I N K M I N I M U M S
_ N O N E _ M U M _ S L I M
T I N _ I L L P R A C T I C E
I C E F L O E _ E C O _ N A S
C E D E _ A I M _ E L E N A
_ U M M A C H I N E _
A S I D E _ S O D _ A T T A
P O W _ E T S _ N E W S I E S
B E A T T O T H E A W _ R A P
S X S W _ T A U _ I T E M
_ T H E D O C T O R I S O U T
R A R E _ K C U P _ K U S H
A D E N _ S H I M _ S T A Y
```

23

```
S A P S _ A L I S T _ H A G
E L L A _ T A S T E _ P U R R
Q U I C K B R E A D _ O G R E
U M A _ E A G E R _ B E G I N
I N N _ N Y E _ T H Y _ A V A
N I T R O _ Q U E E N B E D
_ O B E _ U R L _ E L S E
_ Q U I L T I N G B E E _
S P U N _ V A T _ A I D _
Q U A D B I K E _ L Y M P H
U R N _ U S E _ M A O _ I L O
A S T E R _ S P A N X _ N A B
L U I S _ S T A R T I N G Q B
L I F T _ E E R I E _ F L U E
S T Y _ W A K E S _ L E E S
```

24

```
S M I R K _ T A P _ O P E R A
L E V E L _ E R A _ O R G A N
A T O N E _ R E S _ H I G G S
W A R O P E R A T I O N _
S L Y _ T A O _ S O C C E R
_ S O R R Y O T H E L L O
A S S E S S _ U F O _ E M S
R O P E _ A C T _ B A S E
O R A _ T S K _ S P O R T S
M O N O P O L Y R I S K _
A S K S O F _ E D Y _ N E E
_ C L U E C H E C K E R S
C L O A K _ A R E _ H O R N S
C O B R A _ S A M _ I N D I A
S W I S S _ T B S _ C A S E Y
```

25

```
L O A M . S P A M . A N G E R
A N T E . E L I E . N O U S E
H E A D S T A N D . N B A T V
R A D I O . S T A T I O N . .
. . . C L A M . L I E D T O .
D A T A . T A B L E . Y A R D
A T R I U M . R E S T . N O W
V O I D S . L I D . O B A M A
I M P . B L O T . C R A M E R
S I L T . S L A T E . R O O F
. C E R E A L . A L E C . . .
. P A R T I N G . W O R D S .
P A L I N . P A S S E D O U T
O P A L S . O N U S . E T S Y
T R Y S T . P O P E . S I T E
```

26

```
P A P A . S A N G . P R I M
A L U M . A R E A . R O M A
S P R I N G F E S T I V A L
T O R S O . . . A G E N T .
. . . S C R I P T . . . . .
. R O S H H A S H A N A H .
R E N O . A F A R . O B E Y
E T A L . M A Y A . W O R E
G A L L . P E N S . R U B S
I K E A . S L O E . U T E S
M E R L E . . A Z U R E . .
E S T . C E A S E D . S T S
. . S O N G K R A N . . . .
B E A K . T I E R . E V E N
T A X I . E L I E . R I L E
S T E P . R E N D . D E F T
```

27

```
P E D R O . A H E M . M A V S
A D I E U . S E R A . A B I T
L I N T R O L L E R . D A T A
S T I R . K E G . P E C A N .
. N O G R E A T S H A K E S .
O M G . N A P . H O O F . . .
R A S T A . W E S . I S L A .
C R E A T E D A M O N S T E R
A S T I . L O X . A T E A M .
. . B E A T . O T P . P N Y .
D R A G O N E S H E E L S . .
R E L A Y . E A T . L O S T .
O M I T . P R I D E M O N T H
N I K E . B O Z O . A S I D E
E X E S . S T E W . P A T S Y
```

28

```
L O G S . F I F A . A B I D E
O V A L . I D O S . L U C A S
L E M O N B A R S . A G E N T
C R E P E S . R I G S . D U H
A T S E A . B E S O . G I B E
T I T . T O M A T O M E T E R
S M O G . O W L . D O T . . .
. E P O C H S . P A N I C S .
. F A B . C H I . T I N T . .
B A N A N A G R A M S . I A O
A M O R . B R A T . I N A P T
D O D . R Y A N . A R E N T I
R E E S E . F I G N E W T O N
A B A C I . T A P E . T R I O
P A L I N . S L A W . S O T S
```

29

```
K P O P . A C A I . S P I T
H A Z E . A C O R N . T I M E
A L A R M C L O C K . I V A N
K E R M I T . P E P . L O G O
I R K E D . P E D O M E T E R
. . D I N A R . T A T . . . .
F O E . A L S O . U T I C A .
C O M P A S S . R O L O D E X
C H O I R . Y O D A . S E E .
. . E L F . P E R K Y . . . .
C A M C O R D E R . C O S M O
U T A H . E R R . Q U O T E D
B O N A . S M A R T P H O N E
E N G R . N O T E S . O R S O
S E A T . O M E N . O M A N .
```

30

```
S T E P U P . O D I N . C O T
I O D I N E . N O R A . A R E
C O U L D A . A R I D . R I T
. . C O U R T D I S A S T E R
E L A T E . O A T H . T O N I
L E T . A F R O . L O O T S .
F I E L D Q U E S T I O N S .
. . I O U . . . O M G . . . .
. R I N G A L A R M B E L L S
R I M E S . E G O S . E E K .
O C T A . M A R K . A M I G A
P O O L R E S O U R C E S . .
E T A . O A H U . A U T U M N
I T S . W R E N . S T A R E S
N A T . S A D D . H E L E N A
```

31

```
M A D E A   J O D I E     Z A C
A L I S T   A A B O N D   U G H
J U S T F O R K I C K S   M A E
A M C   I N F O       R B I S
  L E V I S B L U E J E A N S
D O A S E T     I N B O X
A L I A   I M A F A N   R C A
F A M I L Y D I N I N G R O O M
T V S   Y E L L A T   H A S P
    A N G E L     A T E S T S
H A V I N G S A I D T H A T
I K I D       T O T E   H I T
H E X   G O I N G W A Y B A C K
O L E   E A R B U D   R O M E O
N A N   T R A C Y     E A S E S
```

32

```
  M A G S   W I F E     W I E
T O R R E A (TWO) R L D S E N D
G L E A N   P R O M O T I N G
I T S N O T O K   N O R S E
F O O (TWO) R N   S E N (TWO) R D
    O A T   L O R E N Z O
Q U I D   S H I R R   E I N
I B N   T U E S D A Y   S T Y
N E T   I N A N E   F S I X
G R E N D E L     A G O
  R E E S E S   B A R G E S
J U S (TWO) W   L E A S (TWO) R S T
O P E R A G O E R   C R E T E
D O C K Y A R D S   A T E A M
I N T   B E S T   P H D S
```

33

```
P A C K   T I E D U P   W A S
A L A I   A R L E N E   I C E
S I P S   O K E F E N O K E E
T E R S E   N E A   O I L Y
A N I M A N I A C S   M P A A
    E T A L   T E M P E
P C S   V E T   R A D I I
T H I R T Y S O M E T H I N G
S I T A R   M E N   A K A
  U N I T S   A D A M
P E A K   W O R D S W O R T H
A C T I   O L E   S P O R E
C H I N C H I L L A   I D E A
T O O   D I D I O N   N E E D
S S N   C T S C A N   G O D S
```

34

```
G A B S   B A Y O U   B A R T
U V E A   A L U M S   E V E R
M C A T   K O R A N   N E V E
B L T   N E U T R A L   N O M
O U T D O       I R U L E
  B O U R B O N S T R E E T
    M A R D I G R A S
P E E P   B A T T Y   I L K S
V E T O   Y E S   D I O N
C L O U D S   D R E V I L
  U T E R I   G O O S E
D E F   B I G E A S Y   J F K
U P F O R   L A P   A L A I N
S E E Y A   O R E   L I Z Z O
K E E L   O L D   B Z Z T
```

35

```
M E R   S K O P J E   A B C S
A P E   W A L R U S   M E E T
L I V   I N D I G O   U S D A
I C E C R E A M   S I S T E R
  N H L   G A M   D E S
G A G A   J E L L I E D E E L
A G E N D A   B R A   R Y E
S R I   R B I   E L E V E N
P A S T A S A L A D   T E S T
  A R M   N O V   S T D
I M D E A D   G A Z P A C H O
L E I A   R I O T E R   O E R
I N S T   U P F A K E   L A G
A S H Y   G O F R E E   D R Y
```

36

```
B O G I E   I M A C   R E V S
A D E L E   N A P A   U N I T
N E L L Y S A C H S   R O D E
    B O A   H I T M A K E R
  G E R T R U D E E L I O N
S I R   E Y E   S S R
I R A N   R N A   C A M E O
D O N N A S T R I C K L A N D
E N T E R   C D R   A M I D
    B S A   Y U P   A D S
B E T T Y W I L L I A M S
E M I S S A R Y   S R A
N A D A   M A R I E C U R I E
T I E R   P R I M   E V A D E
O L D S   Y M C A   L E G A L
```

37

```
T O A D   L A C E D   H O P E
E U R O   S T A Y S   T H I N
S T E V E U R K E L   M I N D
L I N E N   I E S   B L O G S
A N A   T A U   I D O
    K I M M Y G I B B L E R
C Y N I C S   O H M   R A V E
R O U T E   C S T   H A T E D
O G L E   D O H   L O W E R S
W I L S O N W I L S O N
    R A G   O D D   U S A
S H A D E   I D A   O A T E S
W I R E   F R E D R O G E R S
I D E A   A L L E Y   E R I E
M E A L   B S I D E   G I F T
```

38

```
E S T E   Q U O T E   P A W S
I T S Y   U N B O X   E R A S
G R E E N O L I V E   D E R N
H O T D A T E     J A Y Z
T B S   C A S I N O F L O O R
Y E E S H   S N A C K   U N O
    L O A   A S H   C O E D
    N A S C A R T R A C K
E B A Y   T R U   E M U
T O N   R O A S T   E P S O M
C O N C E R T H A L L   I R E
  B Y O B     R A I S M A N
M A C S   I T S T H E P I T S
I M A M   R A B A T   A L E C
C A M O   A T A R I   M E S H
```

39

```
R I C C I   R I D E   B L O T
A M O U R   A C E R   A I D E
R A M B O   T E A G A R D E N
E X P A N D E D R O L E
    M A D     E S P N
P I C K I N G N I T S   E O N
I M E A N   E T S   S P C A
K H L O E K A R D A S H I A N
E E L S   P H D   P E T R A
S R O   C H I S E L E D A B S
  E S T O     S A C
    B A C K U P S I N G E R
I N B O X Z E R O   A O R T A
D A R N   A M I S   L S A T S
O B O E   R O S A   K E Y U P
```

40

```
G E A R E D   A S P   W A Z E
U L T I M A   L O U   A G O G
F A T B O Y S L I M   F R O G
F I E   E A R P   F E S S
A N N   F   S H E E P L E
W E D I D I T   E D G E D U P
    R A R E S   I S I T M E
E C H O   O T H E R   R O A R
S E E N I N   H B O G O
P E R F U M E   O N E N E S S
  H I D A L G O   E   A P U
S K O L   I M O K   S A N
C A N I   D I S S E N T E R S
A T O N   E R E   L I A I S E
B E R G   N A E   M A G N E T
```

41

```
C A N O N   O B E Y   S O D
E M O T E   S T E V E   A W E
D O T T E D L I N E S   N E W
A R I A   E A S T   E T S Y
R E T W E E T   O B A M A
    A D D E D B O N U S E S
U R A N U S   L O A N   U T E
G E L S   S I X   C I T E
G A L   S P A S   B H U T A N
S L A S H E D T I R E S
  B L E A T   N O N S T O P
B U O Y   O T T O   W A N E
A D A   D A S H E D H O P E S
N O R   A V A I L   B R E A K
E N D   D A Y S   O D D L Y
```

42

```
A S A D A   T B A R   C O I F
R O S I N   U R S A   H I D E
F A K E D   N A S H V I L L E
  K S T R E E T   A S Y E T
    P O S T   T R U E
  S I L I C O N V A L L E Y
S T R A D   O M I T   S A N
N E I N   M U R A L   C P L S
L A N   T O F U   P A N I C
  M A D I S O N A V E N U E
    O P T S   C A T O
C R A G S   D E T R O I T
H O L L Y W O O D   O D D E R
E L L E   A U D I   C L O A K
F L A G   T R O T   K E L S O
```

43

```
S H I N   M V P S   M O T E L
L O C O   R E I N   A D A G E
A V I D   F E T A   D O J O S
V E L O C I R A P T O R
S L Y F O X   S I N   N T H
    F O I S T   E N C O R E
A C E   P T E R O D A C T Y L
C O C O   G O T   S O M E
T R I C E R A T O P S   K E N
E G G D Y E   S H R E D
D I S   E P I   E L A P S E
    B R O N T O S A U R U S
A P B I O   A R G O   B U S T
P E A R L   W E L L   E D I E
P R N D L   E X E D   D E E R
```

44

```
L A C K S   A P E X   B E E T
A L L E Y   F L O E   L A D E
B L O W N G L A S S   A R M S
A T M   C O A T   I N S E T
M O P S   A C E P I T C H E R
B L E E P S   L O S   O S U
A D D T O   A M A N A   T E N
    S P A C E C A S E
Z A G   T I T H E   I C E E S
I R E   A D O   S N O C A P
P O R K B A R R E L   N O S H
F U M E S   O N U S   T I E
I S A Y   H O L D M Y B E E R
L E N O   I D E A   M O U S E
E D E N   P E S T   S O R T S
```

45

```
L A B   T A D A   G A M B L E
O D E   I N I T   R O I L E D
O M G   L A M A   A L T O I D
F A U L T L I N E S   S A Y
A N N E E   T E A S E R S
    A D O R N S   G E O D E
G U T   V I D E O G A M E S
O H I S E E   A S L E E P
D U M P T R U C K S   D R Y
S H E A R   T O E T A P
    P R E S A L E   S H E A F
A P I   C H O P S T I C K S
S H E I L A   G O A L   H I T
P I C K U P   N U K E   O T O
S L E E V E   E T S Y   S A P
```

46

```
O D O R   P S A T   B E E T
H U L U   I A G O   M U N R O
O D D S   G R A F   O R G A N
    M E T E O R O L O G I S T
S H E   W O N   L E I   N E O
W E D D I N G P L A N N E R
A L I E N S   L O N G O
P I A F   P A W   T H I N
    O Y V E Y   A S P I R E
    Y O G A I N S T R U C T O R
S E X   C N N   R A N   I N D
P S Y C H O A N A L Y S T
L I G H T   M A C S   O B I T
I D E A S   E P E E   D I C E
T O N I   S E R A   A G E D
```

47

```
T A P E   J U D O   W H A M S
O B E Y   A S E A   R O B O T
T A K E A W A L K   A N O D E
A C O R N S   T E M P   V E E
L I E O N   B A N D S H E L L
    L U L U   S U E Z
C H A L L E N G E   P R E E N
A O L   I D O L S   R N A
B E L T S   T O L L B O O T H
    S A K E   I R O N
L I Q U I C A P S   R E H A B
I C U   P O L E   I N S A N E
G I A D A   L O O S E E N D S
H E R O S   A N T E   E D I T
T R E E S   N Y S E   D Y E S
```

48

```
  A N T E   G A U L   O C T
A D E A L   O L M O S   B R R
B O W L I N G B A L L   L A Y
U P T O   C H U M   A M I S S
S T A N Z A   M I D N I G H T
E E K   I A N   A G R E E S
  D E F T   O P A L   A D D
    L I G H T N I N G
  S E A   R O A D   Y E L P
M A X I M A   Y E S   A L T
E M P L O Y E E   V E L O U R
D E I S T   A X L E   E T S Y
U S A   I N S P I R A T I O N
S E T   F O Y E R   M O A N A
A X E   G A L A   A N N E
```

49

L	O	A	F	■	N	U	M	B	S	■	O	M	N	I
A	C	N	E	■	B	R	O	I	L	■	R	E	A	M
G	E	N	E	R	A	L	T	S	O	■	B	L	I	P
G	A	U	D	Y	■	S	T	E	M	S	■	A	V	A
A	N	I	M	E	S	■	C	O	L	O	N	E	L	■
R	I	T	E	■	H	O	S	T	■	U	N	I	T	E
D	A	Y	■	R	O	L	O	■	S	I	N	E	S	■
■	■	F	O	O	D	F	I	G	H	T	■	■	■	■
O	A	S	I	S	■	■	I	T	R	Y	■	S	A	G
B	L	I	N	I	■	J	A	D	A	■	M	I	L	E
S	A	N	D	E	R	S	■	■	S	C	U	L	P	T
C	D	C	■	R	E	B	U	S	■	A	T	E	A	T
E	D	I	T	■	C	A	P	N	C	R	U	N	C	H
N	I	T	E	■	A	C	T	O	R	■	A	C	A	I
E	N	Y	A	■	P	H	O	T	O	■	L	E	S	S

50

J	I	G	■	T	D	P	A	S	S	■	D	R	O	P
O	D	E	■	O	R	A	C	L	E	■	R	O	B	E
I	L	L	■	M	A	N	H	U	G	■	E	C	O	N
N	E	S	T	E	G	G	■	R	E	M	A	K	E	S
■	■	■	E	S	Q	■	A	P	L	O	M	B	■	■
L	A	C	E	■	U	Z	I	S	■	T	O	O	T	H
I	R	A	N	■	E	A	R	■	S	E	N	T	R	Y
B	I	N	■	D	E	C	K	O	U	T	■	T	O	M
R	E	D	F	I	N	■	I	N	G	■	M	O	O	N
A	S	Y	L	A	■	A	S	E	A	■	A	M	P	S
■	■	H	O	N	O	R	S	■	R	P	M	■	■	■
S	E	E	S	A	W	S	■	A	R	E	A	R	U	G
E	R	A	S	■	N	O	C	L	U	E	■	E	R	R
W	I	R	E	■	U	N	R	E	S	T	■	E	G	O
N	E	T	S	■	P	S	Y	C	H	E	■	F	E	W

51

A	C	H	O	O	■	E	D	S	■	S	A	L	E	M
P	L	A	N	K	■	N	Y	E	■	U	S	A	G	E
N	E	V	E	R	E	V	E	R	■	R	I	N	G	S
E	R	A	■	A	L	I	■	B	R	E	A	D	T	H
W	I	N	E	■	M	A	R	I	A	■	B	A	E	■
S	C	A	N	S	■	B	E	A	R	S	E	A	R	S
■	■	R	E	A	L	M	■	E	N	A	C	T	■	■
■	■	L	A	D	L	E	■	F	L	A	S	K	■	■
■	■	N	I	G	E	L	■	R	O	Y	C	E	■	■
H	O	V	E	R	O	V	E	R	■	K	U	R	I	A
A	T	E	■	T	E	X	T	S	■	P	E	A	T	■
H	A	L	F	A	S	S	■	N	A	P	■	T	N	T
A	F	O	U	L	■	T	H	I	G	H	H	I	G	H
H	A	N	E	S	■	E	B	T	■	D	A	R	L	A
A	N	G	L	O	■	D	O	E	■	S	W	E	E	T

52

D	I	A	L	O	G	■	E	D	I	T	■	A	L	L
I	G	N	O	B	E	L	■	N	O	R	I	■	T	E	A
M	I	N	G	L	E	I	N	T	H	E	C	R	O	W	D
E	V	O	■	O	S	C	A	R	S	■	■	E	N	D	S
S	E	D	A	N	■	I	P	A	■	A	T	E	■	■
■	O	M	G	■	T	A	N	G	L	E	D	W	E	B
A	C	M	E	■	■	S	T	O	L	E	■	A	T	A
C	H	I	N	E	S	E	■	D	Y	N	A	S	T	Y
E	O	N	■	T	O	T	A	L	■	■	G	N	U	S
S	U	I	T	T	O	A	T	E	E	■	O	U	T	■
■	■	R	A	N	■	T	E	N	■	R	E	C	O	N
W	I	K	I	■	E	A	R	L	A	P	■	L	S	U
H	A	N	G	I	N	G	B	Y	A	T	H	R	E	A	D
E	G	O	■	T	O	G	O	■	I	M	A	N	A	G	E
W	O	W	■	T	R	O	Y	■	S	N	A	R	E	S

53

T	E	M	P	O	■	R	A	M	■	S	E	E	P
K	A	R	A	T	■	J	O	K	E	■	U	L	N	A
O	U	T	R	O	■	O	B	I	T	■	D	E	E	R
■	■	T	H	I	S	O	N	E	S	O	N	M	E
I	T	S	Y	■	T	E	C	■	O	K	A	Y	■
T	O	O	B	A	D	F	O	R	Y	O	U	■	■
A	W	F	U	L	■	P	E	E	T	■	B	R	B
L	E	T	S	L	I	P	■	A	S	H	T	R	A	Y
O	R	G	■	T	R	A	M	■	E	R	U	P	T
■	■	S	H	A	L	L	W	E	D	A	N	C	E
M	A	Y	A	■	B	O	A	■	S	O	D	S
P	A	S	S	T	H	E	T	O	R	C	H	■	■
D	R	A	T	■	I	C	E	D	■	H	A	P	P	Y
A	C	N	E	■	G	R	A	Y	■	I	R	A	T	E
S	H	A	M	■	H	U	M	■	A	T	T	A	R

54

I	P	O	D	■	P	S	A	L	M	■	T	R	A	M
M	E	N	U	■	O	N	S	E	T	■	R	A	C	E
P	R	E	V	A	I	L	I	N	G	W	I	N	D	S
S	U	G	A	R	■	H	A	D	■	H	A	T	C	H
■	■	L	M	A	O	■	E	R	I	N	■	■
P	U	L	L	E	D	S	T	R	I	N	G	S
I	P	A	■	D	O	T	H	■	D	E	L	E	T	E
E	D	Y	S	■	S	I	T	■	E	L	O	N
D	O	U	L	A	S	■	N	O	T	I	■	M	E	D
■	P	E	N	T	A	G	O	N	B	R	A	S	S
■	■	E	D	A	M	■	K	N	E	E	■	■
H	A	R	P	S	■	O	O	H	■	A	F	L	A	T
T	H	E	S	O	U	N	D	O	F	M	U	S	I	C
M	O	N	O	■	G	R	I	L	L	■	G	A	R	B
L	Y	O	N	■	H	A	N	D	Y	■	E	T	S	Y

55

M	A	R	E	S	█	A	S	O	F	█	E	G	O	S
A	W	A	S	H	█	T	O	G	A	█	N	O	A	H
Z	A	P	P	A	█	W	A	L	L	█	V	O	T	E
D	R	I	N	K	L	I	K	E	A	F	I	S	H	█
A	D	D	█	E	E	L	█	█	F	R	E	E	█	█
█	█	█	R	U	N	L	I	K	E	A	D	E	E	R
A	E	S	O	P	█	█	R	E	L	Y	█	G	R	E
F	L	O	W	█	S	W	A	Y	S	█	T	G	I	F
E	M	U	█	A	L	O	T	█	█	G	A	S	E	S
W	O	R	K	L	I	K	E	A	D	O	G	█	█	█
█	B	E	E	T	█	█	N	U	T	█	S	T	S	█
█	W	A	T	C	H	L	I	K	E	A	H	A	W	K
D	O	L	T	█	E	A	R	L	█	J	A	M	I	E
R	O	L	L	█	R	I	M	E	█	O	Z	O	N	E
E	L	S	E	█	S	C	A	T	█	B	E	A	S	T

56

G	O	A	T	S	█	A	B	E	T	█	A	W	O	L
A	R	N	I	E	█	M	Y	N	A	█	C	O	P	E
B	E	E	K	E	E	P	E	R	S	█	T	O	R	N
S	O	W	I	N	G	█	N	O	T	E	█	L	A	G
█	█	█	█	█	O	H	O	L	Y	N	I	G	H	T
O	L	S	O	N	█	O	W	L	█	G	N	A	S	H
Y	O	U	T	U	B	E	█	S	T	U	N	T	█	█
S	U	B	T	L	Y	█	█	A	L	O	H	A	S	█
█	S	A	L	U	T	█	E	N	F	U	E	G	O	█
T	R	E	V	I	█	R	I	M	█	S	T	R	E	W
D	E	C	A	F	L	A	T	T	E	█	█	█	█	█
P	A	T	█	Y	A	M	S	█	S	T	Y	M	I	E
A	L	I	A	█	S	P	E	L	L	B	O	U	N	D
S	L	O	B	█	E	L	L	E	█	S	U	L	K	Y
S	Y	N	C	█	R	E	F	S	█	P	R	E	S	S

57

B	A	R	S	█	G	P	A	S	█	A	S	S	E	T
E	X	E	C	█	R	E	N	T	█	F	I	E	R	I
A	L	S	O	█	O	L	D	E	█	F	L	E	A	S
N	E	T	N	E	U	T	R	A	L	I	T	Y	█	█
█	█	█	E	T	C	█	E	M	I	R	█	A	D	S
S	E	T	█	A	H	A	█	█	A	M	U	L	E	T
P	L	A	Y	P	O	S	S	U	M	█	T	A	T	I
O	L	L	I	E	█	A	U	G	█	S	A	T	A	N
K	E	E	P	█	S	P	E	L	L	C	H	E	C	K
E	R	N	E	S	T	█	█	Y	E	R	█	R	H	O
N	Y	T	█	P	U	T	T	█	G	U	M	█	█	█
█	█	S	H	A	D	O	W	C	A	B	I	N	E	T
A	D	H	O	C	█	G	I	L	L	█	M	A	G	I
S	N	O	R	E	█	A	C	A	I	█	I	D	O	L
P	A	W	N	S	█	S	E	N	D	█	C	A	S	T

58

V	A	N	█	S	P	A	█	L	E	A	D	C	A	R
C	H	E	A	P	E	N	█	A	B	R	E	A	S	T
R	A	W	S	I	L	K	█	P	A	R	A	B	L	E
█	█	█	F	E	E	L	█	E	Y	E	D	█	█	█
O	R	C	A	S	█	E	E	L	█	T	O	W	E	D
B	O	A	R	█	T	A	M	A	█	N	E	R	O	█
S	O	L	A	C	E	█	R	I	D	E	█	I	A	N
█	M	U	S	I	C	A	L	C	H	A	I	R	S	█
A	I	M	█	O	H	I	O	█	D	U	M	D	U	M
Y	E	N	S	█	O	R	B	S	█	P	A	R	E	█
N	S	Y	N	C	█	P	E	A	█	A	L	L	E	N
█	█	█	O	H	N	O	█	Y	O	L	O	█	█	█
S	P	A	C	I	E	R	█	S	W	A	D	D	L	E
Y	O	G	A	M	A	T	█	H	E	R	E	I	A	M
N	E	O	P	E	T	S	█	I	S	M	█	N	G	O

59

S	T	A	F	F	█	B	E	E	F	█	A	M	O	S
P	E	A	R	L	█	A	M	M	O	█	L	O	R	E
Y	A	H	O	O	█	N	O	U	G	A	T	B	A	R
█	█	█	N	O	L	A	█	█	P	O	I	N	T	█
N	E	U	T	R	O	N	S	T	A	R	█	L	G	A
E	A	R	L	█	L	A	P	E	L	█	G	E	E	S
O	R	G	A	N	█	█	O	R	A	T	E	█	█	█
█	█	N	E	W	B	E	G	I	N	N	I	N	G	S
█	█	█	N	A	S	A	L	█	█	P	E	R	I	L
S	E	A	S	█	S	T	E	E	L	█	R	O	L	E
C	N	N	█	N	O	O	D	L	E	B	O	W	L	S
A	S	T	R	O	█	█	B	E	E	S	█	█	█	█
N	U	M	E	R	O	U	N	O	█	A	I	S	L	E
T	R	A	P	█	D	R	E	W	█	S	T	A	I	R
Y	E	N	S	█	E	N	D	S	█	T	Y	P	E	S

60

A	M	P	L	E	█	L	I	A	M	█	M	O	S	H
N	O	O	I	L	█	E	L	S	A	█	A	N	T	I
V	O	O	D	O	O	D	O	L	L	█	L	E	A	K
I	L	L	S	█	W	T	S	█	A	S	T	U	T	E
L	A	P	█	C	L	O	T	H	D	I	A	P	E	R
█	█	█	A	C	U	█	█	A	R	M	█	█	█	█
O	N	R	U	S	H	█	P	R	O	█	D	O	N	S
L	E	T	S	P	U	T	A	P	I	N	I	N	I	T
E	D	Y	S	█	M	A	W	█	T	I	D	I	L	Y
█	█	█	P	A	N	█	█	L	O	O	█	█	█	█
B	O	W	L	I	N	G	L	A	N	E	█	N	B	A
A	C	H	I	E	R	█	I	C	E	█	T	R	O	T
S	H	I	N	█	A	T	M	M	A	C	H	I	N	E
R	E	S	T	█	C	U	B	E	█	P	A	N	D	A
A	R	T	Y	█	E	G	O	S	█	A	N	G	S	T

61

```
VINE  PLASMA  SRI
IDOL  CIPHER  PET
DELLASTREET  ACE
ISAAC  ILK  SCAM
TWELVESTEPS
MCS  SET  ERIES
OAKS  PCP  GAUGE
STICKTHELANDING
SONIA  IMP  STAG
NOTES  ASP  STY
BOYNEXTDOOR
ENDS  PEE  ARGON
LEI  HONEYIMHOME
LIP  ISOMER  EWAN
ELS  CESSNA  ANNE
```

62

```
ESC  CRAGS  ASPER
SAL  MEDIA  BORAX
PHOTOBOMB  SNOTS
RAVEN  MLB  ALF
IRES  TWEETSTORM
TARTARE  WHINER
POSH  ANGST
COMPUTERCRASH
ARNIE  YOLK
BUSMAP  TOSTADA
EMAILBLAST  ARAB
PFC  SIR  CREMA
FLAKE  TECHBOOMS
DEREK  UNDUE  LEE
ASIDE  PACER  ADD
```

63

```
ARCED  LAST  OPED
CELLO  ALPE  NEAR
DAUBS  PIECHARTS
CLEO  BEACHED
WAILS  RADAR
BADEGGS  OPERATE
ELIDES  GOA  EMTS
SPA  SHIPPED  PEE
TALC  URA  LATENT
OCELOTS  ALMONDS
WADUP  DIANA
MUSLIMS  SATE
JUMPSUITS  KTURN
ISEE  FACT  FETID
BAND  IMHO  CROPS
```

64

```
CHILI  ADDTO  ABU
AARON  BEARD  DIP
BLACKCOFFEE  ESS
ODOISTS  SLOE
AHA  LOL  PATENT
SYMBOL  BEALE
IDIOT  REDSPRING
ARGO  MOLDS  ICEE
MOONJELLY  BLARE
IRATE  TRENDS
FOREST  SUE  TSE
EVES  LAUTREC
MIC  ROCKANDROLL
UNO  HALER  EUROS
REN  OFUSE  RESOD
```

65

```
ATOM  ANKA  BASIL
CAME  DIOS  ABIDE
EXITPOLLS  CURLS
DITTO  NECKTIES
LOGS  SAL
ANGELOU  SPATIAL
DOE  BEG  SUNNI
OVERSIZEDCHECKS
RESIN  MAR  ALL
ELEGIAC  FORESEE
FLO  TWIT
TAILFINS  CHEAP
RURAL  NATIONALS
ATONE  ERIN  ISMS
PONDS  DANK  CYST
```

66

```
GOBI  FBILAB  GPS
ENOS  OLDELI  LAT
NOWWEREEVEN  USE
LEN  WAIT  FETA
AHEAD  AMSTERDAM
GARR  SKA  EAU
ASH  RHINO  ZIPIT
STATUES  DAYTONA
PETRI  SWOLE  KFC
ANA  ERA  GEEK
SNOWGLOBE  TARRY
EARL  LISA  OUR
WIG  SPLITSECOND
EVA  GRETEL  HOUR
REN  TORERO  EMTS
```

67

```
H A L L   E G A D S   A R M S
I D E A   L E G I T   L O C H
K E V I N K L I N E   F A D E
E L I D E   S N A R F   D O E
R E S O R T   G R E A T F U N
      F O U L   O R A L B
T G I F   B A R B   G O A L S
M A N   W A R H E R O   R E I
I S T O O   D O N E   R E S T
    T H R O B   Z A C H
F R E E D I V E   P A Y C U T
R O Z   S N I T S   S M O R E
I P O D   G L U E S T I C K S
T U N A   E L D E R   N O E L
O B E Y   D E E D S   G A L A
```

68

```
A S A P   B R A T S     P S T
N A D A   R A B I E S   O H S
O D O R   O M E L E T   W O E
    S P O I L E R A L E R T
A N G L E D   S P I R E S
T O W E R   C E O   L A P S E
T H E Y F O U N D N E M O
N O N   A B O D E     S E A
    S H E K I L L E D B I L L
A C T O N   C A Y   I O N I A
P L E A D S     B A D G E S
H E F R E E D W I L L Y
I R A   A V E R S E   O A T S
D I N   R E V E L S   I D E A
S C I   N I N E S   L E A P
```

69

```
D R A G   S T A R S   R O C K
R O L O   T H R E E   O X E N
O A T S   R E I N S   L E T O
P R E E M I E   T A L L Y U P
    R E A P   A M I   E S E
Y I N   L E A F L E T S
A D A P T S T O   O T O E
N O T E S   E R R   S H O R T
G L E E     C A T W O M A N
    P E T P E E V E   A L A
M I X   G R O   G E S T
A C E S O U T   B U T T O N S
T A N S   E A P O E   O R E O
C M O N   S T E W S   K E E N
H E N S   T O A S T   E D D Y
```

70

```
F I T B I T   A M P   T U R K
I M P A L A   C O O   O N A N
J E K Y L L   T H E V O I C E
I D E A   L I S A   I N T E L
    R I O S   N O S I E S T
F L E E T W O O D M A C
L I L A C   M A N   E G G O
O K S   H O M E S I N   O O O
P E A S   R A G   A D B I Z
    M I C H A E L C A I N E
P I C A S S O   M I L D
O F A L L   G I S T   J A V A
U N C L E S A M   M O O R E D
T O T E   A N A   U N K I N D
S T I R   G Y M   S T E A D S
```

71

```
B I B B   O P E D S   O P E C
C H A I   L A D E N   U R D U
C O N G R A T U L A T I O N S
S P Y   I F S   I P O   M A P
    A S P       B B Q
    O N P A S S I N G Y O U R
A N T I   P A S E O   N E A R
B A R T   F L O A T   Z E T A
L I E S L   T N T   S O N I C
E R E   E Y E T E S T   S O Y
    U N A D O R N E D
A L T P O P     E M E N D S
S O H O   P E N N E   C O I L
A V O N   E M B E R   A N N E
P E R E   D U C T S   F O O D
```

72

```
S I N K   G A U S S   P U B S
I S E E   U P S E T   O N I T
N O W W H E R E W E   E D G E
B L T   A R E S   R E M O T E
A D O   R N S   H E R   S A P
D E N A L I   G E O R W E L L
    L E C A R S     I N K Y
    N O M A N I S L A N D
B L A H   S T E E L E
R O M A T O E S   G U S H E R
A T E   A I L   A R M   A X E
I T G I R L   E V E N   N A P
S E A R   R I D E S A D D L E
E R M A   I N E R T   A L T A
D Y E S   G E N T S   P E S T
```

73

```
FACT  CULLS  TALC
LUAU  UBOAT  ADOS
URLS  BENDS  HOST
BACKWARDS  BOLT
   SANER  BREECH
GIT  YODELER  SAO
ONEON  SET  ACUT
THEBELT  THEREST
HITS  OOH  RENEE
OBO  MINIBAR  TSA
TITIAN  GLUON
 TALL  THEBRIDGE
SILO  WATER  FIND
EVES  ERODE  TRAY
WERE  TOPSY  YEWS
```

74

```
ADZ  SMUG  ESPANA
TAO  AONE  TEACUP
FLO  DOWNJACKETS
IAMB  DERULO  LTE
RISES  DESI  RAYS
SLIDIN  TAZO
TAN  NAOMI  EKES
 MOMENTOFTRUTH
ANEW  HAYAO  HED
 NYSE  STRIPE
ILSA  ALFA  HOOHA
NOT  ITLLDO  OPED
CROSSYOURTS  IRS
ANGLER  BETA  ADE
SAYYES  SPOT  NSA
```

75

```
JELLY  FISH  CMON
EIEIO  ECTO  HIVE
FROND  BEETSALAD
FESTER  DETAIL
 ELECTRIC  EEL
ARAL  SHEEP  ARGO
ROB  STEAD  CITGO
MANTIS  SHRIMP
ODEUM  PASHA  MAE
RIGG  PIQUE  PEND
SEA  CUCUMBER
 TOPEKA  ALEAST
DRILLBITS  BATHE
JOVE  LEIS  OCTET
SEES  ORCA  WHALE
```

76

```
DOGLEG  JAR  APP
OOLALA  GUSHOVER
OZARKS  S[I/DOT] SENORA
MEME  EACH  SUCKY
[I/DOT]TSWAR  USA
YER  ALOES  [I/DOT]MO
XOXO  YEWS  TOAD
LOUANN  CROAKS
OU[I/DOT]S  OPAL  ORSO
NTH  GNOME  OPT
 EMU  LEGUME
LOMAN  KNOB [I/DOT]HOP
THATSSAD  EQUATE
DOTTHE[I/DOT]S  RUBSON
SHH  YES  SEEPED
```

77

```
BLOOP  SMASH  SASS
MAHAL  PIXIE  ECCE
WHITECOLLAR  CTRL
SRO  DARN  ARIEL
GREENSLEEVES
JOYLESS  ECARTE
ATEAT  TORI  PREP
COATOFMANYCOLORS
KERR  OARS  HALOS
 SAVEUS  VAINEST
SILVERLINING
TRAIT  ISEE  APU
IOTA  YELLOWTAILS
CNET  DRIER  INDIE
KYRA  SEUSS  TASER
```

78

```
GASP  WAFT  ALFA
ACELA  ICLAUDIUS
LANAI  STARTOURS
LITTLEDIPPER
 ISTO  ELM
CLAN  SMALLFRIES
HAMUP  HAIL  BAE
ATOMICSUBMARINE
REN  TURF  WADED
MERETRIFLE  TORY
 NAN  ARCH
 MICROSECONDS
AFRIKAANS  ELIOT
WINTERIZE  DELVE
EBAY  ADES  SEEP
```

79

```
B I B L E . D A M E . U C L A
I D I O T . E C I G . R H O S
G U T F E E L I N G . B E N T
K N I T . K I D D . F A R G O
I N N . H E N . S A Y N O . .
D O G M A . T H E K I C K E R
. . . A L L . A Y E . A E R O
S I G N F O R D E L I V E R Y
O N U S . R O I . A P E . . .
B U M P Y R I D E . O R A T E
. . L L O Y D . M O D . M A V
A S I A N . R I C A . F O M O
M I N I . W A T E R B R E A K
E D E N . O G R E . S A B R E
N E S S . K E Y S . S T A I D
```

80

```
B A R B Q S . A S I F . P R O
F R E E U P . W H O A . R O W
L O N G I I S L A N D . E O N
A S E A . C A S K . . B F F S
T E E T H E D . Y O D E L . .
. . . H A R D C C A N D I E S
B A T O N . R A F A . G R E .
I C O N . I T E M S . S H I A
N A P . A S I A . A T T E N .
S I L E N T M M O V I E . . .
. O N T O E . M E G A H I T .
C H A D . . S A I L . M A C E
H I D . C A P I T A L S S I N
E Y E . E X A M . R O U T E D
W A R . L E N S . S U P E R S
```

81

```
T R O P E . M A A M . T V M O M
R E P E L . A L T O . R E I K I
A N T E D . K E E N . A N N A L
C A I R O M E X I C O C I T Y .
E M O . R A D . T H A T . O T C
R E N T A C O P . E R S . R H O
. . A D A . E R R . . S E E N .
. O H I O W A S H I N G T O N .
O V A L . . S T Y . O R E . . .
R E V . D J S . S O D A P O P S
G R E . R A T S . C U D . W O E
. P A N A M A L I T H U A N I A
E A T U P . T O N E . A G I N G
A S I D E . E M I T . T O N T O
U S T E D . D O T S . E G G E D
```

82

```
O R B S . N S F W . O D D S
T H A N . U C L A . F R E T
H I G L I D A Y S . F A M E
E N G . H E R E T O . G E T
R O Y C E . F R E N C R N S
. . . L A O . . E R A T O .
. T A R M A C S . I C O N .
. J U S T A D D W A T E R .
B A R S . R E S I S T S . .
A N N I E . . . T H E . . .
B E A C U S E S . O R A L B
B E L . R E N N E R . T A O
L Y O N . E L E V E N T U R
E R S T . Y A L E . S I G N
S E S H . A I L S . A C H E
```

83

```
R A G U . S U E R . Z E T A
O L E S . J E T L I . I R I S
L E T S H A V E I T . P I N K
E X T R U D E . A Z A L E A S
S A Y . T E R I . B I O . . .
. . S T U D E N T I D C A R D
A B B A S . S I T E . D A Y .
C R U X . G A T E S . J U N E
M A R . P U L I . M A L T S
E G G S H E L L P A I N T .
. . M A S . L A V S . M I A
Y A K U T S K . G O D S O N S
A R I D . W E R E W O L V E S
K I N G . H E A R S . E I R E
S A K E . O P T S . W E T S
```

84

```
A D B I Z . S O S A . R P M S
C I R C E . P S A T . E L O N
T R A I N A R I D E . P A V E
E G G . D R I E S . H O S E R
D E A L A S T R I K E . T A D
. . . O Y E Z . G A Y L I B .
S C H W A . P H Y S I Q U E
O H O K . S T A T E . B U S Y
W E R E C O O L . S I E T E
. C R Y O U T . T H U D . .
S K I . P L A N E A B O A R D
C A F E S . L O S E S . T U O
A C I D . S W I T C H J O B S
R U E D . P A C E . O L L I E
E T S Y . F R E D . P O L O S
```

85

```
AVOID   NTH   SHIRK
PEACE   ERA   LINEN
TAKECOVER   ISSUE
SLY   AREAMAP   TEA
    MYERS   DONALD
CHAOS   URANO
REIN   RATSNEST
ERRATA   EYE   STEW
DRYROT   TANA
    CEE   HOLDS
BATHTOY   ZAP
ELI   ONESHOT   SAI
MAMET   STOOPDOWN
AMIGO   EEL   EULER
DODGE   STY   GOOSE
```

86

```
ICON   SQUABS   PUB
NOVA   AUNTIE   RNA
TREK   LITTLEROCK
OGRE   OPI   ENABLE
WILDROSES   ICEES
   OLIN   HATE
STOIC   ASAP   SUP
TAKEOUTTHETRASH
UPS   NAYS   WANED
   ODOR   LOTT
RETRO   IOWASTATE
ATHENS   RIP   ASIS
SHOOTCRAPS   ILLS
TEN   GOATEE   LADE
ARG   OWNERS   SPEX
```

87

```
BRUT   BIRD   HARP
BONA   TRUE   PUREE
QUICKSALE   EFILE
SETTO   EPICFAIL
   FLEA   ENLISTS
CASUALSANDAL
HILL   LIZ   SYNCS
ADA   BEATLES   ELI
IABOO   EAT   GOOD
   POLICYCHANGE
ADDISON   SHAM
COINTOSS   RENTS
UNTIE   PLUNKDOWN
TUTOR   OUZO   AVIA
ETON   TROD   YANG
```

88

```
CFO   SPAM   BOSOM
URDU   URSA   INTRO
RAIN[BAR]RELS   REECE
3UCHI   MATHCLASS
EDT   SHIN   AHEM
   STYX   EM[BAR]GOED
TAPTAP   TASK   PUR
ICON   EBERT   PERU
FAT   ARON   EGGNOG
DISEM[BAR]K   SARA
   MINI   LOKI   USC
PROTECTED   PINTA
SIKHS   RAISETHE[BAR]
SLEET   ISUP   DIVE
TERRY   OHMY   PET
```

89

```
GEARS   STENO   AHA
ALLAH   ARCHANGEL
HOLDINCAULFIELD
   INURN   STOLI
KEVINBAKIN   PUNS
ALE   YSL   DORITOS
TERM   GOTAC
   ABRAHAMLINKIN
   FRONT   YEAH
SPAREME   AFL   DNA
ARIE   OWINWILSON
VOLES   NTILE
ELIZABETHWARRIN
MONEYTREE   COMMA
EGG   SWARM   SYSOP
```

90

```
ATED   BRAHE   HIMO
HOAR   PARES   OPED
OUST   ISLAS   MANE
RTTEACHER   MEDUS
ASSENT   NOFAT
   TNUT   FORESTS
ACEHORSE   PGATOU
FOG   TEALS   IMAMS
OBAMA   RATON   LEA
OBLETS   NOPARKIN
TSELIOT   PELE
   TOYOU   NIPPLE
CEMAN   DRYMARTIN
AVOW   BABAR   IRON
SELA   ATARI   CANI
ERDY   MENDS   EPSO
```

91

```
VACAY   TAIL   TETRA
OHARE   RUNE   OPRAH
LENIN   ITCH   BEIGE
EATAT   COURSEEXAM
SPA  ASK   REEFS
   LASTED   RCA   TWO
BLOC   IRAN   IOWAN
LAUNDRYDETERGENT
IMPEI   SAHL   REDO
PEE   RNC   PASSED
   BTEAM   TAT   LCD
ANNOYANCES   ADELE
REAIR   AGRO   TIDAL
LOTSA   REID   INUIT
ONSET   DEED   COMMA
```

92

```
NEWB   TKOD   MCJOB
YOHO   MINI   OHARE
UNIONISTS   NEMEA
   STU   HOCKEYMOM
OKEYDOKE   EPEES
RAJ   GPA   STAND
ENURES   FLOWN
SEGO   HAY   EDGE
   BTEAM   ABSORB
   DOUBT   MIA   NAB
   METRO   TURNKEYS
JOCKEYFOR   EEK
AVOID   EMMASTONE
DICTA   DEUS   ENOS
ANTSY   SIRS   LGBT
```

93

```
ONS   BUNCH   OOZE
PEC   ASAHI   PROS
TAIL   DECOR   TERI
ITSOK   DRIER   ORG
MISPLACE   SOSOON
IDO   EID   LOCHS
SERVER   PANKO
MASA   VEX   WRIT
   LAPAZ   GENOME
   RESET   BEG   SPA
GEOTAG   GALOSHES
ORB   PAPER   SHARE
BABY   SOCKS   EMIR
ASIA   URKEL   BAA
GEEK   STORY   OLD
```

94

```
STAGE   EGOT   PERP
EAGER   GREATAPES
WHATAGOODBOYAMI
EOS   AIG   LUG
REPASTS   DECANTS
   SCOTTISHPOET
USTA   UNA   FLU
SPINNINGWHEEL
RUE   OVI   ORES
BRASSSECTION
GYRATES   ODDSOCK
   LAS   YON   BAE
FROMSTEMTOSTERN
HADAHUNCH   OHYAY
ADEN   DDAY   PASTA
```

95

```
SLAPS   IRS   THEME
MADRE   CUE   WAXED
USAINBOLT   ILIAD
GEMSTONE   SNOTTY
   TIS   ZEKE
   PRINCEFIELDER
NAAN   HELPME   ROB
ANSEL   YAS   SPRAY
BAT   ENOKIS   LOSE
   MARGARETCOURT
   ARSE   RBS
SIPTEA   PHOTOIDS
ANAIS   TIMDUNCAN
STINT   ONO   SEEYA
SONGS   OKS   ESTOP
```

96

```
CAPS   SPLAT   FAWN
OSHA   LOATH   ELIE
STAYSALIVE   EFTS
MIS   IVERSE   DAT
ORECK   USERID
   LESSER   ORONO
MACE   EOLIAN   MGR
ERE   ECLIPSE   ELM
GAR   STATES   GOYA
ACTUP   RENTTO
THANOS   AETNA
   NIS   PLAYER   ION
AONE   RAZOREDGED
MILA   ILIKE   ERNE
IDYL   GAZES   REDS
```

97

```
R A M P   L A T E R   A S P S
I K E A   A L I B I   L E I A
C R A M   C O M B O M E A L S
C O N   F I F E   A X L E S
I N S T A N T R E P L A Y
  O W I N G   V E T
S H E E T   S W A N   L A I D
T I L T A T W I N D M I L L S
Y O L O   H I T S   A T O L L
    B U N   S L U E S
  B U R G E R F L I P P E R
A S A M I   E L I A   L E E
B U M P E R C R O P   B A Y S
B E B E   E X U R B   I N O T
A R I D   I X N A Y   B T U S
```

98

```
  I M A G E   I T S O K
  V A L O R   C R A Z E
  A W A I T S   K I S M E T
  B A M B I     C H A P S
G R R   I V S   A K A   S U M
A I D   S T E R N L Y   O N O
P D F S   O N I C E   B N A I
E G A N   B O D H I   A T M S
D E C A T U R   O V E R H I T
  I R A S     T Y K E
G E N E S I S   T H E S I M S
O M G   K N I S H E S   V I E
N A D A   E N E R O   S L A V
Z I O N   S A P O R   R O M E
O L G A   S I T B Y   I W I N
```

99

```
Z A P   T H E D O W   I C E
I L L S   E U G E N E   N H L
T O U C H E T Y P E S   C A L
I N T R O   P T O   D O P E
  G O E S O N T H E L A M E
    E T N A   C A M E R A
A L A N   I F S O   S E T O N
R E V   A T T A C H E   A N A
I T A L Y   A T T A   A X E L
A S L E E P   A N A T
  P A S S E J U D G M E N T
S A N S   Y E N   E M A I L
A R C   G O T D O W N P A T E
N T H   A T T I L A   O C H O
D Y E   L E A D E R   P E N
```

100

```
F I B   K O R U N A S   G S A
A H A   A D D S A L T   O C D
M A T H T E A C H E R   L I E
I D S A Y     C O R D E N
S T I R   S O O N   P E E N
H O N   S P I R A L   O N C E
  C O O L D U D E   R E X
  S L I T   E T O N   A C C
D E A R   T R I P S   T A O
T O Q U E   H U L A   S I M P
E L U D E   E P I   T T O P S
C L E E S E   F U R
H I N T   T R I A L D A T E S
S E C T   S U N F L O W E R S
  S E E   Y E S T E R Y E A R
```

101

```
B L O W S I T   A S I A   R E F
R O N A L D O   T T O P   E M O
R O C K I N G H O R S E   M I G
  S E E T O   E L I   C A N E
A E O N S   W I L D T U R K E Y
R E V   B I D   E S T E E M S
I N E D I B L E   H I E
  D R U N K E N C H I C K E N
    S C I   H A R A S S E S
C R E T A N S   A L T   C T A
R A G I N G B U L L   B L A S T
A M E N   A S K   K O A L A
N O S   P A R T Y A N I M A L S
E N T   O G R E   S E N A T E S
D A S   W O O D   L E G R E S T
```

102

```
U T A H   N A T   H A W A I I
N I N A   ∞ P S   A D A P T S
P E N N   U B E R M E N S C H
C R E D I T S L I P   D O H
    C V S   I N S T A
  L A Y   B O D H I   A W E
S P ∞ R   S E T   I T S C ∞ L
N A I V E T E   B R O N T E S
O N E E A R   O Y E   A I D E
W E S   S A B R E   M R I
  A T W ∞ D   R E F
  E M U   H A A G E N D A Z S
F L I R T A T I O N   O R E O
U M L A U T   N Y E   W I S P
R O A S T S   S A W   N E T S
```

103

```
S O F A   P I P E D   V S I G N
I M A C   L L A N O   O H B O Y
L A Y I T A L L O U T T H E R E
O N E D A Y   L U C R E   T E T
      I N F O   G H O S T
  P I C K U P T H E P I E C E S
G A B   S L E W   E N C O R E
R U S S   C O W L   H A N G
A L E A S T   I O T A   T S A
F I N D T H E R I G H T F I T
      E R O D E   Y E T I
O H M   A S I D E   W I L L O W
S E E T H E B I G P I C T U R E
L L A M A   L A G E R   E X E S
O P T I N   E L O P E   R E S T
```

104

```
M P G   A R C S   L O W E S
A H A   N A O M I   O V A L S
D I S C I P L E S   C U T I N
A L T A   C A L L T I M E
M I R R O R   T E A   R N S
S P O R T E D   S C R U B U P
      T W I N   T O P E K A
P A L E O   P A Y   T I D E S
O L I V I A   B E T H
H O M E I C E   T A K E O F F
L E O   E X O   S O P H I A
  R A I S I N E T   E G G S
F L I N G   S T R I K E O U T
G O D N O   T O T E S   O R E
S W E A R   P E R U   D E N
```

105

```
P A R K   A L P H A   I D L E
I R O N   R U R A L   N E E R
P O D I U M C A S T   S C A R
E M I T S   I M P O S T O R S
R A N   U S A   H E M
  C R A N I U M A P P L E
S H E R Y L   S M O G   I O N
C O P Y   A D A P T   A L S O
A L I   G A I A   I S L E T S
M E D I U M S C H O O L
  E R A   E N D   O V A
S C R I M S H A W   O A S I S
H A M S   T E D I U M T A L K
O P I E   A R E N T   O G L E
T O S S   R A N G E   M E A D
```

106

```
A B B A   R O S S   E M I T
S L O G   O N T A P   L O C I
H O U R   S E E Y A   S P I T
  W R E S T L I N G M A T C H
O H D E A R   N O O R   O L E
B A A   R U B   D I A P E R
O R I G A M I C L A S S
E D N A   B I O   I O W A
  L O W B A L L O F F E R
A R M A N I   A A S   F A T
F I T   I P S O   C H E C K S
E L E C T I O N S E A S O N
W E T S   N A I A D   P L E A
Z U N I   G R O G U   N O S H
S P A S   S N A P   U R S A
```

107

```
A M E N   R E G R O W   J O B
M A G I   O M E A R A   A D O
P H O N E N U M B E R   W E D
M I S T E D   E M B A S S Y
  E L O P E   I D O
  S T N S   A N D C R A F T S
C H A D   R E G A R D   L E A
A E R O S O L   N E S T I N G
P L O   T A L E S E   E F T S
O F T H E D A R K   B E E S
  C I A   R O L E S
M I A S M I C   A S H L E E
O R R   C O L L E C T I O N S
M I D   A T A S T E   R B I S
A S S   R A N D O S   T O D O
```

108

```
B A C K   M I L A N   T L C
E T N A   A D A G E   C H A R
S H O T T H E B O W   R A K E
T O T   A A A S   G O A T E E
  S E O U L   E I L I S H
  K N O C K D R A G O U T
I D I O T   R A I L   N R A
N I C K S   E N T   A R M O R
C S A   M A Y O   L I E N S
H A N D S A M E R I C A
  S T A I N S   C O L B Y
S T E N C H   E L E V   R I M
W E V E   U P S I D E C A K E
A R E S   N A O M I   U K E S
M S N   T Y S O N   B E S S
```

109

A	T	B	A	T			V	A	C	A	Y		M	E	L
M	A	O	R	I	S		A	M	O	R	E		O	L	E
P	I	C	K	E	T	H	L	I	N	E	S		V	I	A
M	L	K		D	U	A	L			B	I	O	S		
		P	U	B	L	I	C	T	O	I	L	E	T	H	
E	C	L	I	P	S	E		H	E	A	T	E	R		
T	H	I	N			A	R	T	S	C	H	O	O	L	
C	A	T		F	A	D	D	I	E	T	H		L	I	E
H	O	T	E	L	B	A	R	S			G	E	N	X	
		E	L	O	I	S	E		P	A	R	A	S	K	I
M	A	R	K	E	T	H	P	L	A	C	E	S			
E	B	B	S				O	A	T	S		L	I	P	
A	B	U		M	O	D	E	L	R	O	C	K	E	T	H
L	O	G		P	R	O	W	L		R	U	I	N	E	D
S	T	S		H	E	X	E	S		E	X	A	M	S	

110

C	A	M	I	S		T	O	R	T		T	R	A	P
L	E	E	C	H		O	V	E	R		H	E	H	E
A	R	E	T	H	A		R	A	D	I	O	D	I	I	T	S
S	A	C		H	U	E		D	O	L	E	O	U	T
S	T	U		S	T	R	E	W		D	U	N	N	E
I	O	T	A		T	O	R	A	H	S		E	A	R
C	R	E	C	H	E		A	R	E	A	S			
		S	H	O	R	T		F	I	L	M	S		
		E	L	L	E	N		S	T	O	O	P	S	
K	G	B		L	Y	R	I	S	T		G	U	R	U
I	R	A	T	E		M	A	L	E	K		L	O	G
S	O	R	O	R	A	L		I	D	A		M	T	A
S	U	P	E	R	S	T	O	R	M		P	C	U	S	E	R
M	O	L	T		M	A	I	L		P	A	I	G	E
E	N	Y	A		E	N	B	Y		A	R	C	E	D

111

P	A	L	S		I	N	C	A		S	A	L	A	D
E	L	A	N		T	E	A	S		A	R	O	M	A
N	O	M	A	T	T	E	R	H	O	W	M	U	C	H
S	T	A	I	R			P	E	N	H				
		L	A	P	S	E		C	O	O	L	T	O	
R	F	K		Y	O	U		F	E	R	R	I	E	D
E	R	I	C		O	R	C	A		S	A	T	E	D
P	U	S	H	T	H	E	E	N	V	E	L	O	P	E
A	T	S	E	A		D	O	N	E		S	U	E	S
S	T	I	C	K	T	O		I	T	S		T	E	T
T	I	N	K	E	R		P	E	S	O	S			
			F	I	S	H		H	A	T	C	H		
S	T	I	L	L	S	T	A	T	I	O	N	(E/A)	R	Y
I	N	D	I	A		A	S	I	A		T	R	I	P
S	T	O	C	K		T	E	E	N		A	S	T	O

112

S	U	C	K	S		A	M	P		A	B	E	T	S
O	R	N	O	T		P	A	R		I	L	L	B	E
N	N	N	N	I	C	S	C	I	E	N	T	I	S	T
			A	I	I	F	Y	C	A	T	S			
W	I	T		T	O	S	S	E	R	S		A	B	S
A	T	O	A	S	T			P	O	P	D	U	O	
I	A	M	B		H	I	C	K	S		A	D	D	S
F	L	O	U	R		C	U	E		K	I	D	D	O
	I	O	T	A		A	T	E		I	N	D	Y	
M	A	O		J	U	N	I	P	E	R		D	M	S
A	N	O		S	T	E	W	S			D	O	O	
R	I	O		I	C	E	P	A	C	K		D	V	R
I	C	O	N	S		V	A	T		E	Y	D	I	E
S	E	O	U	L		E	T	C		Y	O	D	E	L
A	S	O	N	E		N	T	H		S	U	D	S	Y

113

S	E	A	R	C	H		O	W	L		A	M	P
U	M	P	I	R	E		P	O	U	T		F	E	E
Z	I	P	P	E	R	M	E	R	G	E		F	T	C
I	L	L		W	E	I	R	D		A	G	O	R	A
E	Y	E	S		S	N	A	P	D	R	A	G	O	N
		P	A	Y		R	A	Y	B	A	N			
A	S	S	A	D		E	T	E	S		T	O	E
B	U	T	T	O	N	M	U	S	H	R	O	O	M	S
S	S	E		E	O	N	S		A	S	S	E	T
	H	I	S	S	A	T		A	W	L			
P	I	N	S	T	R	I	P	E	S		O	T	T	O
U	M	B	R	A		O	A	T	H	S		R	O	B
D	E	E		F	I	N	D	C	L	O	S	U	R	E
G	N	C		F	R	A	U		E	D	I	C	T	S
Y	U	K		A	L	A		Y	A	N	K	E	E

114

D	E	S	I		J	A	D	E			A	C	M	E
I	M	A	M		E	D	I	T		A	C	H	E	S
C	A	N	O	O	D	L	E	S		T	R	I	E	S
T	I	T		W	I	I	G		F	L	I	C	K	A
A	L	I	A	S		B	O	O	R	A	D	L	E	Y
T	E	A	L			H	U	N				E	R	S
E	D	G	E	S		L	I	M	I	T	S			
		O	X	Y	G	E	N	A	T	I	O	N		
			A	M	Y	T	A	N		S	L	A	S	H
A	H	S		B	R	B					V	I	L	E
T	A	T	T	O	O	E	R	S		C	E	L	I	A
T	R	A	I	L	S		E	A	C	H		F	D	R
I	M	P	E	I		P	A	T	O	O	T	I	E	S
R	E	L	I	C		S	L	U	G		E	L	I	A
E	D	E	N		I	M	P	S		D	E	N	Y

115

```
C H A I █ F I G H T █ W H O M
B O R N █ E N L A I █ H I V E
G R A B B E D A B I T E █ A J A R
B A S E D █ I N H A B I T A B L E
█ T A R T T █ O D S █
█ B L A M E █ R W A N D A N
S R I █ H A Z E █ H E A V E
A B O M I N A B L E S N O W M A N
R O O M Y █ O N T O █ U S E
A D S P A C E █ T E M P T █
█ A L E █ O H A R A █
A B R A C A D A B R A █ I S U Z U
H U T T █ A B C R U N C H E S
O B O E █ R E A D S █ O U R S
R E N D █ S Y S C O █ T H O R
```

116

```
D A T A █ A U R O R A █ S A G
E X E C █ P R O V E S █ E V A
V E N D N G M A C H █ N E S
█ C R E E █ D E B A R K
M A R █ E A N T O █ N E T T E
A L O N G █ T R A P █ L E S T
P E T A R D █ O H A R A █
█ C O V E R Y O U R E Y E S █
█ A T E U P █ K N E L L S
C H A R █ G R E Y █ O D O U R
D E T R O █ T R E D W █ N G S
C A T E R S █ L E N O █
A L L █ N O N E P R █ N T E R
S E E █ O P E N E R █ Y U L E
E R E █ T H E O R Y █ X B O X
```

117

```
L A B O R █ I D S █ E X I S T
A M I N O █ N A P █ R Y D E R
V I N C A █ D R E W A L I N E
A D D E D P U N C H █ E D D Y
█ M U S S █ I S M █
█ O C T A L █ S C H █ C P A
█ D R O P P E D T H E B A L L
M O O N █ C I A █ I D O L
B R O K E T H E R E C O R D
A S K █ B R O █ L O S E S
█ A B A █ J A I L █
O P A L █ S H O T S U B P A R
T O O K A H I K E █ M O O L A
I O N I C █ Y E A █ N U K E S
S H E E T █ A R M █ S T E E P
```

118

```
W H I T E █ M I A █ D E B A R
H I M O M █ E R R █ I N A N E
E H U D B A R A K █ S I E T E
N O S █ A B L E █ I N G R I D
█ B R N O █ I T E M █
I D L I K E T O B U Y A N E
P O U T E R █ N A P █ A L T
O N R E D █ T O R █ W A U G H
D O C █ A R F █ M O R R I E
█ W H (1) (2) L O F F O R T U N (3)
█ S V E N █ I N K Y █
V E R T E X █ O N E D █ A D O
C L E A R █ B O D Y A R M O R
R O A R S █ I Z E █ Y E A R S
S I R E E █ S Y R █ S A J A K
```

(1) BLANK (2) BLANK (3) BLANK

119

```
W O O D █ P A P E R █ V I S
A L F A █ E V O K E █ B E L T
D E F Y █ C E R E B R A L L Y
█ S P O C K █ S I L V E R
A T E █ H A D T O █ L I E G E
T R A D I T I O N A L █ T I N
T A K E N █ A P E X █ B Y T E
█ B A U M █ L E A R █
P F F T █ R O L O █ D A N C E
U R L █ A N N I V E R S A R Y
P E A R L █ D E E R E █ B Y E
P I N U P S █ A P H I S █
E G G B E A T E R S █ A S T R
T H E Y █ N O F E E █ N C A A
S T S █ G I F T S █ G O L D
```

120

```
R A T T A T █ I C E D T E A
I S E E N O W █ H O T D A M N
B E A T S M E █ O A R S M A N
█ T H E B I [GAP] P L E █ P I E
D D A Y █ B A L E
R O S S S E A █ P E A L
A N T █ H E L [GAP] I C T U R E S
G U E V A R A █ C A R R A C E
S T R I K I N [GAP] O S E █ D O L
█ E Y E S █ T H E P I L L
G N A W █ R O I S
O A K █ S I N [GAP] O R E A N █
L O R E L E I █ R E L I E V E
E M O T I O N █ B E E S W A X
M I N D T H E [GAP] █ S E E S T O
```

121

P	A	C	T			B	Y	M	E		H	A	L	T
O	V	E	R		C	R	O	A	T		U	C	L	A
M	E	N	U		H	E	Y	Y	A		H	I	C	K
P	E	T	E	R	O	T	O	O	L	E		D	O	E
O	N	E		A	C	T			E	F	R	O	N	
M	O	R	E	S	O		L	A	I	L	A	A	L	I
		A	T	L		I	P	O		R	I	J	N	
	I	S	A	A	C	N	E	W	T	O	N			
A	R	N	E		T	I	E		A	R	F			
P	A	U	L	R	Y	A	N		S	O	F	T	I	E
R	I	N	S	O			S	T	U		O	N	S	
O	L	D		I	V	A	N	K	A	T	R	U	M	P
P	S	A	T		A	B	O	U	T		A	C	A	I
O	A	T	S		T	B	O	N	E		G	A	T	E
S	T	E	P		S	A	N	K		U	N	E	S	

122

B	A	N	A	N	A	S		P	E	A	C	O	A	T
O	P	E	N	E	R	A		A	D	S	O	R	B	S
F	A	V	I	C	O	N		P	I	T	S	T	O	P
F	R	A	N	K	S	I	N	A	T	R	A			
			T	E	T	E		H	A	N	S	E	L	
R	A	D	I	I		Y	O	U		Y	O	W	Z	A
E	N	T	R	E	E		N	A	P		S	A	I	D
A	G	R	A		E	X	T	R	A		T	I	N	Y
M	O	A	N		L	I	E		W	A	R	N	E	D
E	R	I	C	S		S	T	D		B	A	S	S	I
R	A	N	O	U	T		R	E	A	R				
			N	I	S	S	A	N	S	E	N	T	R	A
A	B	U	T	T	A	L		A	P	A	I	R	O	F
C	A	R	R	E	R	A		D	E	S	C	A	N	T
E	M	B	A	S	S	Y		A	R	T	E	M	I	S

123

Q	U	A	D	S		J	E	W	S		B	R	I	E
E	F	R	O	N		I	M	O	K		M	E	N	U
D	O	C	T	O	R	N	O	N	O		A	F	A	R
		H	O	A	X		B	A	N	J	O	J	O	
A	C	C	E	P	T		L	I	L	A		R	A	P
B	O	O	M		E	M	A	G		C	O	M	M	A
E	L	L	A		D	A	Y		B	R	R			
L	E	T	M	Y	P	E	O	P	L	E	G	O	G	O
		B	E	G		V	I	A		A	J	A	R	
G	O	G	O	L		W	E	E	D		N	A	R	C
A	V	A		L	A	H	R		E	L	M	I	R	A
D	I	S	C	O	C	O		D	I	E	U			
D	E	C	O		M	A	K	E	I	T	S	O	S	O
E	D	A	M		E	M	I	L		H	I	J	A	B
D	O	P	E		S	I	D	E		E	C	O	L	I

124

S	P	A	C	E	J	A	M			D	E	S	K	
O	R	G	A	N	I	Z	E	R		S	I	N	C	E
W	O	E	B	E	G	O	N	E		A	N	T	O	N
S	O	N	A	R			C	E	L	E	R	O	N	
	F	A	R	O	N		T	O	L	E	R	A	T	E
		E	S	E		S	U	M	M	O	N	E	D	
	S	G	T		W	A	H	R			C	R	Y	
T	E	A	S		T	E	A	S	E		T	E	E	S
R	E	L			S	P	E	C		A	D	D		
I	N	A	S	T	A	T	E		H	S	N			
M	O	N	A	R	C	H	S		O	U	T	G	O	
N	E	T	L	I	K	E			R	A	I	S	E	
E	V	I	T	E		T	I	N	D	E	R	B	O	X
S	I	N	E	S		E	Q	U	I	T	A	B	L	E
S	L	E	D			S	T	R	E	S	S	E	D	

125

B	I	G	A	M	Y		E	G	G		A	L	M	A
O	N	E	S	I	E		N	R	A		L	E	I	S
A	S	T	H	M	A		C	O	S		E	C	O	L
S	E	N	I	O	R	P	R	O	J	E	C	T		
T	T	O	P	S		L	U	M	E	T		U	A	W
		A	G	E	S		T	H	O	R	P	E		
B	A	L	L		E	A	T		O	M	E	N	S	
B	R	A	I	S	E	D		D	E	S	I	R	E	E
G	O	R	M	E		S	R	I		T	S	A	R	
U	P	R	O	A	R		I	O	N	A				
N	E	Y		T	A	N	G	O		N	A	B	O	B
	B	R	O	K	E	N	P	R	O	M	I	S	E	
A	S	I	A		I	V	E		A	M	I	N	O	R
M	A	R	V		S	E	T		G	I	S	E	L	E
B	O	D	E		H	R	S		S	E	S	T	E	T

126

A	R	M	A	N	I			P	O	S	I	N	G	
S	E	A	S	O	N	E	D		A	L	L	M	E	N
S	E	T	H	R	O	G	E	N		S	E	E	T	H	R	U
E	S	T	A	S		K	A	N			I	O	U	S
S	E	E	M	E	D		F	L	A	G				
			S	I	N	G	L	E	T	H	R	E	A	D
A	S	T	A		S	I	E		A	L	I	C	I	A
D	A	R	N		T	E	H	R	A	N		D	O	R	M
D	M	I	T	R	I		I	R	E		E	L	S	E
N	E	P	H	R	O	L	O	G	I	S	T			
		A	W	L	S			T	U	G	S	O	N	
N	S	E	C		E	V	A		M	A	N	N	A	
E	H	R	L	I	C	H		H	&	R	B	L	O	C	K
D	E	B	T	O	R		S	E	A	L	A	B	L	E
S	K	E	E	T	S			M	E	S	S	E	D	

127

```
P L A S M A S   O C T   S R O
C A L C U L I   R H O   P E R
T H E A G E D T E A M   E T A
    R A C E W A R   A E O N
D E N E B   B A D G E D D O G
S M O R E S     E R R O L S
L A T     K N E W   I A M
  J A C K I E C H A N G E D
  L O D   W O O S   T A G
S A L U K I     S L E E V E
T V T R A G E D Y   E R R E D
B A H T   N A N E T T E
E T E   V I S A G E D C A R D
D A R   I T E   G L I T T E R
E R E   N E D   S E E S A W S
```

128

```
R E P O   O R B   R O S E S
E L A N   B E L   L A T O Y A
F I R E S I D E   A S T L E Y
E C A S H   D U T C H O V E N
R I D   E S E   Y E A   E X O
S T E E L T R A P   D E F A T
    E V E   F E B   N O M O
    E L E V A T O R C A R
S L U E   E A R   E T C
H A R D G   B A R N S T O R M
A P O   A R B   O T C   T E A
B A C K S T A G E   A P O L O
B L O U S E   O P E N D O O R
A M I N E S   L E G   A L A I
T A N G S   F R O   S E N S
```

129

```
(B)O S N I A   C A B   A V E(O)
A S P E C T   U N U   R A G U
C H E C K M A R K S   A N O S
H A W K   B L A C K L I S T
  T E A L   H O S T
  F B I A G E N T   H E Y H O
T A L E S E   A R C   A F A R
O R U   Y E A R E N D   A Z T
A G E D   S L C   O U T I E S
D O J O S   P O S T C A R D
  A G U A   P E E N
F A C E V A L U E   K O B E
I N K A   M A T C H M A K E R
N Y E R   C P A   A I R I N G
(K)A T S   O S H   M A D E D O(O)
```

130

```
D R O U G H T   B E D   G A B
W E L L N O W   E D U A R D O
A D D U P T O   E Y E W E A R
R A I L   A H A B   T E A M O
F L E A   S I R E E   E S A U
S E S T O   T O A D   K I N G
  E R R   U R G E   E C H
T P S   F O U N D E D   R E S
H O P   F U N D   S A M
O L A F   G I T S   M A S S E
R A M A   H O H O S   T A L L
O R B I T   N E W T   T R O I
U S O T O U R   H A S H O U T
G E T H O M E   A R R A N G E
H A S   L A P   T R O U G H S
```

131

```
E X T O L   E V I T E   R I B
K E A N E   P E N I N   A M A
G R E A T H O R N E D O W L S
    I M A C S     O B I T
S E C R E T H A N D S H A K E
E P A     A A H   R E D
W I S P S   G E I S E L
  C H A N G E O F H E A R T
  C A N O N S   P O I S E
A B A   F A D   C A M
C O M P U T E R H A C K E R S
T R O U   O R I O N
S E E N B U T N O T H E A R D
O R B   I P O D S   O L D I E
N S A   C A P O S   S L O P E
```

132

```
P R O   A N D   C O N
N I V E   K S O U T   B O N O
O F E R   V E R S E   F I D E
M E N A D E S   T R O L L E D
    S I T   C H A
S C I E N C E   G E S T I O N
T O N S   H I B I T   S O D Y
A M S   N E R   N I E
N E T O   G E A L S   S I S T
S T R A I N S   S T R I C T S
    T R A   A I R
F I T E E R S   C L A I M E D
I F E R   L O G U E   N O T E
C H E S   S O R T S   G R A M
T E M   T E S   N T O
```

133

```
R A F T █ G A B S █ S W I S H
E L L A █ O B O E █ C O R F U
A F A R █ H A S N O O O M P H
P A P A D O C █ T H R E A D S
█ █ █ I M U S █ W E D █ █ █
T O O O N E S I D E D █ B E N
O Z A R K █ D E L █ S O L O
T A K E S I T █ B L E W O F F
E W E S █ D A D █ T A L I A
D A N █ Z O O O C C U P A N T
█ █ S E T █ S H A D █ █
B I S T R O S █ E R E C T E D
I G L O O O W N E R █ H E R O
L E O N I █ A E R O █ A R I Z
L T G E N █ M O S T █ D I C E
```

134

```
S T A R D O M █ S P O U S E
M I N O R C A █ C H U R R O S
O D D D U C K █ A U T O B O T
G A S █ G U E S S T I M A T E
█ L O S █ P L U S █ T E N █
█ █ L A Y O P E N █ O H S O
F L U I D █ V E T T E █ I O U
D O N T O V E R T H I N K I T
I C I █ S E N S E █ N O E L S
C H O O █ G O T P A S T █ █
█ N A T █ T A L L █ A B C █
T U R K E Y W R A P S █ A H H
O P E N S E A █ Y A L E L A W
P O P U L A R █ E C O N O M Y
O N S T A R █ R A G T O P S
```

135

```
█ S L A M █ A C I D █ S U L A
S T O R E B R A N D █ A N E W
W E R E R A B B I T █ L I F E
I V E █ C R U S T █ T E X T S
G E N D E R S █ O H M █ █
█ █ O D E █ P O N E █ A P P
P R O P E L L E R B E A N I E
T A K E S F O R G R A N T E D
S T A R B U C K S O R D E R S
D E Y █ E L K S █ A L E █ █
█ █ I N S █ O D Y S S E Y
G L I T Z █ F L O W S █ E M U
L A G S █ P L A Z A H O T E L
A T O M █ I O W E Y O U O N E
M E R E █ T E N D █ W I N D
```

136

```
G A Y M E C C A █ I M B I B E
O V E R L O R D █ F O R C E D
R E T A I N E R █ S C R E E D
P R I Z E █ P I C A S █ M R I
█ █ L E T F L Y █ F A K E
R I P E █ P I T A █ T A C O █
O N A N D O N █ W A R T H O G
M A T R I X █ █ B E L I Z E
A C R O N Y M █ B I K I N I S
C O L T █ B A R D █ P E E I
C U L L █ V A L U E S █ █
A R C █ T E S T S █ K E M P T
M A A L O X █ E Q U A L P A Y
E T R A D E █ R U S T L E U P
L E S B O S █ S E A E A G L E
```

137

```
G O P R O █ D I L I █ G D A Y
A V I A N █ U R A L █ R E P O
E E R I E █ R E Y K J A V I K
A R A L █ K A N E █ O Z O N E
█ S T R A N G E R T H I N G S
O L E O L E █ C I N E █ █
D E B A T E T E A M S █ B B S
D E A D █ D A R K O █ N E A T
S P Y █ S E C R E T S A N T A
█ █ S E E K █ H E I G H T
C L E A N P L A T E C L U B
H A L L S █ E D I E █ C R O P
I R E M E M B E R █ R A I M I
N A N O █ M O L E █ P R O B S
O M A N █ A X E D █ M E N S A
```

138

```
S H I V E R M E T I M B E R S
H O T E L C A L I F O R N I A
E T H N I C R E L A T I O N S
E T A T █ O R A L █ H A R K S
P O P █ L Y N █ T E R M S █
█ █ P I C A █ O D O R S █ █
S T E P H █ D R U G S █ S A X
F U N S I Z E █ D A D J O K E
O T S █ L E V I S █ A Q U A S
█ █ N I K O N █ R Y A N █ █
█ G L O V E █ G T A █ D R E
W H I N E █ A R O D █ S W A B
H A T E R S G O N N A H A T E
I N E E D A H U G E F A V O R
G A R D E N A P A R T M E N T
```

139

F	R	E	S	H	■	S	A	K	E	B	O	M	B	■
L	E	X	I	E	■	A	L	P	H	A	M	A	L	E
E	N	T	R	Y	■	I	M	H	U	M	B	L	E	D
W	O	R	E	■	P	D	A	■	D	A	R	T	E	D
A	V	A	■	E	L	A	N	D	■	■	E	S	P	Y
K	A	M	A	L	A	H	A	R	R	I	S	■	■	■
I	T	I	S	N	T	■	C	O	E	N	■	N	B	C
T	O	L	K	I	E	N	■	P	E	S	K	I	E	R
E	R	E	■	N	A	A	N	■	B	E	A	G	L	E
■	■	■	Y	O	U	V	E	G	O	T	T	H	I	S
I	S	E	E	■	Y	O	L	K	S	■	T	E	C	■
M	I	L	O	R	D	■	N	A	S	■	C	O	V	E
A	L	A	M	A	I	S	O	N	■	A	R	W	E	N
N	O	T	A	F	R	A	I	D	■	R	E	L	I	T
■	S	E	N	A	T	O	R	S	■	T	E	S	T	S

140

P	E	S	T	■	R	A	D	I	O	S	H	A	C	K
A	R	I	A	■	I	R	O	N	M	A	I	D	E	N
T	R	A	P	■	D	E	N	T	A	L	C	A	R	E
H	O	M	E	R	■	S	T	E	N	O	■	M	A	W
■	R	E	S	I	N	■	B	R	I	M	■	■	■	■
O	P	S	■	C	U	B	E	■	S	E	M	P	L	E
F	R	E	S	H	M	E	A	T	■	A	R	E	A	■
F	O	C	I	■	B	E	S	O	T	■	D	O	G	S
A	N	A	T	■	■	S	T	R	I	K	E	P	A	Y
L	E	T	H	A	L	■	R	O	L	E	■	A	L	A
■	■	■	B	A	B	A	■	■	L	E	T	G	O	■
D	N	A	■	I	V	A	N	S	■	P	R	A	W	N
R	O	U	N	D	I	N	G	U	P	■	A	N	N	E
O	N	T	H	E	S	C	E	N	T	■	I	D	E	A
P	O	O	L	S	H	A	R	K	S	■	T	A	R	T

141

S	C	O	F	F	■	R	E	P	E	N	T	S	■
A	I	L	E	D	■	B	E	S	E	R	I	O	U	S
U	N	D	E	R	C	O	V	E	R	A	G	E	N	T
N	E	T	S	■	O	S	U	■	■	E	T	T	E	■
A	M	I	■	B	I	C	E	P	■	B	L	A	Z	E
S	A	M	P	A	N	■	I	P	A	■	P	U	P	■
■	X	E	R	I	S	C	A	P	I	N	G	■	■	■
■	■	Y	E	L	L	O	W	P	A	G	E	S	■	■
■	■	Z	O	O	P	L	A	N	K	T	O	N	■	■
A	S	P	■	U	T	E	■	O	O	Z	I	E	R	■
B	E	A	S	T	■	S	T	A	L	K	■	L	O	O
C	A	M	O	■	U	S	A	■	E	T	N	A	■
T	H	E	C	O	A	S	T	I	S	C	L	E	A	R
V	A	L	K	Y	R	I	E	S	■	P	A	S	T	E
■	G	A	S	L	I	N	E	■	A	N	T	E	D	■

142

B	O	T	H	■	O	S	I	R	I	S	■	H	B	O
R	H	E	A	■	U	P	T	O	N	O	G	O	O	D
A	I	M	S	■	S	E	C	O	N	D	W	I	N	D
T	O	P	N	O	T	C	H	■	■	D	E	S	K	S
■	■	■	T	O	N	E	S	■	G	L	I	N	T	S
I	F	F	I	E	R	■	L	O	A	N	■	■	■	■
R	E	A	D	S	■	B	A	B	Y	G	A	T	E	S
K	A	T	E	■	T	A	P	A	S	■	S	U	R	E
S	T	E	A	D	Y	G	I	G	■	D	I	X	I	E
■	■	■	E	K	E	S	■	D	E	F	E	N	D	■
■	R	A	F	A	E	L	■	V	A	L	I	D	■	■
W	O	R	L	D	■	■	G	A	Y	I	C	O	N	S
A	D	I	O	S	A	M	I	G	O	■	A	C	A	I
R	E	S	P	E	C	T	F	U	L	■	R	A	I	D
M	O	E	■	T	E	A	S	E	D	■	E	T	R	E

143

C	H	E	F	S	K	I	S	S	■	C	L	I	F	F
Y	O	G	A	P	A	N	T	S	■	H	E	N	R	I
B	O	R	N	A	G	A	I	N	■	I	N	D	E	X
E	K	E	■	Y	A	R	N	■	A	N	D	I	E	■
R	A	G	A	■	N	O	T	E	T	O	S	E	L	F
C	H	I	C	K	■	W	E	L	L	S	■	B	A	A
A	B	O	D	E	S	■	D	I	A	■	S	A	N	K
F	A	U	C	E	T	S	■	A	S	K	A	N	C	E
E	R	S	■	P	A	R	E	S	■	A	N	D	E	S
■	■	■	S	I	T	I	N	■	E	T	S	■	■	■
B	I	D	E	T	S	■	G	O	T	A	S	E	C	■
A	C	R	I	D	■	H	A	B	A	N	E	R	O	S
S	A	Y	N	O	M	O	R	E	■	A	R	O	M	A
E	L	L	E	W	O	O	D	S	■	S	I	D	E	D
S	L	Y	■	N	O	F	E	E	■	F	E	T	E	■

144

B	E	D	I	N	A	B	A	G	■	M	A	L	A	R
E	N	R	O	U	T	E	T	O	■	A	L	O	N	E
L	E	A	N	R	I	G	H	T	■	G	O	T	T	A
■	■	G	I	S	T	■	E	O	L	I	T	H	I	C
P	R	I	Z	E	■	R	I	T	A	■	■	A	F	T
R	E	N	E	■	P	U	S	H	U	P	B	R	A	S
E	A	T	■	M	O	N	T	E	R	E	Y	■	■	■
P	R	O	N	O	U	N	■	■	R	E	D	U	C	E	D
■	■	■	G	E	N	E	R	A	L	S	■	H	A	Y
S	H	O	O	T	C	R	A	P	S	■	T	I	R	E
A	O	L	■	E	S	P	Y	■	P	O	O	L	S	■
C	H	I	R	A	S	H	I	■	T	E	R	M	■	■
R	O	V	E	D	■	I	N	D	I	A	P	E	R	S
A	H	E	A	D	■	G	O	N	E	R	O	G	U	E
L	O	R	D	S	■	H	E	A	R	T	R	A	T	E

145

```
A I R . . G P A . . S T E P T O
P R E Q U E L S . . H A T E R S
T A Q U E R I A . . A L A N I S
. Q U E S T . . W I K I . . C O O
. . I S S U E . . S U S H I .
A G R A . . R U M O R M I L L
B L E D . . B R A T . . A T S E A
L E D I N . . O R O . . N O H O W
E A R L E . . Z I N E . . P A N E
. M E L A T O N I N . . F R E D
. A A R O N . . C H E A P .
D O D . . S E E M . . A R D E N
O R I S I T . . L E N I E N C Y
D E N A D A . . B A C K S E A T
D O G L E G . . T E A . . R A D
```

146

```
B I B I M B A P . . V I S A G E
O R A T O R I O . . I M P R O V
B E S T R O D E . . S O L U T E
A S S Y R I A . . M I N I B A R
. . . B I L . . J O G . . T A T S
S E M I S . . G E N O A .
I C E T . . H O T S T R E A K S
T H A T H I T S T H E S P O T
H O L Y S M O K E S . . T O F U
. T A P I R . . S A P I D
A P R S . . L E S . . L E T .
F R E E G A N . . L I N E M A N
L O V E L Y . . S A B O T A G E
A N E M I A . . A V E R A G E S
C E L E B S . . G A L A X I E S
```

147

```
A C T S . . R A N T S . . A D D S
R A V E . . A L O H A . . T O O T
I N S T A N T W I N . . A T T A
. W E L L D A M N . . B L I N I
P E R I O D . . O K B O O M E R
A N I S E . . T R A I N S E T S
P O E T . . B E E G E E S .
I T S . . N O S T A R S . . C P A
. D I G T H I S . . D R A Y
F R Y I N G P A N . . S U I T E
L E A V E S I N . . B E G E T S
E T H E R . . L E M O N A D E
T I E R . . C O V E R S T O R Y
C R A G . . S T E R E . . T U N A
H E R E . . I S R E D . . I T S Y
```

148

```
D R E W B A C K . . O M I T
N E U R A L N E T . . M E M E
A F R I K A N E R S . . A T O N
L I E G E S . . P A T . . N A V Y
A N K H S . . L A C E S . . D E E
B E A T . . B O C K . . T I A R A
. C O W L S . . A S T I R
. Y E A H A B O U T T H A T .
P O S S E . . A S I D E .
H U C K S . . L E T S . . G A S P
S A O . . S O L E S . . T O S C A
T W O S . . R E Y . . T A S S E L
R A T E . . G R E W A S P I N E
I K E A . . S O I L T E S T S
P E R M . . N I C E L I S T
```

149

```
. P H O T O A P P S .
. T H E N E W B L A C K .
. S H O R T S W E A T H E R .
P L I N T H S . . T S E L I O T
I O N I Z E . . T S E T S E
T A L C . . R A I M I . . P E E N
A N Y . . J A M P A C K . . L S D
. G O D F O R B I D .
. O O H I M S C A R E D .
. R H I N O . . G I V E S .
T E E N S . . M A P . . N I C A D
A T M S . . M O M O A . . A L L Y
M E G A C O R P O R A T I O N
E L E N A D E L L E D O N N E
S L E E V E L E S S D R E S S
```

150

```
F R U I T T A R T . . G A S P S
O O M P A H P A H . . A D O R E
T U N A M E L T S . . R U B O N
O X O . . A P A T . . O R L E S S
. . X R A Y L A B . . T R E E
A P P E A L . . E L S A S .
B E E R . . E A S I E R . . V I M
L E T S T H I N G S S L I D E
E R A . . W O M A N S . . A N N A
. B A R A K . . E L W O O D
J O E L . . S T E P D A D .
I N R O M E . . B L O T . . F E W
L E I C A . . V I A V E N E T O
T A C K Y . . A T T E N U A T E
S L A Y S . . R E A R T I R E S
```

151


```
WINNER   ■ ■  PLANBS
WHOOPI   ■  MAOSUIT
IAMBIC   ■  DOUGHBOY
■  TOUCHSENSOR  ■
CERTS ■ WAKE ■ APPT
LIES ■ SITE ■ SMORE
ATF ■ CATHY ■ ASTIN
WHO ■ ZXCVBNM ■ ADD
SERTA ■ HARES ■ TEA
ARMOR ■ BLEW ■ COPY
TEES ■ LALA ■ CASAS
■ PEACEDOLLAR ■
CLEARSKY ■ PILLAR
SEARATS ■ UNMADE
IGUESS ■ SEEDED
```

152

```
ACNE ■ GAME ■ RUSTS
THOR ■ OPEN ■ IDAHO
TONI ■ THATSSOYOU
ICANDOIT ■ CENSUS
COP ■ END ■ SRA
■ HORSE ■ COINFLIP
SOLOS ■ WARPDRIVE
ELOPE ■ ERR ■ SIMON
TIGERLILY ■ HAIRS
ICYSTARE ■ DIRTY
■ WMD ■ TON ■ ECO
ANEMIA ■ SHEEPDOG
DOZENROSES ■ URAL
AGREE ■ UNTO ■ MUSE
MOATS ■ ISAK ■ ANTS
```

153

```
PASCALSTRIANGLE
INTIMATEAPPAREL
TOOTIREDTOTHINK
SSN ■ SCREEDS ■ MGM
AMID ■ HOURS ■ FATE
WINES ■ IMS ■ SACHA
SAGCARDS ■ PHTEST
■ IPOS ■ MART ■
AIMLOW ■ TAKEACAB
TRUER ■ SIR ■ WILLA
LESS ■ PARIS ■ LULL
APE ■ ARMANIS ■ BEL
SETAGOODEXAMPLE
EATDESSERTFIRST
STEADYASSHEGOES
```

154

```
■ BANDMATE ■ CST
■ MOUSEOVER ■ CHAR
TEATASTING ■ RIMA
OTTO ■ KHAN ■ RULED
GUESTS ■ INEXILE
OPRAH ■ OASIS ■ DOW
■ VERBIAGE ■ OVA
WIRELESSCHARGER
ADE ■ OMELETTE ■
RAD ■ RISES ■ EARLS
CRAVATS ■ ADDOIL
RELAX ■ OPER ■ UPTO
AYES ■ EVILEMPIRE
FORT ■ TELLNOONE
TUT ■ CREATING
```

155

```
SMACKDAB ■ ASLANT
EAGLEOWL ■ MOOCOW
IHEARYOU ■ ENTIRE
ZOOMBOMBING ■ DIE
EMUS ■ GABS ■ WRIST
SET ■ PANELTRUCKS
■ SOHO ■ REOIL ■
■ FETED ■ TOTEM ■
■ ATEIT ■ ERAS ■
SWIVELCHAIR ■ KTS
MINER ■ TENT ■ NEAP
USB ■ MOUNTSHASTA
REEBOK ■ OHBOTHER
FUTURA ■ REALTALK
SPACEY ■ MMDDYYYY
```

156

```
EBAY ■ TIKI ■ BEGET
MOLE ■ ONUS ■ AMORE
MOUTHWASH ■ HITON
ATM ■ EACH ■ GODS
■ AIWA ■ SLURPEE
HANDSANITIZER ■
TWEETY ■ KYLO ■ ISU
MEWS ■ ENE ■ PSAS
LDS ■ REDO ■ CREOLE
■ WINDOWCLEANER
OPOSSUM ■ HUNT
AIRS ■ LATE ■ SPA
SETUP ■ SALTWATER
ETHER ■ TYKE ■ HARM
SAYSO ■ USSR ■ ARTY
```

157

```
C O N S U L ■ I N S P I R I T
A P O L L O ■ S E T A D A T E
R E C A N T ■ F A R C I C A L
D R A M A ■ S A T E ■ D E L L
T A M S ■ S C H L E P ■ D Y S
A G E ■ S P R A Y T A N ■ ■ ■
B O R D E R O N ■ S P I C E D
L E A R N E D ■ O M A K A S E
E R S A T Z ■ P L A C E N T A
■ ■ W I Z A R D R Y ■ N A T
P G A ■ N A M E I T ■ R O T H
A R U M ■ T O M E ■ M I N E R
S U R E S U R E ■ M A S A L A
T F A S E R A D ■ O N E D A Y
A L L H E A L S ■ S I N E W S
```

158

```
G I T M O ■ P A L ■ ■ G A H
A S W A N ■ I D I G ■ E R G O
G H O S T ■ C A M E C L E A N
■ ■ P E A S ■ M A T H L E T E
S C O R P I O ■ R A I D E D
A R I A ■ S U N S E T S ■ ■
M A N T A ■ T A P A S ■ S H O
O P T I C A L I L L U S I O N
A S S ■ C R A V E ■ P E R S E
■ R E T W E E T ■ M E T A
R E W I N D ■ N O M I N A L
A L I S T E R S ■ P O T S ■
N U D E S C E N E ■ L O O S E
O D O R ■ O V A L ■ A N N I E
N E W ■ ■ S P F ■ R E G A L
```

159

```
M U S T B E N I C E ■ A P B S
O B A M A B I D E N ■ C H A T
N E W Z E A L A N D ■ T O D O
I R E ■ R Y E ■ S I L E N T O
C E R A ■ C U T A D E A L
A D S L O G A N S ■ T U T S I
■ G E R U N D S ■ P A T E
R I D ■ R A T P A C K ■ G E S
O R I T ■ F O O T A G E ■
B E R R A ■ C L A M B A K E S
A F T E R A L L ■ T A L C
B O B A T E A ■ Y A M ■ F D A
A R I D ■ T V R E P O R T E R
N E K O ■ N E X T P L E A S E
K E E N ■ A S S I S T A N T S
```

160

```
X R A Y E Y E S ■ A R A F A T
X O X O X O X O ■ R E L A T E
X Y L O P H O N E M A L L E T
■ ■ H O O T ■ C Y R I L ■
I P S O ■ H I T O N ■ N E S T
S H O O ■ O C A L A ■ A Q U A
A O L ■ R E V ■ L U R K
I B A R ■ P A T S Y ■ L I V E
D I R E ■ E R A ■ N I T
N A P S ■ T E R S E ■ C O V E
O S L O ■ S T E A L ■ O X E N
■ E R A T O ■ F I N N ■
T E X T B O O K E X A M P L E
R O U T E R ■ O L I V E O Y L
I N S O L E ■ P Y R E N E E S
```

161

```
D C B A S E D ■ K E E P T O
A L I S T E R S ■ O R E L A N
G O T T A C A T C H E M A L L
A V E R Y ■ G I R L S ■ S K A
M E M O ■ T I C O S ■ C A I N
A R E ■ R I N K S ■ C A N E D
■ B O O T Y S H O R T S
■ K I N G O F B E E R S
■ M E D I A C I R C U S
G O T O N ■ O N E H R ■ B E T
O V E N ■ P U G E T ■ M A L E
O I L ■ B A R E D ■ D A M N S
G E O C E N T R I C O R B I T
L A N C E D ■ S N O W C O N E
E D E S S A ■ G O D H O O D
```

162

```
L I F E H A C K ■ L E A N O N
I M A M O R O N ■ A R C A N E
B A R E N E C E S S I T I E S
I R O N S ■ K E A T S ■ L O T
D E E D ■ C E L T S ■ G E N E
O T S ■ P A R E S ■ Y O D O G
■ A I M E D ■ T U B I N G
O L D S O U L ■ D I L A T E S
H A I K U S ■ F I N E D ■
S T E M S ■ B O G G S ■ N Y U
T E T E ■ M O R S E ■ M I E N
O S S ■ S O D O I ■ R O G E R
P H O T O S Y N T H E S I Z E
I O D I N E ■ C E R B E R U S
T W A N G S ■ E S S A Y I S T
```

163

```
. C O D E R E D . . T G I F .
. M A C A R O N I . L I L M O
M A T H T E S T S . E R A S E
U L T R A . T E C H D E M O .
D A R E . M E R G E . D O S E
B Y E . F A R . O A F . R O D
A S A N A S . T L D R . O R E
T I T A N . C O F F E E U R N
H A S I T A L L . A R T S Y .
. . L A V A L A K E S . . . .
. J I F . A P P L E . Y M C A
C A N I T . L O S T S O U L .
O M E L E T P A N . O H A R A
S U P E R S I Z E . T O N E R
A P T . N A N A . S P A S M .
```

164

```
W A S H . T E E M S . E T N A
A L P O . R A M O S . T H O R
F L I R T A T I O N . H E S S
T E E N A G E R S . S I R E .
S N L . B I N . U L C E R S .
. . . L U C . M E S A . M I A
. . S O L O P A R E N T I N G
. W H O A M I K I D D I N G .
P A I N R E L I E V E R S . .
E R R . A D E N . E R E . . .
I M E A S Y . O H O . T B A .
. E L L A . G E N I U S B A R
I D L E . M U S I C S T A N D
S T E P . G A S O L . A L T O
M O S H . S C O N E . B L U R
```

165

```
B O G . H A D U P . B L I S S
A V I . A L E R O . R U N T O
N E V E R F E L T B E T T E R
G R E W D I M . B E N Z E N E
. N O P E . G R A D . L O L .
T A N K A . B R O G A N . . .
U S A . S C R A W L . A G E S
G A M E S H O W N E T W O R K
S P E C . O W L I S H . I R A
. . O O P S I E . E R N S T .
A S H . A P E X . S M O G . .
T H E A T E R . A T A L O S S
B A R B E D W I R E F E N C E
A M B E R . A C T I I . C A M
T E S T S . R E Y N A . E M I
```

166

```
S E A M A P . . F L O A T S
P O P T A R T . S E N S E I
I C E S H O W S . T O T I N G
G E M . S I P H O N . T A N .
O N E W A Y T R I P . W B A .
T E N A M . T I S . T C E L L
. H E W E N T T H E R E . .
. W I N O R G O H O M E . .
. W I N D O W F R A M E . .
P A N E S . A L Y . A N S E L
E K E . G R I N D S T O N E .
T A T . E I S N E R . B E N .
S N O O D S . G R E A T E S T
A D U N I T . D A D V I C E .
T A R O T S . R E S T O N .
```

167

```
F I F T H S . M A D A M .
U N R E A L . O X E Y E S .
J O A N N E . R E L E N T S .
I T T A K E S A L L S O R T S
. N E P A L . A I R I E R .
. S T R O L L S . R A V E S .
. R I S E N . Y U M . H E L L
M I D . D I D . M E H . F E Y
S T E P . T A G . T U D O R .
N A D A L . D E J A G E R .
B O O Y A H . T O P U P . .
C R O S S O F F T H E L I S T
. A R T S I E R . O N E S I E
. S U I S S E . R O T A T E .
. B E T T E . S T E W E D .
```

168

```
C H A R T . S P F . O W L S
R O M A N A C L E F . L E O S
A R E N T W E A L L . D I O N
I S N T . A N Y T A K E R S .
G E T . W I T H . K I N D E R
. R O B O T . O P E D . S E A
B A T O N . C O R D . C O N K
T C H O T C H K E . C R U D E
S E A T . L A Y A B O U T S .
. S T Y L E D . C O N S . .
. . C I O . R H Y T H M S .
P I L A F . R A I S E H E L L
A D U L T S I T E . S A D I E
D E C L U T T E R . T R I M S
S A Y . P L E D . D A Y S .
```

169

```
A S T O N I S H . . . . S T U B
S C R E E N C A P . G O O D E
S H O R T F A L L . E R R O R
A W L . S I L L Y S T R I N G
Y A L L . N E O . P A Y . . .
. . I T I S W H A T I T I S
P R O F I T . S I C . A I D E
H O M E G Y M . M E N S R E A
E L A L . P O P . W O K E S T
W E R E D O N E H E R E . . .
. . S O O . D A S . D O E S
C O N S U L T A N T S . H A H
A D I O S . O L D E L P A S O
M I L N E . M E T R O A R E A
O N E S . . . . D O N T T E L L
```

170

```
O M N I . A B U T . . C L A M
L O I N C L O T H . O H A R A
D O G N A P P E R . C A K E S
. S H U T . P R E S C I E N T
. . M A H . O A H U . G A S
A R S E N I C . T O R M E . .
H O U R . S U P E R S O N I C
A B R A . P R I N T . Z E N O
S O F T T A R G E T . A V I D
. T E E N Y . D O G M A T A
N T H . R I F F . N O B . .
I R E N E C A R A . N I C K
C A N E S . V E L A Z Q U E Z
H Y E N A . O D D C O U P L E
E S T A . R O O T . E S P N
```

171

```
C A R P A Y M E N T . C R A P
O R E O C O O K I E . L O L L
M E D S T U D E N T . A C L U
M O D I S H . . J E T S K I S
A L I T . E S T A . R H I N O
S A T . B A T H T O Y . D A N
. . M A R R Y U P . R O L E
T V G U I D E . R E F I L L S
W O O D . M E A T R U B . .
I T O . S E T P L A N . E B B
H E D D A . S P E C . A M I E
A D V I L P M . A L L O T S
R O I D . H A N D P U P P E T
D U B S . D R I V E S H O M E
S T E T . S T A R S H A P E D
```

172

```
C A T F I S H E S . T O A S T
O N E I N C O M E . R U L E D
L O N G P A U S E . A T L A S
. . S A L S . S K I R T . .
I T T . I D E S . A L O H A S
T O W . N E W H I R E . E D U
A R I D . D I E H A R D F A N
L O T U S . N B A . S E E P S
I N T H E W E E D S . F E T E
A T E . T I S A N E S . L E T
N O R M A N . R O N A . S R S
. . F U D G E . I S L A . .
O P E R A . R A D I O D I A L
W H E A T . O P E N M A T T E
S I D L E . S T A G E M O M S
```

173

```
A S A P . O C H R E . D J E D
P A P E R T R A I L . Y O G A
P A S T A S A U C E . S H O D
. B E A V . S T E P S O N S
. L E T H E . H I N D . .
I A M . R A T . W A X . R A G
T R A V E L E D I N S T Y L E
A R R I V E S O N T H E D O T
L I V E I N T H E M O M E N T
O D E . E T S . T A O . N E O
. L A W S . S A N T A . .
. W O R S H I P S . E V E S
D I V E . O R A T O R I C A L
I K E A . W A T E R S L I D E
S I R S . S N E R D . A G E D
```

174

```
L O G I C . O T I S . T I L T
O P E N I N G A C T . E M I R
B A N K R O L L E D . N O N O
O L E . C R E E P . D U V E T
. . S U M S . L A U R E N . .
C A N O L A . B A R T E R . .
E B O L A . F A N C Y T H A T
L E V A R . I R E . F R E D O
S T A R F L E E T . R A R E R
. . S P I E L S . D E C E N T
. . S C A L E D . W E E K . .
P H O N E . T E E N S . M O M
R A T E . C R U N C H T I M E
E V I L . B I R D H O U S E S
P E A S . S P O T . P E O N S
```

175

176

177

178

179

180

181

```
I M H O ■ S P A C E F O R C E
C O A X ■ T E L E N O V E L A
E N V Y ■ A D A M D R I V E R
P O E ■ C R A N E ■ D U A L
A R A G O R N ■ N A S ■ P R Y
C A P U L E T ■ T H A T
K I L L E D I T ■ I M A C
■ L A P S ■ C O T ■ S P A R
■ N E L L ■ Y A M M E R O N
■ D A I S ■ Q U I T E S O
S T Y ■ W E K ■ U P T O B A T
C H E F ■ A L E P H ■ E R A
R E A L M A T U R E ■ B A I L
I M S O O V E R I T ■ O R E O
M E T R O A R E A S ■ P S S T
```

182

```
S M A C K D O W N ■ W H A L E
T A M A L E P I E ■ H O M E Y
R H I N E G O L D ■ I R E N E
A R T ■ E A R L ■ I T S S A D
Y E O W ■ S T A N D E E
■ B A H ■ O R E O S ■ S P F
B A L L E T ■ D O N A T E T O
O N A L A R K ■ S O L O C U P
W E M A D E I T ■ T E T R I S
E W E ■ C A R O M ■ S E E
■ N O T S P A M ■ S T A T
B A D G U Y ■ G R A S ■ W H O
O C E A N ■ B E A C H C O M B
O R B I T ■ C A C A O T R E E
R O T O S ■ C R A W D A D D Y
```

183

```
B E L T ■ W A L T Z ■ A C T S
O N E A T A T I M E ■ Z A H N
B R A K E F L U I D ■ E P E E
C A D E N T ■ S T R I F F
A G U A ■ S E E S ■ H A T E R
T E P I D ■ G N O M E ■ A D S
■ M A J O R L A B E L S
■ D A R E T O D R E A M
■ L I T T E R B O X E S
C O G ■ G R I E F ■ B Y L A W
H A I K U ■ P D F S ■ R E N O
I N C A N T ■ P L I N K O
C O A T ■ V O O D O O D O L L
H U M E ■ P O W E R L E V E L
I T S Y ■ G F L A T ■ R O S Y
```

184

```
T H A T S A T A L L O R D E R
E A C H O N E T E A C H O N E
A R A I S I N I N T H E S U N
M A K E A F R E S H S T A R T
■ M E L ■ O M S ■ T S E
■ R E U P P E D
S P A R E D N O E X P E N S E
C A M E L I D ■ E C L A I R S
I N C L A S S ■ D I U R N A L
■ O X O ■ T S P
I M A C ■ N A C R E ■ I S A O
R A B A T ■ M L I ■ D E A L T
V I C T O R I A S S E C R E T
I N D E P E N D E N C E A V E
N E E D S T O ■ S L A S H E R
```

185

```
F A C E S ■ M A J O R C A
E R A G O N ■ U S O T O U R
L A N G U O R ■ S T A T U T E
I M I M P R E S S E D ■ G T O
Z I N C ■ M A K E R ■ P H I L
■ S E M I A R I D ■ P R I M A
■ S U C R E S ■ W R I T E R
■ F E A R ■ H A I D
S E L F I E ■ B I T S E C
P L A I N ■ S O R E S P O T
E D E N ■ E U L E R ■ A L I S
C U R ■ U N I T E D F R O N T
I Q T E S T S ■ S O L A N G E
F U E L E R S ■ G O D E E P
Y E S I S E E ■ W E L S H
```

186

```
G R A B B A R ■ P A R A D O R
R E L E A S E ■ A B I L E N E
A T L A N T A ■ L A B E L E D
N O I R ■ E P E E S ■ S I T E
T O N ■ B R E A D E D ■ C O Y
S L O P E ■ R R R ■ E L A T E
■ N I T ■ S P Y ■ C I T E S
■ B E E T ■ ■ O V E N
G O P R O ■ C O T ■ D E B
E R R O R ■ R N A ■ E D A T E
M E I ■ S T E E P E D ■ L E M
I S N T ■ B A S E L ■ S A A B
N O T A L O T ■ D E F E N S E
I M E M I N E ■ U N L A C E D
S E R A P E S ■ P A Y L E S S
```

187

```
BOOPADOOP
SENDALETTER
BIGTICKETITEM
YOS VSHAPES LAP
ESTD TILER SERA
STEEP NIN PLAIN
MORLOCKS REASON
ANSELMO HELLENE
SCOTIA SALLOWED
TRUES BMI AMATO
EELS POORS SITU
RAJ SYNODAL VET
MAJORITYRULES
HOMETHEATER
TEXASSIZE
```

188

```
WIKILEAKS SPLIT
ONADOWNER IRONS
RARECOINS TORTA
DNA AKON CINDER
VITAL NYRANGERS
OMELET EROS
MAKESAUTURN CAP
ITIS OPINE HOBO
TED SISTERWIVES
APSE EELERS
STILETTOS TORRE
NAPLES LOCK BAS
ALOUD HAWAIIANS
KIDDO EVERSINCE
EASES FIRESIDES
```

189

```
MIDMARCH ABUT
MARIECURIE HEME
ORANGESODA HELM
ZYNGA TWERP RAP
ALIENS TONGUE
ROAR TRASHMOUTH
TUN BEANPLANTS
CLAMJUICE
BLOODBORNE JOB
THINKYOUNG PAWL
HUGGED SHANIA
ETA SITBY EMEND
LATE ERRATAPAGE
ANEW TEAMEVENTS
WIDE FMSTEREO
```

190

```
WITCHHUNT AGASP
EMERGENCY RUNTO
ESTATECAR TATAS
DERN DAREDEVILS
STANCES AMALIE
IED ARTISANS
STEEL JIVES BIS
ERAS BODED BOSE
XER FAKER HURTS
CATSEYES GOD
ADHERE DOGSPAS
PETERROGET ELSE
ADOSE NICHOLASI
DONAT ELCAPITAN
ENEWS BLAMEGAME
```

191

```
HALLPASS GAPPY
OLIGARCH SOIREE
PIBBXTRA PANERA
ICET SOBSISTERS
SERRA DBACK NYT
FAIRS ATEAT
NATGEO TURNRIPE
EYEHAND PAYAFEE
WESTCORK COVENS
SOFIA KNEES
OTB DANZA ELLIE
COOKEDKALE BLOW
TRAUMA KETELONE
AIRDAM HUNGOVER
DIDUP STAGGERS
```

192

```
IINSIST COLLATE
STEAMER AVIATOR
LEASETO ROOTFOR
EMPHASISMINE
ANA QED CABS
ZANY GAUL LAPEL
APE BOLA LOLITA
PORTRAITGALLERY
PLURAL JAZZ CUE
ELDON RUBY FEED
ROAM JAM BOO
BOOKPROPOSAL
LEMONDE ONADATE
SCENEIII MERINOS
TOHELEN ESTEEMS
```

193

```
ORGAN   OCTAL  AMO
KOENIG  WHATATRIP
SANCHO  EATATHOME
ONEHALF REDEEMER
 STOODUP    ASADA
  ETRE  LPS
LINMANUELMIRANDA
INALLPROBABILITY
ZOMBIEAPOCALYPSE
   DEN  SWAT
CHURN    SWIFFER
RARAAVIS SOLOCUP
ASIFTOSAY NICOLE
STATELINE SEALER
HEH DESKS  DLIST
```

194

```
TROI  ABUT  DANTE
BOXCAMERA  SPEAR
SPEEDBALL  THATS
PENTHOUSESUITE
   ROY   ADDAMS
AFLAC GABLE  SOY
CLAY NEMEAN  ADD
EAT COLBERT  PEN
TMI ODDITY  DIRE
IBN RESTS  SUNNY
COLADA  GPS
 YOGURTSMOOTHIE
CAVER  INAMORATA
ONENO  PIXELATED
STRAY  STIR  GEMS
```

195

```
BMX  GOTME  CHASM
BODYSPRAY  RANTS
QUIETTIME  IDTAG
SENORITAS  PAST
  MICE  TREFOIL
ASIANS  PRESENCE
CHANG  FOAL  WALT
COM SEALION   LIT
OPAL TRON  BOONE
SAMADAMS  DANGER
THEBEST  VEGA
 ORCA  ERICAJONG
ELIOT  AUTOMAKER
MICAH  MBADEGREE
SCATS  SELES  ADS
```

196

```
DNALABS  BJNOVAK
ROSECUT  YOULOSE
OXIDATE  LUDDITE
OZS INEXILE  DAB
PEAS OPINE  GIRL
EMITS LIE  MONTE
DADJOKE  SWAGGER
  ODE   BRR
MACHONE  CAKEMIX
OMANI  ABU  SEEMS
NIPS STIES  NAPA
ART BAITCAR  NIN
RICOACT  ADAPTED
CTHULHU  RISOTTO
HEATMAP  DEPLOYS
```

197

```
FIFTHESTATE  AHS
IRAROLLOVER  REA
RUMORMONGER  GAD
SLEDS GIAN   REDS
TED PACS  MENLO
 ASIN  EASTON
 BINGEWATCHING
 PAROLEHEARING
SLIPPERYSLOPE
COLLET  TINS
IDEAS MAHI   MSG
EDDY ROME  PROWL
NEO PIRATERADIO
CRU CANTILEVERS
EST BASICSKILLS
```

198

```
RMS  WASABI  ABCS
OAT IPCRESSFILE
CUM COUGHBUTTON
KNOCK BOONE  EST
FARO MANN  TIMER
AKIN ASNER  FETA
NETTER  ESSAY
SAZERAC  TVHOSTS
 SMURF  PAULIV
SARS DIODE  CODE
CLEAT TROD  ATIT
UGG OVITZ  INTEL
FOIAREQUEST  IDA
FRONTRUNNER  NUN
SEND  YEASTY  GPA
```

199

```
P O S T E R I Z E ■ L A S T S
E S C A P E P O D ■ A R H A T
W H A T S M O R E ■ Z A I R E
S A N T O ■ ■ A R M Y B R A T
■ ■ O M A R ■ ■ O B S E S S
C A M O ■ G O S O L O ■ ■ ■
O F F I C E M A X ■ N E A T O
S T A S H ■ A L I ■ E X C O P
T A S T E ■ N U D E S C E N E
■ ■ ■ E R O D E D ■ U S E D
L A O T Z U ■ ■ S U S S ■
I T S A W R A P ■ ■ C E A S E
L E A S H ■ S A Y S A Y S A Y
T A K E I ■ A R I S T O T L E
S T A R Z ■ P A N T S U I T S
```

200

```
R A T P A C K ■ N B A J A M
E U R A S I A N ■ Y E S I D O
A B U D H A B I ■ S E W N O N
P A I R ■ O L G A ■ N A G A T
E D S E L ■ O H M S ■ N O N A
R E M ■ E X O T I C A ■ I N N
■ ■ H A R E M ■ R U S S I A
■ O N E D A Y A T A T I M E ■
G R O M I T ■ R A P I D ■ ■
A D S ■ N E M E S E S ■ P A C
N E L L ■ D A F T ■ M A R S H
G R O A N ■ S U E Z ■ R O S A
S O U P E D ■ E B E N E Z E R
T U C S O N ■ L U K E W A R M
A T H E N A ■ ■ D E T E C T S
```

The New York Times
SMART PUZZLES
Presented with Style

Available at your local bookstore or online at
us.macmillan.com/author/thenewyorktimes

 ST. MARTIN'S GRIFFIN